THE POSSESSION OF BARBE HALLAY

MCGILL-QUEEN'S STUDIES IN EARLY CANADA / AVANT LE CANADA

Series Editors / Directeurs de la collection :
Allan Greer and Carolyn Podruchny

This series features studies of the history of the northern half of North America – a vast expanse that would eventually be known as Canada – in the era before extensive European settlement and extending into the nineteenth century. Long neglected, Canada-before-Canada is a fascinating area of study experiencing an intellectual renaissance as researchers in a range of disciplines, including history, geography, archeology, anthropology, literary studies, and law, contribute to a new and enriched understanding of the distant past. The editors welcome manuscripts in English or French on all aspects of the period, including work on Indigenous history, the Atlantic fisheries, the fur trade, exploration, French or British imperial expansion, colonial life, culture, language, law, science, religion, and the environment.

Cette série de monographies est consacrée à l'histoire de la partie septentrionale du continent de l'Amérique du nord, autrement dit le grand espace qui deviendra le Canada, dans les siècles qui s'étendent jusqu'au début du 19e. Longtemps négligé par les chercheurs, ce Canada-avant-le-Canada suscite beaucoup d'intérêt de la part de spécialistes dans plusieurs disciplines, entre autres, l'histoire, la géographie, l'archéologie, l'anthropologie, les études littéraires et le droit. Nous assistons à une renaissance intellectuelle dans ce champ d'étude axé sur l'interaction de premières nations, d'empires européens et de colonies. Les directeurs de cette série sollicitent des manuscrits, en français ou en anglais, qui portent sur tout aspect de cette période, y compris l'histoire des autochtones, celle des pêcheries de l'atlantique, de la traite des fourrures, de l'exploration, de l'expansion de l'empire français ou britannique, de la vie coloniale (Nouvelle-France, l'Acadie, Terre-Neuve, les provinces maritimes, etc.), de la culture, la langue, le droit, les sciences, la religion ou l'environnement.

1 A Touch of Fire
Marie-André Duplessis, the Hôtel-Dieu of Quebec, and the Writing of New France
Thomas M. Carr, Jr

2 Entangling the Quebec Act
Transnational Contexts, Meanings, and Legacies in North America and the British Empire
Edited by Ollivier Hubert and François Furstenberg

3 Listening to the Fur Trade
Soundways and Music in the British North American Fur Trade, 1760–1840
Daniel Robert Laxer

4 Heirs of an Ambivalent Empire
French-Indigenous Relations and the Rise of the Métis in the Hudson Bay Watershed
Scott Berthelette

5 The Possession of Barbe Hallay
Diabolical Arts and Daily Life in Early Canada
Mairi Cowan

The Possession of Barbe Hallay

Diabolical Arts and Daily Life in Early Canada

MAIRI COWAN

McGill-Queen's University Press
Montreal & Kingston • London • Chicago

ISBN 978-0-2280-1403-4 (cloth)
ISBN 978-0-2280-1404-1 (paper)
ISBN 978-0-2280-1498-0 (ePDF)
ISBN 978-0-2280-1499-7 (ePUB)

Legal deposit fourth quarter 2022
Bibliothèque nationale du Québec

Reprinted 2024

This book has been published with the help of a grant from the Canadian Federation for the Humanities and Social Sciences, through the Awards to Scholarly Publications Program, using funds provided by the Social Sciences and Humanities Research Council of Canada.

Financé par le gouvernement du Canada | Funded by the Government of Canada | Canada | Conseil des arts du Canada | Canada Council for the Arts

We acknowledge the support of the Canada Council for the Arts.

Nous remercions le Conseil des arts du Canada de son soutien.

McGill-Queen's University Press in Montreal is on land which long served as a site of meeting and exchange amongst Indigenous Peoples, including the Haudenosaunee and Anishinabeg nations. In Kingston it is situated on the territory of the Haudenosaunee and Anishinaabek. We acknowledge and thank the diverse Indigenous Peoples whose footsteps have marked these territories on which peoples of the world now gather.

Library and Archives Canada Cataloguing in Publication

Title: The possession of Barbe Hallay: diabolical arts and daily life in early Canada / Mairi Cowan.

Names: Cowan, Mairi, 1974- author.

Series: McGill-Queen's studies in early Canada ; 5.

Description: Series statement: McGill-Queen's studies in early Canada / Avant le Canada; 5 | Includes bibliographical references and index.

Identifiers: Canadiana (print) 20220260133 | Canadiana (ebook) 20220260257 | ISBN 9780228014034 (cloth) | ISBN 9780228014041 (paper) | ISBN 9780228014980 (ePDF) | ISBN 9780228014997 (ePUB)

Subjects: LCSH: Hallay, Barbe. | LCSH: Demoniac possession—Québec (Province)—History—17th century. | LCSH: Witchcraft—Québec (Province)—History—17th century. | LCSH: Québec (Province)—Religious life and customs. | LCSH: Québec (Province)—Social life and customs—17th century. | LCSH: Canada—History—To 1763 (New France)

Classification: LCC BF1517.C3 C69 2022 | DDC 133.4/260971409032—dc23

This book was typeset by Marquis Interscript in 10.5/13 Sabon.

Contents

Figures vii

Preface ix

Acknowledgments xi

Abbreviations xiii

Introduction 3

1 Across the Atlantic 13

2 The Servant, the Miller, and the Infested Seigneurie 44

3 Missionary Demonologists 71

4 A Deliverance from Demons 102

5 To the Other Shore 122

Conclusion 153

Glossary 159

Notes 163

Bibliography 223

Index 265

Figures

1.1 France and New France on the Atlantic. Map by Marcel Fortin and the University of Toronto Library, 2022. 14

1.2 The region around Québec. Map by Marcel Fortin and the University of Toronto Library, 2022. 28

1.3 The town of Québec in 1660. Jean Bourdon, "Vrai plan du haut et bas Québec comme il est en l'an 1660." BAnQ Québec E21, S555, SS1, SSS22, P61. Courtesy of Bibliothèque et Archives nationales du Québec. Map by Marcel Fortin and the University of Toronto Library, 2022. 30

1.4 Detail from the town of Québec in 1663. Jean Bourdon, "Le Véritable plan de Québec fait en 1663." Bibliothèque nationale de France, département des Cartes et plans, GE SH 18 PF 127 DIV 7 P 3. Courtesy of Bibliothèque nationale de France. 32

2.1 Engraving of the manor house of Beauport as it looked in the nineteenth century. "Montcalm's Headquarters with a distant view of Quebec." BAnQ Québec P546, D3, P11. Courtesy of Bibliothèque et Archives nationales du Québec. 46

2.2 Photograph of the manor house of Beauport as it looked in the nineteenth century. L.P. Vallée, "Beauport – Avenue Royale – Manoir Robert Giffard – Domaine Darnoc – Résidence." BAnQ Québec P600, S6, D2, P52. Courtesy of Bibliothèque et Archives nationales du Québec. 46

3.1 Jean Bourdon, "Le Véritable plan de Québec fait en 1663." Bibliothèque nationale de France, département des Cartes et plans, GE SH 18 PF 127 DIV 7 P 3. Courtesy of Bibliothèque nationale de France. 81

3.2 Frontispiece from *La vie de la mere Catherine de Saint Augustin: religieuse hospitaliere de la misericorde de Quebec en la Nouvelle-France.* JCB Archive of Early American Images. Courtesy of the John Carter Brown Library. 87

5.1 Marque of Jean-Baptiste Hallay on a marriage contract from Greffe de Pierre Duquet de la Chesnaye (1663–87). BAnQ-Q, CN301, S95, 27 July 1670. Courtesy of Bibliothèque et Archives nationales du Québec. 128

5.2 Detail of an "habitation" from Jean-Baptiste Franquelin, "L'entrée de la Rivière du St Laurent, et la ville de Québec dans le Canada." Bibliothèque nationale de France, département des Cartes et plans, GE SH 18 PF 127 DIV 6 P 1 D. Courtesy of Bibliothèque nationale de France. 142

5.3 Jean-Baptiste Franquelin, "L'entrée de la Rivière du St Laurent, et la ville de Québec dans le Canada." Bibliothèque nationale de France, département des Cartes et plans, GE SH 18 PF 127 DIV 6 P 1 D. Courtesy of Bibliothèque nationale de France. 143

5.4 Robert de Villeneuve, "Carte des Environs de Quebec en La Nouvelle France Mezuré sur le lieu très exactement en 1685 et 86 par le Sr Devilleneuve Ingénieur du Roy." Bibliothèque nationale de France, département des Cartes et plans, GE SH 18 PF 127 DIV 7 P 4. Courtesy of Bibliothèque nationale de France. 144

Preface

I first came upon this story, or perhaps I should say this story first came upon me, a few years ago during a family vacation in the Old Town of Québec. Thinking that we could read a primary source from New France to learn about our environs from someone who had lived there centuries ago, I packed into our bags a selection of letters by the seventeenth-century Ursuline nun Marie de l'Incarnation. It quickly became apparent that not everyone on the trip shared my taste in holiday reading material. As soon as I read Marie's first account of a mysterious demonic infestation, though, I was hooked. Riveted. One might even say (if one were thinking in technical terms of demonology) obsessed. I felt that I needed to know what had happened to the supposedly possessed servant and the person accused of using witchcraft to torment her with demons. I became curious about whether this episode resembled other cases of bewitchment in Europe and North America, or if it took on unique qualities from its setting in and around Québec. I wondered if fears of witchcraft and demons were more widespread in New France than I had thought.

With no immediate answers to these questions in Marie's letters, I started to search for other primary sources that touched on the matter, and I began my survey of other historians' research. Before long, I was learning about efforts to improve Canada's reputation in France, recurring spats between the vicar apostolic and the governor in Québec, heated debates and vibrant enthusiasms in French baroque Catholicism, and the jostling of people on both sides of the Atlantic as they tried to move through an *ancien régime* social hierarchy whose boundaries were inflexibly brittle in theory but often porous in practice. My investigation then got pulled into complex networks as it progressed, joining this tale from Québec to France, other European colonies in the Americas, and Indigenous nations who controlled access to most of the territory in what the French king called New France. What struck me most forcefully was the vulnerability of the colony. Reading Marie de l'Incarnation's letters during a stay at a hotel near the Ursuline convent made it obvious that the settlement of Québec had survived, endured, and thrived over the centuries. This outcome was not clear to the colonists in the seventeenth century. They recognized that their future in North America was contingent on alliances with Indigenous nations, help from France, and good fortune. None of these conditions was something they felt they could count on in 1659, when Barbe Hallay arrived, and their anxieties about the future of New France continued to grow over the next few years.

I tell this tale because I find the origin stories of research projects interesting in general, and because this one in particular helps to explain how a book began spontaneously from reading a single letter about "diabolical arts," then grew into a much larger study of broad and deep concerns about religion, authority, and even the very survival of the French colonial project. I came to the sources with the training of a medievalist and the curiosity of a traveller; I now hope that this book will bring to its readers some of the same enjoyment as the research has brought to me.

Acknowledgments

I started this book as a newcomer to research on the history of New France. Somewhat timid at first, and trying not to intrude as a blundering trespasser onto a well-established field, I soon found that the scholars who specialize in New France and colonial North America are a welcoming and generous group. Thank you to the historians, librarians, and archivists who helped me. Emma Anderson, Carl Benn, Arnaud Bessière, Leslie Choquette, Luca Codignola, Natalie Zemon Davis, Catherine Desbarats, Dominique Deslandres, Helen Dewar, Fannie Dionne, Alexandre Dubé, Robert Englebert, Joseph Gagné, Peter Gagné, Allan Greer, Benoît Grenier, Gilles Havard, Lauric Henneton, Katherine Ibbett, Gregory Kennedy, Kathryn Magee Labelle, Susanne Lachenicht, Chantal Lacombe, Yann Lignereux, Jean-François Lozier, Michel Morin, Caroline Nadeau, Joy Palacios, Jean-François Palomino, Christopher Parsons, Stephanie Pettigrew, Geneviève Piché, Joshua Piker, Carolyn Podruchny, Josée Pomminville, Allan Potofsky, Léon Robichaud, François Rousseau, Adina Ruiu, Brett Rushforth, Gordon Sayre, Erik Seeman, John Steckley, Charles André Téotonio, Marie-Claire Tremblay, Laurier Turgeon, Andrew Wegmann, Sophie White, Thomas Wien, and the reviewers of the book have all offered valuable assistance. Thank you also to historians of other times and places who continued to lend their support to this research, including Elizabeth Ewan, Elizabeth Ferguson, Whitney Hahn, Lucas Harris, Daniel MacLeod, Donna Trembinski, and Christopher Young.

Thank you to the many faculty, staff, and students at the University of Toronto who have assisted with this project in one way or another. Julia Armstrong, Dianne Ashbourne, Sidney Aster, Carrie Atkins, Andreas Bendlin, Shawna Browarsky Quigley, Elspeth Brown, Nicole

Charles, Isabelle Cochelin, Boris Chrubasik, Kevin Coleman, Carla DeMarco, Ken Derry, Tyler Evans-Tokaryk, Marcel Fortin, Sherry Fukuzawa, Brian Gettler, Joe Goering, Duncan Hill, Sanja Hinic-Frlog, Grégoire Holtz, Robert Johnson, Hammad Junejo, Michael Kaler, Rachel Kulick, Jessica Kulpa, Nicole Laliberté, Alex Logue, Julie MacArthur, Stuart Macdonald, Kimberly Main, Sharon Marjadsingh, Preksha Mehta, Sarianna Metso, Mark Meyerson, Shabina Moheebulla, Andreas Motsch, Barbara Murck, Alexander Murray, Jan Noel, Nicholas Overgaard, Carol Percy, Christopher Petrakos, Enrico Raffaelli, Ajay Rao, Fiona Rawle, Martin Revermann, Jean-Olivier Richard, Sarah Richardson, Christoph Richter, Catherine Rubincam, Adam Sarouji, Chester Scoville, Joan Simalchik, Nicholas Terpstra, Heather Thornton, Yayo Umetsubo, Shafique Virani, David Wilson, and Rebecca Wittmann make this university a supportive institutional base for research and writing.

Several organizations have contributed to this project through financial assistance, including the Social Sciences and Humanities Research Council of Canada, the Omohundro Institute, and the University of Toronto. I acknowledge this support with appreciation. McGill-Queen's University Press has also contributed resources to bring this book to publication, and I am grateful for that continued investment. Thank you in particular to Kyla Madden, who spotted the potential of this project before I did, and whose encouragement and wise counsel kept the book on a true course.

Finally, I would like to extend a note of gratitude for the patience of friends and family who have been listening to me go on and on (and on) about a weird case of demonic possession from centuries ago. Katarina Bulat, Hilary Evans Cameron, John Cowan, Norma Cowan, Corina Eberle, David Farrell, Bruce Fraser, Linda Meyer, Todd Meyer, Christopher Munro, Emmet O'Reilly, Jessica Riley, and Reed Thomas have spent a lot of time with this story already, and I hope they will enjoy the result. Warmest thanks to the members of my household Chris Meyer, Daphne Cowan, little miss Titi, and floofy house panther Delilah. In return for your company on research trips and conversations around the dining room table, I promise that I have never put any ground-up bones into your drinks.

Abbreviations

AAQ	Archives de l'archidiocèse de Québec
AJC-GLC	The Archive of the Jesuits in Canada
AMHDQ	Archives du Monastère de l'Hôtel-Dieu de Québec
ANOM	Archives nationales d'outre-mer
ARSI	Archivum Romanum Societas Iesu
ASJCF	Archives de la Compagnie de Jésus, province du Canada français
ASQ	Archives du Séminaire de Québec
AUQ	Archives des Ursulines de Québec
BAnQ-M	Bibliothèque et Archives nationales du Québec, Montréal
BAnQ-Q	Bibliothèque et Archives nationales du Québec, Québec
BNF	Bibliothèque nationale de France
DCB	Dictionary of Canadian Biography
JR	Jesuit Relations
LAC	Library and Archives Canada
MNF	Monumenta Novae Franciae
PRDH	Programme de recherche en démographie historique (Université de Montréal)
RAPQ	Rapport de l'Archiviste de la province de Québec

THE POSSESSION OF BARBE HALLAY

Introduction

Not long after the ships left Québec to return across the Atlantic in the autumn of 1660, residents of the small French settlement on the banks of the St Lawrence River began to worry about evil forces in their midst. People saw a comet in the sky with its rods pointed towards the earth. Then they saw a man of fire, a canoe of fire, and a crown of fire in the air. They heard confused voices of women and children along with lamentable cries, and later a thunderous, horrible voice. The Ursuline nun Marie de l'Incarnation reported that these signs terrified many people. She took them to be sinister portents of woes ready to befall the colony. The signs were linked, in her mind, to a discovery of "witches and magicians in this country." Among these witches and magicians was a miller using "the tricks of his diabolical art" in an attempt to corrupt and then marry a young woman.[1] The young woman, a teenaged domestic servant named Barbe Hallay, began to see demons in a variety of terrifying forms. She identified Daniel Vuil, the miller with the diabolical tricks, as the witch responsible for sending the demons to frighten her. Then Hallay started to act as if possessed, unable to control her thrashing limbs or utterances of demonic speech.

As stories of Barbe Hallay's possession circulated among the colonists, people attempted to contain the demonic threat. Priests went to the estate where Hallay worked and tried to end the demonic infestation through prayer. Nuns at the Hôtel-Dieu hospital cared for Hallay's body and soul while they battled against the demons that threatened their patient. A bishop had Vuil imprisoned and investigated for signs of witchcraft, then a governor had Vuil executed. Finally, an elite laywoman delivered Hallay from her demonic torments.

A historical investigation into the possession of Barbe Hallay yields much more than just a description of this series of strange events, fascinating as they are. It provides an exceptional opportunity to survey the French colony, observe the everyday experiences of people who lived there, and extend our analysis into the social and religious history of New France. The world of Barbe Hallay was one of both small and big spaces. French settlement in the town of Québec, and in New France more widely, was much less secure in reality than the confidence of royal edicts would suggest. The settlers had crossed a vast ocean to colonize what to them was still a fairly new world. They proceeded to insert themselves into the complex networks of Indigenous North America and struggled to adapt both socially and physically to the environment. As the decades passed, it became clear that they were not having as easy a time as they had expected, and they grew increasingly anxious about the future of New France.

The basic outline of events in the possession of Barbe Hallay can only be reconstructed by combining information from different sources, and so right away we are brought into the challenges of comparing documents against one another, assessing competing claims, and assembling disparate clues into a cohesive narration. To understand not just what happened, but also how people in the midst of events understood their experiences, we need to interpret the evidence in ways that respect the perspectives of those who generated the evidence during the seventeenth century in coordination with the insights we have today. This book draws from a diverse array of sources to engage readers in a story that might seem small – how one domestic servant was believed to be possessed and then liberated from her demonic torments – but which, through the little details, allows us to think about much larger themes. By investigating the possession of Barbe Hallay, we can see the texture of daily life in seventeenth-century Canada from up close, while perceiving also from afar how people's beliefs and actions were shaped by historical forces of migration, empire, colonization, class, gender, religion, and authority.

The possession of Barbe Hallay runs as a narrative path through this book from beginning to end. Little or no prior knowledge about seventeenth-century New France is presumed among its readership, and therefore enough historical context about the world of Barbe Hallay is provided so that readers new to the field may follow how this suspected case of possession developed, and, if they like, engage with some of the enduring debates in the historiography of early modern North America. Much of this context will be familiar to historians of New France, colonial North America, and early modern Europe, and these experts may find that the book contributes something new to our understanding of how early modern people understood natural and supernatural forces, and of how the French colony on the St Lawrence fits into the larger early modern world.[2]

The first chapter, "Across the Atlantic," traces the migration of Barbe Hallay from Europe to North America in 1659. It situates Hallay's family within larger trends of French mobility, considers what immigrants knew about Canada before embarking on their oceanic voyages, and describes how the town of Québec would have appeared to Hallay when she landed. Then it introduces two of the people who made the trans-Atlantic crossing at the same time as Hallay and who would come to play central roles in the story of her possession: Daniel Vuil, the miller accused of using magic and sorcery, and François de Laval, the vicar apostolic of Québec whose decisions shaped the fates of both Vuil and Hallay. From this assembly of passengers arises the question of how important Catholicism was to the colonial designs of New France. By law, since 1627, all colonists were supposed to be Catholic. Laval obviously met this standard. Not only was he a Catholic priest, but he would also become the first bishop of Québec. The Hallay family was conventionally Catholic by all accounts as well, undergoing baptisms and confirmations and marriages and burials according to Catholic rites, but their Catholicism differed in some ways from that of Laval. Daniel Vuil's religious identity was more complex. He was a Protestant when he embarked from France. Like other Huguenot migrants, he was supposed to renounce his Protestantism before settling in Canada. Although he seems to have done so, those who came to suspect him of engaging in dark arts remembered his Huguenot past. Set against the larger backdrop of religious geopolitics in the colony, Vuil's presence sounded a discordant note between New France's theoretical formation as an ideal Catholic colony and the messier reality of a place inhabited by many people who were either not Catholic at all, or not Catholic in a way that met with the approval of religious leaders.

Barbe Hallay first showed signs of possession while working as a domestic servant at Beauport, a seigneurial estate just outside the town of Québec. There, she encountered terrifying demons and spectres. Other people reported hearing phantasmal music and seeing stones that flew by themselves. Chapter 2, "The Servant, the Miller, and the

Infested Seigneurie," shows how the early stages of Hallay's torments at Beauport followed the expected course of French demonic possessions in some ways, yet deviated from expectations in others. Witnesses' accounts were shaped by both widespread assumptions and local conditions. As an adolescent female from a humble background, Hallay fit easily into early modern European ideas about typical demoniacs (people believed to be possessed by demons) in terms of her age, gender, and social status. Similarly, the person she identified as responsible for the torments, Daniel Vuil, matched contemporary descriptions of witches in some respects, especially with his anti-social behaviour. The reason given for Vuil's launching of demons against Hallay – the rejection of his offer of marriage – was known in Europe too, but its social context was very specific to New France in the early 1660s. Two local features were particularly significant: the demographic situation of French settlements along the St Lawrence, with their severe sexual imbalance among colonists, which put unusually high pressure on Hallay to wed, and the insecurities of the French colony, both physical and metaphysical, which sharpened the anxieties of settlers.

The third chapter, "Missionary Demonologists," turns to the efforts of nuns at the Hôtel-Dieu hospital who tried to help Hallay. Their care drew from therapeutic spheres of medicine and religion, with practices influenced both by the hospital's institutional origins in Europe and also by its initial missionary purpose in New France. Chapter 3 examines how earlier stages in the development of the Hôtel-Dieu hospital conditioned the treatments that the nuns provided, and then expands to a broader examination of missionary work in New France. As members of the same Catholic Church, the missionaries all shared certain fundamental beliefs about demons, but they disagreed about exactly which challenges they were facing in New France and about how to counter whatever demonic forces they might find there. The demonology that the missionaries developed was complex and sometimes contradictory, pierced through with a deep disappointment that they were not achieving the results they had hoped for in the conversion of Indigenous people. This disappointment left its mark on how the Hospitalière nuns responded to Hallay's symptoms, and on how their supporters recorded their efforts.

Barbe Hallay continued to exhibit signs of possession after she left the hospital and returned to work as a servant at Beauport. "Deliverance from Demons," the fourth chapter, discusses the intervention of someone who took charge of freeing Hallay from her demonic torments back at the *seigneurie*. This person was Marie Regnouard, wife of the *seigneur* at Beauport. As described in unpublished accounts from the Jesuit archive in Montréal and the archive of the Hôtel-Dieu in Québec, Regnouard's care for Hallay extended across several registers of responsibility. It constituted a form of healing, which was well within Regnouard's normal responsibilities as female head of a household. The care was also a kind of deliverance, which took on the shape of a religious ritual theoretically permitted but normally forbidden to women – especially laywomen. When measured against manuals of Catholic ritual and compared with descriptions of religious practices in Europe, Regnouard's actions look very much like an exorcism. Regnouard's high social status in the colony and her personal connections to both medical and religious leaders help explain why she was encouraged to care both medically and spiritually for her servant. What comes through even more clearly in the accounts of Regnouard's intervention is an insistence that the real power to free Hallay from her demonic tormentors was that of a holy martyr. Marie Regnouard could wield sacred power and petition holy forces for help, but she was careful to imply that the true agent of deliverance was the deceased Jesuit priest Jean de Brébeuf.

Chapter 5, "To the Other Shore," offers an account of Barbe Hallay's life after the possession. Having been relieved of her demonic torments, Hallay returned to the town of Québec to work as a servant, first in a merchant's household and next in the Hôtel-Dieu hospital. Then she married Jean Carrier, a man who had also been working as a servant at the hospital. The two of them settled in the seigneurie of Lauzon across the river, set up a successful farm, and raised several children. The course of Hallay's life after her deliverance from demons is strikingly normal for a seventeenth-century colonist in the St Lawrence Valley. In trying to understand the significance of such normalcy, this chapter takes a step back from the case of possession itself and surveys New France within a broader context of later seventeenth-century developments on both sides of the Atlantic. Even as the colony departed from some of its earlier ideals, and especially the religious goals of its founders, its security increased both politically and economically. When the settlers became more confident that New France would endure, their general and specific anxieties about invisible threats diminished. They did not stop believing in witches and demons, but their concerns about the power of these dark forces shrank in scale. Meanwhile, intellectuals in Europe were becoming more skeptical about reports of demonic interference. They did not deny the existence of witches and demons altogether for the most part, but they did increasingly question whether witches and demons really were responsible for all the things popularly attributed to them. The colonial leaders in New France adopted a similar attitude. When presented with claims of witchcraft and demonic activity in the later seventeenth century, they hesitated in ascribing the observed manifestations to supernatural forces, preferring instead to seek natural causes. No one seems to have been worried that Barbe Hallay's earlier encounters with witches and demons would endanger anyone around her, and no large-scale witch hunt or mass possession ever took hold in New France. The colony had changed since Hallay's arrival, and the earlier stories of possession, while never denied, cast no dark shadow over her later years.

The possession of Barbe Hallay will already be known, at least in the basic outline of events, to some readers. It has been mentioned in studies of Quebec folklore and religion, although usually just in passing. The possession has been dismissed as unworthy of more sustained attention,[3] and reduced to a single medical cause.[4] It has been featured briefly as a rare example of witchcraft in New France,[5] and used to illustrate disputes between civil and ecclesiastical jurisdictions.[6] Somewhat more attention has been given to elements of the case that show connections between holiness, authority, and fear in the colony.[7] Each of these studies offers valuable insights into the history of New France, but none provides a sustained and context-rich analysis of the case itself.

The materials for such an analysis exist in primary sources that touch on this possession directly, in those that provide details about its historical context in seventeenth-century New France, and in the scholarship on early modern European and colonial North American history. Together, these materials form the basis of this study of a small group of settlers in New France and the currents of early modern history swirling around them. Inspired by the analytical and narrative power of microhistories such as Carlo Ginzburg's *The Cheese and the Worms*, Natalie Zemon Davis' *The Return of Martin Guerre*, and Allan Greer's *Mohawk Saint: Catherine Tekakwitha and the Jesuits*, this book takes a microhistorical approach.[8] Perhaps the simplest way to describe microhistory is to say that it focuses on small things but addresses big questions. With what Ginzburg calls a "minute analysis of a circumscribed documentation" and an "insistence on context," microhistory analyzes from up close but draws expansive conclusions.[9] There exists no definite set of principles that define what a microhistory is, nor do its leading practitioners all agree on core characteristics, but some common traits have emerged that describe the approach. Most conspicuously, microhistories focus on a single object with great attention to detail and a close reading of sources. They combine the small scale with larger ones, both through insisting on the importance of wider historical context when interpreting evidence, and by asking questions with broad historical and contemporary resonance. In making connections between small and large scales, microhistories stress the agency of people, presuming that people in the past acted consciously in their world even when constrained by external forces beyond their control. Microhistories often focus on a topic somewhat outside the mainstream historical field, presenting a seemingly weird or unusual case as a way to show the complexity of historical societies. Further to show this complexity, microhistories tend towards transparency about their methods of investigation and limits to knowledge, typically including discussions of problems with evidence and gaps in the record not as methodological asides, but rather as central features of the main presentation. And microhistories frequently accomplish all this with a narrative style that makes them accessible to a wide audience beyond academic specialists.[10]

Since their emergence in the 1970s, microhistories have been critiqued and praised. Those who admire them find special value in how their tight focus allows us to see the past in new ways, and in how they bring us into the methods of historical investigation with a charming, playful streak.[11] When done well, they have ably served what Edward Muir says is microhistory's purpose, which is "to elucidate historical causation on the level of small groups where most of real life takes place and to open history to peoples who would be left out by other methods."[12] Recently, discussions have turned to how microhistories can help us better understand the much larger scope of world history and the "global turn."[13]

This book enters into the microhistorical tradition with less source material created by its central characters than readers might expect. In the absence of writings directly by the demoniac Barbe Hallay herself, it uses what evidence is available to illuminate the world of a teenaged domestic servant who could not write, but whose remarkable tale of possession is told by those around her, and even (if we for a moment accept the claims of some sources) by a demonic entity within her body. But really, how ought we to treat such claims? As the object of historical study, a case of demonic possession might seem to present some formidable challenges to the historical researcher. Even after finding enough sources to assemble a coherent narrative and construct a sound argument, what is a scholar to do when faced with claims that are, frankly, difficult to accept in a plain reading of the texts? Must one decide whether to believe in supernatural activities, possession by evil spirits, and the healing powers of relics in order to analyze the case? No. A person may remain fundamentally agnostic on these matters, or subscribe to a religious belief, or be firmly atheist, and still think clearly and historically when considering the sources. Rather than asking questions that require access to metaphysical truths, we should ask questions that can be answered using evidence available to everyone for consultation and evaluation. Instead of asking "was the person really possessed by demons?" for example, ask "why did some observers believe the claims of possession more readily than others?" or "in what ways did the demoniac's behaviour appear similar to or different from other supposed possessions of the time?" We certainly need to read the sources with a critical eye. People who wrote about possession may have deliberately misrepresented what they observed in order to increase the appeal of their accounts, heighten fears of demonic interference, or demonstrate the power of the person fighting the demons. Alternatively, they may have unintentionally misled their audiences because they misunderstood what they were observing, or because they saw what they expected to see, or because they heard second- or third-hand accounts. But whatever the motivations and misunderstandings, the sources do tell us what people believed to be true, or at least what they wanted to convince others was true.[14] Most early modern Europeans believed in demonic possession. For us to understand their ideas, as Stuart Clark says, "depends on taking the culturally perceived reality of possession for granted."[15] We can ask what meaning demonic possession had for historical people, and how it made sense to explain their world.[16] If the sources are difficult to use, they are not impossible. A careful study of something that was classified as supernatural in the past demands that we consider as much context as we can, and that we take people's reported experiences as seriously as possible within that context.[17] In historical studies of demonic possession, this approach can mean seeing a case of possession as closely bound with questions of authority, and as something that was at the same time very local yet dependent upon larger forces.[18]

The possession of Barbe Hallay unfolded in the French settlements along the St Lawrence River in the 1660s, but it was also influenced by forces extending beyond that place and time for many leagues and many years. Some of what we find in the story's unfolding is familiar, some is strange, and much is surprising. This is as it should be when studying history. The historian Johan Huizinga said that the "mainspring of all historical knowledge" is "our perpetual astonishment that the past was once a living reality."[19] Surprise is a central, and delightful, feature of historical investigation. It shows us that people in the past did not always think or behave as we would expect, which, in turn, should remind us that our expectations are built on our own limited perspectives. The more we find to surprise us in the historical record, the more we expand our view to admit a richer complexity to the world of the past, along with new possibilities for human experience then and in our own time. As we try to understand what happened and why, both the diabolical arts and the daily lives, we see how people lived and what they thought. We catch glimpses of where they travelled. How they slept. Why they married. What they feared. Who they were. In these little details lie paths to questions that probe deeper layers of early modern North American history, where spiritual authority and social discipline were bound to anxieties about the precariousness of the colonial project.

A NOTE ON LANGUAGE

Translations from French and Latin are my own, unless otherwise indicated. Where the exact wording of the original is especially important, it has been included in the notes.

Generally, I have followed the principle of calling people what they called themselves. "Marie de l'Incarnation" is used here rather than "Marie Guyart," for example, because that is the name she used once she became a cloistered nun. Some people's names are spelled many different ways in the records. In such cases, I have opted for whatever form seems to appear most commonly in the sources. Thus Barbe Hallay / Halay / Halle / Halé / Hallé / Haslé is presented as "Barbe Hallay" in this book, and Daniel Vuil / Vvil / Voil / Vuril / Vril / Wril as "Daniel Vuil."

I have chosen names for groups of people according to the same principle of respecting self-designation. For the sake of clarity, I have sometimes glossed the names with additional descriptors, or paired them with terms that might be more familiar to modern readers. Many if not most of the French migrants to New France during this period considered themselves French, but I have often called them "settlers" or "colonists," or something like "the French in New France" when it is important to distinguish them from French people in France.[20] "Indigenous" is a counterpart to "European" as a label that covers many distinct nations. When describing a more specific group, I have usually employed the term that the people of the group employ for themselves in English. Exceptions occur when adopting the perspective of an outsider, such as when the French called the Wendat the "Huron" or when the Wendat called the Jesuits "Black Robes." The French word "sauvage" is especially problematic to translate, but it appears often in French sources about Indigenous people and so cannot be ignored. When paraphrasing or quoting directly, I have usually chosen to translate it as "Indian" or "Native" in an attempt to render into modern English something of what the early modern French authors meant. For them, the word remained closer to the Latin ancestor "silvestris" – belonging to the forest or growing wild – than the more obvious English cognate "savage," which now is a much more jarringly offensive term. "Sauvage" did have connotations of untamedurociousness in some uses, and in such cases it was inaccurate, so the slightly discordant tones of "Indian" and "Native" perhaps succeed in conveying the off-ness of the seventeenth-century French word.[21] A glossary following the conclusion explains how other terms are used in the book, and may be especially useful to readers not already familiar with the terminology of New France.

As names for places, "Québec," "Canada," and "New France" are related, but not coterminous. Each is used in this book to represent roughly what French writers in the seventeenth century meant when they used the terms. "Québec" refers to the town (not the modern province), and "Canada" means the area of French settlement along the St Lawrence River (not the modern state).[22] "New France" is the least precise of the three. At its greatest extent, it could mean all the lands in North America claimed by the king of France, but this was more an imagined possibility than any kind of recognized territory over which the French had meaningful control. As historians have already shown, and as this book continues to argue, the imperial idea of New France certainly did not always fit neatly upon the experiences of people living there.[23]

1

Across the Atlantic

There was no quick or easy way to cross the Atlantic Ocean in the seventeenth century. If all went well – that is, if the winds and the currents were favourable and no storms struck; if enemy vessels kept their distance; if the captain avoided all treacherous sandbanks and shoals; if, in short, nothing arose to challenge the course of a ship under sail – then the voyage between a port in France and the town of Québec could be expected to take about two months. Some crossings lasted much longer. Ships might spend fifteen weeks, twenty weeks, or even more at sea. The passengers aboard the *Saint-Sébastien* in 1665 had to wait a hundred and eleven days before reaching their destination, and those on the *Maréchale* in 1688 were on board their vessel for a hundred and twenty-nine. For many of these days, the passengers did not know how much more time would pass before they could disembark.[1]

Captains often used dead reckoning and were guided on their way by stars when they could see them. Their main navigational instrument was the compass, whose magnetic needle showed the orientation of the ship. To calculate latitude, they could use the astrolabe. Longitude was more difficult to calculate, and their methods, which included combining estimates of orientation with distance travelled, remained unreliable. Captains tried to maintain a course between the forty-third and the forty-seventh parallels when sailing from France to Canada, but, once they lost sight of land, they simply did not know precisely where they were until they reached the Grand Banks of Newfoundland. Then they could turn to pilot books with information about courses and approaches, and nautical charts with diagrams of coastlines and place names. Their journey was still not yet over. They had to make it

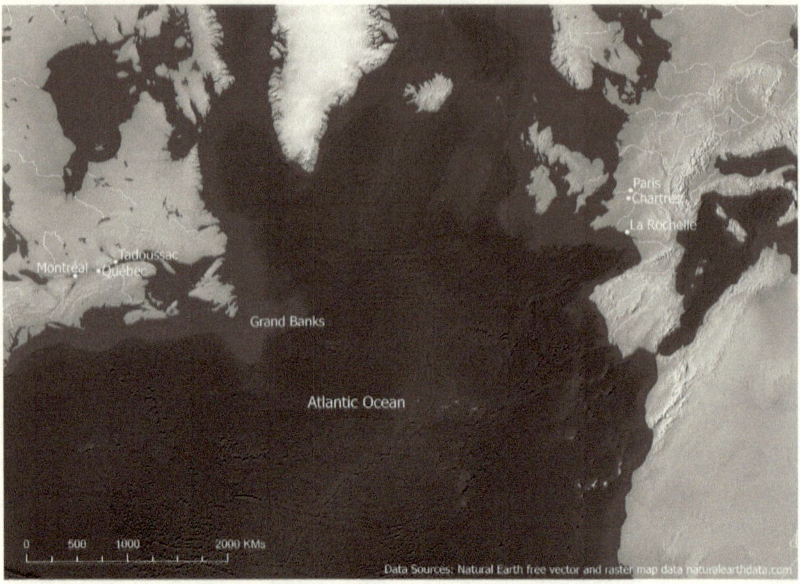

1.1 France and New France on the Atlantic

up the St Lawrence River, whose winds, tides, currents, islets, sandbanks, rocks, and shoals made this waterway notoriously difficult to navigate safely.[2]

The voyage was filled with uncertainty. At any point from beginning to end, the winds might be too heavy or too light. A topmast might break. Fever might take hold. A serious leak might damage supplies and equipment, or perhaps endanger the vessel. Even on the smoothest crossings, passengers were afflicted with the typical discomforts of long sea voyages. Close quarters, stale food, and foul water made the experience an ordeal. Jean Talon, Intendant of New France, described the voyage as "rough and long."[3] The Franciscan missionary Gabriel Sagard had not imagined that sea sickness could be so disagreeable until he experienced it for himself. Then it seemed to him that he had never in his life suffered so much in his body as during the three months and six days of crossing "this great and terrible ocean."[4] Most passengers survived, but not all. It has been calculated that about 5 per cent of all those sailing from France to Canada during the seventeenth and eighteenth centuries perished at sea.[5]

Barbe Hallay was one of those who made it across. We do not have accounts written by her or by members of her family about what their crossing was like, nor do we have any direct evidence about why they decided to make the voyage. What we can do is take information about when her family came, join this information with research on French mobility more generally, and see how this one small group fits into larger patterns of early modern migration. From the perspective of the French crown, the family of Hallay presented an ideal migrant profile: they were strong enough to work, willing to remain in the colony, likely to increase its settler population, and Catholic.

Barbe Hallay's journey from Europe to North America provides background for the story of her possession. We can consider what she might have known about New France before leaving, which features of Québec she would have noted upon arrival, and how the colony's official Catholic identity was understood both by those who directed its affairs from afar and by the inhabitants of New France. All the colonists were supposed to be Catholic. In practice, the colony's religious identity was not so straightforward. The Catholicism of New France may have looked firm and confident in directives from France, but when seen from up close it appears shifting and unstable, and its adherents felt vulnerable to attacks both human and demonic.

MIGRATION FROM FRANCE

France was among the richest and most populous countries in seventeenth-century Europe, but all was not easy within its borders. The kingdom was beset by war, civil strife, plague, and the real possibility of famine. It was also sufficiently diverse in geography and culture to resist any simple generalizations. Depending on where they lived, French people spoke different languages and dialects, wore different clothes, ate different foods, obeyed different laws, and used different weights and measures.[6]

Barbe Hallay was born in the parish of Saint-Julien du Coudray.[7] Her father was named Jean-Baptiste Hallay, and her mother Mathurine Vallet. She had an older sister, Marie, and a younger sister, Elisabeth, both also born – like Barbe – in Saint-Julien. (When Barbe's mother crossed the Atlantic, she was pregnant again: another sibling, Jean-Baptiste, was baptized in Québec a few months after they landed.)[8]

Saint-Julien du Coudray was in an agriculturally rich area about eighty-five kilometres south-west of Paris. The nearby city of Chartres, its bell towers visible above the fields, was the closest urban centre. Chartres had grown significantly from the eleventh to the thirteenth centuries, when it became especially famous for its cathedral and scholars. The Hundred Years War in the fourteenth and fifteenth centuries brought considerable damage to the surrounding countryside. Even with the economic recovery afterwards, the city never regained the intellectual prestige of earlier years. The Wars of Religion in the sixteenth century caused further destruction. By Hallay's time, the importance of Chartres had diminished from its medieval height, but the city was nonetheless still a significant regional economic centre with a population of about 14,000. Local religious leaders were trying to improve the quality of pastoral care, but the bishops thought that clerical behaviour remained mediocre at best.[9]

When the family of Barbe Hallay travelled from France to Canada in the summer of 1659, they joined a small but growing wave of migration. Thanks to an abundance of sources on the demographics of the colony, historians have been able to study the migrant population of New France in considerable detail. One of its most striking features is its youthfulness. Both mean and modal ages of migrants were in the twenties.[10] Another notable feature is geographical. Although all regions of France contributed migrants, those on or near the Atlantic coast and those north of the Loire contributed the most. A perhaps surprising feature, considering the rural destinations of many migrants to Canada, is that about two-thirds of them came from towns and cities. Elites, artisans, and labourers made up a disproportionately large number, whereas the very poor were underrepresented.[11]

The total number of migrants from France to the St Lawrence Valley during the entire period of the French regime was about 30,000. At least 14,000 came to the Laurentian settlements in the seventeenth century alone, with a peak in the decades around Barbe Hallay's arrival.[12] Such numbers might seem to suggest large groups of French people in North America, but many of these migrants went back to France.[13] French immigration to the Americas was actually quite small when compared with immigration from other parts of Europe. Gross migration from France to all of New France for the period 1608–1700 was around or slightly above 15,000, whereas England, with only a third the population, sent about 380,000 to the Americas during the same period.[14] The discrepancy in size between colonial settlements becomes even more obvious when looking at specific towns. Mexico City's population was already about 100,000 at the start of the century, and Potosí, a centre of mining in South America, reached about 150,000 at its peak.[15] Further north, Boston had exceeded 2,000 people by the early 1660s. The largest French settlement in New France was the town of Québec, and it had nowhere near such numbers. In 1659, its population was under 800.[16]

Although leaders of the colony were aware that many people were leaving, they were uncertain about why. New France's governor at the time of Barbe Hallay's arrival, Pierre de Voyer d'Argenson, thought that the departures greatly weakened the country, but he said that he was not sure he could retain them.[17] Historians, with the benefit of hindsight, have been able to analyze the problem that the governor could not solve. One general difficulty was that of transforming visitors into colonists.[18] At a personal level, many migrants lacked the tight family connections that would hold them in North America. Distant kin, friends, and patrons were all important in early modern Europeans' networks, but during the seventeenth century the immediate family was coming to take precedence over the rest. Many were trying to plan for the maintenance of the family group beyond the lifetimes of individual members, and such planning was stretched beyond feasibility when individuals were separated from one another by thousands of leagues of ocean.[19] Family units had been favoured in the recruitment process during the early years of French colonization, but authorities started to change their minds about the value of this policy when they calculated the high costs of sending families and supporting unproductive children. By the time Hallay's family arrived, most French migrants to New France came as single people without spouses, children, or parents.[20] Barbe Hallay's family, because they came together, brought the ties of kinship with them.

Members of Hallay's family probably knew people already in the colony. Barbe's father had been given possession of land in the seigneurie of Beauport on 23 January 1656, so he must have come to Canada before the rest of his family, in 1655 at the latest.[21] This connection to settlers in New France might have helped attract the family, and recruiters in France might have encouraged them more directly. Prior to New France becoming a royal colony in 1663, migration was closely connected with private commercial interests. The crown granted trading monopolies to private companies, and these companies were obligated to find settlers.[22] Recruitment was not an easy task. The two biggest obstacles were motivation and reputation: much of the audience being addressed favoured the familiar, and the destination being proposed was widely perceived as unattractive. Peasants in early modern France were often hesitant about taking risks and suspicious of novelty. Historians have characterized this attitude as backwards, but it was actually very reasonable. When vulnerable to famine, disease, and war, when lacking capital and the means to purchase new equipment, a decision to continue with proven practices that would at least ensure subsistence was much safer than trying something new that might fail.[23] The peasants were not unaware of changes around them or uninterested in new developments; they were selective in their innovations. When times were good, peasants sold their surplus to urban markets, increased the size of their landholdings, used credit, and accumulated capital. When times were bad, they created cottage industries, looked for work in the growing cities, or moved to different rural areas.[24]

It is not only historians who assume backwardness in early modern peasants. Writers from the seventeenth century sometimes showed the same assumption in their complaints.[25] The Jesuit Paul Le Jeune devoted a chapter of his 1636 *Relation* to "Some Advice to Those who Desire to Cross Over into New France." In it, Le Jeune listed what could be accomplished with the right attitude and hard work. A poor man "who can handle the axe, the hoe, the spade, and the plough," if willing to work, "could become rich in a little while in this country." Le Jeune believed that New France would someday be "a terrestrial Paradise," provided that God continued to bestow his blessings on it. In the meantime, however, Le Jeune thought that the inhabitants would need to labour as did Adam in the original Paradise, "not to stay there and do nothing." Convinced that migrants could have an excellent life in New France if they worked hard enough, Le Jeune pondered why more people were not coming. He was especially puzzled about the "strong and robust peasants in France who have no bread to put under their teeth," and wondered if the poor were simply held in place by the forces of familiarity. "Is it possible," he asked, "they are so afraid of losing sight of the village steeple, as they say, that they would rather languish in their misery and poverty, than to place themselves someday at their ease among the inhabitants of New France, where with the good things of earth they will far more easily find those things of heaven and of the soul?"[26] Le Jeune thought that peasants allowed fear of change to get the better of their judgment. This interpretation might have made sense to him once he was in Canada, but it underestimates what migrants would need to do to get there. The mobility and change undertaken by peasants within France paled in comparison to what was required of those leaving to cross the ocean.

Anyone contemplating migration would have found it difficult to assess exactly how much difference they should expect between France and New France. Early French explorers' accounts were distorted by hopes for riches and a passage to Asia.[27] The descriptions of New France circulating by Barbe Hallay's time had become more realistic in some respects, but they were still neither coherent nor consistent.[28] The problem for those in Europe who wanted to learn more about North America was not only a shortage of reliable accounts, but also uncertainty about how to interpret the information that came their way. Some writers characterized New France as a place that strongly resembled France (or would do so soon), while others emphasized differences.[29] As many of these writers knew, their readers had already formed a negative opinion on the subject. A private letter from 1651, probably written by the gentleman Simon Denys in Québec to his brother-in-law in Tours, contrasts what the writer perceived as the true positive aspects of New France with its bad reputation. Among the "blessings by which God has favoured this country" were good health for the inhabitants, fertile soils producing wheat and vegetables of excellent quality, healthy waters and even healthier beer, an abundance of fish and fowl as well as game, and plenty of firewood. Moreover, the people were friendly and generous, "visiting one another as do brothers," and inviting anyone who passed their habitation to come in and drink some milk or wine. The letter also described what must have seemed quite a remarkable change to the class system of ancien régime France. In Canada, all were noble, free from taxes, tributes, military requisitions, and other similar exactions. The writer further claimed that men, women, and children of illustrious birth dressed and adorned themselves as well as in Paris, and he asserted that Québec lacked nothing in comparison to any city in France. Exaggerations and implausible assertions aside, the general point of the letter-writer was clearly supposed to be that life in New France could be just as comfortable as in France, and this point needed to be made because the colony had a poor reputation: "If you hear about Canada at all in France," he said, "you imagine a certain horrible and uncultivated wilderness."[30] This image was on the mind of Pierre Boucher, Governor of Trois-Rivières, when he wrote the *Histoire véritable et naturelle des mœurs & productions du pays de la Nouvelle France* in 1664. As Boucher said near the end of the book's first chapter, he wished to "remove the bad opinion that the vulgar hold" about Canada.[31] Denys and Boucher, sharing mercantile interests that led them to consider the colony in terms of its suitability for investment and potential for profit, were confident in the bounty of the land and optimistic about the future of commerce and agriculture.[32] But they also knew that Canada's reputation was unfavourable in France, and that this reputation was proving difficult to dismantle.

The French government did not always do much to help. Jean-Baptiste Colbert, chief minister for the king, thought that France was at risk of decline if too many people moved away: he worried that the kingdom was shrinking due to wars, plague, and poverty. In 1666, in response to efforts by New France's intendant to make Canada a "great and powerful state," Colbert replied that "it would not be prudent" for the king "to depopulate his kingdom as he would have to do to populate Canada." Instead, Colbert argued that the best way to strengthen New France would be to empower justice, establish a good police force, protect the inhabitants, and help the colonists win against their enemies. When these things were well observed, Colbert said, the population would increase gradually on its own.[33] The government in France also took direct measures to increase the colony's population. To encourage marriages, they put in place a housing construction program, financial incentives for newlyweds, and fines for fathers of boys still unmarried at age twenty and girls still unmarried at sixteen.[34] With measures like these, the government was hoping that a few French people would move to New France, and then grow the population by natural increase.

Although the number of immigrants was still small when Barbe Hallay crossed the Atlantic, New France was no longer really all that new to those in France. Europeans had been thinking about the Americas for more than a century and a half by this time, and struggling to reconcile direct observations with readings of ancient texts whose authors were ignorant of the Americas' existence.[35] In trying to assimilate information received from travellers with the ways of thinking inherited from antiquity, early modern Europeans found that they could only squeeze so much new knowledge into old categories.[36] The Americas did change ideas in Europe, but often slowly and partially. The shift in European writings about New France in particular follows the same broad pattern as for European writings about the Americas generally. French travellers came with literary and philosophical ideas already in their minds. Their interpretations of what they observed were shaped by these preconceptions, but their observations also challenged the older ideas.[37] On the whole, the French tended to perceive more familiarity in New France than did Spanish writers visiting places further south in the Caribbean, Mesoamerica, and South America. Some of this difference can be attributed to chronology, since texts about New France were written later, once the writers were more aware of the Americas. Geography played a role too. The climate in temperate Europe was closer to that in the St Lawrence Valley than to that of the tropical Americas.[38]

The climate in New France was not identical to that of France, however. Weather was a famous example of a notable difference between the two places, and likely one of the topics that would have reached Barbe Hallay before her departure from France. French writers were particularly struck by the coldness of the Canadian winter. Some reported that a person really had to be in Canada themselves to understand winter completely,[39] but many still tried to explain it to readers far away. Their accounts show an expectation for similarities, a curiosity about differences, and a predisposition to try and change what they did not like. Pierre Biard wrote in his Jesuit *Relation* of 1616 that one of the reasons behind the name "New France" was because the lands are parallel to France. Although Biard thought that New France ought to have the same influences and temperatures as France, being in the same climate and at the same latitude, he was forced to admit that the two areas actually differed greatly from one another in both weather and seasons. Uncertain why winters were so much harsher in New France, Biard suggested that it was because Canada had more water and less cultivation. About the water, there was not much French settlers could do; they could, however, cultivate more land: "If the land were inhabited and cultivated, from it and from the dwellings of the inhabitants would arise exhalations, that is, warm and dry fumes; furthermore, the sun would find it prepared to feel its rays, and to scatter the cold and fogs."[40] For Biard, therefore, the less desirable aspects of weather could be modified by human settler activity. It was an idea of climate with imperial implications, since settlers could alter the weather to make it more like that of France.

Biard's discussion of weather was part of a larger discourse among early modern Europeans interested in climates. The system they favoured came from classical Mediterranean geographers, most often represented by Ptolemy (c. 90–168 CE). Within this system, as it came to be understood in the early modern period, several latitudinally arranged bands of hot and cold wrapped around the world. There was a frozen zone at each of the poles, a torrid zone in the tropics, and temperate zones in between. This theory told them that climate should be constant at any given latitude anywhere on the globe, yet travel taught otherwise. In the tropics, European travellers noticed that some areas near the equator were temperate rather than torrid, summers were cooler and wetter than expected, and prevailing winds blew in different directions than in Africa and Eurasia. In North America, travellers became increasingly aware that the winters were far colder than in Europe.[41]

Several seventeenth-century French writers noted that Québec was south of Paris or on a parallel with La Rochelle, yet had a much harsher winter.[42] They were long perplexed about why.[43] Among the explanations offered, two were especially common: winds passing over snowy mountains, and extensive forests.[44] The Récollet missionary Gabriel Sagard wrote in his *Le Grand voyage du pays des Hurons*, published in 1632, that wind from the north-west brought the cold, and the country was not yet sufficiently inhabited or cleared of its forests.[45] When the Jesuit Paul Le Jeune tried to explain in 1633 why there were frosts every month of the year, he said that they had a chain of mountains on the north, probably always covered with snow, and that wind coming from that direction brought the cold air. In addition, they lived in the midst of large forests and on the banks of large rivers. Le Jeune concluded that the harshness of winter was not inevitable. He reported that the river was still frozen and the ground still white with snow in April, but thunderstorms indicated heat in the air, "and these snows and this cold were accidental and contrary to the nature of the climate." His suggestion was to clear the country as far as the mountains: "Experience teaches us that the woods engender cold and frosts." When an area is cleared, it is sooner freed from snow.[46] Similar ideas about Canada's cold were still circulating around the time of Barbe Hallay's arrival. When Asseline de Ronval tried to explain in 1662 why winters were so cold and snowy in Canada, he said that the land was almost entirely covered by thick and high trees, and the sun could not pierce the trees to warm the ground.[47] François Joseph Le Mercier wrote in his *Relation* of 1664–65 that once forests were exchanged for cities, the lands, since they were in the same climate as France, would "also have the same benign atmosphere."[48]

The connection between forests and weather in the Americas went back in European minds at least to the 1490s with Spanish travellers in the Caribbean.[49] It continued through the seventeenth century with English travellers noting colder temperatures to the north.[50] European writers were optimistic that the cold in North America could eventually be tempered, yet French leaders eager to increase the number of colonists in Canada knew that in the meantime stories about the cold would dissuade potential immigrants. So they tried to adjust Canada's wintery reputation by contending that this cold was bearable and even beneficial. Pierre Boucher reassured his readers that although the land in New France was covered with snows, and the cold was a bit bitter for the five months of winter, it was not entirely disagreeable. Rather, the cold was actually joyful. Most of the days were beautiful and serene, and people walked around everywhere with the help of snowshoes. "In truth," Boucher confided, "the snows here are less troublesome than are the muds in France." Elsewhere in his book Boucher said that there were some very cold days, but that this did not stop people from doing what they needed to do: they put on more clothing, they made good fires in their houses, and they rode sleds. Moreover, the air was especially healthy in winter. Boucher seemed to be saying that the winter was unpleasant for those not yet accustomed to the cold, but not really so bad as many believed. In his list of the most bothersome things about New France, the length of winter ranked not first, nor second, but third – after attacks by the Iroquois, and mosquitoes.[51] New France's intendant Jean Talon also struggled against the harsh reputation of Canada's winters. When he wrote to Jean-Baptiste Colber in 1665, Talon admitted that the climate of New France made people apprehensive because of its great cold, but added that the country was nevertheless so healthy that people were rarely sick and lived for a very long time.[52] Boucher and Talon were optimistic in their assessments of the colony's progress so far, hopeful that things would continue to improve in the future, and convinced that the current state of cold actually brought some advantages.[53]

Their optimism was not shared by all, and immigrants like Barbe Hallay may not have felt entirely convinced by it. The intendant Jacques de Meulles wrote in about 1684 that "Canada has always been regarded as a country at the end of the world, and as an exile that might almost pass for a [sentence] of civil death."[54] Even accounting for some possible exaggeration by de Meulles, the French settlements on the St Lawrence truly were cut off from France for much of the year because of ice on the river and in the Gulf of St Lawrence. When François Dollier de Casson wrote his history of Montréal in 1672, he chose to divide his chapters by year. The division between one year and the next was not that of the standard calendar, however, but was placed rather at the point when vessels departed from Canada to

France.[55] The first vessels from France arrived in Canada between May and September, and the last to depart left at some point between September and November. If vessels arrived relatively early and left relatively late in the season, Québec was isolated from France for only seven months; in other years, the isolation could last as long as eleven.[56]

Stories about winters, remoteness, and isolation had real force in France. In combination with tales of hostile neighbours, they impeded the efforts even of those most determined to migrate. When three Hospitalière nuns tried to leave La Flèche for Canada in 1659, the same year as the Hallay family came, the townspeople gathered around the Hôtel-Dieu to try and prevent the departure because they had learned the sad lots of children sent to Canada a few years earlier who had died from misery or had been killed by the Iroquois. It took assertion by the men accompanying the nuns, with swords raised in hand, to clear a way through the crowd.[57]

Those who decided to migrate to Canada might have calculated that the chances for success were actually quite good in spite of the challenges. It was easier in New France to own land and climb the social ladder, which might help explain why, on average, settlers in Canada were slightly better educated than their French contemporaries who stayed in Europe.[58] People were moving across France to seek economic or social advancement too, and their movement across the ocean extended these migratory patterns into an expanding Atlantic economy.[59] However remote New France was thought to be, it was in reality firmly embedded within early modern global networks.

To take one example of how these networks wove through people's lives, consider an enthusiastic account of foods that Marie de l'Incarnation included in a letter to her son in 1668. She was sending him the seed of a squash, which she called "the pumpkins of the Hiroquois," that the French had received from the Wendat. Marie knew that this food would be new to her son, and indeed so new to France that she was unsure whether the *terroir* there would change its taste. She explained that the French in Québec prepared the squash in diverse ways, baking them in the oven like apples, or braising them like pears.[60] Already in this account, Marie was showing how the settlers were adding new elements to their diet, and incorporating North American foods that were prepared using methods recognizable to Europeans.[61] The nuns may not always have understood the histories of these foods. They imported sunflowers from France, for example, even though the plant was originally cultivated in the

Americas.[62] They certainly were aware that some of their foods were new to them. Along with melons (possibly musk melons) from Montréal that she declared "as good as the best of France," Marie de l'Incarnation also received a different kind of melon, one that she called "des melons d'eau," or watermelons. She explained that these were in form like pumpkins, and eaten like melons – some people salting them, and others adding sugar. The French found them excellent.[63] They were only the latest group to appreciate the watermelon. It had probably first been grown in western, central, and southern Africa, where it was highly desirable not only as a food, but also as a vital source of water in arid regions. From here, the watermelon spread to south-western Asia and northern Africa, where its seeds were placed in Tutankhamun's tomb. It had reached India by the ninth century, Baghdad and al-Andalus by the tenth, and China by the twelfth. The watermelon was probably brought to the Americas by Spaniards and Africans. It was growing in Brazil by 1613, Massachusetts by 1628, and Barbados by 1648. Its cultivators were sometimes European settlers, but more often it was Africans growing the plant and Indigenous peoples who spread its seeds – including in the Great Lakes region, which may have been watermelon's point of departure for Montréal and from there to Marie de l'Incarnation's convent in Québec.[64] Marie provided no indication that she was aware of watermelon's long global history, but this food that was new and excellent to her was ancient and widespread for others, linking Canada to people thousands of leagues away. As its path to Québec shows, New France was not in all respects nearly so isolated as some French writers declared.

SAILING TO QUÉBEC

Once Barbe Hallay's family made the decision to migrate, they had to get to a port and then cross the ocean. The cost of their travel was not negligible. The fare for a passenger sailing to New France was between sixty and eighty *livres*, an amount of money that would have taken a skilled craftsman about a year to accumulate.[65]

In attempting to identify which vessel carried Hallay's family, we can narrow down the possibilities to the three ships that set out for New France in 1659. We know that this is the year of Barbe's journey, which is more information than we have for most migrants.[66] The French maritime commercial code mandated that passenger lists be maintained, but these lists could be quite sloppy when they were drawn up, and the registers of the Quebec Admiralty have disappeared while many in French ports have been destroyed through fire and negligence.[67] All three ships sailing for New France in 1659 departed from the port of La Rochelle. One of them, the *Prince Guillaume*, let off people and merchandise in Acadia and only went up the St Lawrence to collect some debts. The *Sacrifice d'Abraham*, about 300 tons, arrived in Québec on 16 June. The *Saint André*, also about 300 tons, arrived in Québec on 7 September.[68] Since members of Hallay's family are recorded at Québec in August of 1659,[69] she must have been on the *Sacrifice d'Abraham*. François de Laval, who sailed on the same ship, found the journey not too harrowing or dangerous.[70] Passengers on the *Saint André* had a more difficult journey, marked by storms and sickness. A fever broke out, many became ill, eight to ten died at sea, and then the contagion spread through the town of Québec.[71]

This town was fairly new as a French settlement when Barbe Hallay landed, having been founded fifty-one years earlier by Samuel de Champlain, but human habitation on the site went back thousands of years. Indigenous groups had hunted, fished, and farmed along the shores of the river, which they used as a highway for the circulation of people, goods, and ideas.[72] The French presence was more recent. Jacques Cartier sailed up the St Lawrence in the 1530s and 1540s. He spent the winter of 1535–36 just outside the St Lawrence Iroquoian town of Stadacona, the location where the town of Québec would later be built.[73] When Champlain sailed up the St Lawrence in 1608, European and Indigenous societies were being transformed by earlier contacts. A trade was developing that sent beaver furs to Europe, where they would be turned into felt for fashionable hats, and objects of iron and glass beads were being passed along into the interior of North America, where they were prized for their usefulness and beauty.[74] Champlain could find little trace of the people of Stadacona or the other agriculturalists of the St Lawrence Valley, but he and the French king had reasons to make another attempt at settlement: the trade provided an economic incentive, and the English were founding colonies to the south, which meant that there would be competition from another European country for access to the resources of northeastern North America.[75]

In 1608, twenty-eight Frenchmen built a "habitation" at the base of the cliff where the St Lawrence River narrowed between the end of the estuary and the start of fresh water. The site was well chosen to control trade. All watercraft sailing between the ocean and the interior had to pass by this very spot. It was also defensible. With a promontory rising about forty metres from the shoreline, the French could protect the location with cannons on high ground. The cliff face made it difficult for potential attackers to reach the promontory from the river, yet a level area along the shore provided a place for commercial buildings with access to the water.[76] Soon, the habitation had a storehouse for supplies, lodgings for the men and for Champlain, a forge and workshops, and even a dovecote to house pigeons, all protected by a palisade, encircled by a ditch, and guarded by cannon. Symbols of France were there too, including a flag flying from the roof and the escutcheon of Pierre Dugua, Sieur de Mons and the holder of the trading monopoly, in the courtyard. Around the fort Champlain planted some gardens – useful for food, ornamental, and symbols of French order.[77] In spite of their efforts, however, the French attempt at settlement barely survived the first winter: of the twenty-eight who had arrived in the fall of 1608, only eight remained alive the following spring, and they were weakened by scurvy and dysentery.

This French attempt at establishing a permanent settlement would have failed were it not for relief from French ships in the spring, and, more importantly, ongoing help from Indigenous allies. The French had inserted themselves into the international relations of Indigenous North America by allying themselves with the Innu, the Algonquin, and the Wendat. Because of the international system already in place, French alliance with some groups made them the enemy of others, and relations were especially fraught with the Haudenosaunee.[78] The settlement at Québec also generated tensions with allies, as Innu oral history records: "At first, [the French] did not plant very much [...] They must have grown only what they needed to feed themselves [...] They had to surround their garden with a wooden fence. Then, while the Innu were not there, while they were gone inland, the French must have expanded it, they must have increased the land on which they grew wheat [...] They must have made it bigger and bigger, and the Innu must have ended up leaving their land of Uepishtikueiau."[79] Champlain's planting of gardens, much like French writers' optimism about changing the climate of New France, had imperial implications for a group hoping to settle permanently.[80] By the time the Hallay family arrived, half a century after Champlain's horticultural experiment, French gardens and farms had spread some distance from the initial habitation into the replication of French agricultural practices along the river.

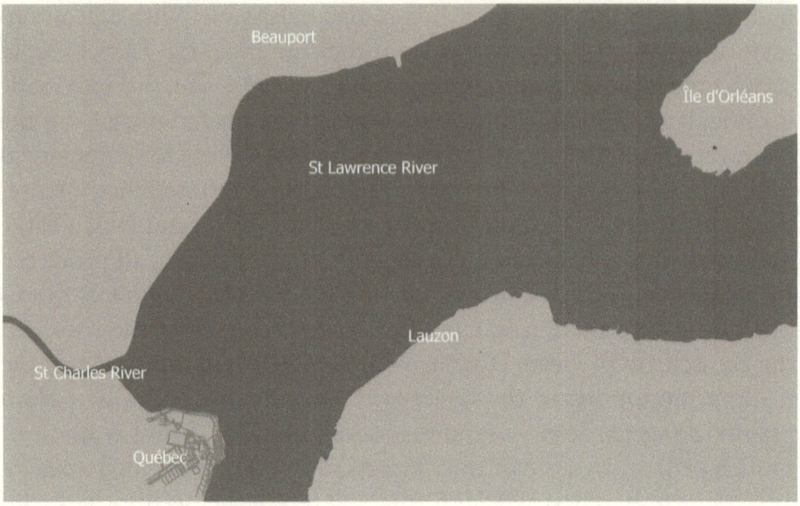

1.2 The region around Québec

Barbe Hallay's first view of Québec would have been from the deck of the ship. Ocean-going vessels could not dock; they had to moor in a deep part of the river, and then smaller boats took people and cargo ashore. What would she have seen? The basic features of the town would have looked much as they did to Asseline de Ronval, a traveller from Dieppe who described Québec three years later. One thing Asseline noted right away was that the city was divided into two parts, upper and lower. The Upper Town was where most of the religious buildings were located. These were well built, Asseline said, places where the inhabitants could live almost as comfortably as in France. Overlooking the Lower Town was a small fortress set against the side of a small steep mountain. A person went from one part of the town to the other along a steep road. The Lower Town was on the banks of the river and was the centre of commercial activity, "the dwelling place of the merchants and the place with all the shops."[81]

This traveller's description accords with visual evidence from the period. A plan of the town drawn in 1660 shows a small crowd of buildings in the Lower Town. They are arranged along an irregular grid of roads, hemmed in between the cliff and the river. A narrow path leads to the Upper Town with its more spacious arrangement of mostly religious buildings and a few roads leading out of the town in a radial pattern.[82]

Another plan from a few years later shows a collection of small and medium buildings clustered in the Lower Town, and more widely spaced religious and government buildings along with a few houses in the Upper Town.[83]

The impression from both these plans is of a settlement that was crowded and confined in the Lower Town, open and ready for expansion in the Upper Town, and altogether very small. It could easily be seen in its entirety during the day, but once night fell so too did visibility. The moon and the stars provided some light, brighter in the winter than in the summer because of reflection off the snow. On cloudy nights and during the new moon, the darkness of night was very dark indeed, and the only artificial sources of light available to people were candles and lanterns.

Perhaps the first building that would have caught Barbe's attention from the deck of the ship was the one called, rather grandly, the Château Saint-Louis. Construction was still ongoing in 1659 for this, the third governor's residence to be built overlooking the river. It was the base of power for the governor, who was the king's representative in New France, head of the armed forces, and responsible for official diplomacy with Indigenous nations. For all its importance, the structure of the residence itself might not have lived up to the expectations generated by its name. A stone building of a single story measuring slightly under twenty-eight metres long and eight metres wide, it had four main rooms, two of which had a private chamber or closet, and a kitchen with a ladder leading to a cellar. This was not quite the "château" of baroque French imaginations, although along the side facing the river it did have a private terrace that offered beautiful views of the surrounding area, and also a garden with vegetables and possibly ornamental plants for the governor's private use.[84] Other notable buildings were the college of the Jesuits, the Ursuline convent, and the Hôtel-Dieu hospital, all substantial stone structures in the Upper Town.[85]

Some of the domestic architecture would have looked familiar to Hallay, some less so. The houses were a mixture of different styles. The dwellings of a group of Wendat near where the path to the Lower Town passed by the church, a kind of fort within the fortified city, had been established in 1656 after the Wendat were dispersed from their territories in the west.[86] The French settlers' houses were varied in appearance, reflecting the building traditions of the different regions from where the settlers had come. These houses were constructed of stone, of wood,

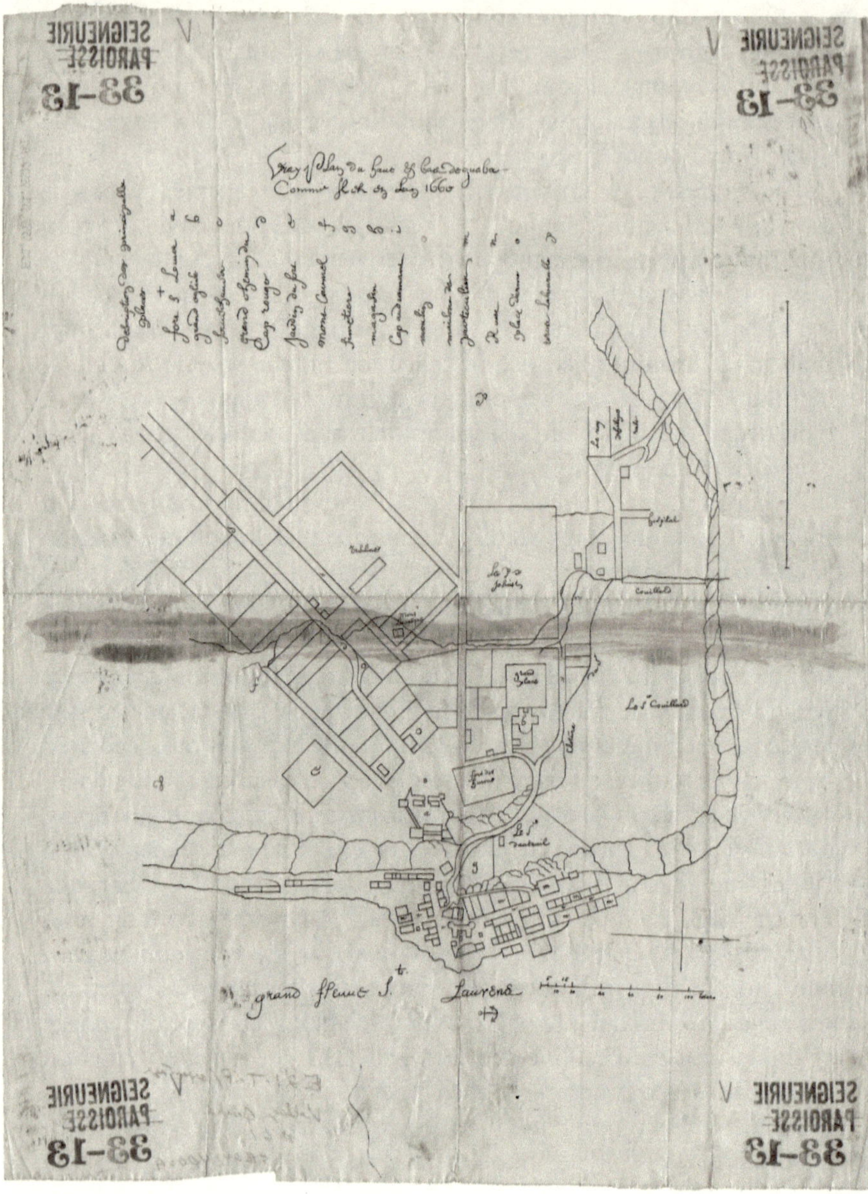

1.3 The town of Québec in 1660, from a plan probably by Jean Bourdon

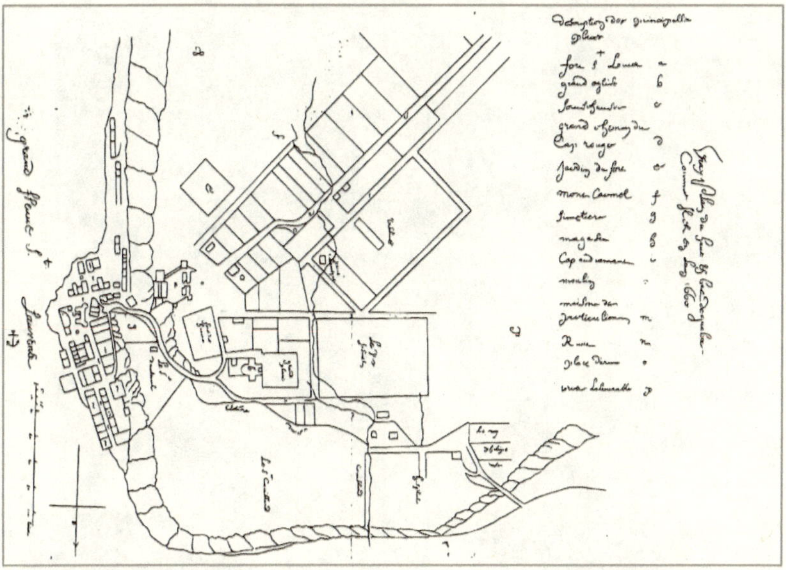

Ursuline Convent
Mill
Place d'armes
Fort Saint-Louis
Store
Cemetery
Huron Fort
Jesuit College
Notre-Dame Church
Lower Town
Upper Town
Hôtel-Dieu Hospital
N
St Lawrence River
0.5 KM

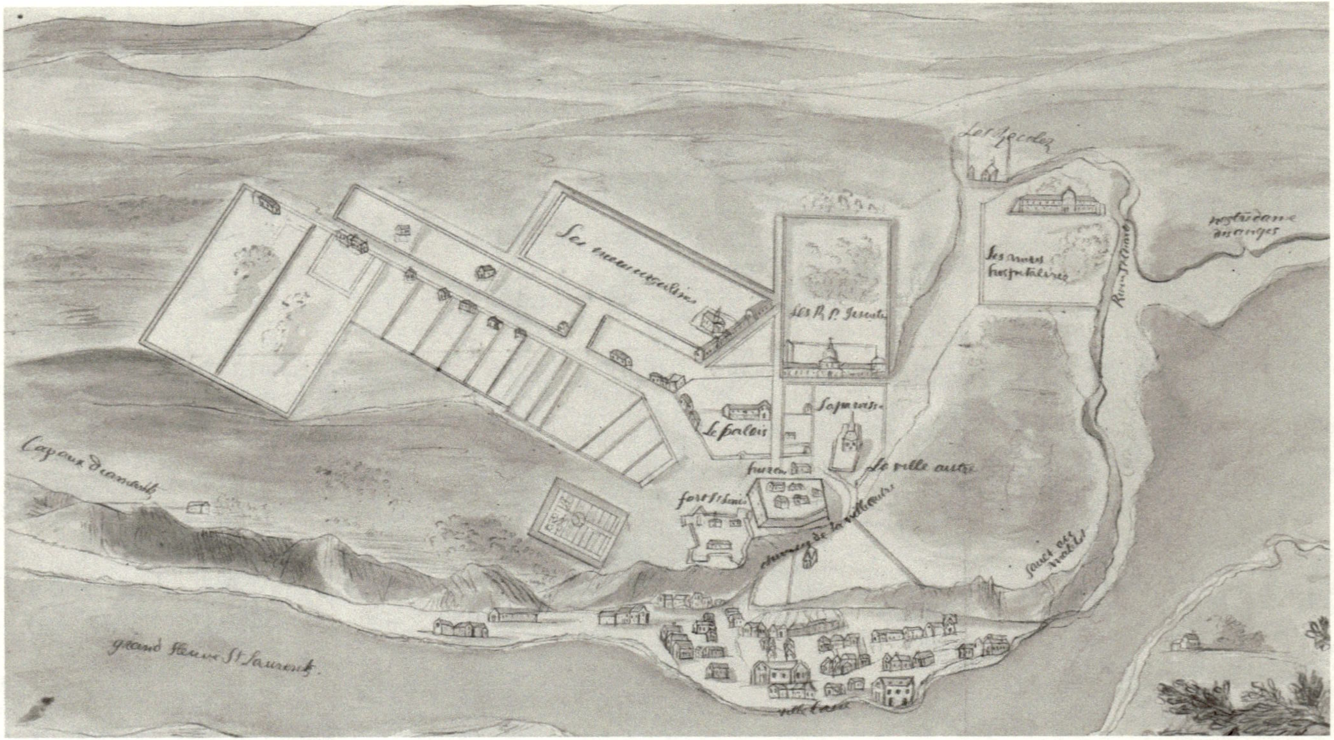

1.4 The town of Québec in 1663, detail from a plan by Jean Bourdon

or a combination of both, with roofs made from wooden boards that were steeply pitched to shed snow and rain. If there was a dominant form of house construction, it was probably a one- or two-storey house made of "colombage pierroté," a method sometimes called "half-timbered," in which timber frames were filled in with stones and mortar. Colonists desired stone and half-timber houses because these were of high status back in France, but such constructions were actually less comfortable in the climate of Canada than houses made entirely of wood, a material that insulated against the cold more effectively than either stone or rubble.[87] It took some time for builders to learn how to modify France's architectural styles to suit Canada's climate. One house, for example, had different floors from different stages of construction. In its older section was a wooden floor lying directly on top of hard-packed earth. This would have been very cold in the winter, which was possibly why a later section had a floor raised with a crawl space underneath. Some houses in Québec were quite comfortable for the time. Guillaume Couillard and Guillemette Hébert had a house in the Upper Town that they expanded in 1653 with a timber-framed and plaster-covered addition of almost six metres in length, enhanced with two chimneys and white-washed interior walls.[88]

Some of Québec's soundscape would have been recognizable to Barbe Hallay. Early modern people listened carefully to the sounds of nature such as wind, water, and especially thunder.[89] Because of Québec's location and its small size, these sounds were probably slightly more prominent in the soundscape than what Barbe had known in France, but not of an entirely different sort. Physiologists in seventeenth-century Europe thought that the loudest sounds people heard besides thunder were cannon-fire and bells.[90] Both were heard in Québec. Cannons were fired not only when defending the town against attack, but also to announce the arrival of a governor and on the morning of New Year's Day. They were additionally fired at moments of civic religious significance during processions, at the elevation of the host during mass on New Year's Day and on the feast of St Louis, during the Christmas Eve midnight mass, and on the eves and mornings of the feast days of St Joseph, St Ignatius, the Conception, and the Annunciation.[91] Perhaps more pleasing to the ear were bells. These could be sounded in different ways – quickly or slowly, regularly or in bursts, pealed in a church or rung through the streets. They marked the beginning, middle, and end of each day, called parishioners to prayer, summoned people to remembrance of the deceased and the celebration of weddings, and raised the alarm.[92] As musical as the bells were the birds around Québec. They would have been especially tuneful at the time of Hallay's arrival, which coincided with the annual peak of breeding birdsong. The songs of some of the warblers and sparrows would have been new to a migrant from France. So would the calls of the blue jays and northern cardinals, whose brightly coloured feathers may have appealed to Hallay's eyes too. The songs of winter wrens, barn swallows, and some owls could have sounded more familiar to Hallay, since similar species were also found in Europe. Depending on how observant she was, Hallay might have noticed songs that were similar, but not identical, to what she had heard from birds in France. The song of the American robin, for example, is close to that of the European blackbird.[93]

At least one aspect of Québec's soundscape would have struck Hallay as notable for its absence. In European towns, horses were a principal means of transport. Their hoof-beats, whinnies, and snorts were everywhere, and the clattering of wooden and iron-rimmed wheels on roads generated considerable din in the urban environment.[94] But there were no horses in Québec when Hallay's family arrived. A horse had been brought over in 1647 as a gift from the Compagnie des Habitants to the governor, but it seems to have been the only one of its kind. Not until 1665 were more horses brought to the St Lawrence Valley.[95] When Hallay disembarked, therefore, there were no equine noises in the soundscape of New France.

The music in the churches would have sounded basically familiar to Hallay in form. Psalms, hymns, motets for one or two parts, with or without basso continuo, and polyphonic masses could be heard at the convent of the Ursulines, at the Hôtel-Dieu, at the chapel of the Jesuits, and at the church of Notre-Dame-de-la-Paix.[96] There was a viol being played at the Ursuline convent,[97] and violins and flutes sometimes accompanied mass at the church.[98] This church had an organ too, but unlike instruments in France it was paid for in both money and beaver.[99] Also unlike French music were some of the languages used in singing. A ceremony in the Hôtel-Dieu in 1659 featured the singing of hymns in four languages: French and Latin, which would have been used in France, also Wendat and Algonquin, which would have sounded new to the ears of Hallay.[100]

The precise extent of linguistic diversity among settlers in seventeenth-century New France cannot be measured with certainty. France itself was a polyglot kingdom, and its political leaders accepted linguistic plurality in its empire.[101] Historians and linguists disagree on whether French settlers in North America all spoke the same form of French, or at least closely related forms that were mutually understandable.[102] Even with some regional variation, they were likely able to communicate with one another. Hallay may have heard a greater variety of French dialects spoken in Québec than what she would typically have heard around her hometown in France, but she probably would not have had much trouble understanding or making herself understood by other French colonists.

The smells of Québec would almost certainly have been less strong than in European cities of the time, although it should probably not be said that the smells themselves were "bad" in absolute terms. Smell is especially subjective, and the same scent could be deemed unbearable by one person, yet hardly noticeable to another.[103] It is possible that milder odours were a reason behind the numerous assertions that New France had such healthy air. For early modern Europeans, noxious airs were stenches that seemed to emanate from sources of corruption and were believed to cause disease, even death. The putridness of air, or the smell of putrid odours, was noted as a concern for health, and there were fewer such odours in the towns of New France than in urban Europe.[104] This is not to say that Québec had no scents that would have been considered noxious. Beaches by the river's shore were used as a dump not only for building materials, ceramic items, glass containers, pieces of fabric, and broken tools, but also for the much more odoriferous contents of emptied privies and carcasses of butchered animals.[105] The church of Notre-Dame was running out of room for burials, and by a couple of years after Hallay's arrival people noted a "bad smell exhaling from the bodies that have been buried there." This smell went beyond unpleasantness into danger according to early modern medical reasoning, since it created "contagious and pestilential" air that would be detrimental to health.[106]

Taste might have been the last sense that Barbe Hallay engaged directly within the town of Québec, but once she ate a meal, she probably would have enjoyed the fresh food as a welcome change from the dry and salted provisions of the ship. The settlers' diets in seventeenth-century New France were healthy by the standards of their time. Archaeological excavations from the site of a fairly affluent colonist's house show that the occupants ate meat from numerous sources. The findings indicate that the most common meats from domestic livestock were pork and beef, and that the inhabitants also ate some lamb, goose, and probably chicken. Game meats included beaver, moose, duck, wild goose, partridge, and passenger pigeon. Catfish and sturgeon were common among the fish in their diet, along with some imported haddock.[107] Written sources add further information about diet. Records from the Ursuline convent show a mixture of European and North American foods. The nuns' meals were recognizably French in some ways, but the Ursulines were under no illusions that the foodways in New France could be transferred directly from France, and they adapted to the environmental and cultural realities of their location. Turkeys were eaten at the convent alongside fowl of European origin, and the nuns bought moose from hunters. Sometimes, the records specifically mention the purchase of moose tongues and muffles (the nose and upper lip of the animal), considered a delicacy in local Indigenous food cultures. The nuns ate some maize (corn) too, but much less of it than wheat. More often, they used maize to make *sagamité*, an Indigenous corn stew, for Indigenous visitors and students.[108] In general, the diet of French settlers – a diet based on bread, with varieties of meat and fish, dairy mostly in salted butter and cheese, eggs, vegetables and fruit, seasonings of salt, pepper, sugar, spices – resembled that of the French in France, although the proportion of game was higher. The settlers' drinks were similar to what they had known in France too, with milk in the summer, also water, beer, wine, cider, and the harder liquor of *eau-de-vie* year-round.[109] Barbe Hallay's first meal in Québec was likely to her taste.

THE RELIGIOUS IDENTITY OF NEW FRANCE

Barbe Hallay would have understood much of Québec's religious culture when she arrived, but not all its connections to colonialism. Colonial leaders built Catholicism into the political construction of New France, and defended colonization as a kind of religious geopolitics.[110] They used religion to distinguish the colony from the colonies of Protestant countries such as England and the Netherlands, and to justify incursions into Indigenous territories.

Missionary endeavours themselves were not new. Since the earliest days of Christianity, some adherents thought they should be persuading as many people as possible to join their religious group.[111] That same energy was still to be found among Christians more than a millennium later. The propagation of the Catholic faith was among the duties outlined in the 1486 papal bull *Orthodoxe fidei propagationem* and confirmed in the *Inter caetera* papal bulls of 1493. This obligation was given increased institutional support in 1622 with the founding of the Sacred Congregation "de Propaganda Fide," which, among other things, was to spread Catholicism among non-Catholics and protect Catholicism where Catholics lived alongside non-Catholics.[112] Secular leaders encouraged proselytizing too. The argument that French exploration and settlement in Canada brought spiritual benefit to both French and Indigenous peoples had been used since the time of Jacques Cartier in the sixteenth century. In the dedication preceding the account of his second voyage, Cartier (or someone in Cartier's name) wrote that it pleases God "that all human beings inhabiting the surface of the globe" have knowledge of Catholic Christianity. This dedication assured the king that efforts at colonization in Canada, with its fertile soils, its rich river, and its immense numbers of peoples, would improve France both materially and spiritually: "These things fill those who have seen them with the sure hope of the future increase of our most holy faith and of your possessions and most Christian name." When King François I commissioned Cartier for a third voyage, he said that the earlier voyages had been undertaken because the king was "desiring to learn of and be informed about several countries that are said to be uninhabited, and others to be possessed by savage peoples living without knowledge of God and without the use of reason." The lands of Canada – which the king believed were connected by land to Asia on the west – were "provided with several valuable commodities," but the main intention of the French, at least officially, was "to do something that is pleasing to God our creator and redeemer and that will be to the exaltation of His holy and sacred name and of our mother the holy Catholic Church."[113]

By the time Barbe Hallay arrived in 1659, New France had become even more deliberately a Catholic colony. The exclusion of non-Catholic colonists was launched in 1627 with the foundation of the Compagnie de la Nouvelle-France, the Company of New France, whose charter called for the peopling of the colony with "naturels François catholiques." This category of French Catholics was determined by religious allegiance. According to Article XVII of the company's charter, descendants of the French living in New France along with Indigenous people who professed Catholicism would be counted as "French naturals."[114]

Since religious allegiance determined French nationality, and since alliances with Indigenous peoples were necessary for the survival of the colony, missionaries were indispensable to the French colonial effort.[115] From the 1630s, members of the Society of Jesus, the Jesuits, were especially important. They raised funds and sent priests, strengthened alliances with Indigenous peoples, and brought settlers over as indentured servants.[116] The Jesuits were also able to shape their experiences into a rhetorically effective presentation of worthy asceticism. They saw Canada as well suited to arduous struggles in a fallen world, and they interpreted their struggles in a way that showcased potential for the colony's future. Paul Le Jeune, for example, described Canada in 1634 as a land that had borne little besides thorns before the arrival of missionaries, but he emphasized the likelihood of improvement, and he enumerated positive aspects of Indigenous people in order to demonstrate that they were good candidates for conversion. Le Jeune said that their bodies were strong and powerful, their minds of good quality; they only lacked education and instruction. Employing a metaphor that would have made sense to French people keen to clear forests and plant crops, Le Jeune said of Indigenous people that "their soul is a soil which is naturally good, but loaded down with all the evils that a land abandoned since the birth of the world can produce."[117] Souls and soils: for Jesuit missionaries, both could be prepared to receive seeds – spiritual or material.[118] Elsewhere, Le Jeune advised that if those holding the reins of government were zealous for the glory of God, there would be established in New France "a new Jerusalem blessed by God, composed of citizens destined for Heaven." He went on to emphasize that the time was right to start the improvements off well. "It is very easy in a new country," he wrote, "when the families arrive all disposed to receive the laws that will be established, to banish the bad customs of some places in old France, and to introduce better ones."[119]

All the settlers in New France had experiences shaped by the colony's religious identity. Two of these settlers, François de Laval and Daniel Vuil, also played particularly important roles in shaping the responses to Hallay's demonic possession as it developed in the years after her arrival. We know much more about the one than the other. Laval was a priest who came to Québec as New France's Vicar Apostolic. He wrote many documents, and much was written about him. Daniel Vuil was a miller. We have nothing written by him, nor even a paraphrase of his words in the writings of others. We do know that both these men became involved at the centre of Barbe Hallay's possession, which will be explained further in chapter 2, and that each of them occupied places along a spectrum of Christian identity in New France.

Laval arrived at Québec on 16 June 1659, at about 6 o'clock in the evening. His activities over the following days indicate his priorities. On the 17th of June, he was received into Québec with a procession that went along the shore of the river and to the Jesuits' church. On the 22nd, he had a feast with Indigenous people and spoke with them in a room at the Jesuit college. On the 29th, he celebrated a high mass, and after vespers he attended the abjuration of a heretic.[120] With these activities, Laval entered the town and helped establish the community's territory. Then he put himself forward as an evangelist to Indigenous inhabitants, performed a solemn rite in Québec's main church, and oversaw a settler's formal rejection of one form of Christianity in favour of another.[121] Each of these actions showed a dimension of New France's religious activities: colonization, settling, conversion.

Laval had chosen Canada as his destination not in spite of its roughness, but because of it. He said that he preferred "a savage country, rather than … a civilized one."[122] And he was optimistic that savagery (as he saw it) could be turned into civilization (as he hoped). A few months after his arrival, Laval wrote that Roman Catholicism flourished where French colonies were fixed, and that Christian converts, when not prevented by distance or the disruptions of war, came to the French regularly to be instructed and to receive the sacraments.[123] These points presupposed that the French settlers would be good Catholics, but such a presupposition was undercut by fissures in the religious foundations of the colony.

One of the things that we know about Daniel Vuil is that he had been a Protestant when he left France. We do not know if he converted to Catholicism in Canada, nor what his sincere beliefs might have been, but his Protestant past tainted him with suspicion. Catholic settlers perceived Protestants as a threat.[124] Protestants were thought to menace the colony from outside because the rival colonial powers closest in space to New France were Protestant, and these colonies' Indigenous allies were particularly strong. As Laval put it in a report to the pope, the Iroquois, a "wild and very cruel people, accustomed to war," were allies with the "heretical Dutch and English."[125] The Protestants were also thought to be dangers from within. They were considered potentially traitorous due to their ties to co-religionists beyond New France's bounds, and their very presence interrupted the ideal of a fully Catholic society.[126] In 1635, the Congregation for the Evangelization of Peoples in Rome directed the nuncio in

France to see that the French king not allow heretics (by which he meant Protestants) to enter Canada.[127] In official Catholic discourse, Protestantism was not even a real version of Christianity. It was typically referred to by the abbreviation "RPR," which stands for "Religion Prétendue Réformée," the "so-called reformed religion."[128]

In spite of their official exclusion, Protestants were present in New France. There was no church of any Protestant confession established, nor any clear leaders of a Protestant community (except for briefly when a Lutheran minister served during the Kirke brothers' occupation from 1629–32), but Protestant colonists, sometimes called "Huguenots," can certainly be found in the records.[129] Individual Protestant merchants from Europe made annual visits to New France, and maritime commerce remained largely in the control of Protestants for the first half of the seventeenth century.[130] Sometimes larger groups crossed the Atlantic. Marguerite Bourgeoys, founder of the Congrégation de Notre-Dame de Montréal, wrote with exasperation of her experiences on a voyage back to France in 1659, saying that the ship on which she travelled "was all Huguenot." Only seven or eight of the passengers were Catholic, she reported, and these hardly left their chamber. The Huguenots, by contrast, had a much louder presence on the ship. They sang their prayers "evening, morning, and other times," and it took the determination of Montréal's formidable nurse Jeanne Mance asking them not to sing for them to stop.[131]

Protestant arrivals in New France were expected to convert to Catholicism, which some did. Paul Le Jeune wrote in his *Relation* of 1635 of a young Protestant who came to New France as a soldier and visited the Jesuits' residence several times. After having been instructed on the principal points of Catholic belief, as Le Jeune put it, "he wanted to bring back to Old France the treasure of truth that God had made him find in the New."[132] Some form of instruction was supposed to be the norm for converts, according to the oath recorded in the "Registre des Abjurations d'Heresie depuis 1662 jusqu'à 1757." At the beginning of their declaration renouncing all heresy, "and particularly that of the supposed reformed religion," the person abjuring Protestantism was to state that they had been instructed on what Catholicism contains and teaches.[133] Many people probably abjured without much formal instruction though, undertaking instead the simple process of signing or making their mark on an act of abjuration in a church or chapel.[134]

Catholicism was the religion of most French migrants to New France by any simple measure. Like other French settlers, the members of Hallay's family were baptized Catholic as infants, married in Catholic ceremonies, and buried with Catholic rites. Many migrants were also confirmed, receiving the sacrament that was meant to strengthen and reaffirm the commitment of baptism upon reaching the age of reason.[135] Clearly, civil and religious authorities were able to obtain outward conformity to Catholic practice from most French settlers. The level of inward commitment to Catholicism is impossible to gauge, though this did not stop people from trying to assess it, sometimes with sour disapproval. An anonymous "Mémoire" from 1664 complained that people coming to Canada from La Rochelle were for the most part lacking in conscience and "almost without religion, loafers and very lazy in work," adding that they were "misleading, debauched, blasphemers."[136] La Rochelle may have been singled out in this document because of its associations with Huguenots, but colonists were criticized regardless of their place of origin. A set of rules for interments in the church of Notre-Dame in Québec published in July 1661 said that most inhabitants wished for their kin to be buried in the church, but that space was running short. The drafters of the new rules, not presuming the best of intentions among the parishioners, stated that requests for burial were often made "through vanity and ambition" rather than devotion.[137] Unacknowledged was that care for the burial of kin was typical among European Catholics at the time. Its presence among settlers in New France is evidence for a very conventional European Catholicism.[138]

This Catholicism could still include a wide variety of beliefs and behaviours, even though the boundaries between licit and illicit practices were becoming firmer, religious observances were facing growing scrutiny for whether they were truly orthodox, and secular pursuits in church buildings were increasingly being deemed inappropriate.[139] One distinction that could confuse believers then and historians now is the one between "magic" and "religion." Some scholars place the dividing line according to whether a person was trying to effect a change themselves, or asking a greater power to do so: magic is operational, in which practitioners try to control supernatural forces to get results, and religion is supplicatory, in which practitioners ask a supernatural power for assistance. With magic, people try to harness supernatural power; with religion, they try to influence divine power.[140]

Such a distinction between magic and religion can be analytically useful, but it becomes fuzzy when applied to how people of the past actually behaved.[141] Consider how the residents of Québec tried to cope with a threat to their crops. They held a procession against caterpillars. After vespers on 15 July 1646, priests, cantors, a domestic worker with the Jesuits, and two Abenaki leaders went to the Hôtel-Dieu hospital and the Ursuline convent with bells, a banner, a cross, candlesticks, and a small reliquary. Only one of the Abenaki was Christian, which seemed to displease the Jesuit superior who added to the journal entry (in Latin) that he "tolerated and concealed" it. They sang litanies and said "appropriate prayers."[142] The Jesuits' journal does not record the contents of these prayers, but the priests may have been guided by a document of about the same age, now kept in the archive of the Séminaire du Québec. It is an "Exorcismus Contra Locusta Brucos & alia Nociva Animalia," an exorcism against locusts, wingless locusts, and other harmful animals. In a text excerpted from a manual in Constance, it directs a priest, dressed in a stole and holding a cross, and an assistant, carrying holy water, to come to the place where the harmful animals are. The priest is to ask God to bless the fruit that he has made for humans and pour out his blessing so that the priest will be effective at throwing down demons and driving away diseases. Then the priest is to sprinkle the water on the boundaries of the fields, ask for mercy, and bless the fields. He is to read a psalm, a passage from the Gospel of Mark, and another prayer asking God that they be freed from the harmful animals, so that through God's power the expelled things harm none, "and leave intact these fields or gardens, until these things which had appeared serve your Majesty through Christ." Then the priest is to sprinkle the holy water on the fields three times in the form of a cross, asking for the blessing of God to descend and remain over the fields or gardens and their fruits.[143]

This activity would have been considered conventionally Catholic by those who participated in it. In France, many examples can be found of religious rituals against "harmful" animals. Pope Paul V authorized the exorcism of dolphins decimating the population of fish at Marseille in 1612. That same year, the bishop of Autun issued an authorisation for the exorcism of harmful creatures. There were adjurations of caterpillars at Aix-en-Provence in 1623 and 1636, in several parishes within the diocese of Clermont in 1670, and in the diocese of Grenoble in 1673. Often, perhaps even most of the time, the request for the ritual was made by the parishioners – it was not the clergy's initiative, though they did acquiesce to the request.[144] The formula would differ from time to time and place to place, but it was considered religious rather than magical because it called upon divine power to eject undesirable elements from a habitat.[145]

Attendance at mass, religious instruction, processions against caterpillars. This was the religious world shared by Catholics in France and the French settlers in Canada. New France as a geopolitical space was shaped, perhaps even in some sense defined, by the religion of its inhabitants, but its Catholic identity was also challenged by the realities of daily life where the borders of Catholicism wavered at the edges of French clerical influence. From erstwhile Protestant European migrants to Indigenous people who resisted missionary attempts at conversion, people living in the territory claimed by the French king as New France made religious geopolitics much messier in practice than they were meant to be in policy. Catholicism was an important element in the political formation of the colony, where all settlers were supposed to be Catholic, but it was not a simple or homogeneous system. Simmering disagreements and open disputes interrupted the utopian dream of a perfectly Catholic society. As will be shown in chapter 2, the weaknesses and insecurities in the colonial Catholicism of New France influenced the course of Barbe Hallay's possession and helped determine where the blame would be placed for her torments.

2

The Servant, the Miller, and the Infested Seigneurie

Barbe Hallay went to work as a domestic servant at the *seigneurie* of Beauport, about six kilometres north-east from the town of Québec. This estate was the first site of the demonic appearances that would continue to trouble Hallay for several years. Witnesses said that at Beauport they saw frightening spectres, heard phantasmal music, and encountered flying stones.

In some respects, these early stages of what became known as a demonic infestation followed a pattern already established in early modern European reports of demonic occurrences. They were also rooted in circumstances specific to the place and time of New France during the early 1660s. Both the vast extent of the French empire and the very local conditions of Canada helped determine how people tried to make sense of what they were seeing and hearing, who was thought to be a likely instigator of the demonic attacks, and why the settlers' anxieties about colonization amplified their fears about this suspected case of demonic interference.

A DEMONIC INFESTATION BEGINS

There is nothing to indicate that Barbe Hallay's place of employment was regarded as strange or frightening prior to the first reports of demonic appearances.

The manor house of Beauport was built in 1642 on a location next to the Beauport River. It is recalled in the name of a nearby street, "rue du Manoir," but this name was only given in 1948. The street's earlier name, "rue des Carrières," referred to quarries whose stones were used for some of the most prestigious buildings in the town of Québec, including the seminary and the bishop's residence.[1] The manor house cannot be visited today, because it was destroyed by fire in 1879, but an engraving and a photograph from the mid-nineteenth century provide an idea of what it looked like. They show a façade of about eighteen metres in length and very thick stone walls. The steep slope of the roof was good for preventing an accumulation of snow, while the multiple stone chimneys rising above the roofline indicate the presence of several fireplaces where wood was burned to heat the building through the long, cold Canadian winters. In addition to living space, the house also contained a chapel for religious services, a public area for the seigneur's administration of justice, and an office where he collected seigneurial dues.[2] Sturdy and imposing, this building stood as a symbol of seigneurial authority.

Seigneurialism was a system adopted from France, but with some important modifications in North America.[3] In 1627, the crown granted North America as a fief to the Compagnie de la Nouvelle-France, the Company of New France. This company, as vassal to the king, granted portions of its estate as subordinate fiefs to settlers. These subordinate fiefs were the seigneuries, of which there were sixty-eight in New France by 1663. Fiefs along the St Lawrence were generally granted in *censive* tenure, meaning that the vassals, the *censitaires*, owed dues and obligations to the landlords, the *seigneurs*, who could be either individuals or religious orders. Some of these seigneurs brought settlers over, but for the most part the seigneuries were still ongoing formations during the seventeenth century.[4]

The seigneur at Beauport was Robert Giffard de Moncel. The seigneurie had been conceded to him by the Compagnie des Cent-Associés (another name for the Compagnie de la Nouvelle-France) in 1634. Its lands were desirable because they were productive and well positioned on navigable rivers near the town of Québec. An area called the domain was reserved for Giffard's own use. By about 1660, it extended to both shores of the Beauport River. The rest of the lands were held by tenants. Some of the tenants' holdings were in an unconventional shape and orientation, because when Giffard was first granted the seigneurie he did not know the land well and divided it into parcels of unequal size and along an unusual axis. Over the years, Giffard increased the extent of his holdings. In addition to the manor house, Giffard also built a watermill and a windmill on the seigneurie, along with a strong house that could be used as a fortress to protect the inhabitants in times of attack.[5]

2.1 Engraving of the manor house of Beauport as it looked in the nineteenth century

2.2 Photograph of the manor house of Beauport as it looked in the nineteenth century

Barbe Hallay came to this seigneurie to work as a domestic servant. Most domestic servants in New France were men, because the colony's administration wanted to put land under the plough and they were accustomed to thinking of this as men's work, but the colony's domestic labour force included women too. Female servants were usually young single women, like Hallay, often placed in service by their families. Many were Canadian-born. Barbe was not, but since her father, Jean-Baptiste, held land in this seigneurie, he did have a connection there. In general, as in France, servants were hired both to show the fortune and rank of the head of the household, and also to take care of material needs in a world where little was mechanized. The details of the labour they performed are not always clear in the records, but surviving contracts for hiring a servant indicate that commonly expected tasks included caring for farm animals, tending to the garden, and doing the laundry. Often the contracts referred to work in much more general terms, and assumed that readers would understand a servant's duties without needing to have them spelled out. Contracts stated, for example, that the servants were to do all that they were judged honestly capable of doing, or to do all the ordinary tasks that people of that sex were accustomed to do. Servants could be paid wages, or instead they could work in exchange for lodging, food, and goods such as shoes, clothing, textiles, wheat, tobacco, alcohol, and animal skins. Barbe Hallay probably knew, in basic terms, what was expected of her while she held the job and how she would be compensated. She may not have planned on holding the job for very long. Domestic servitude was often a period of transition. Provided with the necessities of life, a bit of income or some goods, and the opportunity to gain experience in tasks essential to running a household, young domestic servants were engaged in a form of training for full adulthood.[6] Hallay's entry into the position of servant at the seigneurie of Beauport was therefore a stage in her lifecycle.

Not long after Barbe Hallay started this rather typical job, the young servant found herself at the centre of some very strange events. The Ursuline nun Marie de l'Incarnation wrote that demons and spectres terrified Hallay. She reported that François de Laval, the vicar apostolic, sent priests to perform exorcisms, and that Laval even went himself to chase away the demons, but to no avail. The manifestations became stranger. Marie wrote that phantoms were seen, and a drum and flute were heard. Stones detached themselves from the walls and flew here and there. The Jesuit priest Paul Ragueneau said that these stones passed in front of about twenty people, travelling with such a noise and force that they seemed to have been launched by a strong arm, yet did not injure any of the people they crossed. Every day, according to Ragueneau, there was a dreadful upheaval and racket. Only Hallay saw demons appearing, and these arrived under a variety of forms – men, children, beasts, and spectres of hell. Both Paul Ragueneau and Marie de l'Incarnation reported that it was the miller on the seigneurie who was causing the infestation, and Marie supplied a name: Daniel Vuil. Barbe Hallay had identified him. He appeared to her day and night, sometimes alone, sometimes accompanied by two or three others. Marie also supplied a motivation for Vuil's actions: vengeance. He had wanted to marry Hallay, and, after being refused, he wished to arrive at his ends by using the "tricks of his diabolical art" to corrupt Hallay and then make her marry him.[7]

The demonic infestation had begun.

SIGNS AND SYMPTOMS

People observing the strange events at Beauport came to different conclusions about what kind of situation they were facing. François de Laval was the most general in his assessment, writing that Barbe Hallay was "afflicted" by "some malefice."[8] With these words, Laval was indicating that an external malevolent force was affecting Hallay, but nothing more specific about what this force was. Marie de l'Incarnation was more precise, but still uncertain. She wrote in one letter that Hallay was "vexed with demons." In another, she used two terms that were related, but not synonymous, writing that Hallay was "possessed or obsessed."[9] Possession generally meant that a demon was controlling a person's body from within, whereas obsession was a form of demonic attack from outside.[10] Paul Ragueneau explained the distinction by emphasizing agency and awareness. Possession, he said, is a "malignant operation, by which the devil makes himself master of the person's power." Speech was an important sign for Ragueneau. If the devil was speaking from inside a person, then the person was possessed; if the person was still the speaker, then that person was obsessed. Because possession caused a person to lose reason and liberty, a possessed person was not free to direct their own actions and might not even be aware that they were possessed. With obsession, the person knew that their afflictions were caused by demons.[11] In his assessment of Hallay's case, Ragueneau was exact, writing that Hallay was "possessed."[12]

These different and sometimes ambivalent conclusions about what was happening to Hallay show that observers were having difficulty with discernment. That difficulty would not have surprised them. European intellectuals who wrote about demonology advised caution, since appearances could be misleading and signs that indicated possession looked much like symptoms of illness or suggestions of fraud.[13] When people described a case of possible possession, whether their own or that of someone else, they drew upon cultural presumptions of what was expected in the actions of demons, and their description was believed or not according to whether it met others' expectations of demonic activities. To use an explanation favoured by Brian Levack to account for stories of demonic possession, people implicated in a suspected case were "playing roles and following scripts that were encoded in their respective religious cultures."[14] The observers of Hallay's case noted several things that suggested to them a genuinely demonic presence. The cultural performance was in the tradition of France, but the plot changed somewhat in the theatre of New France.

The reports of the infested seigneurie were preceded by ominous signs. As Marie de l'Incarnation put it in a letter to her son, Hallay's demonic troubles were foretold by sinister portents. Appearing in the sky was a comet with its rods pointing toward the earth. In the air were a man enveloped in fire, a canoe of fire, and a crown of fire. Strange things could be heard too, including a child crying inside the body of its mother, indistinct voices of women and children with lamentable cries, as well as a thundering and horrible voice. These things, Marie wrote to her son, gave as much fright as he would think.[15]

Marie's expectation that her son back in France would sympathize with her fear depended on a shared understanding about what the signs meant. For many early modern Europeans, comets were links between the microcosm and macrocosm, wondrous appearances that foretold disasters. By the late seventeenth century, educated opinion was beginning to deviate from popular views on the significance of comets. While a strong current of popular belief continued to hold that comets heralded the wrath of God, some writers were raising the level of doubt and even expressing scorn for the idea that comets were foretellers of misfortune.[16] Observers of this comet and the other celestial phenomena over Canada in 1660 were not yet so skeptical. The Jesuit *Relation* for 1660–61 offers an interpretation that helps elucidate what Marie thought. The lamentable voices were perhaps an echo of the voices of those taken captive by the Iroquois, the canoes of fire a portent of the canoes of the enemy, the comet an "omen too clear of our mourning and our sad adventures."[17] These occurrences were all reported locally – in the town of Québec itself, on nearby Île d'Orléans, in Trois-Rivières – and they were interpreted as indicating local circumstances, but their imagery was a transatlantic mixture of symbols. The Jesuits and Marie de l'Incarnation were joining ideas that they would have known in Europe about strange things in the sky to a specifically North American situation. To them, these signs meant something bad was about to happen in New France.

Marie de l'Incarnation's description of the portents was made with hindsight, after events at the seigneurie were already causing concern. This concern arose because the manifestations reported at Beauport were consistent with what demonologists in early modern Europe identified as signs of malevolent supernatural activity. Witches and demons were believed to throw stones, and strange drumming was sometimes associated with witches and demons too.[18] People who witnessed or heard about Hallay's symptoms would also have been directed to thoughts of demonic possession because she, as an adolescent female, fit the profile of a typical early modern European demoniac in terms of age and gender.[19] Some men believed themselves possessed in early modern Europe, but most demoniacs were women or children. Europeans in the seventeenth century were aware of this preponderance among the possessed, and they had their ideas as to why. The dominant theory in theological and medical discourses was that physical and spiritual weaknesses made women and children especially susceptible. As the French physician Barthélemy Pardoux wrote in his book *De Morbis animi*, published in Lyon in 1649, "demons especially afflict women and children because of their fragile and infirm condition."[20]

Another feature of Hallay's situation that would have led observers to an interpretation of possession was her claim about the involvement of witches. The association between witchcraft and possession was an old idea with a new dimension. It was a form of the traditional belief that witches were employers of *maleficium* (harmful magic, like the "maléfices" described by Laval), augmented by the more recent notion of witches cooperating with the devil. According to the theory that possession could be initiated through the actions of a witch, demoniacs were not to blame for their possession. They had not invited it in the first place and were not responsible for their actions while possessed; it was the witches who were the willing inflictors of harm.[21]

The witches of early modern Europeans' imaginations displayed a variety of characteristics, but, most basically, they were thought to cause harm by uncanny means. Witches were commonly believed to harbour a generalized hatred for humanity and society; to direct their destructive magic towards people they knew; to use magic as an illegitimate means of dealing with feuds or rivalries; and to draw upon techniques and resources obtained through inheritance or initiation. They were also believed to be stoppable. Witches could be forced to lift their curses, and they could be legally prosecuted.[22] Although early modern witchcraft in Europe tended to be associated with women, and although women made up a majority of those accused and convicted overall, men actually outnumbered women among those suspected of witchcraft in parts of France.[23] The suspected witch in the case of Barbe Hallay, and the witchcraft he was supposedly practising, fit neatly into most of these expectations. Daniel Vuil was a suspicious person of bad customs attacking someone known to him; his motivation was vengeance for a refusal of something he desired; he worked with other magicians; and he could be stopped.

Vuil's occupation as miller might have added further suspicion, since both literary and real millers were negatively associated with exploitation and dishonest work.[24] Several factors contributed to millers' bad reputation. First, the cost of the mill gave the person working there an air of exclusivity that generated a sense of separation from the rest of the community. Mills were expensive to build and maintain. In seventeenth-century France, it was mostly seigneurs who undertook the project of constructing mills and also seigneurs who chose the millers who ran them. The miller, therefore, had a relationship with the local figure of authority that could be perceived as unusually close. Second, the running of the mill demanded special training and a somewhat unusual lifestyle. A miller required advanced technical knowledge to work with the machinery of the mill, and his dwelling was often removed from the rest of the village in order for the mill to take advantage of wind at the top of a hill or running water in a river. Partially isolated both in knowledge and location, the miller's distance from others in the community generated suspicion about what was really going on in the noisy mill. Third, the terms of the miller's employment bound him financially to the mill and its success in ways that were liable to breed resentment. Millers' leases usually required that they maintain all parts of the mill to keep it working. As payment, they kept a portion of whatever was being brought for grinding. In New

France, this was a customary right, usually fixed at every fourteenth measure of flour, which was slightly higher than in France. Tenants were forced to pay it, since they were required to make use of the "moulin banal" – the mill on their seigneurie. They could neither take their grain to a mill elsewhere that offered a better rate, nor build their own mill. When farmers were prevented by law from either grinding their grain themselves or bringing it to whichever mill offered the best deal, the cost of having their grain ground at the seigneurie's mill might well have felt exploitative even if the miller was honest in all his dealings. And sometimes the millers were dishonest. In France, millers were reported to use vessels with a false bottom that could be moved either up or down depending on whether they were measuring the grain being brought to them or the flour they were returning to the farmers.[25] Bearing such a reputation, a miller had a somewhat privileged position in early modern society, but he was not always to be trusted.[26]

A SPURNED PROPOSAL

According to Marie de l'Incarnation, the specific incident that led Daniel Vuil to instigate the demonic infestation was a refusal. He wanted to marry Barbe Hallay and said that she had been promised to him, but, because he was a man of bad customs, nobody wanted to listen. Vuil was so "irrité," Marie wrote, that "to avenge himself for this refusal, he wanted to have by his ill-will what he had not been able to obtain by the right path."[27]

It is easy to be misled into a false sense of familiarity when seeing a term from a historical document that looks the same as what we would use today, and we must be sensitive here to how words describing emotions have changed over time.[28] "Irritated" in the modern sense does not capture the sense of what Vuil was reported to have been feeling. "Irrité" did not mean "stirred up" or "exasperated, provoked, annoyed"[29] when used by seventeenth-century French writers. It meant something much stronger. The *Dictionnaire françois* from 1680 defines "irriter" as "to provoke, excite the anger of a person," and the "anger" being excited is, specifically, a desire for vengeance.[30] Writers in seventeenth-century New France used "irriter" to mean the incitement of a potentially destructive anger that, when felt by God, could lead to the punishment of sinful people, and, when felt by a person, could lead to murder.[31]

The notion of Vuil as "irrité" would have made sense to those around him who knew of the spurned proposal, although it would not have excused his behaviour. For early modern Europeans, displays of anger could be acceptable or unacceptable, depending on social context. The most acceptable displays were moderate and with good cause.[32] Vuil's anger, immoderate and caused by a rejected offer of marriage, might have been believable, but it would not have been acceptable. It would also have been perceived as potentially harmful to others because emotions were not just inner feelings for Europeans at the time. They were directed outward and thought to cause real damage.[33] This was especially so when the anger was focused through the use of witchcraft, and Vuil's anger did resemble an emotional state commonly associated with witches.[34] A witch's use of harmful magic was often believed to have been triggered as retribution for being refused something they desired, or for violations of social bonds. The devil or diabolical creatures were often believed to help the witches with their revenge, and the use of love magic by a male suitor on a female was thought to be a significant cause of possessions.[35] When Marie de l'Incarnation chose to describe Vuil's emotional state as "irritated," therefore, she meant that Vuil had been sent into a rage by having his design thwarted, and she was making a connection between unregulated emotion, witchcraft, and love magic that was already well established among early modern Europeans.

The demographic situation in Canada contributed another dimension to people's interpretation of what was causing Hallay's torments, and specifically the significance of a broken promise of marriage. New France had many more French men for every marriageable French woman than France did, and this imbalance led to changes in how marriages were formed among French settlers.

In law, marriage was based on the free exchange of vows, as it had been in the medieval period. Over the course of the sixteenth and early seventeenth centuries, its formation took on additional requirements in both canon and civil law that accumulated into layers of public acknowledgment and parental consent. The Tridentine decree *Tametsi* in 1563 stated that a marriage needed to take place before witnesses to be valid, and that it was not binding without a priest's verification of the public affirmation of consent. French royal edicts from 1556, 1579, and 1639 insisted upon consent by parents, the proclamation of banns, and the presence of four witnesses at the wedding. Minors who married in secret or against their parents' wishes could be deprived of financial assets, disinherited, in theory even put to death. Notwithstanding changes to the law, social practices did sometimes continue as before. Couples could still celebrate their weddings privately, or begin their sexual relationship after the marriage contract was signed or a verbal agreement was made but before the wedding itself. Parents could still advise and encourage their children to choose a suitable spouse without resorting to the courts. But the severity of the new penalties for disobeying the rules, and the new rules themselves, amounted to stricter control over forming a marriage. Church and state were making greater claims on who had the right or requirement to participate, and reinforcing the role of patriarchal authority within the family.[36]

One reason why church and state were so deeply invested in forming a marriage was that the choice of a spouse was so important. A married couple constituted the basic economic unit of survival, and the bond, once forged, was very difficult to undo. Barbe Hallay's ability to make her own decisions regarding her marriage would have been partially determined by her age, since both law and custom granted a person more control over whom to marry as they grew older. A challenge when examining this case is that Hallay's precise age at her arrival in Canada is difficult to establish. In both the 1666 and 1667 censuses, she is listed as twenty years old, meaning that she would have been born sometime between 1645 and 1647, and would therefore have been between eleven and fourteen years old at the time of her arrival at Québec.[37] Neither of these censuses, however, is entirely reliable on age. A person's age is given in more than 97 per cent of cases in the 1666 census, but these ages are better regarded as estimates rather than certainties. When measured against other documents that provide dates of birth, the ages as reported in the 1666 census are off by at least one year in about a quarter of the cases. Most often, the discrepancy is from one to three years, and sometimes it is as many as twelve years.[38] The census of 1667 is probably slightly more accurate.[39] There was another census in 1681, and here Hallay's age is given as thirty-six, making her year of birth 1644 or 1645 and meaning that she would have been about fourteen or fifteen when she came to Canada.[40]

Given these possibilities, it is reasonable to conclude that Barbe Hallay was probably between twelve and fourteen years old when she disembarked at Québec. This would put her at the low end of the range for age at first marriage in seventeenth-century New France, where most women were first wed between the ages of fourteen and twenty-three and their median age at first marriage was twenty. We do not know how old Daniel Vuil was, but he was probably older. Men in New France were most often first married between the ages of twenty-two and thirty-two, with a median age of twenty-eight.[41]

Even at such a young age, Hallay would have reached the legal age of consent for marriage (twelve for girls), and she would have been legally able, with parental consent, to choose her spouse. Marie de l'Incarnation's letter is ambiguous about who, exactly, was agreeing to the marriage when saying that Hallay had been promised to Vuil.[42] Regardless of whether it was Hallay or her parents, that promise would have established an agreement; in the space between official law and customary practice, breaking a promise to marry was considered something like a breach of contract. By law, Hallay was perfectly within her rights to withdraw from an agreement to marry if she chose, and her parents were perfectly within their rights to withhold consent. In custom, a promise was still a promise. And the demographic situation in New France would have brought still further pressure to bear on Hallay to follow through with any nuptial agreement that had been made.

Hallay and her family arrived in Canada toward the end of a period of rising migration, but the French population in all of New France had still only reached about 1,700. The population in the town of Québec itself was under 800.[43] Leaders of the colony were hoping to increase the colonial population, and they put in place policies and incentives to bring this about through both immigration and natural increase. As discussed in chapter 1, however, New France remained a notoriously unattractive destination for French migrants. This was especially so for female migrants. Among French settlers, there were six or seven marriageable men for every marriageable woman. When looking just at young adults (aged sixteen to thirty) during the 1660s, the figure rises to more than twelve unmarried men of French origin for every unmarried woman of French origin.[44] With a large supply of men and a high demand for women, so to speak, the marriage market was tilted decidedly in women's favour, which would have allowed a young unmarried woman like Hallay considerable choice in partners.[45]

Men generally had to establish themselves in Canada before they were able to find a spouse, while unmarried women tended to marry quickly after arrival, and usually within a year. Some women changed their minds about whom to marry, and sometimes quite suddenly. At least 10 per cent of female immigrants signed a marriage contract with a man they would never wed, often shortly before marrying someone else.[46] In backing away from a promise of marriage, therefore, Barbe Hallay was not alone. And she might have had good reason to object to the promise, because Daniel Vuil did not appear to be an attractive potential spouse. While still on the ship he had obviously not established himself in the colony, and reactions to him once he was in Canada indicate that he was not considered suitable for the companionship that early modern French people expected from marriage. Their ideal union was one that joined together a good personal relationship between spouses, the aspirations of their families, and the maintenance of a good reputation.[47] Marie de l'Incarnation alluded to Vuil's "bad customs" in her first account of the demonic torments, and in a later letter she added that Vuil's offer of marriage had been refused because he was suspected of "*maléfices*."[48] As will be discussed later in this chapter, his few appearances in the records from Québec all point to a disruptive and even criminal figure.

So Barbe Hallay may have had very good reasons to avoid marriage with Daniel Vuil, promised or not. Unlike most women who rescinded an agreement to wed, however, she did not enter into another engagement soon after. Women had quite a lot of choice in deciding whom to marry in New France, but, aside from those who took religious vows, they were not really given the option of simply not marrying at all. The French crown was strongly in support of more marriages. Before Hallay's arrival, French officials encouraged intermarriage with Indigenous populations in the hope that this would "Christianize" and "Frenchify" the new families.[49] When this policy failed, they instituted policies to favour marriages between settlers.[50] In time, their efforts brought some success. As will be discussed in chapter 5, more women did migrate, more marriages did take place, more babies were born, and the settler population increased.[51] But these developments were not yet very far along when Hallay arrived. She was a close observer of the formation of other marriages, including the signing of her eighteen-year-old sister Marie's marriage contract in September 1660, and she probably knew very well that young women in Canada were expected to wed.[52]

If a delay in marrying or the avoidance of marriage altogether was Hallay's desire, there was no easy way for her to maintain a celibate state for long. Her status as demoniac, whether consciously adopted as a strategic response to unwanted pressures or not, shielded her from nuptials. As mentioned above, early modern demonologists attributed the large numbers of women and children among the possessed to a weakness in body and mind. Historians explain the overrepresentation of these groups differently, pointing to their status as subordinate in the social hierarchy of early modern Europe: women were expected to submit to patriarchal control by husbands and fathers, and children were expected to submit to parental control and the authority of their elders. Possession interfered with this hierarchy by granting a kind of contradictory agency to the demoniac. According to early modern demonologists, the demoniac's speech and actions were directed by the demon, not the person whose body the demon was inhabiting. So, although the demoniac was deprived of their normal agency while possessed, a diagnosis of possession allowed the demoniac to break and even mock social expectations. Whether consciously or unconsciously, in fraud or in sincerity, the performance of possession gave new power to the possessed.[53] In losing their agency to a possessing demon, demoniacs gained it in the world. Women believed to be possessed were granted licence to do things normally forbidden to them, and they could become active participants in the discernment of what was vexing them without needing to take full responsibility for whatever statements they voiced.[54]

Using the evidence we have, there is no way to know whether Barbe Hallay really believed herself to be possessed or not. We do know that the fear and anxiety building in the colony conditioned the responses of those around her.

COLONIAL INSECURITIES

In October 1660, while Barbe Hallay was in the early stages of her demonic torments, François de Laval wrote a report on the state of New France to Pope Alexander VII. Laval cast Canada in a positive light for the most part, at least in terms of its colonial potential. He also alerted the pope to some of the challenges and dangers still troubling the French. The rivers were more noble than the rivers of Europe, but frequent rapids made navigation difficult. The air was healthy because it was cold and dry. It hardly rained all winter, while deep snow covered the ground. Sicknesses were neither so numerous nor so varied as in Europe, women were pregnant more often, and infant death was less common. Commerce was infrequent, but it was hoped that the export of skins would soon increase. Laval said that the exercise of Catholicism thrived where French colonies were fixed, although he judged the situation to be more complex away from French settlements. There were Christians among the "barbarians," he wrote, often quite distant from Québec, including some who had once been Huron but were now living among the Iroquois. Laval singled out the Iroquois as a "wild and most cruel people, and accustomed to war," allied to the English and the Dutch heretics. Violence in the "rough and bloody wars" led to the torture of captives and the destruction of entire peoples.[55] Laval's report portrayed New France as ripe with promise for continued French settlement, but also as a difficult and dangerous place to live. The natural environment was salubrious, the economy was promising, and religious conversion was making some progress. At the same time, travel was difficult, commercial development was stunted, and Indigenous Christians were often isolated from a supportive community. Most seriously, violence threatened people's safety and sometimes their very existence. From this perspective, the colonial project of New France was not secure.

The colonists living in Québec during the years of Hallay's possession wrote in a particularly anxious tone about the Five Nations of the Haudenosaunee, called the Iroquois by the French. Settlers did not fully understand the complex international relations and obligations arising from alliances formed back in the time of Champlain. The French knew, though, that they and the Iroquois had been at peace since 1653, until the eruption of warfare again in 1660.[56] And they were scared about what would happen next. A rumour reached Québec in the spring of that year about a group of Iroquois preparing for an invasion.[57] The scribe of the *Chronique de l'Hôtel-Dieu de Québec* reported that when the Augustinian nuns heard news of the Iroquois army, they deliberated about what they should do. They were advised that they could not safely stay the night in their monastery since their defences were insufficient against sudden attack. Probably adding still more to the nuns' dread, they were also told that the Iroquois usually approached by night without being perceived. So, except for a few nuns who stayed behind to care for the sick, the Augustinians went every day before sunset to the College of the Jesuits to spend the night there.[58] The scribe of the *Annales des Ursulines de Québec* also recorded feelings of alarm, in her case when she heard a report from Montréal that the Iroquois were descending to Québec. Laval came to their convent and found that it was not sufficiently strong. He ordered the nuns to leave each night and, as with the Augustinians, sleep at the Jesuit College. During the day, they stayed in their own convent, guarded by soldiers.[59] Marie de l'Incarnation's letters describe the preparations for war. The bishop had the Holy Sacrament removed from the Ursuline church, and the governor ordered two corps of guards to be placed at the convent. Redoubts were built, windows were fitted with shutters, and narrow slits were carved into walls through which projectiles could be fired. "In a word," as Marie put it, "our monastery was converted into a fort guarded by twenty-four very resolute men." The Ursulines took still more precautions by making provision of gunpowder and lead, and by borrowing weapons that were always ready in case of alarm.[60]

All this took a toll on the nuns, who were exhausted and afraid. Marie wrote that they had not rested day or night over the course of five weeks, and that she was "extremely tired" from attending to the guards and providing them with what they required for war and food.[61] In a letter to her son, she admitted a feeling of vulnerability that must have been shared by many French colonists: with the freezing of the St Lawrence River from late fall until spring, they were stuck in North America for half the year, and, if they were attacked when no ship was in port, they could not save themselves.[62] They heard gruesomely frightening details of attacks. In the same letter where Marie introduced the arrival of witches and magicians, she also reported having been told by Marie-Barbe de Boullongne, widow of a previous governor, Louis D'Ailleboust, that several farmers near Montréal had been taken by surprise in the woods, and that the settlers did not know where these farmers were or what had become of them. Nobody dared search, nor even go out, because they feared being taken by the same misfortune. The place of the farmers' death was finally discovered because dogs were seen coming back daily "satiated and full of blood." When the French came to the place where the dogs had gone, they found corpses lying scattered, some cut in half, others "butchered and stripped of flesh," with heads, legs, and hands scattered to all sides.[63] The imagery was nightmarish, as was the French retaliation of burning Haudenosaunee prisoners in the town of Québec.[64] An additional source of worry was that not all the Haudenosaunee attacking the French had always been Haudenosaunee: some had once been Wendat, allies of the French, suggesting perhaps to the settlers that their alliances were not so firm as they had hoped. The *Journal des jésuites* called such Haudenosaunee "Hurons iroquisés," and, in the minds of French settlers, they could be as threatening as the rest.[65]

Most of the attacks happened to the west of Québec – as Marie de l'Incarnation put it, Montréal was "the principal theatre of their carnage"[66] – but the threat was felt throughout the French settlements along the St Lawrence. The Jesuit *Relation* covering the period of summer 1660 to summer 1661 reports that the French settlers were on the edge of a precipice, and very close to total ruin, yet at the same time full of vigour and courage. "In a word," the report said, "never have we been more feeble and never more powerful."[67] Such an assessment seems to ring with determination inspired by a Christian sense of weakness-as-strength in the face of possible martyrdom. But this assessment was written for publication back in France, informed by an awareness that readers were potential supporters of the mission. Jesuit writings not intended for public view express fear more unguardedly. In August 1660, Jérôme Lalemant wrote to the Superior-General of the Society of Jesus in Rome about "trepidation" in the whole colony.[68]

Historians have calculated that the number of French settlers killed or taken captive in the early years of the Iroquois wars was low, reaching a height of perhaps 5–7 per cent of the total settler population, and they point out that the Five Nations of the Iroquois Confederacy had many international concerns beyond the small French settlements. But the colonists did not have this benefit of historical hindsight, and they knew that they were vulnerable. They were too few to have the initiative, and they were so weak that the Haudenosaunee could have expelled or exterminated them if this were their goal.[69]

Regardless of the precise number of fatalities and the real designs of the Haudenosaunee warriors, the French settlers were living in a nervous state of apprehension as the drama of Hallay's possession unfolded. Their future in North America seemed deeply uncertain. Asseline de Ronval, traveller from Dieppe, said in 1662 that "life in this country is more in danger than that of a bird on a branch."[70] As historian Louise Dechêne explained it, the French positions were in "extreme vulnerability," and always on the defensive. The colonists did not know what was happening to them, nor what would happen in the future. They were "plunged into a world where they did not know how to read the signs. Events were unforeseeable and incomprehensible," and a "climate of terror" reigned in the colonial imaginary.[71]

In the midst of these existential uncertainties about the future of the colony arose the suspicion that enemies within were using witchcraft to launch an assault of dark supernatural forces. It was not a suspicion that could be either confirmed or dismissed quickly. Arriving at a legal decision in a case of witchcraft was long and convoluted, as Marie de l'Incarnation understood. She closed her discussion of the case in her letter of September 1661 by reporting that the magician Vuil had not yet wished to confess anything, and "it is not easy to convict persons of this nature of crime."[72] So, Vuil was brought into Québec and imprisoned. The jail was probably in the governor's residence, the Château Saint-Louis, where an inventory drawn up in 1660 indicates a tower that served as defence and prison.[73] Here, Vuil awaited his trial.

THE CRIMES OF DANIEL VUIL

In October 1661, Daniel Vuil was executed at Québec. This much is clear from multiple accounts. The accounts diverge, however, on exactly how and why the execution took place. The manner and significance of the execution can only be understood through a careful comparison of sources within the context of a dispute between representatives of crown and church in Canada.

Historians writing about Vuil's execution have disagreed about both Vuil's crime and the means of his death. Some have concluded that he was executed for illegal trade in alcohol.[74] Other historians have favoured a religious infraction as the capital crime.[75] Most have thought that he was shot,[76] but one found that he was hanged.[77] Historians' disagreements have arisen from contradictions between sources and even among different versions of the same source, and their assessments depend largely on which source they make most central to their interpretation.

The only account of Vuil's execution to have been published during the seventeenth century is Paul Ragueneau's 1671 book *La vie de la mere Catherine de Saint-Augustin*. It states that Vuil was hanged for pronouncing blasphemies and profaning the sacraments, having by a simulated conversion abjured Huguenotism.[78] Using this source as the main piece of evidence leads to a conclusion that the reason for the execution was blasphemy and profanation, motivated by a secret Protestant belief, and that the means of execution was hanging. Although Ragueneau's *Vie* is the only source *published* within a few decades of the execution, it was not the only source *written* close in time to the event. Other sources created in the seventeenth century deserve at least as much attention, and especially an entry from October 1661 in the *Journal des jésuites*.

This source needs to be taken very seriously not only because of its chronological proximity to the execution – it was written closest in time to the event itself – but also because of the conditions of its composition. The *Journal des jésuites* was the book in which one of the Jesuits, usually the local superior (at this time, Jérôme Lalemant), recorded daily events affecting the order.[79] It was therefore written more quickly and unselfconsciously than many of the other documents that survive from New France. Its timing and purpose give it an important immediacy, which can be heard in the tone of this entry: it states that Vuil was "hanged, or rather shot," as if the scribe were correcting himself partway through his writing.[80]

In all versions of the *Journal de jésuites* – the original manuscript held at the Séminaire de Québec and the three later printed editions – the entry says that Vuil was shot with a musket. Beyond this point, any easy interpretation is hindered by an ambiguity in the phrasing. The 1871 edition has the following: "Le 7. Daniel Vvil pendu ou plustost arquebuzé, & le 11. vn autre nommé la Violette; & un f8eté le lundy 10. pour auoir traité aux sauuages de l'eau de vie." "The 7 Daniel Vuil hanged or rather shot with an arquebus, and the 11 another named la Violette; and one whipped Monday 10 for having traded liquor with the Indians." In the margin on the side, it has "Executions pour la traite," "Executions for trade."[81] Based on this edition, it looks as though Vuil was shot for having traded liquor with Indigenous people.

The entry as it appears in the Thwaites edition of *The Jesuit Relations and Allied Documents* adds a semicolon that might change the reader's interpretation: "le 7. Daniel Vvil pendu ou plustost arquebusé; & le 11. vn autre nommé la violette; & vn f8eté le Lundy. 10. p^{r}. auoir traité aux sauvages de l'eau de vie." In the margin, it also has: "Executions pour La traite." The semicolon suggests the *Journal* is reporting that Vuil was executed for a different reason and by a different means than Laviolette. The English translation provided by Thwaites continues with this possibility: "On the 7th, Daniel Vvil was hanged – or rather shot – and on the 11th another named la violette; and one was flogged on Monday, the 10th, for having traded brandy to the savages." In the margin, "Executions for having traded."[82] The main text of this edition might be leading the reader to think that the person being flogged was punished for trading brandy, but that Vuil and Laviolette were executed for something else. The information in the margin, however, is clearer: executions – in the plural – for trading.

The entry in the *Monumenta Novae Franciae*, published in 2003 and generally considered the more reliable edition of Jesuit writings from New France, has this: "Le sept, Daniel Vuil pendu, ou plustost arquebusé, et le 11 un autre, nommé Laviolette. Et un foueté le lundy, 10, pour avoir traité aux sauvages de l'eau-de-vie." Above, it has written "Exécutions pour la traite."[83] Here with a full stop after "Laviolette," the main text again leaves open the possibility that trading liquor was the crime of the person whipped on the 10th, and that Vuil and Laviolette were executed for something else. Once more, however, the writing in the margin points to all three prisoners having been executed for trading.

These three published editions have minor variances in spellings and punctuation markings, but none of the differences would alter some basic facts in a basic reading: Daniel Vuil was executed by arquebus on 7 October, Laviolette was executed on 11 October, and someone else was whipped on 10 October, all for having traded liquor illegally.

An examination of the original manuscript of the *Journal des jésuites*, held at the Archives du Séminaire de Québec, makes this reading seem less certain. It has: "Le .7. Daniel Vvil pendu ou plustost arquebusé; & le .11. vn autre nommé la violette; & vn f8eté le Lundy .10. p^r auoir traité aux sauuages de l'eau de vie." The first thing to note is that the marks after "arquebusé" and "la violette" are semicolons, meaning that the entry might be saying that Daniel Vuil was hanged or rather shot with an arquebus; that another person named Laviolette was also shot; and that yet another person, unnamed, was whipped for having traded liquor. The phrasing makes it unclear whether trading in liquor was the crime of only this third, unnamed, person, or of all three. The second thing to note is that the marginal text, "Executions pour la traite," is in a different hand than the main body of the text. Written by a different person, the note in the margin may not accurately reflect what the scribe of the main text intended, and so we should perhaps not give it too much weight.[84]

An entry from earlier in the *Journal des jésuites* reports the reason for Vuil's imprisonment, and it was not trading liquor. This entry says that in February 1661 a sentence was brought by Laval against Vuil, who was a prisoner, relapsed heretic, blasphemer, and profaner of sacraments. As of February 1661, therefore, Vuil was in prison because of religious crimes. This sentence was brought eight months before the execution, an unusually long duration, so it is possible that the crime for which Vuil was imprisoned in February was not the crime for which he was executed in October. It is even possible that he was imprisoned multiple times for separate offences.[85]

Local context is important here, especially the precarious situation of Québec as outlined in the previous section and the disagreements between leaders in the colony about how to proceed against Vuil as a disobedient colonist. The imprisonment and execution of Vuil occurred during a time of serious challenges for the French colony. We have already seen how some of these challenges influenced the stories of Hallay's possession. First, New France was having trouble attracting immigrants, especially marriageable female immigrants like Barbe Hallay. It was believed that Vuil instigated the demonic infestation because his desire to marry her had been refused. Second, as will be described in upcoming chapters, the ideal of creating a truly Catholic society was proving difficult to sustain when the French populace was insufficiently devout in the eyes of some clerics, conversions among Indigenous people were lower in number than the missionaries had hoped, and colonial rivals on the continent were Protestant. Part of what made Vuil suspicious was that he had been Protestant too. Third, many settlers feared for the future of the colony itself. It was isolated and vulnerable to attack.

This was the atmosphere in which the accusations against Vuil developed, and two of the most powerful leaders in the colony clashed over how to respond. An entry from February 1661 in the *Journal des jésuites* puts it this way: "Great quarrel between the powers," where the authorities were about to come to extremities over the sentence brought against Vuil.[86] The powers being alluded to were Governor Pierre de Voyer d'Argenson and Bishop François de Laval.

Voyer d'Argenson did not always recognize the authority of Laval, whose ecclesiastical position in Canada was unusual. Laval was not the titular bishop at this time, but rather the vicar apostolic, and the scope of such a position was uncertain. The Parlement of Paris denounced "the supposed quality of vicar apostolic in the province of Canada, which is a new quality and unknown in France," while the Parlement of Rouen objected to the "new introduction of a vicar dependent immediately to the Court of Rome, counter to all order and rule of the Church." If the objection in Paris was largely because the authority of the position was not well understood, the objection in Rouen was more about what it meant for Rouen, the diocese chosen to have spiritual authority over New France. The Archbishop of Rouen would not accept the nomination of vicar apostolic and continued to consider New France as part of his own diocese. The king tried to solve the problem by having Laval's authority recognized as Archbishop of Petra (which is in Palestine) while awaiting the erection of a bishopric under the dependence of Rouen. The Archbishop of Rouen agreed, and, shortly thereafter, the king's mother, Anne of Austria, wrote to the governor of New France to have Laval recognized as vicar apostolic and bring all ecclesiastics in line. In spite of these efforts, the situation was still confusing. On the one hand, royal authority recognized that Laval had jurisdiction in New France as vicar apostolic. On the other hand, the Archbishop of Rouen was presuming that he would have supremacy in a future diocese once it was established.[87] Laval was a bishop, yes, but as Marie de l'Incarnation wrote, he had "the title of Bishop of Petra and not of Québec or Canada." She went on to explain that the title was the subject of a disagreement between the court of Rome and the court of France. The pope thought he had a particular right in foreign nations, while the French king wanted the Bishop of Canada to depend on him.[88] She was explaining, from her perspective in Québec, that the disagreement was tied up with a dispute between what historians sometimes call "Gallicanism," French efforts to increase royal control over the Catholic Church in France largely free from papal authority, versus "Ultramontanism," a position favouring control from Rome.[89]

Caught in the political push and pull between Rouen and Rome, neither governor nor bishop was keen on compromise. They were both from noble families, both in their thirties, both recently arrived in Canada, and both accustomed to getting their way. Voyer d'Argenson wrote to his brother that Laval had such an adherence to his own sentiments and such zeal bringing him beyond his lawful scope that he had no difficulty encroaching on the power of others and listened to nobody.[90] Laval wrote to Voyer d'Argenson's brother complaining about the governor's suspicious attitude towards him.[91] The very next day, Voyer d'Argenson wrote that Laval would accomplish much in Canada once he understood "that the practices here are very different from the speculations he had made."[92] In her letters, Marie de l'Incarnation portrayed the two men as self-assured in their uprightness. She described Voyer d'Argenson as without reproach, and said that all he spoke about was God and virtue.[93] She described Laval as zealous and inflexible, and said that he would never give up if he became persuaded that the glory of God was at stake.[94]

Both the governor and the bishop were headstrong and determined to solidify their positions in New France, and both were also highly sensitive to any perceived slights. In September 1659, there arose what the journal of the Jesuits called "a great contestation" between the two of them about where the benches of each should be placed in church. A few months later, another "great contestation" arose. This time, Laval had ordered the thurifer rather than a deacon to cense the governor at Christmas. Voyer d'Argenson, upset by what he felt was an improper precedence, did some research, and argued that according to the Ceremonial of Bishops he was supposed to have been censed immediately after the bishop, by both the deacon and the priest, and before the priests of the choir. Laval did some research of his own. He answered that the Use of France was different from what they were doing in Québec, noting that since the beginning of services there they had been proceeding in a way that was explained in an act found in the archives. Yet another quarrel arose in Holy Week 1660. The Jesuits prepared two cushions in their church, one each for the bishop and governor. The governor arrived first, and knelt down too close to the cushion designated for the bishop. Things did not improve from there. At Easter, the governor was going to be presenting the blessed bread in the church. He was presuming to present it in what was an ordinary fashion for him, with drums "et cetera," perhaps as the soldiers had done a few months earlier when they were presenting bread while playing fifes and drums, "which powerfully shocked the bishop." This time, the bishop did not want to suffer it, and so it was decided that the bread would be brought in before the service and taken out afterwards, in order to avoid any interruption. In November 1660, without first discussing the matter with Voyer d'Argenson, Laval announced at a meeting of churchwardens that the governor should no longer hold the rank of honorary churchwarden. Two days later, the governor came to another meeting of the churchwardens anyway, and declared that the bishop did not have the power to remove him. Laval must have been particularly upset about this episode, because the journal of the Jesuits reports that he said "several things not very respectful." In February 1661, tensions were rising yet again between the two, this time about who should have precedence at the Jesuits' school. The governor said that he would not attend if the bishop were saluted before him. The Jesuits decided that it would be a good idea for the schoolchildren to have their hands occupied, presumably so that none of them could salute anyone, and told their students to salute neither the governor nor the bishop. But two of the children disobeyed, and saluted the governor first. This "powerfully offended" Laval, whom the Jesuits "strove to appease," with the result that the two children were whipped the following day.[95]

These disagreements no doubt seem petty to modern readers, but public acknowledgment of precedence mattered to seventeenth-century Frenchmen jostling for status in a highly hierarchical society. The Jesuits understood. Knowing that the bishop and governor did not get along, knowing also that inviting one without the other to dinner after an ordination ceremony would cause jealousy since neither wanted the other to have the first rank, they simply decided not to invite anyone.[96]

The Jesuits were themselves caught up in the dispute, and aware of its implications for their authority in New France. So long as Québec remained a vicariate apostolic rather than a bishopric, Jesuits were subordinate to the Sacred Congregation for the Propagation of the Faith in Rome, not to the Archbishop of Rouen.[97] The Jesuit Paul Ragueneau wrote a letter to the general of the Jesuit order complaining that "the governor was always very unfair both to our society [the Jesuits] and to the Lord Bishop of Petra [Laval]."[98] The king took a different view. He acknowledged that those who had made the most faithful and objective reports of Canada had always said that the Jesuits' piety and zeal contributed a great deal to attracting people to the colony, but he told the new intendant in 1665 that the Jesuits had assumed an authority beyond the bounds of their rightful profession, which should be only consciences. The king thought that the Jesuits were being manipulative in their support of Laval. To maintain their positions, they were very happy to name Laval to perform episcopal functions, bringing him into their dependence, and they also tried to influence the choice of governor. The king insisted that "it is absolutely necessary to hold in fair balance temporal authority that resides in the person of the King and in those who represent him, and spiritual [authority] that resides in the person of the said Lord Bishop and the Jesuits."[99] This framing of the conflict in terms of spiritual versus temporal authority was one of very long standing by this point, and certainly not concluded yet.[100]

The power struggle between bishop and governor magnified the significance of Daniel Vuil's misdeeds. The *Journal des jésuites* entry for February 1661, the same entry that begins with a statement of there being a great quarrel between the powers, concludes with a statement that one or the other courts assumed for itself the claim to judge Vuil's crime, and an intriguing suggestion of further information in "a long story, about which elsewhere at length."[101] Interestingly, these phrases are written in Latin, a language that appears to be preferred over the more common French when discussing sensitive matters. It is not known where this additional information is, but the remark points to wider discussions.[102]

Another item in the Québec seminary archives offers further tantalizing clues. This is an inventory compiled by Laval of all the pieces touching on the affairs between him and Voyer d'Argenson.[103] It is undated, but it mentions episodes from 12 February to 15 March 1661, and so was likely assembled while Vuil was imprisoned. One of the sections is about "a certain girl infested with demons, and who for more than a year continues to be tormented." Among the documents listed are some about the diabolical infestation: by what marks it was recognized; the innocence of Hallay; proofs against Vuil, accused of witchcraft. Other documents are about the judicial process: permission to initiate inquiries about Vuil; an appeal made to the governor; permission to publish a monition against Vuil and other witches; the governor's refusal of the appeal and the bishop's response; another appeal to the governor. This inventory does not say where the documents were sent, and the documents themselves have not been found. What is clear from the inventory alone is that with this dossier, Laval was trying to build a case of witchcraft against Vuil and establish who was responsible for prosecution. Perhaps he was trying to have Vuil brought before the recently established ecclesiastical tribunal called the Officialité, although there was some question about which cases were properly within this court's jurisdictional domain and such a tribunal would have had to hand Vuil over to the secular court for capital punishment. Or perhaps Laval was trying to establish that he had the authority to judge Vuil himself.[104]

Laval's efforts did not work at first. But in August 1661, Voyer d'Argenson asked to go back to France because of his infirmities. Contemporaries wondered if he was really pushed out by complaints about him in Québec and quarrels with Laval. In any case, he left. His replacement pronounced judgment against Vuil – a sentence of death.[105] Laval had gotten his way.

Whether Vuil's execution was for illegal trade or for a religious crime, his punishment would have been unusual if not unprecedented in the colony. People certainly were executed for crimes in New France, more than a hundred of them between 1608 and 1760, but neither trade in liquor nor blasphemy was a common reason.[106] A dispute about the liquor trade raged for years. The dividing line often cut between civil and religious authorities at high levels, with Voyer d'Argenson tolerating and Laval opposing it. For Laval, the issue was one of utmost importance, at least rhetorically. He wrote that the practice not only led to public scandal, but also put all Christianity in danger of total ruin.[107] Deliberations were held at the Sorbonne on the matter and repeated warnings of excommunication were issued for those who engaged in the trade. In April of 1661 (therefore after Vuil was put in prison but before he was executed), a man named Pierre Aigron was excommunicated for trading liquor. He had already been absolved with the promise that he would never again engage in such a trade, and then he refused to receive public absolution for having fallen back into the same sin.[108] This was punishment for a repeat offender, and it was nowhere near a death penalty.

Blasphemy was taken seriously as a form of *Lèse-Majesté divine*, an outrage against the majesty of God.[109] As a crime against authority, it was placed at the summit of the hierarchy of crimes.[110] Several items in the archives of the seminary in Québec report the grisly fates of people found guilty of it in France in 1661, one of whom was brought to the market to have his upper and lower lips cut, his body broken on a scaffold then burnt and reduced to ashes, his goods confiscated to the king,[111] but no such punishment was meted out for the crime in New France.

As for witchcraft, there had as yet been only one trial for it in New France. This was the 1658 trial of René Besnard dit Bourjoly, charged after tying knots in a cord – a spell, known as the *aiguillette*, to cause impotence in a groom. Besnard, about thirty years old, had been courting Marie Pontonnier, about fourteen. Pontonnier chose instead to marry twenty-five-year-old Pierre Gadois. Besnard went to Pontonnier to tell her that he was a witch, and then announced that her forthcoming marriage to Gadois would be sterile. Pontonnier informed her future husband and her priest right away of the vengeance being planned, but the couple decided to marry anyway. The wedding ceremony took place at the church in Montréal on 12 August 1657. A friend of Gadois gave him advice on how to counter the hex: recite the psalm *Miserere* in Latin and backwards while the nuptial blessing was being said. Gadois tried this counter-magic, but it did not work. He was impotent. The couple confessed to their priest, the bishop exhorted them to go to Québec to receive a nuptial blessing again, and the governor decided to charge Besnard. On 2 November 1658, Besnard appeared before the seigneurial court in Montréal. Witnesses accused him of witchcraft. He was found guilty despite his claim that he had only been joking to frighten Gadois, and his punishment was banishment from the town. He moved to Trois-Rivières and married.[112]

So if those who traded liquor were excommunicated, and a man found guilty of witchcraft was banished, why was Daniel Vuil executed? We cannot say definitively. It seems likely that Laval wanted Vuil convicted of witchcraft, Voyer D'Argenson refused, and the court hearing the case did not recognize Laval's episcopal authority.[113] When a new governor arrived, he allowed Laval to assert his will.[114] The witchcraft itself might have been the transgression that most bothered Laval. Or perhaps Vuil was actually up to all sorts of no good, with witchcraft being Laval's choice for most the prosecutable offence. In early modern Europe and its colonies, the severity of punishment was supposed to be proportional to the social danger of the crime, not to the damage it caused, so the potential harm of Vuil's religious nonconformity as relapsed Protestant and witch might have seemed especially disturbing to the bishop.[115] Criminal punishments were meant to inspire fear among onlookers and deter them from committing the same offence themselves.[116] Laval probably hoped that the execution of Vuil would put an end to heresy and witchcraft in the Catholic colony. If he were worried about people not properly recognizing ecclesiastical authority in a society whose religious ideals were being eroded at a time of existential threat, then he might have considered the execution of Vuil to be proportionate and appropriate.

We may never know whether Vuil was executed for witchcraft, or for blasphemy and profaning of sacraments, or for trade in liquor. In the end, perhaps neither he nor Laval cared about precisely which criminal offence was the capital one. We do know that Vuil's imprisonment and execution did not end Barbe Hallay's torments. While he waited in prison, she was sent to the hospital. Her treatment there by missionaries with their own demonological designs is the subject of the next chapter.

3

Missionary Demonologists

In December 1660, about a year and a half after her arrival in New France, Barbe Hallay was brought from Beauport into Québec. She was placed in the Hôtel-Dieu hospital, where she helped care for the other patients when she could, and one of the Hospitalière nuns battled with the demons that continued to vex her.

A hospital may seem somewhat unsuitable as a place to care for someone thought to be demonically possessed. For the nuns at the Hôtel-Dieu, however, sickness was not just a corporeal concern. Their care for Hallay was fully within the hospital's purview even – or rather, especially – when it encompassed both medical treatment and spiritual protection. The overlap of care for the body with care for the soul was imported from European hospitals. The origins of the Hôtel-Dieu in Québec as an institution for the conversion of Indigenous people in North America added a new missionary dimension to the nurses' work in Canada. Their general assumptions about supernatural forces retained many features of what Catholics in Europe believed, but their more specific worries changed when they learned that the people the missionaries had come to convert would not simply follow all the missionaries' directions. The hopes and disappointments in the mission field influenced the care that Barbe Hallay received at the Hôtel-Dieu, and also how this care was recorded and promoted.

TREATMENT IN THE HOSPITAL

The *Journal des jésuites* reports Barbe Hallay's admittance into the Hôtel-Dieu in December 1660 with a few lines: "In this month Barbe Halé was brought from Beauport, infested by a démon folet for the past five or six months, but on several occasions. She was put at the start in a room of the old hospital, where she spent the night in the company of a guard of her sex and some priest and servants."[1]

Although brief, this entry nonetheless offers several interesting details about the case. In calling the infesting creature a "démon folet," the scribe was evoking the "follet" elf-like creature that was believed to entertain itself by causing mischief without doing any real damage.[2] Perhaps the scribe was indicating that he thought the demon to be annoying, but mostly harmless. This idea is reinforced by a marginal note to the side of the entry. Under "Barbe Halé" is written "Esprit follet," which was the name for a creature usually described as a nuisance more than a danger, and treated as imaginary rather than real. One seventeenth-century dictionary defines "esprit follet" as a kind of spirit believed to make noises in houses,[3] and another gives the English translation of "An Hobgoblin, Robin-goodfellow."[4] By choosing to describe the demon this way, and by writing that the infestation had been ongoing but not continuous, the scribe was indicating that the problem was neither overly threatening nor relentless.[5]

The entry in the *Journal des jésuites* concludes with the same Latin phrase as the scribe used when describing the great quarrel between the bishop and the governor discussed in chapter 2. Here, again, was "a long story, about which elsewhere at length."[6] While the surviving records may not yield all the information hinted at in the scribe's words, they do offer enough additional information to provide a sense of how Hallay spent her time at the hospital.

The *Chroniques* of the Hôtel-Dieu reports that Hallay was placed there by the order of Bishop Laval, and that he had judged this necessary for the good of the girl, who was afflicted by "some kind of malefice."[7] This phrase points to the use of harmful magic against Hallay, but is otherwise not very precise. If Laval's concern sounds unclear or ambiguous, that is because physical illness could resemble spiritual sickness, even demonic torment, to early modern observers. When the nun Antoinette de Sainte-Marie died at the Ursuline convent in Québec, the community's *Annales* reported that she had suffered for two years from a "strange illness." None of the nuns' attempted remedies had any effect, and the Ursulines suspected malefice in what ailed her.[8] On another occasion, Marie de l'Incarnation wrote that several people, including she herself, had erred in diagnosing the torments of the Augustinian nun Catherine de Saint-Augustin.

She had thought that Catherine's languor and excessive thinness were signs of a serious disease, but then Marie decided instead that these symptoms were caused by demonic obsession.[9] Paul Ragueneau wrote that Catherine's infestation by demons sometimes caused sicknesses that physicians were unable to understand.[10]

With this much possible confusion or disagreement around the diagnosis of physical and spiritual malaise, the people at the Hôtel-Dieu may well have been unsure of what exactly troubled Hallay when she arrived. They interpreted Hallay's afflictions as due possibly to illness as well as to possession, describing Hallay not only as demonically troubled, but also as "sick."[11] It is not clear what this sickness was, but a severe illness did take hold in Québec at around the time that Hallay went to the Hôtel-Dieu. Marie de l'Incarnation called it a "universal malady," and characterized it as both highly contagious and deadly. None was free of it, she wrote. Almost all the children of Indigenous people and many of the children of the French were dying. Marie described the illness as a kind of whooping cough or mortal rheum that terminated in a pleurisy accompanied by fever, and she also said that people believed it was caused by witches and magicians poisoning the air.[12] Physical illness could be caused by supernatural means according to seventeenth-century French settlers, and so it made sense to them that Hallay could have been sick in body because of a demonic infestation.

The hospital had a newly built room for the sick at the time of Hallay's arrival. Connected to the chapel and illuminated by light coming through three windows onto the interior courtyard as well as four windows facing south, it would have been quite pleasant for the patients occupying its ten beds under eleven-foot-high ceilings.[13] But Hallay did not go here; she was put into a little room next to the parlour.[14] The records of the Hôtel-Dieu do not say whether Hallay received the usual treatment for sick inmates, which, according to the hospital's constitution, meant a doctor or surgeon examining her at admission and then visiting at least once per day under the supervision of a Hospitalière nun accompanied by the apothecary.[15] One source reports that Hallay herself helped in serving the sick. This care was given presumably during daylight hours, since the same source states that the demon did not appear during the day but "wreaked havoc by night, agitating the girl in a strange manner" and giving Hallay an unwelcome view of the magician who appeared to her accompanied by many others.[16]

The leading figure in protecting Hallay from supernatural threats at the hospital was the nun Catherine de Saint-Augustin. At one point, she sewed Hallay into a sack to cover her from the insistent visitations of a magician who kept himself invisible to all except Hallay.[17] Marie de l'Incarnation wrote that demons, angered by how Catherine guarded the girl, appeared in hideous forms and beat the nun. The sores and bruises that remained on Catherine's body showed that these beatings were realities and not illusions, according to Marie, and Catherine's confessor told her that he had once seen Catherine's arm black as ink from the hits she had received.[18] This confessor was the Jesuit Paul Ragueneau. He wrote in his biography of Catherine that it was thought "nobody would be more capable of rendering the necessary charity to the poor sick girl [Hallay] than Mother Catherine de Saint-Augustin, who was always ready to relieve the afflicted." For a long time, day and night, Hallay received from Catherine a care "worthy of a truly Christian heart, and of a charitable Hospitalière." Ragueneau thought very highly of this care, but, according to his account, the demons detested it. They were enraged against Catherine for the contempt in which she held them, and because she tore their prey away. The demons, apparently, were not fair fighters. Unable to intimidate Catherine with threats, they tried to surprise her with tricks, transforming themselves into illusions of angels of light. But Catherine was the stronger force, more able to preserve the innocence of the possessed girl than was all hell to carry her to sin.[19]

Ragueneau's report of how Catherine cared for Hallay shows a greater concern for spiritual than for medical matters. One factor that helps explain this balance of metaphysical and physical attention is the scope of practice in the Hôtel-Dieu as an institution. Its responsibility to care for the sick was meant to include attention to the soul. Another factor is the careful construction of Catherine's reputation. She was not only a nurse in the colony, but a mystic as well. To understand why the Hôtel-Dieu was so concerned with saving souls, and why Ragueneau was so keen to disseminate evidence of the nun's mystical powers, it is helpful to go back to the original missionary foundation of the Hôtel-Dieu in New France and trace the institution's development as it moved from a Jesuit mission into the town of Québec.

THE HÔTEL-DIEU AS A MISSIONARY INSTITUTION

A hospital served multiple functions for early modern Europeans. It cared for the sick in body and soul, provided poor relief, and offered a visible outlet for charitable donations by the wealthy.[20] This Hôtel-Dieu followed largely in the same tradition, but during its early years in North America it took on the overarching goal of converting Indigenous people to Catholicism.

The Jesuit Paul Le Jeune called for such an institution in his *Relation* of 1634, saying that if there were a hospital in New France, all the sick and the elderly of the country could go there.[21] He bragged the following year (although he said it astonished him) that many nuns wanted to come over from France. He advised that they delay their departure, since there was not yet a place for them to live. Then, with dramatic rhetorical flourish, Le Jeune berated the French ladies for their spending habits and called upon them to help:

> Alas! My God, if the excesses, the superfluities of some ladies of France were employed to this so holy a work, what a great blessing would they bring down on their families! What glory in the sight of angels to have gathered the blood of the Son of God to apply it to these poor infidels! Is it possible that earthly possessions touch us more closely than life itself? Here are tender and delicate virgins, all ready to throw their lives into danger on the waves of the ocean, to come to seek the little souls in the rigours of air much colder than the air of France, to endure work that even astounds men. And cannot some brave lady be found who will give a passport to these Amazons of the great God, giving them a house, to praise and serve his divine majesty in this other world? I do not know how to persuade myself that our Lord does not dispose someone to this act.[22]

Le Jeune's call was answered by the French aristocrat Marie Madeleine de Vignerot du Pont Courlay, marquise de Combalet, better known as the Duchesse d'Aiguillon.[23] This wealthy widow and niece of Cardinal Richelieu gave the sum of 22,400 *livres* to the foundation of a hospital in Canada.[24]

From the perspective of the hospital's founders, the Hôtel-Dieu's goal of converting Indigenous people was an extension of what hospitals were trying to do in France, which was to correct Christians who were in the wrong sect (for French Catholics, this meant Protestants) and teach the proper observance of religion to those who were ignorant (for the elite, this meant the poor).[25] A seventeenth-century French handbook for parish priests explained bodily care as a conversion strategy by saying "it is certain that by the cure of the body one can as often cure souls as with sermons and good advice."[26]

The hospital's missionary goal was more obvious and ambitious in New France, where documents were explicit in stating that the nuns were not only to provide medical assistance to those who needed it, but also draw people to Catholicism.[27] As the royal letters establishing the foundation stated, the hospital was one of the "means of attracting the wild peoples and the infidels of New France to the true religion."[28] Missionaries' hopes for its effectiveness were high. In his *Relation* of 1635, Paul Le Jeune wrote that if a hospital were set up in New France, its charity "would do more for the conversion of the Indians than all our actions and our words."[29] Conversion of Indigenous people to Catholicism was not politically neutral; as discussed in chapter 1, it extended French sovereignty in North America. The 1627 charter of the Compagnie de la Nouvelle-France declared that Indigenous people who professed Catholicism would be counted as French, and the crown understood that Catholic converts would help the French colony survive.[30] The hospital founders' missionary goals for religious conversion, therefore, were well in line with the political goals of the French crown.[31]

The first three Augustinian nuns came to Canada in 1639. They were from the Hôtel-Dieu in Dieppe, a newly reformed institution praised by Le Jeune as "one of the best run in Europe."[32] Its nursing nuns took the standard monastic vows of poverty, chastity, and obedience, as well as additional vows to remain cloistered and serve the sick.[33] Construction had not finished on their monastery in Québec when the nuns arrived, so they set up their hospital in a house belonging to the Compagnie de la Nouvelle-France. In July 1640, they relocated to the Jesuit mission of Sillery, a few kilometres upriver from the town of Québec. They established themselves a little to the west and around a hill in the next cove over from the Jesuits' house.[34] The Hôtel-Dieu's time at Sillery was short, but influential. It strengthened the connection between the hospital and the missionary goals of New France, while exposing the limitations and failures of French efforts at conversion.

The mission of Sillery, also called the mission of Saint-Joseph in some French sources, had been founded in 1637. It was named after Noël Brûlart de Sillery, a French nobleman who had been a diplomat before taking holy orders. He donated 12,000 *livres* to establish the mission, stating in the foundation document that arresting and assembling wandering Native people in a convenient place was the most powerful means of converting them.[35] The importance of settlement as a step toward conversion was emphasized by other missionaries too. In 1632, Paul Le Jeune, then superior of the Jesuit mission in Canada, wrote that nations in a stable location would be more easily converted than "vagabond" nations.[36] In his *Relation* of 1634, doubtless influenced by a winter spent with the Innu in which he struggled not all that valiantly to keep up with his travelling hosts, Le Jeune explained why he thought that the Jesuits would not advance much with conversions until the Natives were settled: you can instruct them today, he said, but tomorrow hunger will take them away, forcing them to find their food in rivers and woods. In order to follow them, there would need to be as many missionaries as there were cabins, and fewer than ten missionaries out of every hundred would be able to endure the work.[37] By 1638, Le Jeune still maintained that settling the travelling groups was a means of conversion, but he admitted the difficulty involved, saying that "golden chains" were required for the task.[38] Sillery, the Jesuits hoped, would succeed in fixing would-be Christians in place.

As envisioned by its founder and its Jesuit administrators, Sillery would gather Indigenous people from different nations and help them learn to be farming Christians. But the mission did not develop exactly as its founders hoped. Although the colonial authorities presumed that the missionaries were in charge of the mission, this settlement was actually not under complete control of the French. The Indigenous inhabitants asserted a considerable amount of independence. Often their independence was supported by the missionaries, but at times it was invisible to French settlers, and once in a while it came into conflict with the missionaries' designs.

The location of Sillery, for example, was chosen not by the founder back in France, nor by the Jesuits who administered the settlement, but by its Indigenous inhabitants. The site of Kamiskouaouangachit, where Sillery would be established, was on a point of land extending into the St Lawrence. Because of the rocky river bottom at this spot, it was an excellent place for eel fishing and had been so for Indigenous people, as the Jesuits put it, since "time immemorial."[39] Indeed, Algonquian groups had long been using the site as a seasonal fishing location.[40] It was not the French missionaries' first choice of site for the mission, but they deferred to Indigenous preference. As the Jesuit superior Barthélemi Vimont wrote to the Dieppe Hospitalière nun Élisabeth de Saint-François in 1640, "the soil is better at Québec, but the Natives like to reside at Sillery."[41] French missionaries soon learned that residents at Sillery were also going to retain Indigenous methods of housing construction,[42] foodways,[43] and leadership,[44] and that they would mount objections to French methods of corporal punishment.[45]

One of the reasons why people came to live at Sillery, even when French missionaries tried to impose unpopularly strict codes of behaviour there, was because it provided a way to maintain some coherence as an Indigenous society in the face of unprecedented existential threats.[46] Confronted by epidemic disease, ecological disruption, military invasion, and economic realignment, settlement at Sillery brought with it the possibility of medical and spiritual care as developed by the newcomers who were able to recover from the strange new diseases, legal protection over natural resources in the midst of a growing population of colonists, fortification against attack from hostile forces, and privileged access to European technology, trade goods, and literacy.[47] As Jean-François Lozier demonstrates in his study of seventeenth-century Christian missions, the St Lawrence Valley was an area of renewal and regeneration for different Indigenous peoples during a time of upheaval. The settlement of Kamiskouaouangachit/Saint-Joseph/Sillery in Lozier's analysis was "fully a joint creation" between French missionaries and Indigenous inhabitants, "the intersection of Indigenous and French desires, needs, and priorities."[48] This intersection was not always smooth, and the reconfiguration of kinship in particular could be painful to the excluded.[49] But this reconfiguration also established new bonds. People baptized at the church were declared brothers of those already living in the settlement,[50] and Christian visitors were treated as kin.[51] Conversion shaped new political identities as well. One convert expressed the idea that for the Christians at Sillery, "prayer and belief have a strange force, since from several nations they have made but one."[52]

The Hôtel-Dieu was supposed to help with conversions at Sillery by attracting people to Catholicism. The nuns were there to assist in "the relief of the sick and the conversion of the poor Indians," as the Duchesse d'Aiguillon wrote,[53] and they did engage in both medical care and proselytizing. They transplanted European medical techniques to North America, and reported that Indigenous patients responded well to remedies brought over from Europe. They also adapted their treatments to meet Indigenous expectations.[54] Sometimes Indigenous people came to the hospital to get medicines, which they then took into their own cabins, and the nuns provided residents in the settlement with food, blankets, kettles, and firewood.[55] Such practices were a departure from the Hôtels-Dieu back in France, and they took on special significance in Indigenous North America. The nuns were not just giving gifts; they were participating in an exchange. During the nuns' first winter in Québec, when they were sick and short of food, their Indigenous neighbours had brought them moose and beaver, which helped to restore the nuns' health. At Sillery, when the nuns were sick and short of food again, the Indigenous residents gave smoked meat. Even if the nuns did not fully understand the system of gift exchange in which they were participating, and although they were not quite so appreciative as they might have been (they said that they pretended to accept the gift of smoked meat with pleasure but, not being accustomed to this type of food, they felt they would rather die of hunger than eat it), nevertheless, in receiving gifts and giving them in return, they were tying themselves more closely into the fabric of Indigenous societies.[56]

Nuns made further adjustments in their hospital to accommodate Indigenous patients. Indigenous people who visited sometimes slept on top of skins on the floor rather than in hospital beds, and they ate sagamité rather than French food.[57] They would not leave sick kin, so the nuns had to feed not only the individuals who arrived with a sickness but also the family members who stayed with them, and the sick insisted on sharing food and drink with kin, so the nuns gave medicines that could be shared for different maladies.[58] The nuns adjusted religious instruction as well. They started to learn Indigenous languages for teaching the principles of Catholicism to Indigenous patients "so that they could cure by their instruction the souls as well as the bodies,"[59] and they taught not only patients but visitors too.[60]

Baptisms occurred regularly at the hospital.[61] These new Christians did not simply convert to the Christianity of the missionaries, however; they formed a Christianity based on Indigenous priorities. They heard its messages through Indigenous languages in the hymns sung at the chapel,[62] and through the prayers by the Indigenous "Captain of Prayers."[63] Two examples of death and burial from 1643 show the range of Christian diversity at the hospital in Sillery.[64] One, Pierre Trigatin, the Captain of Prayers, died in the Hôtel-Dieu and was buried "à la françoise" (as the Jesuits put it) in a simple sheet. Another, Ursule Chiouabougoukoue, daughter and wife of political leaders at Tadoussac, was brought to the Hôtel-Dieu in her illness, then later moved to a cabin near the hospital's door. Her Christian mother had decorated this cabin "tout à la sauvage" (in the words of the Jesuits) with bark, leaves, robes of beaver and moose, and also a crucifix and candles borrowed from the hospital. Ursule said prayers with the help of a nun and received extreme unction, and then died. Her mother placed beaver pelts, wampum beads, and other goods into her grave. When the nuns complained that they and the Indians were poor and that these goods did not serve the dead, Ursule's mother pointedly invoked their hypocrisy, reminding the nuns that they had buried one of their own two years previously with her nice habit and all the honour they could. If what she did offended God, she said, she would stop; but because God did not prevent it, she wished to honour the dead.[65] Two burials of Indigenous Christians at Sillery, one by all appearances in conformity with the missionaries' expectations, the other sparking complaints from the nuns (and a good retort by an Indigenous resident). The variance in these Christian approaches to death is reflected more broadly in the archaeological record at Sillery. Some people were buried in a fetal position and wrapped in bark, in accordance with traditional Indigenous customs, while others were stretched out in a coffin, in typical French fashion. Some were interred with clearly Christian goods such as a cross, some with goods not obviously related to Christianity, such as a pipe, a necklace, or a gun, and some with no goods at all.[66] Expressions of Christianity at Sillery were widely varied, and largely under the control of Indigenous Christians.

The nuns at the hospital may have succeeded in attracting some people to the settlement (though their effectiveness here is impossible to measure with precision), but they did not stay for very long. In 1644, the hospital was moved back to Québec because of fears that its placement at Sillery made it too vulnerable to attack by the Iroquois.[67] The original missionary goals of the founders, if not a failure, were at least seriously curtailed. But the legacy of those goals still influenced what happened during Barbe Hallay's stay at the Hôtel-Dieu and how the events were described in missionary sources.

3.1 "Le Véritable plan de Québec fait en 1663," by Jean Bourdon

THE HÔTEL-DIEU IN QUÉBEC

When the Hôtel-Dieu moved from Sillery into Québec, and French settlers increased in number among its patients, the features that the institution retained from European hospitals became more pronounced.[68]

Many different people provided medical assistance in the hospitals of early modern Europe: nurses, physicians, usually a surgeon, sometimes local apothecaries, and even the patients themselves.[69] Barbe Hallay's rotation into patient care, therefore, was not entirely unexpected. Most of the care in European hospitals was provided by nursing sisters though, and this responsibility continued in New France.[70]

French hospital nuns were expected to be simultaneously gentle and authoritarian, obedient and courageous, humble and competent, all while showing compassion towards the sick.[71] These traits were expected among the Hospitalières by the colonists in Canada too. The Jesuit *Relation* in 1648 said that the nuns were never happier than when exercising the functions of their institution by "truly heroic" charity.[72] A more detailed description of ideals for hospital nuns can be found in their obituaries. These notices were meant to honour the recently deceased, contribute to the collective memory of the community, and present models for behaviour.[73] The obituary of Marie Hiroüin, one of the nuns who had been at the hospital both in Sillery and again in Québec when Barbe Hallay arrived, praises this nun's simple obedience, her respectful deference towards her superiors, her unchangeable gentleness, her patience, and her equanimity. According to Hiroüin's obituary, she excelled in humility and offered herself for the most difficult and lowliest tasks while showing the contentment that she felt in the work.[74]

As the contents and tone of this obituary convey, the role of the nurses was not always recognized as primarily medical. Their tasks were regarded as integral parts of their religious devotion and features of their feminine nature. The nuns did receive medical training that combined elements of practice and theory, building their skills through hands-on work in their communities while also developing their theoretical knowledge through information networks that kept them informed about current medical thinking. As part of the hospital staff, the nurses regularly performed minor surgeries and acted as apothecaries. Beyond caring for the bodies of patients and the physical space around them, nursing sisters purified hospital spaces in a sacralizing sense too. They were often instructed to avoid cases deemed shameful (such as sexually transmitted disease), and they were expected to uphold cleanliness and neatness in all things. One unintended by-product of this connection between spiritual and physical purity was an improvement in the hygienic state of hospitals, which, in turn, likely contributed to a reduction in mortality among hospital patients.[75]

A French Hôtel-Dieu was reserved for the sick, and especially for the sick poor, rather than for the permanently invalid, women in childbirth, or those too aged or infirm to work. Many if not most of the patients at the Hôtel-Dieu in Québec fell into this category of sick poor, and a few months after Hallay's arrival, the Hospitalières received from colonists Guillaume Couillard and Marie Guillemette Hébert some lands to use as a cemetery for the poor who died at the hospital and others who wished to be buried there.[76] Unlike most Hôtels-Dieu in France, the Hôtel-Dieu in Québec provided respite for newly arrived migrants too, including some with contagious fever.[77] As nuns of the Augustinian order, the nurses there were instructed not to accept cases of "mal dangereux," such as plague, leprosy, smallpox, skin rashes, epilepsy, raving, and other diseases believed to be malignant, whether incurable or not. In cases where contagion was suspected, a secular woman was to accompany the sick person to an apartment separate from the hospital, where she was to stay for at least three days.[78] This procedure might explain why Hallay was placed not in the main room for the sick when she arrived, but rather in a small room next to the parlour: it was to protect the other patients. Even if the scribe of the *Journal des jésuites* thought that the supernatural force bothering Hallay was not very dangerous, the presence of the guard and the priest in the room with Hallay suggests that someone was worried she might become threatened or threatening.

Whether the nuns at the hospital in Québec thought that Barbe Hallay was suffering from a physical illness, a demonic possession, or both, they considered the Hôtel-Dieu to be an appropriate place to care for the patient. An inventory of books shows that by 1800 the institution had at least two seventeenth-century demonological texts, and the nurses' intellectual networks connected them with medical and spiritual developments in Europe.[79] The hospital had inherited from France a presumption that medical and theological discourses overlapped, and its *Constitutions* state that the service the nuns render to the poor for the health of the body regards the salvation of the soul.[80] Marie de l'Incarnation judged this overlap to be a good thing when she said that Hospitalière nun Catherine de Saint-Augustin was very charitable, helping the sick spiritually and corporally in an admirable manner.[81] Catherine, for her part, desired her work to extend still further.

THE APOSTOLIC ASPIRATIONS OF CATHERINE DE SAINT-AUGUSTIN

From a young age, Catherine had been involved with nursing. As a child she lived with her grandmother in a house that served as a makeshift hospital, then at twelve she entered a convent of Hospitalières in Bayeux. While still too young to make her final profession as a nun, Catherine grew determined to come to Canada. Her father opposed this plan, even petitioning the court to prevent her departure, but Catherine's ardent desire won him over and eventually he consented. She arrived in New France in 1648.[82] Here, she joined a community that was developing a reputation for apostolic work. Vincent de Paul, French priest and founder of the Sisters of Charity, viewed Québec's Hôtel-Dieu very positively. In a letter that he wrote to the Superior there in 1652, he singled out especially the community's work "for the spiritual and corporeal assistance to the poor and the sick, which is the height of Christian charity," and he praised the "holy souls who have the happiness of working there as truly apostolic," deserving the approval and help of the church.[83] Catherine took the apostolic mission very seriously, but not everyone agreed that such a mission was suitable for her. Those writing about her apostolism needed to frame it carefully so that it would be acceptable to readers outside the convent who might question whether a woman could be truly apostolic. In this context, the treatment of Barbe Hallay at the Hôtel-Dieu helped to demonstrate that Catherine's spiritual power was used appropriately for the good of the colony.

Much of our information about Catherine's work in the hospital comes from the biography *La vie de la mere Catherine de Saint Augustin*. This text, written by the Jesuit Paul Ragueneau at the request of Bishop Laval, fit into an already well-established genre. Such biographies of religious women were very popular in seventeenth-century France. Sometimes they were written by the nuns themselves, but more often they were authored by the nuns' spiritual directors, as in this case, or by other male clerics with direct knowledge of their subjects. They were intended to provide examples for admiration and models for how to live a holy life.[84] These biographies could serve a wider propagandistic purpose too. Ragueneau's *Vie* promoted the Hôtel-Dieu's ecclesiastical mission and raised the status of Canada relative to more prestigious missionary postings in Asia, Spanish and Portuguese America, and Protestant areas of Europe.[85]

Such a promotional purpose does not mean that Ragueneau's biography ought to be discarded as a historical source. Based largely on Catherine's own writings as well as the observations of a spiritual director who knew her directly, the *Vie* offers what is probably a fairly reliable reporting of basic events. Even where its accuracy is questionable, the text is still useful as an idealized portrait of behaviour meant to be admired and emulated.[86] It also demonstrates assumptions and attitudes of the intended audience. A pious biography carrying a hagiographic intent could not impose any narrative unilaterally on what local people knew of its subject: if the author of a would-be hagiography departed too far from what the audience held to be true, then the account would not be accepted.[87]

As a testament to Catherine's mysticism, the *Vie* describes many of Catherine's visionary experiences, including visions of hell, visions of heaven, and visions of holding the infant Jesus. It even relates a remarkably detailed and intimate vision of being breastfed by the Virgin Mary.[88] As evidence for the power of Catherine's intercessions, the *Vie* reports that souls in purgatory appeared to Catherine and asked for her prayers, and that she obtained deliverance for many of them.[89] Ragueneau's *Vie* also presents Catherine's successes in bringing about conversions, an echo of the Hôtel-Dieu's years in Sillery. At one point (the book does not say whether this happened before or after her interactions with Hallay), Catherine prayed for the conversion of a man who was in the service of the devil and in commerce with witches. Her prayers led him eventually to confession and conversion.[90] She also converted a Huguenot sailor by giving him water into which she had dipped some relics of Jean de Brébeuf, a Jesuit priest who had died some years previously while on a mission among the Wendat.[91]

The *Vie* reports at length on Catherine's battles against demons. The demons tried to trick her under various appearances including Jesus Christ, the Holy Virgin, a guardian angel, Jean de Brébeuf, and her confessors, but Catherine was not fooled. However much these demons in their rage fought against Catherine, and in such great numbers that they amounted to entire armies of demons, they were always vanquished by her soul.[92] According to Ragueneau, Catherine took the demons on willingly, even to the point of saying that she was happy for them to remain in her body if it was agreeable to God that they should stay.[93] Ragueneau insisted that it was she, not they, in control. Her soul was so faithful to the grace of Jesus Christ that the demons were never able to obtain her consent for even the smallest thing that they desired. Far from possessing Catherine, the *Vie* says, the demons were themselves captured within her.[94] Such an embodiment was almost a reversal of exorcism, where someone attempts to cast the demons out of a body; here, by contrast, Catherine was capturing the demons inside herself. The captivity was difficult for Catherine, the burden of embodying the demons heavy. They inspired a rage in her heart against God, drew her towards impurity, tempted her to return to France, made holy water feel like burning fire, caused her to be terrified about taking Communion, hardened her heart, and gave her a furious disgust of her vocation.[95] The demons moreover corrupted her imagination, infected her mind, and reduced her often to despair until she believed herself "the most criminal person in the world and worthy of a thousand hells."[96]

Clearly, the interactions with demons were very difficult for Catherine. Ragueneau was confident that her susceptibility was a mark of holiness, permitted by God so that her virtue would be proven. Obsession, he said, was the same conduit that God had given to "great saints," including Anthony, Clare of Montefalco, Catherine of Siena, Angela of Foligno, and others, and he also said that God continued to permit obsession for the "most holy souls" even in his own time.[97] Catherine may have surpassed them all: the biographer calculated that her sufferings were so great that it would be hard to find among the lives of saints an example where so many demons made such a terrible and obstinate war.[98] His biography also emphasized that Catherine was more than a match for demonic tormentors. The frontispiece of the book shows a demon being trampled under an angel's foot, and part of the description reads that Catherine "is victorious over demons." She was a spouse of God who was fortified against the horrible torments of hell.[99]

Catherine's relationship to demons was for the most part willingly antagonistic, where she accepted the pain of fighting them for the good of the colony. On at least one occasion, however, in disapproving of the colonists' ungodly behaviour, Catherine entered into something almost like an alliance with the demons. A powerful earthquake shook New France soon after Barbe Hallay's stay as a patient in the Hôtel-Dieu. It began early in the evening of 5 February 1663, the day preceding Mardi Gras. People heard a loud noise underground, then the earth itself seemed to erupt. Rocks rained down hard enough to destroy roofs. Church bells rang, and doors on houses opened and

3.2 Frontispiece from *La vie de la mere Catherine de Saint Augustin: religieuse hospitaliere de la misericorde de Quebec en la Nouvelle-France*. The caption includes the phrase "Elle est victorieuse des Demons."

closed by themselves. The ice covering the St Lawrence River at a thickness of about two metres was broken into pieces, and the water of the river from Québec to Tadoussac took on the colour of sulphur. Landslides changed the shape of the shoreline at several places, and large areas of forest were uprooted. The quake could be felt from Montréal to Acadia to New England. Aftershocks lasted for at least six months. Modern seismologists have estimated that the earthquake's strength was probably between 6.5 and 7.5 on the Richter scale.[100]

Catherine understood the earthquake as a divine punishment. She wrote in her journal that on the day of the quake she was praying to the Jesuit martyrs in Japan. During these prayers, she had a presentiment that God was ready to punish Canada for the sins of its inhabitants, especially the contempt in which they held the church. She did not exactly disapprove. In fact, she wrote, "I could not help but wish for this punishment whatever it was, because then I had no idea what it could be." When the quake started, she saw in her mind four demons occupying the four sides of neighbouring lands and shaking them strongly as if they wanted to overturn them. A few days later, Catherine had a vision of St Michael. He was holding in his hand three arrows that were punishments for three kinds of sin common in Canada: impiety, impurity, and a lack of charity. She asked the angel to have patience and not launch his arrows yet.[101] In her journal's account, Catherine approved of divine and saintly punishment, but took on the role of mystic mediator to ask that the punishment be tempered with mercy.

Les Annales de l'Hôtel-Dieu de Québec provides a similar report about Catherine's interpretation of the earthquake, although it leaves aside the request for lenience. In this source, Catherine knew that God was very angry against Canada, and she could not stop herself from asking him to bring some divine punishment that would open the eyes of sinners. Immediately, she saw four furious demons at the four corners of the lands around Québec, shaking it so roughly that they were about to overturn the whole colony. After the quake began, all were filled with fear, and especially those who felt their consciences charged with crimes that had risen in number during Carnival; the quake stayed the course of their debaucheries and changed their entertainments.[102] In a detailed description of the earthquake that was translated into Latin and sent to the general of the Jesuit order in Rome, the Jesuit Charles Simon wrote about the quake too, and added an even more direct connection between the earthquake and Catherine's volition. In Simon's report, Catherine felt that God was vehemently angry and provoked by the sins committed in New France. Kindled by a zeal for the justice and the glory of God, she was hoping for and ardently demanding from God some notable vengeance and public example and terror to all, when suddenly there appeared four furious demons at the four corners of the region of Québec, trying to overturn the whole area from its foundations.[103] Similarly, according the Marie de l'Incarnation, Catherine knew that God was ready to punish the country for the sins people committed, and above all for the contempt in which they held the ordonnances of the church, and she could not prevent herself from desiring this chastisement.[104]

Catherine's hope for demonic chastisement may have been especially ardent, but she was not the only colonist in New France to approve of the earthquake. The Jesuit Jérôme Lalemant claimed that it brought about conversions among French and Indigenous people, adding that "many people actually wished for an increase rather than a decrease of this scourge."[105] Harsher punishment sounds like an unlikely desire for Carnival-celebrating colonists at large, but some missionaries did agree that the earthquake brought positive outcomes. The annalistes of the Hôtel-Dieu thought that the earthquake moved the consciences of the most hardened sinners and made them think seriously about their salvation.[106] Marie de l'Incarnation wrote that the earthquake was one of the extraordinary effects of God's power for converting the guilty, "as indeed it changed entirely diabolical souls, and put into a better state those that were already on the right path."[107]

It was quite common for early modern Europeans and European colonists to interpret natural disasters as catastrophes sent by God to punish people for their misdeeds or lead them to a better life, and some believed that earthquakes were a divine response to bad behaviour.[108] Most who wrote about earthquakes, however, including religious leaders who were not shy about chastising people for misbehaviour, made no reference to divine or diabolic intervention.[109] They assumed that God's permission was required for earthquakes to happen, but not that God caused them directly. For example, in his 1616 book about earthquakes, Louis du Thoum said that nothing is done without the will of God, who is the true cause of a quake, although not always the immediate one, since God often accommodated himself to secondary causes of the planets, earth, fire, water, and wind.[110]

Along the spectrum of theories about the causes of earthquakes, Catherine de Saint-Augustin placed herself clearly at the divinely demonic end. Nuns at the nearby Ursuline convent were more practical. They took spiritual steps such as kneeling and reciting the *Miserere* in order to appease the divine justice that was angered against the country, but they also slept fully clothed on straw mattresses on the floor so that they could more easily leave the house in case of a quake's intensification.[111]

The earthquake was not the only example of Catherine being keener than others to presume demonic activities. In a letter to the Jesuit Joseph Poncet, Marie de l'Incarnation reported that Catherine suffered strange temptations and persecutions by demons day and night for years both before and after the arrival of Hallay. Marie was somewhat hesitant, however, in sharing her thoughts on Catherine's purported encounters with demons. "Between you and me," she wrote, "I am not too knowledgeable about her affairs." With what seems a cautious tone, Marie admitted knowing that from the outside Catherine was in the communal life, as a good nun needs to be. Marie passed along pieces of information that she had received from others – the governor, the bishop, another Hospitalière nun, and Barbe Hallay – but, of her own opinion, she was reticent to share with Poncet as much as he wanted to know. She begged him to dispense her of the request, "seeing as people of knowledge and virtue suspend their judgment, and remain in doubt, not daring to trust in extraordinary visions of this quality."[112] Marie's writing here was almost certainly a gesture of humility, but at the same time it may also have been a gentle expression of skepticism.

The confessor's statement that he had seen physical evidence of Catherine's fight against demons – her arm blackened from hits – was perhaps a pre-emptive response to skepticism of that sort. The bruised arm was supposed to show that Catherine had been fighting against a strong force capable of causing physical harm, and it was perhaps also meant to be evidence against any charges of false sanctity.[113] In France, most such charges were made by ecclesiastical authorities worried that the current enthusiasm for interior spirituality could inspire unorthodox religious behaviour among women.[114] They were also worried about misinterpretations. Early modern writers on spiritual discernment cautioned that extraordinary religious experiences should not be taken at face value: they had to be carefully examined by the correct authorities, who were often male clergy.[115]

In his descriptions of Catherine's mystical visions and battles with demons, Ragueneau was applying exactly this clerical assurance of veracity. Such support was becoming increasingly important for female visionaries to be taken seriously. Leading theologians in France and elsewhere in Europe were trying to curtail female mysticism and women's religiosity more generally. Women could still earn recognition as spiritual authorities whose guidance was sought within the convent and beyond, but the role of mystic was becoming more contested in religious life by the mid-seventeenth century.[116] Theologians worried that supposedly mystical women's physiological and mental frailties made them all too likely to be ruled by carnal desires and melancholic natures. Jean Chéron wrote in his *Examen de la théologie mystique* of 1657 that the majority of mystics were actually poor creatures suffering from melancholy. They were mostly women, he said, because women were morally and physically weak, and had a propensity to be moved by their passions.[117] Even when determined to be authentic, mystics were thought to embody a particularly feminine paradox of power within weakness: they were ignorant of much human teaching but taught by God. In attributing their teachings directly to a divine source without human intermediary, women mystics entered into another paradox: their claims to mysticism liberated them from many of the hierarchical structures of the church, but placed their words under the surveillance and control of male directors.[118] Many of these directors were especially concerned with how to know if mystical women were experiencing visions of saints or communication with demons.[119] Ragueneau's characterization of Catherine as obsessed rather than possessed might have been a way to clarify the distinction, and an attempt to separate her experiences from what people would have heard about convent possessions in France, most infamously that of Loudun a few decades earlier.[120]

Ragueneau himself admitted near the start of the biography that readers should exercise caution when faced with accounts of extraordinary things. "It's a very reasonable demand," he wrote, "to want to know what assurance we can have of the truth of so many visions, apparitions, and revelations so extraordinary and so frequent, with which all this *Vie* is filled." He confirmed that prudence was merited since people had been deceived so often. He even granted it as all too true that "the imagination, especially of girls who are inclined to piety, is easily mistaken," with the result that these girls confuse their imaginations with reality. Ragueneau advised a middle way. A person should not be too credulous about extraordinary things, but neither should they be too stubbornly incredulous and believe only what they have seen and heard for themselves, "as if their eyes and their judgment were the only infallible rule" while all the other people in the world were more subject to error and illusion. Ragueneau was acknowledging the reasonableness of caution, but asking his readers to accept the possibility of a world beyond their own limited sense perceptions.

The biographer was particularly concerned that people would disbelieve the remarkable things seen by Catherine because she was a woman. He reminded his readers that the resurrected Jesus Christ had first appeared to women, although the male apostles did not believe them, and that God sometimes chose to make himself seen by women rather than by men.[121] Ragueneau clearly anticipated that Catherine's gender would be an obstacle to people accepting the truth of her visions, her battles against demons, and, ultimately, his book. He was probably especially worried that Catherine's gender would interfere with people's reception of her apostolic ideals. Women were active participants in church reform movements in seventeenth-century Europe, but they knew that many men in positions of ecclesiastical and civic authority wanted to silence their public teaching. In response, women with a missionary function along with their supporters were careful to explain the women's role as that of teacher rather than preacher. They emphasized the teaching activity as a domestic activity, even if the actions in reality often amounted to preaching.[122] Claude Martin demonstrated this careful distinction in his biography of his mother, Marie de l'Incarnation, when he wrote with a nimble nomenclature that if his mother could not be given the name of "Apostle," she could at least be called an "apostolic woman."[123]

Many ecclesiastical leaders back in Europe opposed female missionaries' eagerness for active service. They advocated instead contemplation and enclosure for women religious. Historians have argued that such gender restrictions were by necessity more flexible in the frontier conditions of a North American colony.[124] While this was probably the case, we should not underestimate the abilities of women in Europe to subvert or sneak around patriarchal structures either. Some embraced the cloister as a protection against scandal as well as a space for solitude and sacrifice. A group of nuns in Toulouse, for instance, explained to an abbot "that they had bodies capable of suffering, and that they had wills and desires as generous as men to undertake to make the sacrifice of their bodies."[125] Some religious women advocated for a less rigid enclosure so that they could continue an active apostolate within the wider community.[126] Even from within the cloister, women in France could pursue heroic asceticism, they could take on charitable service, and they could obtain respect for their work at the centre of social assistance.[127] Enclosure certainly did not seal religious women away from having an effect on the larger world either in Europe or its overseas colonies. But it did impose certain limits, and these limits were tested by women who saw their mission as apostolic.

Ragueneau's *Vie* stresses that Catherine de Saint-Augustin's commitment to an apostolic mission extended even to the possibility of martyrdom.[128] It was a stance likely to resonate strongly with readers. Martyrological literature was very popular in Europe, where people read books about martyrs and wrote about martyrdom in both official treatises and personal correspondence.[129] When the superior of Catherine's old community in Bayeux wanted to recall Catherine to France, knowing the infirmities and sickness that she endured in North America, Catherine refused, saying that she was "attached to the cross of Canada." Three nails held her in place: the will of God, the salvation of souls, and her vocation in the country along with the vow she had made to die there. Catherine added that even if all the other nuns wished to return to France, "she would stay alone in Canada there to employ her life in the service of the poor Indians and the sick of the country."[130] With such imagery, Catherine was proclaiming herself to be a living martyr in a missionary institution. Catherine's connection with martyrdom was further reinforced in the *Vie* through its account of how she bound herself spiritually to one of the most well-known of local martyrs, Jean de Brébeuf. She had arrived in New France a few months before Brébeuf's death and never met him in person, but this chronology did not prevent Catherine from regarding him as a spiritual director.[131] Catherine had multiple visions of Brébeuf, who told her several times in these visions that he would take care of this country.[132] He also, according to Marie de l'Incarnation, assisted Catherine in treating Hallay. Marie wrote that God had fortified Catherine in this work through Brébeuf's help: "Finally the demons and magician withdrew through the intercession of this holy man who shed his blood for the support of faith in this country."[133] The circumstances of Brébeuf's death and the colonists' attempts to understand what this death truly meant for them will be more fully discussed in the next chapter. In the context of the Hôtel-Dieu, Catherine's linking of herself to Brébeuf created an association between her role in the institution and Canadian martyrdom. This association amplified the sacrificial tone of her description of herself as crucified to Canada, which drew upon the traditional Christian desire to imitate Christ while adding a layer of emotional fervour specific to the New France mission.[134]

Canada's reputation as a difficult and dangerous place led to divergent responses from would-be missionaries. It discouraged people from coming if they thought the mission was too demanding, yet attracted others who actively sought martyrdom.[135] When Jesuits in Europe declared a preference for Canada as their destination, they cited the death of a Jesuit martyr in New France as inspiration.[136] Female missionaries were not supposed to be so eager for a violent death, but Canada's reputation for suffering and violence could appeal to those hoping for spiritual heroism, regardless of gender.[137] Catherine de Saint-Augustin was one of these people, and her battles against demons to save Barbe Hallay were among her heroic acts.

These acts were given increased significance for Ragueneau as Catherine's biographer when he measured Catherine's commitment and success against recent setbacks in New France's missionary endeavours.

THE DISAPPOINTMENTS OF A MISSION FIELD

During the first part of the seventeenth century, French colonists presumed that Indigenous people in North America would willingly, even enthusiastically, embrace conversion to Christianity.[138] Early French efforts at proselytizing met with a courteous hearing. Samuel de Champlain in 1603 explained the basic points of Catholic doctrine as he understood them to people at Tadoussac; they listened patiently and responded politely that they approved of what Champlain said.[139] Such courtesy was sometimes misinterpreted as full acceptance by the French, who had political motivations supporting such a misreading. Conversion was one of the stated objectives of territorial expansion, and inseparable, at least rhetorically, from the search for riches. As the lawyer Marc Lescarbot put it in the dedication to the king from his 1609 *History of New France*, "there are two principal causes which as a rule excite kings to make conquests: zeal for the glory of God, and desire to increase their own possessions."[140] Lescarbot was already claiming progress in one of these areas. In the dedication "To France" from the same book, he told his readers that it is "a shameful thing … to allow so many reasoning creatures formed in God's image to live in ignorance," and he alleged that the Indigenous peoples encountered by the French "all love the French, and desire nothing more than to conform themselves to us in civilisation, morality, and religion."[141] As the French colonists would soon learn, if they did not know already, Indigenous people did not want to become French in the ways Lescarbot was describing. But it took many of them a long time to admit it.

French travellers seeking political and financial support for their voyages had a clear interest in making their goals seem both righteous and obtainable. Some also sincerely believed that people would quite simply want to become French and Christian once they saw what French Christian society was like. Chapter 1 showed how early modern Europeans were drawing upon ancient ideas about the changeability of weather. They were also building upon ancient ideas about how people would change according to where they lived. Hippocrates, writing in approximately 400 BCE, thought that Europeans were more courageous and warlike than Asians not because of anything inherent in the individual persons, but because of differences in their natural climates and political institutions. The uniformity of climate in Asia engendered slackness, which in turn fed cowardice, whereas climatic variation in Europe fostered endurance, which in turn fed bravery. In political institutions, Asia had kings, whose rule discouraged people from taking risks, but Europeans did not have kings and so were more independent and likely to take risks on their own behalf, "willing and eager to go into danger, for they themselves enjoy the prize of victory."[142] Hippocrates thought that Europeans were in many ways superior to Asians, but because of circumstance rather than innate qualities. If a person born in Asia moved to Europe, they would presumably take on the characteristics of Europeans.

French writers in the early seventeenth century still believed that some societies were superior to others – with European Christian societies the best of all – and they also still believed that people would change depending on the where they lived. The hierarchy in their minds was one of societies, not of individual people: a person had the capacity to move up or down the societal hierarchy when they moved from one society to another.[143] The Jesuit Paul Le Jeune discussed this idea as an inheritance from Aristotle, placing the nomadic Natives in North America at the first of three stages along the development of human societies.[144] His elite French readers would have thought that many less elite French people were likewise at an earlier stage of Aristotle's developmental system, and, indeed, the missionaries knew that French society as a whole had changed over time. Well aware that the Christian religion had been imported into Europe, Le Jeune wrote that there had been barbarism in Germany, in Spain, in England, and even in France before the coming of Christianity. Le Jeune extended this trajectory in his imagination to the point where he hoped Indigenous people would help New France exceed the Old to become regenerated and improved, a Jerusalem composed of citizens destined for heaven.[145]

Missionary writers repeatedly stated that Indigenous people in New France were of very sound mind and body, and they insisted that Indigenous people had the same souls as all other humans. These writers also thought that Indigenous societies lacked laws and religion – at least in institutionalized form. The deficiency, in their view, was cultural rather than natural. French writers subscribed to a theory of monogenesis, which was the idea that all humans were descended from the same original parents of Adam and Eve.[146] This common descent gave all people a shared disposition to understand universal truths. In the words of Jean de Brébeuf, the Native peoples of North America, as humans, "could not misrecognize God altogether."[147] Missionaries thought they detected a divine imprint on Indigenous languages and cultures, and even some hazy memories of Old Testament content in Indigenous stories, such as a tradition of Noah's flood in the Innu story of Messou repairing the world lost in water.[148] Speculating that they had found an echo of their own Christian understanding in North America, these missionaries believed they were not introducing Indigenous people to an entirely new religion; they were bringing them back to a forgotten truth.[149]

The theory that all peoples were related and had the same capacity to learn partly explains the missionaries' aims and methods. Another crucial element was the missionaries' presumption of the universality of their own religious system. They believed that the truths of Christianity were equally true in every part of the world, regardless of whether the people living there were Christian or not.[150] Consider how Jean de Brébeuf responded to a group of Wendat after they shared with him their creation story of Aataentsic.[151] Brébeuf informed the French readers of his *Relation* that when the Jesuits prodded their hosts with questions about the details of the story, the Wendat had no answer except to say that they did not know. When the Jesuits tried to preach about God and the Christian mysteries, the headstrong among the listeners answered that this was good for the Jesuits' country, but not for theirs; every country has its ways of doing things. Here, in a Jesuit's words, we see the missionaries' insistence upon Christianity's global applicability, and a paraphrase of a Wendat response that Christianity is not equally and necessarily true for all. The Jesuits in Brébeuf's report tried to make their case more concretely by using a globe to show that there is only one world. The Wendat did not reply.[152] They were probably being polite to their guest, whose use of a prop did not undermine their acceptance that different people could believe different things and that these different things could all be true.[153]

Missionary sources often transmit Indigenous voices saying politely but firmly that religious truths can be variously true for different people. This perspective was not shared by the French missionaries. Traditional Indigenous societies accepted pluralism in spirituality, whereas the European Catholic missionaries expected their religion to be exclusive and universal. This presumption of Christianity's universal reach made the missionaries think they saw the same demons that they knew from Europe in North America. When trying to find specific demonic presences, they sometimes had to perform convoluted interpretations of Indigenous spirits of *manitou* and *oki* in order to make them conform to European expectations of demons.[154] But they did what they could to persuade their French readers and themselves that the demons were trans-Atlantic. As Jérôme Lalemant wrote, the country of the Wendat and neighbouring areas seemed to him a principal fortress of demons, but all the nations of the world were given to Jesus Christ and all would serve him.[155]

French settlers' theory of individual mobility through a hierarchy of societies alongside their confidence in the superiority of their own civilization and universality of their religion contributed to the missionaries' optimism. In New France, they thought, they could make a better France.[156] To get there, the political leaders in France decided to implement "francisation," a policy of assimilation that had at its core religious conversion to Christianity and cultural adaptation to at least some French norms.[157] All missionaries participated in some way to advance the crown's assimilationist policy, although precise goals and strategies varied according to what the missionaries thought the relationship should be between becoming Christian and becoming French. The differences in approach aligned broadly with differences between Catholic religious orders.[158] The Récollets were generally more culturally assertive, for example, advocating that Indigenous peoples become like the French before becoming Christian.[159] Friar Joseph Le Caron explained a Récollet perspective by saying that as the number of colonists grew, they would "humanize the barbarians," and "police them by the laws and ways of living in the French manner, in order to render them capable of hearing reason on such elevated mysteries."[160] The Jesuits on the whole were less concerned with having potential converts accept so many aspects of French culture, emphasizing instead religious instruction.[161] Pierre Biard in 1616, for example, prioritized teaching the Indigenous peoples in Acadia diligently about Christianity before being baptized.[162] Jesuits did sometimes argue that it was desirable to fix Indigenous communities in a location, as with Sillery, but for the Jesuits this plan was mostly to assist with conversion rather than a good in and of itself: it was simply easier to evangelize a group who stayed in one place.

The crown and its agents were more insistent than the Jesuits on the importance of cultural transformation, and they thought that formal education would be helpful in advancing francisation. The most famous missionary school in Québec was that of the Ursulines. Its foundation charter stated that the Ursulines were to be held in perpetuity to instruct the Indigenous girls of New France in knowledge of the Catholic religion, in reading and writing, in the catechism, and "generally all that is necessary to know for a true and faithful Catholic Christian."[163] The community's *Constitutions* of 1647 reinforced the importance of education. It directed that as part of the Ursulines' fourth vow (a vow of education taken in addition to the three conventional monastic vows of poverty, chastity, and obedience), the nuns were obliged to offer education to girls who presented themselves for instruction, and added that it would be a mortal sin to refuse without reasonable cause.[164] By providing Indigenous students with instruction in religion, language, and domestic skills, the Ursulines supported the crown's hope that Indigenous girls could become French women and marry French settlers.[165] This education was in line with the crown's policy for the first few decades of the school's operations. But then, around the middle of the seventeenth century, the crown changed its policy of francisation to one that required Indigenous people to abandon more of their Indigeneity to become French. In a departure from this changing policy, the Ursulines continued not to insist that their students abandon all aspects of Indigenous identity. They supported their students' retention of languages: students spoke, read, and wrote in French, but they also sang, conversed, and wrote letters in Indigenous languages. They catered to Indigenous food preferences: visitors were regularly fed sagamité, and the nuns purchased foods from both European and Indigenous North American cuisines. They allowed students' alterations to French Christian practices: girls built little cabins out of leaves, lined them with greenery, and spent nights there to pray alone or in small groups.[166]

The different missionary orders disagreed among themselves, and sometimes with the crown, about the relative importance of cultural and religious conversion, but they all agreed that Indigenous peoples could and should become Christian. The French crown and the missionary orders invested a lot of time, energy, and effort into converting Indigenous peoples. By the 1650s, however, it was clear that their efforts were not leading to the results they had expected. While many Indigenous people could see value in learning French skills and adopting French technologies for their own purposes, most were not eager to abandon an Indigenous identity altogether to become French. Furthermore, some were accusing the Black Robes – not without reason – of bringing discord and death into their communities, even of benefitting from sickness and mortality to increase the numbers of baptisms and demonstrate spiritual power.[167] And some of the missionaries' earlier apparent successes, notably the Huronia and Sillery missions, were falling apart.

The disappointments of the mission field coloured how Catherine de Saint-Augustin's biographer interpreted her battles against demons. By the 1660s, Jesuits in New France had largely ceased warning about demons as a real force, and were instead writing about demons metaphorically as an abstract power that made people behave in bad ways. Those who became violent when drunk, or even drunkenness itself, for instance, were "demons."[168] Ragueneau, however, continued to treat demons as real in the world. At some point after November 1661, he wrote a letter to someone associated with the bishop of Chalon-sur-Saône in France. He was gathering information so that he could inform priests (including Laval) in Canada about a recent report of demonic possessions in an Ursuline convent in Auxonne, "as we have in Canada people possessed in the same way."[169] This concern with demonic forces represented a change in Ragueneau's beliefs. Back in the 1630s and 1640s, when Jesuits in New France were writing more frequently and more credulously about demonic interference, Ragueneau had held fairly moderate views in comparison to other members of his religious order.[170] Paul Le Jeune at first mistrusted and even mocked Indigenous reports of spiritual forces, but became more concerned as time went on that Indigenous people really were somehow engaged with demonic forces.[171] Jean de Brébeuf thought that Indigenous people might have been in contact with demons, but he remained open to the possibility that he misunderstood what he was observing and presumed for the most part that Indigenous people were correctly disposed in intent even if sometimes misguided in action.[172] Jérôme Lalemant believed in the real, powerful, and pervasive presence of demons and also in Indigenous people's willful communion with them.[173] Ragueneau was in the middle of this range of Jesuits' beliefs. He was keen to distinguish the natural from supernatural when he thought he could, he expressed uncertainty about many of the Indigenous claims to supernatural power, and he readily acknowledged limits to his understanding. Ragueneau admitted that he did not know whether Wendat items called "aaskouandy," a kind of amulet, could really bring good fortune, for example, and he cited a Wendat proverb in support of his preferred interpretation: "industry, strength, and vigilance are the most powerful aaskouandy that a person can have."[174] When trying to determine whether sorcerers could cause death through the casting of spells, Ragueneau said that after examining all the available evidence he had not "yet seen any foundation sufficiently reasonable to believe that there truly are here those that meddle in this hellish trade."[175] His advice to fellow missionaries in 1648 was to be similarly cautious. He instructed them not to condemn too quickly those Indigenous customs that were at odds with European ones, and he warned that "it is easy to accuse something as being irreligion when it is but foolishness and to take as a diabolical operation that which is nothing more than human."[176] Ragueneau was a cautious demonologist in the 1630s and 1640s, but he became one of the most enthusiastic champions of Catherine de Saint-Augustin's visions of demonic dangers a few decades later.

The missionary context had changed significantly in the intervening years, as will be discussed more fully in chapters 4 and 5. By the time he was writing Catherine's biography, Ragueneau had witnessed the destruction of the Huronia mission, overseen the burning of the mission town of Sainte-Marie, presided over the funerals of Jesuit martyrs then had their remains disinterred and brought into Québec, and gone back to France to ask for more troops for Canada. Having known the dashing of missionary hopes, he grew more determined than ever to establish the importance of missionary efforts and fix them in the minds of people near and far. He wrote in 1652 that Satan, seeing Old France being torn apart by its own children, wished to destroy New France so that he could re-establish the domain that he was losing through the conversion of Indigenous people.[177] Ragueneau wanted to make people understand how high the stakes were on a cosmic scale.

With such significance in mind, the Jesuit biographer reconsidered what fighting diabolical agents might look like when missionaries shifted their focus away from evangelizing Indigenous peoples and towards caring for French colonists. He found a worthy subject in Catherine de Saint-Augustin and her desire to be an apostolic martyr for Canada. Her devotion to Jean de Brébeuf and her sense of their connection supported Ragueneau's goal of developing the cult of his fellow Jesuit and friend. Writing about Catherine's fight against demons allowed Ragueneau to show how veneration to Brébeuf could help the settlers in the colony of New France, and it invested missionary disappointments with meaning. In Catherine's visions through Ragueneau's pen, what might seem like the failure of missionaries in New France could be transformed into an inspiring story of courage for the colony's precarious present and hope for its uncertain future.[178] Catherine's ongoing battles with demons, including the ones troubling Barbe Hallay, provided Ragueneau with material to show that evil forces were still amassing against New France, and that missionary defenders were willing and able to sacrifice themselves to save the colony.

The elites of New France thought that the Hôtel-Dieu would be the best place for Barbe Hallay when she was brought from the infested seigneurie into the town of Québec. The Hospitalière nuns were prepared to administer both medical and spiritual remedies, and Catherine de Saint-Augustin in particular was an experienced fighter against demons. Was she successful in her efforts? Marie de l'Incarnation's letter, with its report of demons removing themselves, suggests she was, at least temporarily. As the next chapter will show, the possession persisted after Barbe Hallay's departure from the Hôtel-Dieu. Efforts to deliver her from demons when she returned to the seigneurie at Beauport continued to draw upon the intercessory powers of Jean de Brébeuf, but the scene shifted to the domestic space of the household.

4

A Deliverance from Demons

At some point between the autumn of 1661 and the autumn of 1662, Barbe Hallay left the Hôtel-Dieu in Québec and returned to work as a servant at the *seigneurie* of Beauport. Several attempts had been made to end the demonic interference by this time, and none was successful. Neither the priests visiting the seigneurie when the infestation started nor the Augustinian nuns treating Hallay at the hospital in Québec were able to cast out the demons entirely. Even after the man suspected of using witchcraft to summon the demons had been executed, Hallay continued to show signs of possession. Once back at Beauport, these signs got worse.

Barbe Hallay's behaviour while in the throes of possession was strange and violent, much like the typical presentation of early modern Europeans believed to be possessed. The person who led the efforts to help Hallay at Beauport also acted typically up to a point when responding to the disturbing symptoms. At the seigneurie, it was Marie Regnouard, wife of the *seigneur*, who took charge of freeing her servant from the demonic torments that had been troubling Hallay for more than two years. In providing physical care, Marie Regnouard conformed to expectations for someone of her gender and class. She was the female head of her household, and as such had a responsibility to look after those under her authority. She was to keep them as healthy as possible, treating illnesses and injuries when required. Regnouard's care for Hallay also reached into more contested areas within a spiritual domain. Although the language used to describe Regnouard's activities evokes domestic health care, the actions themselves formed the shape of a religious ritual normally forbidden to women. This apparent transgression can be explained partly through

Regnouard's social status in the colony and partly through her proximity to medical expertise. Still more importantly, Regnouard's actions were accepted, even encouraged, because they could be narrated to focus not on her, but on a martyr moving toward sainthood.[1]

AN ACCOUNT OF DELIVERANCE

Marie Regnouard provided a vivid account of her efforts to end Barbe Hallay's possession. This account survives in three unpublished copies. One, which is conserved in the Archives des Augustines du Monastère de l'Hôtel-Dieu de Québec, includes a line saying that it was signed by Marie Regnouard at Beauport on 25 February 1663.[2] The other two, which are conserved in the Archives des Jésuites au Canada, include lines saying that they were signed by Regnouard at Beauport on 8 March 1663.[3] The Jesuit archive versions also contain additional material in a second section that is dated 9 April 1663. This appended section was signed by Charles de Lauson de Charny, once acting governor of New France and by this time a priest.

The handwriting of the first section of Marie Regnouard's account is different in all three copies. Her signature is not identical across the three, but it is somewhat similar, and resembles her signature on other documents dating from the 1630s to the 1660s.[4] It is therefore quite possible that different scribes wrote out Regnouard's words, but that she signed the documents in her own hand. The handwriting of the appended section of the account is different in the two Jesuit archive copies, and does not appear to match the handwriting of the first part on any of the copies.[5] Charles de Lauson de Charny's signed name on the first of the Jesuit archive versions looks like the handwriting in the rest of that section, but his name on the second version resembles Lauson de Charny's signature on a document from 1664 in the Hôtel Dieu archive.[6] Lauson de Charny, therefore, may have written and signed one of these versions himself, and someone else the other.

Regardless of whoever physically put quill to paper, the first section of the account in all three copies uses the first person singular to convey Regnouard's story as told in her own words. It begins by saying that on about 15 October, 1662, between 10 and 11 in the evening, Barbe Hallay was sleeping when a demon came to torment her as was the demon's custom. Marie Regnouard immediately got out of bed to help, as she was accustomed to doing. She had already gone "many other times" to Hallay in this state and put on her "the relics of many saints." On this night, the demons were tormenting Hallay worse than Regnouard had ever seen before. It came into her mind to put onto Hallay a rib bone of the deceased Jean de Brébeuf, which the Reverend Father Paul Ragueneau had given to her upon his return from the Hurons. Regnouard placed the rib bone against the side of Hallay, and immediately the demon became agitated. In the words of Regnouard's account, "the demon caused [Hallay] to make several contortions of [her] arms and [her] legs and generally all [her] body," and this demon told Regnouard several times to remove the relic because it burned.[7] Regnouard conjured the demon in the name of the living God and by the merits of the very holy Virgin Mary, and she demanded that the demon tell her the name of the person whose relics he was insisting she remove. They argued. The demon said that he would not answer, and Regnouard said she would not remove the relics until he did. Then the demon said that it was a relic from a saint martyred among the Huron by the Iroquois. Regnouard conjured the demon again to tell her the name of the saint. The demon spoke as if in anger and so quickly that Regnouard could not understand what he was saying. He repeated his demand that she remove the relic, and Regnouard told him that she would not remove it unless he consented to leave the girl. The demon refused, because, he said, the girl was his. Regnouard responded forcefully, "you have lied, damned spirit that you are; you have nothing; she [is] mine. Our good God, and her father and her mother gave her to me."[8] Regnouard placed the relic on the side of the girl at the place of her heart. The demon began once again to agitate Hallay's whole body and cry loudly that he could not tolerate it any longer, that he was burning. He made her contort as if she were a very weak person while throwing her arms and head from side to side, then cried out with a languid and dying voice, over and over again, "remove this from me, woman, because I cannot bear it; remove it, remove it quickly, I cannot bear it, I am burnt."[9] Regnouard conjured the demon as before, this time also adding that she was conjuring by the merits of the saint whose relics she was using, and ordered the demon to depart. She saw something "like a breath" leave from the mouth of Hallay, who "began immediately to speak and to say 'Jesus, Mary, Joseph' and to make the sign of the cross on her forehead, on her mouth, and on her heart."[10]

These words and gestures signified the departure of the possessing demon and the return of Hallay's control over her own body. For Hallay though, the liberation was not yet complete. Regnouard's account continues with Hallay saying that the demon left, but that two witches who had been accompanying the demon were now at the foot of the bed. These witches had previously brought the girl something to eat that caused her to vomit, and now they returned. Regnouard conjured them as well in the name of God, and she told them to leave the demon that they served. The witches spoke several words to Regnouard, but she could not understand them, hearing only a low buzzing or hum. Hallay relayed the witches' speech: they had come to bring her to the Sabbath but – as the copy at the Hôtel-Dieu concludes rather abruptly – since that day, the girl had neither seen nor heard either demon or witch, and she was of a freer mind than she had been for the two and a half years during which she had been agitated by demons.

The additional section on the archive of the Jesuits copies signed by Charles de Lauson de Charny switches to the third person to continue the account. It says that four and a half months after this deliverance, Hallay met a certain man suspected of witchcraft. He tried to put her on a cart that he was driving, and said some impertinent things to her. She resisted, then was tormented by demons again for eleven days. The demons made a very large noise in the room of Hallay, and threw a stone from the chimney with such force that Seigneur Giffard rose from his bed thinking that the chimney had fallen; the report added that it has been verified that this chimney, which had smoked earlier, smoked no longer. The same people as before once more prayed to Brébeuf asking for a second recovery for the girl, and she has since then remained entirely delivered.

THE POSSESSION

As discussed in earlier chapters, people witnessing Barbe Hallay's torments thought that she was experiencing some kind of demonic intrusion. In the early stages, they saw phantoms and heard ghostly music at the seigneurie where she worked. Hallay had a spectral vision of the magician who had sent the apparitions, of his companions, and of demons in various forms. Stones detached themselves from walls and flew around on their own.[11] Once Hallay was brought into the Hôtel-Dieu hospital, she continued to see spectral apparitions of the magician, and a demon agitated her by night. Hallay's main protector at the Hôtel-Dieu, the Hospitalière nun Catherine de Saint-Augustin, reported that she too endured attacks from demons, and her confessor reported that these demons left bruises on her arm. Up to this point, observers sometimes called what was happening an infestation, sometimes an obsession, sometimes a possession.[12]

Marie Regnouard's treatment of Hallay shows that she thought her servant was suffering from a demonic possession. Symptoms for possession as described in texts from early modern Europe were numerous and varied. Not all the principal symptoms that Sarah Ferber has identified in French cases were displayed by Hallay. There was no levitation, exceptional strength, understanding of hitherto unknown languages, or knowledge of distant events, for example.[13] When the demon spoke its language was French, which was somewhat unusual. Most often in Europe, the demonic language of choice was Latin, but Greek and Hebrew were sometimes claimed to be understood or spoken by the possessing demon, or even a contemporary European language other than the one normally spoken by the demoniac.[14] Many aspects of Hallay's presentation would have suggested possession to French demonologists, however, including her physical convulsions and contortions, her babbling and speaking in an altered voice, as well as the repeated failure of attempts to end the symptoms, and the demoniac's display of revulsion when presented with a relic.[15] Hallay convulsed and contorted by thrashing her limbs and moving her head from side to side; some of what she said could not be understood, and some of it was in a strangely low-pitched voice; efforts to end the demonic torments had been ongoing for many months, and were intensifying once back at Beauport; the touch of a relic caused the demon to demand and plead that Regnouard remove it, saying over and over that it burned him.

Much of what happened in Regnouard's account was consistent with a pattern from early modern Europe, where observers were struck by the intensely physical character of possession. They particularly noted the twisting and pains of the demoniac, which were thought to increase during efforts to remove the demon.[16] The same characteristics were present in Regnouard's account. Furthermore, as mentioned in chapter 2, most demoniacs were young and female. Barbe Hallay's status of a servant added yet another marker of a subordinate group.[17] The possessed in Europe were often servants, and they were frequently treated on beds. In cases where a male priest was exorcising a female demoniac, especially when she was young and unmarried, witnesses of the act or readers of the written account might have detected a sexual element of submission and lust: a celibate man tending to a woman on the verge of an active sexual life, writhing and rolling on a bed, her clothes twisted to reveal a body over which she was not in control.[18] Regnouard's account does not seem to adopt a sexualized tone at any point, and Hallay's bed might simply have been the most convenient place to treat her, although it is possible that the account's readers could have seen an erotic dimension in knowing that female heads of households and their female servants were often intimately well aware of each other's bodies.[19] Whether meant erotically or not, Regnouard's position of power is emphasized repeatedly in the account. The account refers to Regnouard as a woman and to Hallay as a girl. Regnouard said that Hallay's parents had given Hallay to her, and Hallay called Regnouard "Madame."

One feature of Regnouard's approach that was very clearly in line with European ideas of possession was its differentiation of the demon from the demoniac. Regnouard presumed that the demon was inside Hallay's body, yet she made a distinction between what the demon did and what Hallay did. Her account asserts that it was the demon causing Hallay to contort her limbs, and the demon speaking through Hallay's mouth ("the demon made her make several contortions," "he told me right away," "he was speaking too quickly"). This distinction between the demon's agency and that of the demoniac is maintained even at the level of grammar in the account. When the demon is quoted, he uses not the feminine grammatical forms that Hallay would use, but rather the masculine grammatical forms of a male speaker (e.g., "Je suys tout brulé," except once in the first of the Jesuit archive versions, where – possibly as a result of scribal error – the demon is reported as saying "ie suis tout bruleé"). By contrast, after the account indicates that the demon has left Hallay's body, Regnouard's paraphrases of Hallay's speech take the feminine forms of verbal endings (e.g., "qu'elle auoit esté agittée"). Regnouard and the scribes considered Hallay to be a separate entity from the possessing demon: the demon was in Hallay's body, but the two had distinct voices. They were also treated as having two separate wills. Regnouard believed that so long as the demon was possessing Hallay, the demon was in control of Hallay's actions and speech. When the body moved, the demon moved it; when the body spoke, the words were those of the demon. The signal that the demon had left Hallay's body was when Hallay said the names of Jesus, Mary, and Joseph, and made sign of the cross. It was a return to speech and gesture in conformity with Catholic religious practice that indicated her regaining of control over her body. The distinction that Regnouard maintained between the actions of the demon and the actions of the demoniac was the same distinction made in early modern France. The demon was thought to seize control of the body and mental faculties of the person it was inhabiting, and so the demon was responsible for the actions of the possessed.[20] This distinction travelled to New France, where Ragueneau put it in his biography of Catherine de Saint-Augustin as discussed in chapter 2. In Ragueneau's definition, possession was a "malignant operation, by which the devil makes himself master of the person's power" and "responds personally by the mouth of the person possessed."[21]

The presence of witches in Regnouard's account also fits with an early modern European understanding of possession as the consequence of witchcraft, and of the possessed person as victim.[22] In the specific case of this possession, the appearance of witches at Beauport helped to explain why the demon was still tormenting Hallay even after the person thought to have first provoked the trouble (Daniel Vuil) was executed, and it provided additional reassurance that Hallay was not to blame for the years of demonic infestation. The presence of witches created an arc of continuity stretching from the end of the possession right back to its beginning, when Marie de l'Incarnation had expressed concern about witches and magicians arriving in New France. Now, several years later, witches and demons were still tormenting Barbe Hallay, and it was the turn of Marie Rengouard to bring about a deliverance.

THE DELIVERER

Marie Regnouard's account tells a story of determined efforts. It is clear that she considered herself to be engaging in a vigorous fight against a demon occupying the body of her servant. Her words were confident and assertive as she questioned and commanded her supernatural adversary.

Less obvious, perhaps, is the account's delicacy in naming exactly what Regnouard was doing to bring an end to her servant's hellish torments. Regnouard's actions are characterized in the account as a deliverance ("*delivrance*"), a relief ("*soulagement*"), and a healing ("*guerison*"). Such words convey wholesome ideas of removing harmful forces, easing pain, and restoring health.[23] Looking beyond these words to the procedure being described, however, one might be struck by a conspicuous resemblance to something else: an exorcism. Regnouard did not employ the full rite as laid out in the *Rituale*

Romanum, the text that guided official exorcisms in the Catholic world,[24] and the word "exorcism" itself is not used in any of the sources about the event,[25] but the essential elements were nonetheless present in what Regnouard did, even more clearly than in Catherine de Saint-Augustin's actions as described in the previous chapter. By summoning the possessing demon with a ritual invocation, Regnouard used adjuration; by asking the demon whose relics she was holding, she used interrogation; by calling upon the names of God and the Virgin Mary, she used prayer; and by touching her charge with a relic, she used a sacred object.[26] All these steps were present in official and public exorcisms of the seventeenth century. Even the adjustments that Regnouard made to the procedure as it was laid out in manuals were exorcism-like. Regnouard's appeal to a local holy person for assistance (in this case, Jean de Brébeuf) was typical of exorcisms of the time, as were alterations to the rite as published in the *Rituale Romanum*. In fact, the spoken formulae of exorcisms varied considerably from place to place and practitioner to practitioner, often modifying the Roman Rite by assembling elements of the liturgy together with paraliturgical practices and even traditions of folk magic.[27] Furthermore, Regnouard described herself as speaking with the demon, not with Hallay, and her performance had the expected effects of exorcism in agitating the demon and causing the demoniac increased suffering during the procedure before finally casting out the possessing force.[28]

So, if Regnouard's actions amounted to an exorcism, and a successful one at that, why did her account not describe them as such? A simple answer is that Regnouard's gender and lay status rendered her categorically unsuitable to perform that ritual. In a slightly earlier period, people who sought an exorcist showed little preference for either a man or a woman, clerical or lay; they cared more about personal reputation and geographical proximity than about gender or profession. But starting in the late sixteenth century, ecclesiastical authorities tried to prevent laypeople from practising exorcism, and women who claimed to be able to discern a supernatural cause for an illness became more vulnerable to accusations of witchcraft.[29] Women may have been permitted to exorcise in theological theory, but it was only male clerics were who were granted institutional authority to perform the rite in practice.[30] By the early seventeenth century, the exclusion was made more complete, and the 1614 *Rituale Romanum*'s section on exorcism states that only a priest or another lawfully appointed officer of the church can exorcise.[31] Marie Regnouard was neither.

Such attitudes and regulations may explain why Regnouard's actions were not called an exorcism, but they raise perhaps an even more interesting question: Why did she perform these actions at all, if they constituted some form of exorcism in all but name? Regnouard's actions took place in her house rather than in a public space, but she was certainly not acting in secret. A record was taken of her account, three copies of which survive. The second section in the account even states that some people had read what was written above in the first section, indicating that the account was disseminated shortly after being written. The person writing that second section, Charles de Lauson de Charny, had known people central to the development of Hallay's possession for years, and so he understood what had already been attempted. He had first arrived at Québec in 1652, and promptly married Louise Giffard, daughter of Marie Regnouard and Robert Giffard. Louise died at the Hôtel-Dieu in 1656, two weeks after giving birth to a daughter, Marie. Marie Regnouard was one of the infant's godparents. The following year, Lauson de Charny placed his daughter in the care of her grandparents and went back to France. He entered holy orders, became a priest in 1659, and returned to Québec on the same crossing as François de Laval, Daniel Vuil, and Barbe Hallay. He was appointed an ecclesiastical judge in September 1659, then vicar general in 1660, and therefore may have been involved in the legal cases against Vuil.[32] Lauson de Charny, leader in both state and church, was familiar with the case, and supported Regnouard's intervention. Regnouard was further supported, and indirectly assisted, by the Jesuit priest Paul Ragueneau, who had given her the rib bone of Jean de Brébeuf that she used in the procedure. As discussed in chapter 3, it was also Ragueneau who supplied a relic of Brébeuf to Catherine de Saint-Augustin, the nun caring for Hallay at the Hôtel-Dieu hospital. Jesuits were leaders in the European campaign to exorcise growing numbers of possessed, and also enforcers of a clerical monopoly on exorcism, so it seems especially noteworthy that the two women who attempted to rid Hallay of demons used the relics of a martyred Jesuit given to them by another Jesuit.[33] Because Ragueneau was Catherine de Saint-Augustin's spiritual director, he would have known not only her public role as a nurse in the Hôtel-Dieu hospital, but also her secret record of battling demons. Marie Regnouard was not a nun or a nurse. She was a laywoman on a seigneurie outside of Québec.

To understand how Marie Regnouard's involvement in Hallay's deliverance was accepted by Lauson de Charny, Ragueneau, and others, we need to consider her position in the colonial society of New France, as well as her connection with medical care in Québec. As an elite woman and head of a household, she was fulfilling a responsibility to look after those who lived beneath her roof. As someone closely connected to people with professional medical expertise, she had access to knowledge in the domain of healing.

Marie Regnouard held a powerful position in New France. Much of her power had been passed to her through inheritance in France, and more was accumulated once she reached Canada. She was born in the Perche region of northwestern France to a family of quite high status. Her father, Charles Regnouard, was the *sergent royal* in the city of Mortagne, her godparents were nobles, and her brother was a prior. Her father had died by the time her contract of marriage was signed on 11 February 1628, but the continued strength of her family connections is shown by the list of the kin who came to bear witness: her mother, her brother the prior, and several noblemen with their wives. The bridegroom provided the sum of sixty *livres*. Her recently widowed mother, Jacqueline Michel, promised to feed and lodge the couple for two years, and to maintain the future bride as befitted "her quality."[34]

Marie Regnouard's spouse, Robert Giffard, was also from a Percheron family of high status. Both his father, Guillaume Giffard, and his mother, Louise Viron, counted nobility among their kin.[35] His time in Canada started in about 1620 or 1621, when he travelled there as a ship's surgeon. After a stay near the Beauport River for several years, he returned to France. In 1627, in front of the king's attorney general and the clerk of the Admiralty of France in Paris, he swore that he knew the country of New France well, that he had been there for an uninterrupted stay of five or six years, that the St Lawrence River could return 15,000 beaver, and that the vessel bringing supplies to the habitation of Québec required ordinarily a hundred men to sail it. In the spring of 1628, not long after his marriage to Regnouard, Giffard returned to Canada as ship surgeon for the Compagnie des Cent-Associés. His flotilla was captured by the British after a skirmish at Tadoussac, but Giffard's detention did not last long. By 13 November 1628 he was once again in France, and he attended the baptism of his daughter Marie on 28 December of that same year.[36]

Robert Giffard must have been determined to return to New France, for he successfully petitioned the Compagnie des Cent-Associés for a seigneurie in Canada. In 1634 he was granted, in perpetuity, land along the St Lawrence River that was one league in length by one and a half leagues deep. He contracted with a master mason and master carpenter that they and their families would clear and cultivate the lands in return for travel expenses and all their necessities for at least three years, plus he would have houses built for their families.[37] As described in chapter 2, Giffard increased the size of his holding, and he built a manor house, a watermill, a windmill, and a strong house that could also be a fortress in times of attack. He put land under the plough, and laid out the plans for the village of Fargy (named by reversing the order of syllables in the name "Giffard").[38] Giffard's migration to New France drew others to follow his migratory path. The region of Perche in France would not seem especially likely as a source for immigrants, either by location or economy. It was a landlocked, rural area of isolated farms in a hilly and forested landscape, with little urbanization. Yet it provided migrants not just to Canada, but also to England, Holland, and the Caribbean. One main reason for the region's abundant emigration was encouragement from leading residents. In the case of Canada, Robert Giffard was very encouraging. At least thirty-three Percherons came to Canada with Giffard in 1634, and by 1635 about a third of French migrants in Canada had their origins in Perche.[39]

When Marie Regnouard arrived at Québec in 1634, she was thirty-five years old and able to sign her own name. Having borne two children already, she was heavily pregnant with her third, and she gave birth in the Château Saint-Louis eight days after coming ashore.[40] The child's godparents were Guillemette Hébert, member of one of the most important land-holding families in the colony, and Samuel de Champlain, commander of New France.[41] The following year, Champlain put in his will that Marie Regnouard was to receive a tableau of the Virgin Mary that was in his room.[42] With such notable colonists already among her friends and supporters, Regnouard was clearly well connected to leading figures from the start of her residence in New France. By the time she was delivering her servant from demons decades later, Regnouard was over sixty years old and a figure of some importance in the colony. She appears to have met the criteria for the ideal exorcist as laid out in the *Rituale Romanum*, except obviously for gender and clerical status: she was a mature person who demonstrated good character, piety, wisdom, and prudence.[43] Furthermore, her position as wife of a seigneur was an important marker of high social status.

This status was part of the system of land tenure established by settlers in New France, often called "seigneurialism."[44] Regardless of how extensive the seigneurs' powers really were over the lands claimed by the French king, they brought with them from France a perception of themselves as in some ways separate from their neighbours. They were usually the biggest landowners in a French village, and not shy about exercising seigneurial rights such as presiding over a seigneurial court, collecting dues for a range of services, and forcing peasants to use their wine-press, oven, or mill.[45] To be sure, the material conditions of Marie Regnouard and Robert Giffard's life in New France were not characterized by ease and abundance: when she needed to line sleeves in 1645, Regnouard did the sewing herself and used black cloth from old soutanes given to her by the Jesuits.[46] But however much she needed to employ thrift in her household economy, Regnouard was nonetheless high up in the ancien régime hierarchy. Robert Giffard's title of seigneur cast seigneurial authority onto her as well as a prominent seigneuresse.[47]

Such a position came with responsibilities. Heads of households frequently cared for sick servants in seventeenth-century France.[48] Noblewomen were widely recognized as healers elsewhere in early modern Europe too,[49] and older women were often portrayed as intelligent observers of, sometimes practitioners in, medical care, even if physicians complained of their intrusiveness into what the physicians viewed as their own professional domain.[50]

The provision of healthcare was one area in which gender transcended class, for it was not just among the nobility that women were expected to provide it as a domestic responsibility. French agronomist Olivier de Serres explained at the start of the seventeenth century that although people sometimes needed to call upon medical doctors, these doctors might be far away and take a long time to reach the house. It was therefore sensible for people to know how to look after their own sicknesses as well as those of their children and their servants, and the father and mother of the family should understand how to help themselves and their families when illness or injury occurred. Women were better suited to this than men, de Serres said, because of their charitable nature, and so the mother of the family should open her mind to such things.[51] De Serres was recommending that the female head of a household be ready to provide healthcare to those living under her roof, which was in practice a normal function for the women of early modern Europe. Professionals could be called in for assistance, but female family and friends provided most of the care to the sick, the injured, and the incapacitated. Women in Europe and European colonies were therefore expected to learn the necessary skills for managing illness and administering remedies. In the home they performed diagnoses, prepared medicines, and provided physical and emotional comfort to those who needed it. An early modern European household was the site of a wide range of activities to cure illness and maintain health, a locus of care for the body, and so medical practice could be counted among a woman's domestic skills.[52]

The tradition of women providing health care in the home was carried across the Atlantic. In New France, a female head of a seigneurie was normally expected to care for all who lived under her authority.[53] Regnouard was assertive in this capacity. Her forceful response about Hallay belonging to her, not to the demon, shows her strong sense of responsibility for the well-being of her servant, and demonstrates her confidence that her role as caregiver was widely accepted. Much of this confidence probably came from her elite status as wife of a seigneur, but perhaps additional assurance came from her familial connections to the Hôtel-Dieu hospital.

Marie Regnouard's knowledge and skills as a medical practitioner were almost certainly enhanced by her association with two people in her immediate family who had formally recognized medical expertise.[54] Her husband Robert Giffard was a ship's surgeon when he first arrived in Canada.[55] Following the surrender of Québec to the English in 1629, he was listed as a master surgeon and as an apothecary.[56] Upon his return to New France, he was the surgeon at the Hôtel-Dieu in Québec, and between 1634 and 1668 he was sometimes also described as a physician and as an apothecary.[57] In these various positions, Giffard was a practitioner and not just a theoretician. For example, he assisted an Algonquin woman with a difficult birth, in which both mother and child survived, and he tended to a nun at the Hôtel-Dieu who was suffering from several illnesses.[58]

A second member of Regnouard's family with an officially recognized medical role in the colony was Françoise, the daughter born just after Regnouard's arrival at Québec. Françoise became a pensioner at the Hôtel-Dieu at the age of seven, and the first Canadian-born postulant five years later. As a nun of the choir, she took the name Françoise Marie de Saint-Ignace, then at the age of sixteen made her profession and went into perpetual claustration. As was shown in chapter 3, the nursing sisters at the Hôtel-Dieu were central to healthcare in the colony.

Yet the decision to enter the order had not been an easy one for Françoise. According to the *Chroniques* of the Hôtel-Dieu, she had been strongly tempted by the devil, who tried to persuade her that a life lived in the world would be holier than if she remained celibate. It was not until Françoise addressed herself to the Holy Sacrament and made her vow that she was calmed and could recognize her earlier hesitation to have been a satanic trick. Françoise was not able to continue her nursing work for very long. In 1656 she was struck with an illness that caused her great discomfort. The *Chroniques* report that her body was covered with a painful rash that broke open as if her skin had been flayed. Her wounds poured forth such corruption that her clothing needed to be changed four or five times each day, causing her still more pain. In the end, she was so thin that her bones pierced her skin, which on her back was so sore that she could no longer tolerate her bed. She spent eleven days in a chair without being able to sleep, and died on 15 March 1657.[59] Her life and death made a strong impression on the Hospitalière nun Catherine de Saint-Augustin, who reported several visions of Françoise. They started a few days after Françoise's death when Catherine went to the vault where the body had been buried "because of the particular affection that they had for each other." When Catherine returned to the choir to pray in front of the Holy Sacrament, Françoise offered to deliver Catherine from her temptations. Two months later, Françoise appeared to Catherine in her sleep. During part of their conversation Catherine asked whether Françoise's sister would be leaving purgatory, but Françoise – perhaps with post-mortem discretion – would not tell her. She did reassure Catherine that God had bounty for all who serve him, and that Catherine would know this herself one day.[60]

Marie Regnouard was not an "authorized healer" as were her husband and daughter, but even in the absence of occupational markers she was a healer nonetheless.[61] Her role as a woman in charge of a household and her family connections with medical personnel helped ensure it. French people of the seventeenth century did not consider elite and popular medicine as being in opposition or even entirely separate from one another. Those providing medical care, whether formally trained or not, the "medical core and penumbra" as two historians of medicine put it, shared much of the same medical discourse.[62] Regnouard had probably learned theories and practices from her medically trained family members, and she could put her learning to use in caring for her servant.

The category of bodywork as developed by Mary Fissell as a way to think about attending to the human body goes some way to explaining Regnouard's care for Hallay. Fissell argues that "using bodywork as a category enables us to start at the bedside of the sufferer, attending to the physical labor entailed in the cure of the sick." Regnouard's attendance at Hallay's bedside to alleviate Hallay's pains, a role emphasized in words such as "deliverance," "relief," and "healing" from her account, can be seen as part of this labour. Fissell does not say much about exorcism in particular except in the context of men doing the labour, giving the example of pastors who exorcised the demons that tortured physically as well as spiritually. For Fissell, this healing by men was a second-order effect of gender roles, with not the healing itself being gendered, but rather the social roles through which that healing was done.[63] Such an interpretation might help to explain why Regnouard's care for Hallay was described using the language of healing rather than that of exorcism. If she were to perform an exorcism in name, Regnouard would have been taking on a social role normally gendered masculine in early modern Europe, extending her activities into an area within the sphere of religion where both ecclesiastical and civic leaders were trying to push women further out of public life. Even if Regnouard could benefit from the delay in such patriarchal trends taking hold across the Atlantic and establish for herself some divergence from patriarchal limitations,[64] those keen to publicize the deliverance were trying to emphasize not Regnouard's skill, but rather the power of someone else.

Regnouard was tenacious in her efforts. She was the wife of a seigneur and a settler with many years of experience in the colony. She had borne children, run a household, and cared for her servants. But the demon was fierce. It was also vulnerable to spiritual power, and Regnouard sought help from a powerful intercessor.

THE MARTYR AS MEDIATOR

Not everyone in New France agreed on the scope and effects of demonic activity in the colony, but contemporary observers who wrote about the possession of Hallay did agree on this: it was help from Jean de Brébeuf, Jesuit priest and martyr, that brought about the departure of the demons. Ragueneau's *Vie* of Catherine de Saint-Augustin emphasized the importance of Brébeuf's relationship with the nun,[65] and Marie de l'Incarnation wrote that when Hallay was at the Hôtel-Dieu, the demons and the magicians finally took themselves away because of Brébeuf's intercession.[66] The accounts signed by Regnouard were careful to credit the success of her efforts to Brébeuf as well, noting that previous attempts with the relics of other saints had failed.[67] Even the demon possessing Hallay acted as a witness to the power of Brébeuf. In Regnouard's argument with the demon, when she demanded that he tell her whose relic she was using, the demon answered that "it's a relic of a saint who had been martyred among the Huron by the Iroquois." Charles de Lauson de Charny, the signatory of the second part of the account, provided an interpretation for the return of demons following Brébeuf's first intervention that actually managed to increase rather than diminish the claim being made for Brébeuf's importance after Hallay suffered a relapse into demonic troubles. The demons' return, he said, was reasonably to be attributed to the intention of God, to show the glory of his servant. Brébeuf had chased the demons away the first time, and only after more devotions were made to him did Hallay become and remain entirely delivered.[68]

Clearly, it was Jean de Brébeuf who was supposed to be the real hero of this tale. Two of the three copies of Regnouard's account have titles, and these make the point triumphantly: on the Jesuit archive copy it is "Account of the deliverance of a possessed person by the mediation of relics of the deceased Reverend Father Jean de Brébeuf of happy and holy memory," and on the Hôtel-Dieu copy it is "Account of the relief of a possessed person by the mediation of relics of the Revered Father Jean de Brébeuf of happy and holy memory."[69] Brébeuf had been important to the colony during his life, and his memory as a charismatic champion of Catholic Christianity would continue to sustain the colony after his death. Supporters of Brébeuf's cult knew that if they were going to have him officially recognized also as a saint, they would need vivid and persuasive stories of his post-mortem assistance.

Jean de Brébeuf was born in Normandy in 1593. He joined the novitiate of the Society of Jesus in 1617, studied and taught at the Jesuit college in Rouen, and became a priest in 1622. He first arrived in New France in 1625, but had to leave when the colony came under English occupation in 1629. Once he returned in 1633, Brébeuf remained in New France for the rest of his life. He spent most of his time among the Wendat, in what the French thought of as the Huronia mission, where he was known as Echon or Hechon.[70] In comparison with other Jesuits in New France, Brébeuf was inclined to ascribe positive value to Indigenous cultures, and he got along quite easily with others. He was noted for his skill in learning languages quickly, and also for his physical strength and endurance. As superior of the mission to the Wendat, Brébeuf encouraged Jesuits to live as much as possible according to Indigenous customs, and he required that missionaries take care not to offend or annoy their hosts. In his instructions to priests, Brébeuf urged the missionaries to have a sincere affection for the people among whom they lived, and he ordered that they endure unpleasant things without saying anything or even appearing to notice them. The missionaries were to conduct themselves in such a way that they would not be troublesome to anyone. Brébeuf's missionary work did not meet with the approval of all the Wendat, and there were several times during outbreaks of epidemic disease when hostility to the Jesuit presence grew to the point of almost dissolving the mission. But over time Brébeuf proved to be one of the more effective missionaries in learning languages and customs, and in encouraging Indigenous people to accept baptism and maintain alliances with the French. His ties to the Wendat served French colonial interests by providing trading partners with access to the vast interior of the continent, powerful allies, and, most importantly from the missionaries' perspective, many souls to convert.[71]

The Jesuits' work in what seemed like such a promising mission field was interrupted by the death of key Wendat leaders, the development of opposing factions for and against the French, and escalating warfare between the Wendat and their traditional enemies the Haudenosaunee.[72] On 16 March 1649, Brébeuf and fellow Jesuit Gabriel Lalemant were captured by Haudenosaunee warriors as they were visiting a nearby settlement, and taken to the Wendat village of Saint-Ignace/Taenhatentaron. Their final hours were reported by Christian Wendat who had escaped. Much of what the Jesuits endured were traditional torture ceremonies in an Indigenous context where the captives were political enemies, but to French readers the torments seemed like those of martyrs. Brébeuf was beaten with cudgels, stripped, and tied to a post. His fingernails were torn out and his scalp was ripped off. He had boiling water poured upon him in mockery of Christian baptism. He was burnt by red-hot hatchets and roasted by a belt of bark covered in resin and set on fire. Pieces of his flesh were cut off from his body, roasted, and eaten before his eyes. Witnesses reported that Brébeuf endured it all like a rock, insensible to the fire and flames, preaching continually to those who tortured him until they cut off his nose, tongue, and lips. His courage impressed even his tormentors, who were reported to have eaten of Brébeuf's flesh and to have drunk his blood in order to become courageous like he was. After the Iroquois departed, Jesuits in a nearby village went to St Ignace and brought back the remains of Brébeuf and Lalemant. They buried the bodies and left them in the ground until it was time to leave Huronia. Then they dug the remains back up, boiled them in lye, scraped the bones, and dried them in a small clay oven. When the bones were ready, the Jesuits wrapped them in silk, placed them in chests, and carried them to Québec.[73]

News of the destruction of the Wendat villages and the Jesuits' deaths did not reach Québec until the night of 20 July.[74] As information of Brébeuf's end spread among the French in North America and Europe, the story of his life and death was made to fit into the established hagiographic pattern of Christian martyrs.[75] His fellow Jesuit Charles Garnier explained that Brébeuf was declared a martyr both because he chose death to save souls, staying behind in a village under attack rather than abandoning it, and also because his enemies made him suffer all sorts of cruelties out of their hatred for Christianity.[76] Early modern European Catholics believed that the sacrifice of martyrs, even if not yet declared saints by the church, made them saints in heaven,[77] and Brébeuf's physical remains were soon prized as powerful relics especially beneficial for Catholicism in Canada.[78] Marie de l'Incarnation described Brébeuf as "a holy man who spilled his blood for the sustenance of faith in this country."[79] Catherine de Saint-Augustin used his relics as a tool of conversion, feeding a dying Protestant sailor some water into which a bone had either been dipped (according to Ragueneau's *Vie*), or added in the form of ground up powder (according to Le Mercier in his *Relation*). The relic-infused drink led the sailor both to the recovery of health and conversion to Catholicism.[80] In 1674, Thierry Beschefer wrote that he and other Jesuits helped end the "phrénésie" of a fellow Jesuit, François Boniface, with the help of Brébeuf. They had tried opium to calm the frenetic priest, but it was a series of prayers to Brébeuf and the touching of the head with Brébeuf's bone that finally brought Boniface back to his senses.[81]

Jesuits in New France, seeking more support from France, harnessed the martyrdom of Brébeuf to their cause. They used it to make the case that Canada was a land well suited to mystical spirituality, asceticism, and spiritual transformation. Stories of the miracles obtained through prayer to Brébeuf had the potential to transform the seeming failures of missionary endeavours, even the violent death of one of the most beloved missionaries, into proof of the Jesuits' evangelical commitment to Canada and of divine support for New France.[82] The most prominent champion of Brébeuf was Paul Ragueneau, once Brébeuf's superior, later a caretaker for the martyr's relics and reputation. It was he who ordered that the remains of Brébeuf be disinterred and boiled in lye so that they could be recovered and brought into Québec, and he who most compellingly imbued Brébeuf's death and the larger story of the end of the Huronia mission with meaning through messages of courage and hope.[83] It was also Ragueneau who gave relics of Brébeuf to Catherine de Saint-Augustin and Marie Regnouard. As Catherine's confessor, he gathered her writings to be sources for a hagiographic biography. Raguenaeu's connection with Regnouard is less clearly documented, but her family maintained a good relationship with the Jesuits. Ragueneau spent Christmas 1659 at Beauport, and the following month four Jesuits dined at Beauport with Giffard.[84] They also exchanged Epiphany and New Year's gifts over the years. Exactly what the Jesuits gave is not recorded, but Giffard's gifts included spiced wine and capons.[85] The rib bone of Brébeuf that Regnouard used in her deliverance of Hallay might be thought of as part of the gift-giving tradition between her family and the Jesuits. Regnouard's account reports that the bone was not delivered just to help Hallay, but that Ragueneau had shown charity to Regnouard by giving the bone to her when he returned from his Wendat mission.[86] Ragueneau had given the precious bone to Regnouard, and then ensured that its power would be recorded for posterity. In Regnouard's own account of her actions, this bone was the true instrument of "deliverance," "relief," and "healing."

Centuries later, stories about the powers of Brébeuf's relics were still being told. Brébeuf was canonized in 1930, and declared one of the patron saints of Canada in 1940. Among the files kept in the Vatican Apostolic Archive are those of the Congregazione dei Riti, the office charged with the process of beatification and canonization. Within are items from the early twentieth century attesting to the miracles of Jean de Brébeuf, including several about the demonic torments of Hallay. These accounts shrink the time and space of the efforts by Catherine de Saint-Augustin and Marie Regnouard in order to create more room for emphasizing the role of Brébeuf as heavenly mediator. The Hospitalière nun Marie Sara de Saint-André said that Brébeuf had helped Catherine de Saint-Augustin against magicians and witches, especially for a young girl possessed by a demon given into her care by Monseigneur de Laval after trying vainly to exorcise her himself. This girl received much care at the Hôtel-Dieu, but, after returning to Beauport, the diabolical operations started again. In another account, Pierre-Auguste Fournet, priest, said that a possessed woman had suddenly been delivered by a touch of Brébeuf's bones. Arthur Melançon, a Jesuit, said that he knew from an original copy preserved at the Collège Sainte-Marie that a woman possessed by a demon for two years was instantly delivered when touching one of the bones of Brébeuf. Edouard Désy, another Jesuit priest, produced documents in support of the case, including the "Récit du soulagement d'une possédée par l'entremise des Reliques du R. P. Jean de Brébeuf, d'heureuse et saincte mémoire" – that is, the account by Regnouard. Henri Arthur Scott, priest, who had seen two copies autographed by Marie Regnouard, said that a rib bone of Brébeuf had been given to Madame Giffard, wife of the seigneur of Beauport. He added that it was not known what had become of it.[87] Its location remains unknown today.

The bones of Brébeuf had migrated in a living body from France to New France, and then were carried as a relic from the contact zone of Wendake/Huronia to Québec. A piece was transported to Beauport and given to Marie Regnouard. She, in her role of caring for her servant, used it in a ritual that succeeded where earlier attempts by priests and nuns had failed. Barbe Hallay was delivered, and her life continued. As the next chapter will show, Hallay's life ran along a course back to the Hôtel-Dieu, then into a house in Québec, and finally across the river to a farm where she contributed to the increasing strength of the colony. Her long and painful torments by demons were left behind.

5

To the Other Shore

As of March 1663, Barbe Hallay was "entirely delivered" from demons.[1] This deliverance may have marked the end of her possession, but it does not conclude her story. Hallay lived for another thirty-three years in New France, and the course of her life after the deliverance from demons is almost textbook typical: if one were to put together a composite figure of a female French settler in later seventeenth-century Canada, that person could closely resemble Barbe Hallay. In this sense, the rest of her life was unremarkable. Considering all the attention that her earlier demonic troubles had received, one might even say that the rest of Barbe Hallay's life was remarkably unremarkable.

The steps of Hallay's post-deliverance time in New France take us through such quotidian matters as earning a wage, getting married, setting up a farm, having children, and facing death. The strange events described in earlier chapters left few traces in her subsequent years, and no witch hunt or mass possession followed in the wake of this case of bewitchment and demonic infestation. An analysis of later seventeenth-century Canadian society starts to explain why so little concern was expressed about entanglements with diabolical arts. One significant development is that the colonists of New France became less anxious about threats from within and without. Some aspects of the colony turned out very differently from what the early planners had intended, and their religious goals in particular were mostly unmet, but the colony nonetheless grew and prospered. Another development that helps explain Hallay's unremarkable later life is a change in beliefs about demons. Doubt was becoming more prominent in European intellectuals' discussions of demonology. Many people continued to believe in witches, and some still believed that these witches were working with diabolical forces, but learned opinion was moving towards finding non-magical explanations for strange events. So when situations arose that could look like witchcraft or demonic possession according to the standards applied to the case of Barbe Hallay, slightly later observers instead chose to interpret the signs differently.

A SERVANT IN QUÉBEC

At some point after the spring of 1663, Barbe Hallay moved out of Beauport and back into the town of Québec. On 27 December 1665, at a ceremony of baptism at the parish church of Notre-Dame, she became godmother to her niece, Marie Barbe Girard, daughter of Barbe's sister Marie.[2]

This sister had recently experienced a supernatural encounter of her own, as was reported in the Jesuit *Relation* for 1665. Marie, "a very virtuous woman," was struggling with her parental duties. She had three children, the eldest of whom was only four years old. Living far from the parish church, she found it difficult to do her devotions. She still managed to go to the Chapel of Saint-Jean, although she worried about leaving her children unattended. One day, Marie left the children asleep in the house while she went to the chapel. She was surprised upon her return to find them neatly dressed on their beds, and eating breakfast in the usual manner. She asked her eldest daughter who had dressed them, and the child could not say except that it was a lady clothed in white. The child added that this lady had just left, and so her mother ought to have met her upon entering. Several people believed that this apparition was the Virgin Mary. According to the Jesuits, the Virgin's appearance meant that she chose to calm Marie's worry and let her know that, after having taken the ordinary precautions for the children, she could leave the rest to the protection of the Holy Family.[3] It was just a few months after this reported vision that Marie chose Barbe as godmother to her fourth child. For someone whose reputation for goodness led to her vision of the Virgin Mary being included in the Jesuits' annual reports, such a decision would surely have been unthinkable if Barbe Hallay were considered spiritually suspect.

Barbe Hallay's employment also shows no sign that people were concerned about her past. By 1666, as the census of that year records, she was working in the town of Québec as a domestic servant. The household in which she was employed was that of Jean Maheu and Marguerite Corriveau.[4] Normally in the census, the head of the household is listed at the top of the entry, and the other members are listed beneath, along with information on their relationship to the head of the household or their occupation.[5] In this entry, Jean Maheu, age twenty-three, is listed first, followed by Marguerite Corriveau, age forty, next to whose name is written "sa fem. vevfe de René Maheut," meaning "his wife [i.e., wife of Jean Maheu] and widow of René Maheut." Also in the household were Jean Paul Maheu, age seventeen, and Louis Maheu, age fifteen, the children of the deceased "Maheu"; an indentured servant, Jacques Jore, age twenty-one; and "Barbe Halle," a servant, age twenty. Certain features of this household seem surprising. The first is that the husband Jean shared the same last name as his wife's deceased husband René and their children. The second is that the husband was much younger than his wife.

The shared last name between René and Jean was likely coincidence rather than indicative of a family relationship.[6] The two men had different parents and were from different places.[7] The entry for the marriage of Jean Maheu and Marguerite Corriveau in the parish registry adds further evidence that the new bridegroom was not related to the previous husband. It states that there was no lawful impediment to the union, which there would have been had the deceased spouse been a close relation of the next one.[8] The second surprising feature, the age difference between spouses, was indeed uncommon. For a first marriage in New France at around this time, the husband was on average about twelve to thirteen years older than the wife.[9] In the case of this couple, the age difference was reversed and even larger: when they wed in 1663, she was about thirty-seven and he was about twenty. It is worth noting that this was not a first marriage for Corriveau, and the composition of her household points to the strong position of widows in New France. Widowed female settlers under the age of fifty frequently remarried, often soon after the death of their first husband, and often to younger men who had never been married before.[10] Marguerite Corriveau had been married twice previously. By the time she reached her late thirties, her economic position, with several landholdings in and around Québec, offered financial stability to a prospective third husband.[11] She was also active in protecting her own interests and those of her children. In January 1664, she appeared before the Sovereign Council as part of a dispute with the surgeon Annet Goumin. Goumin was asking her to pay

476 *livres* for having bandaged and medicated her, but Corriveau argued that the bandages and medicines could not have amounted to such a considerable sum given that the records he had provided earlier came to less than a hundred *livres*. In March of that same year, she appeared again to report an error in an account rendered to Jean Guyon sieur du Bisson as guardian of the children. A month later, she decided to replace Guyon with another in the role of guardian. Corriveau seems to have been involved in some slightly sketchy commercial dealings as well. In April 1665, she was accused of selling wine above the set price, insisting that people pay twenty-four *sols* for a pot, rather than the regulation twenty *sols*.[12]

Barbe Hallay's labour in this household was not in any way unusual. A quarter or even more of the settler workforce in New France worked as servants at this time.[13] With her earlier experiences of demonic torment, however, including while she was working as a servant at Beauport, Hallay's employment history was not exactly smooth. The fact that the independent and resolute Corriveau employed Hallay to work in her household suggests that Hallay's presence was not considered in any way detrimental to the family.

Barbe Hallay's innocuous reputation is suggested even more strongly by her next place of employment. In the 1667 census, she is listed as a "pensionnaire" of the Hospitalières at the Hôtel-Dieu.[14] This designation implies that Hallay was a boarder at the hospital, paying money in return for her room and food. A slightly later document indicates that she took on paid work at the Hôtel-Dieu. Among the "active debts" of the hospital in 1671, the amount of 100 *livres* was owing "to Barbe Halay for the remainder of her wages."[15] Chapter 3 discussed Hallay's experiences as a patient in the Hôtel-Dieu; here she was, back at the same institution, but as a paying guest and then as a paid employee.[16] Overall, this was a good place to live and work. The Hôtel-Dieu's financial receipts provide a sense of material conditions there. The most common grain in the diet was wheat, probably consumed mostly in the form of white bread. They also had meats of beef, veal, suckling pigs, sheep, moose, and other game; fowl including chicken and turkey; fish including cod, eel, shad, and salmon; and eggs. Among their fruits and vegetables were plums and grapes, cabbage, beans, and peas. Their fats were mostly lard, butter, and olive oil. Their other foodstuffs included vinegar and salt (both for seasoning and for preservation); jam; sugar without stated purpose and sugars specifically for making jam and syrup; and spices. For beverages they had wine (sometimes specified as being from Bordeaux), eau-de-vie (distilled spirits probably for medicinal use by the apothecary and possibly as a beverage for the servants), and milk (not often drunk by healthy adults, but thought to be particularly well suited to the sick). Among the other necessities and comforts were drugs, wood, coal, candles, stoves, pewter tableware, hay and straw, linens, sheets, towels, and soap.[17] By the standards of seventeenth-century Québec, or indeed anywhere else, the conditions at the Hôtel-Dieu were quite comfortable. This is not to say that Barbe Hallay did not work hard during her employment there. Some kind of illness spread through the town in the spring of 1668, and the hospital probably took in some of the sick. It started with a rash like that from measles, then led to fevers, sore throats, coughs, and other symptoms. Marie de l'Incarnation reported that many were near death.[18] If Hallay fell ill, she recovered.

It is not known precisely when Hallay concluded her employment at the Hôtel-Dieu, but, before her final wages were handed over in 1671, she had made an important decision.

MARRIAGE

On the afternoon of 27 July 1670, Barbe Hallay signed a contract to marry Jean Carrier.[19] Carrier, an immigrant from the parish of Saint-Georges in Xaintes, France, was living in the seigneurie of Lauzon, the area across the St Lawrence River from Québec.[20]

Their courtship is not recorded. Perhaps they met at the Hôtel-Dieu. In 1666, according to the census of that year, Carrier was a thirty-year-old domestic worker at the hospital, and it is possible that their appointments at the institution overlapped.[21] Or perhaps they met in Lauzon, where several members of Hallay's family were living by the time of the engagement.[22]

An important part of a marriage contract was its recording of the couple's consent to wed. As stated in this contract, Hallay and Carrier recognized that they had made promises to take one another as a true and lawful spouse, and to solemnize the marriage in front of the church. Another important part of a contract was the recording of what each partner brought to the union. A French proverb of the time said that "love causes rage, but money makes the marriage."[23] For this marriage, the monetary transfer was carefully spelled out. The bride was to receive a payment of 200 *livres*, and the groom recognized that she brought with her 500 *livres* in money and goods, of which

200 *livres* would go into their goods held in common and 300 *livres* would remain proper to her. The contract was signed in the house of Barbe's father, in the presence of named witnesses. Such a location was quite typical, and the number of invited guests was about average.[24] Also noted in this contract was that Barbe Hallay, her parents, and Jean Carrier said that they did not know how to write or sign. Jean-Baptiste's signature, the "marque" of Hallay, is a small cross with dots in the top right and bottom left corners.[25]

The wedding itself occurred a little over three months after the signing of the contract, with the ceremony taking place on 4 November 1670 in the parish church of Notre-Dame in Québec. The banns had been published three times, and no lawful impediments were made known.[26] This husband was in many ways different from Daniel Vuil, the candidate for marriage that Barbe Hallay had refused more than a decade earlier.[27] Most significantly, Jean Carrier was established in the colony, and he was Catholic. He acted as a witness in January 1661, indicating that he had been in Canada since at least the autumn of 1660. He was confirmed at Québec on 1 May 1662. On 5 June 1666 he received land measuring three arpents fronting the river by forty arpents in the seigneurie of Lauzon near the Pointe de Lévy. He was among the inhabitants of Lauzon who on 1 August 1667 appealed a decision from the lieutenant-general that had required them to make a path for public convenience on the gravel bank close to the tide line. Carrier and the other inhabitants argued that there was great difficulty in the task. They lost the appeal – each would have to maintain and enclose their own portion – but they did not have to pay a fine.[28]

In terms of the expectations for an early modern French marriage, the union of Hallay and Carrier was a success. It produced children, ran a farm, and lasted until the death of one of the spouses.[29]

AN *HABITANT* FAMILY

Most married couples in early modern Europe and its colonies desired children, and many married couples in French settlements along the St Lawrence had a lot of them.[30] Intendent de Meulles reported in 1684 that on Canadian farms "couples frequently have ten to twelve children and even fifteen, sixteen, or seventeen."[31] Barbe Hallay and Jean Carrier did not live up to this demographic boast, nor quite reach the average number of 7.1 offspring.[32] A main reason was probably age. When they married, Hallay was approximately twenty-five years

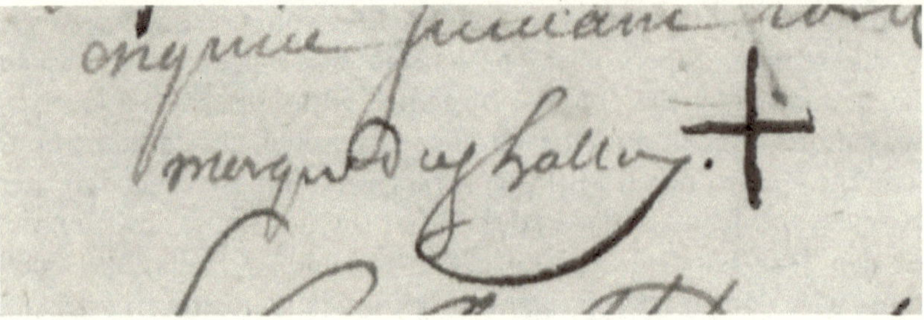

5.1 The "marque" of Jean-Baptiste Hallay on Barbe's marriage contract

old, leaving several years of potential child-bearing behind her. But they were a fertile couple. About a month after the wedding, Hallay was pregnant, and Ignace Philippe was born on 5 September 1671. Other pregnancies followed. Marie Anne was born on 16 January 1674, Charles on 23 December 1678, and Jean on 10 December 1682. These children all lived beyond childhood and left descendants.[33] After the first birth, the children were born in December or January, placing their conceptions around March or April. This pattern was typical for New France, where, as in many other preindustrial societies, conceptions were most frequent in spring and early summer.[34] The intervals between births were fairly typical as well, although a bit longer than most.[35]

The Hallay-Carrier family developed a successful habitation.[36] Their work here would not have been easy, and certainly not at first. Building a shelter, clearing the land, and planting crops were difficult labours.[37] As Marie de l'Incarnation explained in a letter to her son, wheat, vegetables, and all sorts of grains grew abundantly in the excellent soil, but "when a family begins a habitation, it takes two or three years before they have enough to feed themselves, not to mention clothing, furniture, and the endless little things necessary for the maintenance of a house." She went on to describe how, with time and guidance, the family would move beyond these difficulties to live comfortably. At first the habitants lived off their grains, their vegetables, and the winter hunt. For clothing and household utensils, they sold roofing planks and timber. Then, having obtained what is essential, they began to trade, and so advanced little by little.[38]

Barbe Hallay's family followed this trajectory. In the 1681 census, the household is listed as consisting of Carrier, Hallay, their children, and Barbe Girard, age sixteen, who was the niece and goddaughter of

Hallay. Perhaps, given the young ages of Hallay's children, Girard was there to help with agricultural work or childcare. The family had one gun, five cattle, and fifteen arpents of land.[39] The census does not say anything about their fields or crops, but they were probably growing wheat if they could (since this was the preferred grain among French settlers), perhaps some oats, and legumes. They would have rotated their crops on a biennial basis, or, if their land was especially good, they could have divided it into three sections for rotation. The habitation might have included some natural meadow as well, which could produce good grasses for fodder. In addition to the cattle listed on the census, the farm might also have had poultry and pigs, but the livestock probably did not provide sufficient manure for all the fields. Many habitants reserved this fertilizer for use in a garden and vegetable patch where they grew cabbage, carrots, and turnips, by the end of the century also onions, shallots, garlic, cucumber, and chervil.[40]

Barbe Hallay's family continued to prosper. In 1690, a new priest arrived at the parish at Lauzon and had benches installed in the church of Saint-Joseph. Parishioners who wished to reserve a place in these benches could make a donation. This donation went to the "fabrique," which was the elected parish council that held title to church properties, maintained the cemetery, kept the building heated and in good repair, and assumed financial responsibility for providing candles, wine, and wafers. Barbe Hallay and Jean Carrier had a bench on the right side of the altar, for which they paid around four *livres* and twenty *sols* per year.[41]

Hallay remained connected to this church until and beyond her death. On 18 June 1696, she was buried in its cemetery.[42] If her burial was like that of most other colonists, her body was wrapped in a shroud and placed in a coffin, and then laid in a common or an individual grave without any marker bearing the name of the interred.[43] Hallay was about fifty years old when she died, which was somewhat early as an age at death for a person who had reached adulthood.[44] The entry in the burial register does not provide information about the cause of death, but it was unlikely that Barbe had evaded all the pains of aging. In contradiction to Simon Denys's claim that in New France arthritis, fever, and catarrh were unknown,[45] studies of skeletal remains show that many who survived childhood did suffer from illness and discomfort. They had to endure cavities and tooth abscesses, and arthritis was common for people by their forties.[46]

Many people in Barbe Hallay's life had predeceased her. Her father, Jean-Baptiste Hallay, was buried on 19 March 1672 in the cemetery of Côte de Lauzon. His body had been found in the woods the previous day.[47] Her mother, Mathurine Vallet, died on 14 March 1686 at the age of seventy-seven, and was buried in the same cemetery as her husband.[48] Robert Giffard died on 14 April 1668 and was buried two days later at the foot of the cross of the church in Beauport.[49] Marie Regnouard survived her husband. Her date of death is not known, but she was still alive in September 1673 when she made a concession of land.[50] Jean Carrier outlived his wife for some time, and was still alive in 1715 during the signing of a contract between two of his sons.[51]

CHANGES IN THE COLONY

If Barbe Hallay paused near the end of her life to look back on her time in New France, she could have noted many changes since 1659. The colonists certainly continued to face challenges, some of them severe. A fever came with new arrivals in 1687, attacks by the Iroquois grew more frequent in the countryside to the west between 1688 and 1694, and several poor harvests in the early 1690s threatened famine.[52] In spite of these challenges, the colony's leaders had grown more confident about the economic potential of New France and the likelihood of the colony's long-term survival. The settler population continued to increase, and the colony became more secure.

Much of the colony's growth and security was due to the French crown taking a more direct interest in its affairs. It was an interest that had been fervently encouraged by some of the colonists. The Jesuit Paul Le Jeune wrote a plea at the start of the *Relation* for 1660–61 that drew upon rather heavy tropes and emotions to arouse King Louis XIV's sense of paternalistic obligation to his religion and his kingdom. It begins with a presentation of New France at His Majesty's feet. Le Jeune asks the king to hear New France's languid voice and last words: "Save me," she cries, "I am going to lose the Catholic religion; the Fleurs-de-Lys are going to be taken from me by force." New France speaks with "sighs and sobs," saying that she will no longer be French, that she will fall into the hands of foreigners when the Iroquois will have taken the rest of her nearly spent blood. She will soon be consumed in their fire, and the demon will take away many nations awaiting the king's piety, power, and generosity. Le Jeune appeals to the king's sense of responsibility, and perhaps His Majesty's vanity, by saying that perfidious enemies are going to rob the king's crown of one of its finest jewels and that many peoples will be lost if they are not rescued. Le Jeune also appeals to the king's sense of his own grandeur, flattering him that if he considers the French name, he knows that he is a great king, and that if he considers the good of his state, his mind will recognize how much the loss of such a large country will damage his kingdom. Le Jeune concludes with something part way between an ancestral guilt trip and a hagiographic promise by comparing what Louis XIV had not yet done with what Louis IX, crusading king and saint, had accomplished centuries earlier. Only the king, wrote Le Jeune, by saving the lives and goods of his French colony, and the souls of a very large number of nations, will oblige them all to pray to God that he will give the king the name of saint, just as he did to the king's great ancestor.[53]

A few years after penning this dramatic entreaty (although almost certainly not as a result of his plea), the Jesuit got his wish for more support. In 1663, Louis XIV and his minister Jean-Baptiste Colbert turned New France into a royal colony. They quickly dissolved the Compagnie des Cent-Associés and established the Sovereign Council to be a court of justice at Québec.[54] They also made large financial investments in New France. Over the next decade or so, the French state spent more than a million *livres* on establishing industries and developing commerce in Canada.[55] The first intendant, Jean Talon, arrived in 1665. The memo from the king containing Talon's instructions listed several things that were still daunting from the crown's perspective. The Iroquois remained a menacing presence, the habitants established their habitations wherever it pleased them rather than in close proximity to one another where mutual aid would be easier, and more artisans were required for the manufacturing of goods needed in daily life. Nonetheless, the king's memo expressed hope that, in time, there would be considerable growth in New France.[56] Intendant Talon's memo of 1667 expressed a similar optimism about New France's demographic and economic potential. The French settlers were producing many children, the women bearing a child nearly every year. (The Natives were less frequent in childbearing, although Talon thought that this obstacle could be surmounted by regulation – exactly of what kind, he did not say.) Canada was capable of all the same productions as France, Talon thought. In his mind, the colony could benefit from its place in a wider empire, since its products such as flour, legumes, fish, wood, oil, and other things not yet discovered could aid in the subsistence of the French Antilles. Canada could also help France's imperial ambitions by bringing war against English, Dutch, and Swedish colonies.[57]

As the crown tied itself more closely to the colony, immigrants continued to arrive on the ships. In October 1668, Marie de l'Incarnation wrote that the vessels landing at Québec carried French passengers in addition to Portuguese men, German men, Dutch men, and men from which nations she did not know, as well as Portuguese women, French women, and women from other countries. Marie reported that the first to wed was a Moorish woman who married a French man.[58] This woman was probably Espérance du Rosaire, who married Simon Longueville on 9 October 1668, although the Canadian records are ambiguous and possibly confused about her origins, whether Indigenous to the Americas, African, or both. She is described in her marriage contract as a Native from Brazil, in the registry of her marriage as a Moor who had been baptized in Lisbon.[59]

Even more than immigration, natural increase contributed to settler population growth. The crown was aware of the ongoing difficulties in attracting female immigrants and decided to invest in sending marriageable women to New France by assisting with recruitment and paying for transportation. The crown provided dowries too, sometimes in cash, but more often in household goods. Financial support from the royal treasury is what led to the label of "daughters of the king" for this group of immigrants. The *filles du roi* were young overall, but not overwhelmingly so. They ranged from adolescents to mature women, with an average age of twenty-four. Many came from poor or at least humble families, although some (about 12 to 15 per cent) were from the bourgeoisie and lesser nobility. More than half had lost their fathers, and about a fifth were widows. Over 800 young women came as filles du roi from 1663–73, contributing in just one decade almost half the total number of women immigrants during the entire period from the first years of French settlement to the British conquest a century and a half later. With so many more eligible men than women looking for marriage partners in the early filles du roi years, these new arrivals could make considered if quick choices, and four out of five married within six months of landing in New France. They remained in robust good health, likely due both to the salubrious Canadian environment and to selection, since recruiters were instructed to pick strong women and shipboard deaths would have claimed some of the less hardy. Those who reached the age of forty could expect to live, on average, until about seventy. Deaths in childbirth, at eight per thousand, were considerably lower than the ten to twenty per thousand in France. Colbert explained to Frontenac, just after listing the king's expense to send sixty filles du roi to the colony, that nothing was more important or more necessary for the satisfaction of the king than to work for the growth of the colony by marriages. With perhaps some exaggeration for the sake of optimism, Intendant Talon reported between 600 and 700 births in just the one year of 1671. Whatever the real number of babies born, the settler population of Canada was certainly growing. It had numbered only about a hundred in 1627 and roughly 3,000 in 1663, then tripled between 1663 and 1673, expanding to 10,000 in the 1680s. This growth shifted the demographic balance between the sexes. In the 1681 census, there were about twice as many men as women in the category of people aged thirty and higher, but for those under thirty, there was a rough balance.[60]

The crown also sent military reinforcements. In 1665, about 1,200 men of the Carignan-Salières regiment arrived with their equipment and provisions. They had been sent to defend the colony against one of its most powerful enemies, the Haudenosaunee. In the words of instruction from the king to Talon, the nations of the Iroquois were all "perpetual and irreconcilable enemies of the colony." In response to the Iroquois' hindering of the colony's growth by the "massacre of many Frenchmen" and "the inhumanities that they exercise against those who fall into their power," the crown planned a genocidal response, resolved "to bring war to them right to their homes to exterminate them entirely."[61]

This they certainly did not accomplish. Nor did the Carignan-Salières regiment achieve all its other aims. Without adequate intelligence about the realities of warfare in colonial North America, the troops were improperly equipped and insufficiently trained. After building and repairing forts, their first expedition into Mohawk country in January 1666 was a disaster for the French, with most of the soldiers dying from hypothermia and starvation. During their second campaign, in September of that same year, the soldiers burned several villages and destroyed crops, but the Mohawks prevented the French from killing or capturing many people by adopting a strategy of deserting their villages before the arrival of the troops. In 1667, the Mohawks and Oneidas made peace with the French, as had several other Iroquois nations two years previously. Much of the Carignan-Salières regiment returned to France, although the men were encouraged to settle. About

450 did so. Some stayed in the St Lawrence Valley, and others travelled away from the main French settlements.[62]

The division between those who preferred to stay in the Laurentian settlements and those who moved further into the interior of the continent reflected a wider tension that existed between colonial officials in North America and ministers of the crown in France about exactly how the colony should grow. The intendant Jean Talon envisioned extending New France continentally, and advocated for a state that would stretch from the St Lawrence to Mexico. The authorities back in France, by contrast, preferred to focus their efforts on building the colonial population within the St Lawrence Valley. One of the reasons behind this preference for a "compact colony" was likely Colbert's desire for New France to remain economically dependent on France and fully within the mercantile system without depopulating the kingdom. The other preference, that for an "extensive colony," was predicated on extending French sovereignty westward and southward. The extensive model mostly won out in the end, but it was an extension that required little actual French settlement except for places with strategic commercial, missionary, or military importance. Linked through missions and trading posts, French influence stretched west to the "Pays d'en Haut" of the Great Lakes, north towards Hudson's Bay, and south down the Mississippi. This was not, however, the same kind of settler colonialism as was being undertaken in the St Lawrence Valley. The French push into the interior of the North American continent was based not on settling French colonists so much as on France claiming possession of territory and making alliances with Indigenous peoples who lived there.[63]

Whether New France was to remain densely concentrated in the St Lawrence Valley or spread into the interior of the continent, the people directing the colony's affairs from France recognized that it would need more people in order to grow. The crown's support for migrants, especially the filles du roi, certainly helped with this plan, but Colbert's concern about the negative effects of depopulation on France also led him to advocate for growing the population of New France through miscegenation between a small group of French settlers and the Indigenous population on the territory claimed by France. This was an assimilationist approach of "francisation" that the French hoped would turn Indigenous people into French people. As Colbert put it in 1666 when describing how to increase the colony, "instead of waiting to benefit from the new settlers who could be sent from

France, nothing would contribute more than to try to civilize the Algonquins, the Hurons, and the other Natives who have embraced Christianity, and to persuade them to come establish a community with the French to live with them, and raise their children in our manners and customs."[64] As earlier chapters have shown, efforts at francisation largely failed. Indigenous people did adopt some aspects of French culture, but they carefully picked and chose which and how. They might accept alliances but not give up their independence, and find uses for European objects but keep them in an Indigenous context. When it came to forming marriages, Indigenous women did not marry French settlers in large numbers, and when such marriages did occur it was usually not in French settlements but in Indigenous communities where the French men accepted Indigenous terms and customs.[65]

Rather than admit the failure of francisation outright, most leaders of the colony changed their goals for the program. They moved away from an earlier conceptualization of francisation as largely conversion to Catholicism and acceptance of military alliance with the French, and by the late 1660s were demanding a more complete assimilation of Indigenous people into colonial society. French and colonial officials started to insist on compulsion and exclusion: people should be required to take on French customs, abandon Indigenous ways, and become entirely subsumed into the colonial population. The most committed supporters of the plan were convinced that Indigenous people would agree, or should be made to agree, to cease being Indigenous and instead become French. In 1673, Governor Frontenac wrote to Colbert that he was scandalized to find Indians only two leagues from Québec who knew as little French as if they had never seen French people, whereas the English in New England provided a good example by forcing the Indians to learn their language and even their trades.[66] At around the same time, families and religious institutions were still being encouraged to raise Indigenous children "à la française."[67] But by the end of the century, instead of presuming that Indigenous inhabitants of New France could be made into French subjects, elites in France were questioning whether the "sauvages" of North America could ever become French at all. They were starting to think that differences between French and Indigenous peoples were not cultural but biological, and assuming more and more that Indigenous people were inherently inferior to the French.[68]

Not all the colonists were thinking the same way. Some of the missionaries, notably the Ursulines at Québec, knew that the new form of francisation being pushed from above would not succeed.[69] More broadly, missionaries were coming to realize that their earlier ideal of creating a New France to exceed the Old was proving unattainable. One of the largest religious projects in seventeenth-century New France was that of the Société de Notre-Dame founding the town of Ville-Marie, known also as Montréal. As Louise Dechêne has described it, "its avowed purpose was to create an alternate, autonomous settlement, fundamentally religious in nature." This settlement was to be an orderly and prosperous model for further missionary work. In spite of the strong currents of reforming zeal in France and support at the highest levels, the project failed at this purpose. The town itself succeeded, thrived even. But in contrast to the religious aspirations of its founders, it was, according to Dechêne, "no different from other commercial outposts." As Montréal grew into a more commercially driven settlement, its religious elites refused to abandon its founding ideals, and some chose to remember the early years of the French settlement very selectively. The annalistes of the Hôtel-Dieu there wrote with more idealism than accuracy that the early colonists had lived "like saints," where "in short, Montréal in its beginnings embodied all the principles of the early church."[70]

By the time nuns in Montréal were writing this remembrance, the religious priorities for New France had been reordered around them. The missionaries were finding that their successes were, at best, limited among Indigenous peoples, while a growing population of French settlers was in need of their services. Religious orders redirected their energies away from missions and toward the colonists, who came to form the majority of pupils in the schools and patients in the hospitals. As ecclesiastical leaders tried to reproduce forms of religion from France and keep the faith among French Catholics, the church in New France shifted from what might be characterized as a "missionary church" to a "colonial church."[71] Bishop Laval was behind many of the initiatives. He founded the Québec Seminary in 1663 to train clergy and the "Petit Séminaire" in 1668 as a residence for students. In 1664, he introduced the parochial system with the single parish of Notre-Dame-de-Québec, which remained the only parish until 1678 when Laval erected fourteen more. In 1674, Laval's office of vicar apostolic was turned into a bishopric, with the result that there was finally a Bishop of Québec in Québec.[72]

Religion continued to be a paramount concern for supporters of the colony, at least officially, and it remained closely tied to state concerns. Church cooperated with crown in 1663 when the bishop worked with the governor to nominate the first members of the Sovereign Council. Crown cooperated with church in 1664 when Louis XIV issued an edict stating that he saw in the establishment of the colony principally the glory of God and the salvation of the Natives.[73] An oath that the clergy took in 1672 insisted on a continued closeness between church and crown. They swore not only to labour with all their strength "for the maintenance of the Catholic, Apostolic and Roman Religion," but also "to be faithful to the King." The clergy even promised that if they came to know of a matter "which is contrary to His Majesty's service" they would advise the governor of it, and if the governor did not remedy the situation, to "inform His Majesty thereof."[74]

Catholicism remained the exclusive official form of Christianity in the colony, although Protestants were arriving in growing numbers. In the Carignan-Salières regiment Protestants were hastily catechized, and unconfirmed Catholics were quickly confirmed.[75] It was not just soldiers whose ranks included Huguenots. In 1670, Bishop Laval asked that French authorities stop merchants from sending Protestants to Canada, and his reasons suggest a concern that the Protestants might attract additional followers: they held discourses, lent devotional texts, hosted religious assemblies, and generally made a favourable impression on those around them. Laval also tried to make the case that these Protestants were less loyal to the king than Catholics, and that, given the proximity of Boston and other English settlements, their mere presence might foment rebellions. Perhaps in an attempt to limit the dangers of a Protestant presence in New France while admitting that the presence itself could not be eliminated, Laval in 1676 had the Sovereign Council adopt a rule curtailing some of the Protestants' activities. The Huguenots could not assemble for worship, but they were granted permission to stay in the colony during summer. They were forbidden from staying in the colony over winter except for legitimate reasons and with special permission, on condition that they live "as Catholics without scandal." With this ruling the presence of Protestants was acknowledged, but it was clearly circumscribed and probably permitted only as a reluctant concession to the economic interests of the colony.[76]

Protestant migrants were not the clerics' only concern. Some worried that the Catholic colonists were not sufficiently devout, or even sufficiently rule-abiding. Marie de l'Incarnation fretted about the quality of immigrants. It was true that many came from France, she wrote, and also true that the country was being peopled with these new arrivals, but among the honest individuals were scoundrels who caused much scandal. She calculated that it would have been better for the church to have a few good Christians than to have a large number of people causing so much trouble.[77] Other sources hint at the kinds of trouble that may have been on Marie's mind. Ordinances issued by the bishop prohibited parents from baptising or having their children baptized at home unless they were in peril of death, suggesting some reluctance or at least indifference about bringing children to church for the rite.[78] Behaviour in church did not always meet with ecclesiastical approval either. In 1679 priests were given a guideline of conduct to instruct their congregations about being modest and reverent in church. It included warnings against crossing legs, making movements meant to attract attention, staring at people, wearing untidy dress, and creating too much noise during services.[79] In 1682, Bishop Laval issued a "Mandate against the Luxury and Vanity of Women and Girls in the Church." He claimed that girls and women, wishing to please the eyes of men, clothed and ornamented themselves with the pomp of Satan, which was a disorder that God holds in extreme horror. Women appeared in indecent clothing, allowing people to see scandalously bare arms, shoulders, and throats, contenting themselves to cover these parts "with transparent cloth that only serves to give more lustre to these shameful nudities." They also had their hair "curled in a manner unworthy of a Christian." Worst of all, according to Laval, was not only that these women in their lacy fabrics and curled hair looked more prepared for a ball or a play than they did for church, but they even dared to approach the sacraments, present the blessed bread, and make the offering. Their "indecent state" profaned the mysteries and brought great scandal to the faithful, some of whom could not look upon this disturbance without indignation; others, more feeble, could not look upon it without danger to their salvation.[80] (The bishop said nothing in the mandate about men's clothing and hair, nor did he order or even advise the faithful to worry about things other than women's appearance while in church.)

When the bishop was comparing women's dress in church with what they wore to balls and plays, he was alluding to some local possibilities for socialization and entertainment. Religious authorities complained about these too. The first ball in Canada was held on 4 February, 1667. The scribe of the *Journal des jésuites* wrote, crankily, "may God grant that this not become a precedent."[81] In 1694, a quarrel erupted over the performance of Molière's play *Tartuffe*. Back in France, this play had been censured by a group of particularly devout people because it ridiculed asceticism and zealotry, and they succeeded in having it banned several times before it was finally staged as a great success. Governor Frontenac arranged to have the play performed in New France as part of the Carnival festivities, with a member of his household staff named Mareuil in the leading role. Bishop Saint-Vallier issued a mandate declaring that *Tartuffe* and other such plays were not only dangerous, but absolutely bad and criminal, and added that a person could not attend them without sin. Therefore, he condemned the play and forbade anyone from his diocese going to see it. Mareuil was charged with impiety and blasphemy, and was arrested, but then escaped from prison and broke into the grounds of the seminary to do some sort of mischief there. Governor Frontenac started proceedings in the Sovereign Council to determine whether plays previously performed were wicked or vicious. On appeal of the case to Versailles, it was determined that the bishop had the right to denounce the theatre, but nothing was offered to enforce the moral code.[82]

Sometimes, the people took it upon themselves to enforce codes of behaviour. The Confraternity of the Holy Family was established in 1664 to provide edifying examples of upstanding morality as well as severe rules for leading an acceptable life. This confraternity was set up by Laval and approved by the clergy, which makes it sound like a clerical initiative to control lay behaviour, but laypeople were willing and sometimes even eager to participate. Membership was open only to women, and at first only to married women. Any woman who wished to join needed to demonstrate a particular devotion to the Holy Family, to show proof of good will to correct her faults, and to live a life free from scandal. The type of scandal that members were supposed to avoid most assiduously was anything related to chastity. In the practice of this virtue, members were required to dress modestly and abstain from attending any balls.[83]

The Confraternity of the Holy Family was meant to provide positive reinforcement for good behaviour. People also tried shaming. In 1683, Québec had its first recorded charivari. This was a mob form of social censure described by Natalie Zemon Davis in her classic study as "a noisy, masked demonstration to humiliate some wrongdoer in the community." The target of the charivari in early modern France was often someone who had married inappropriately, especially in a second marriage with a large age difference between a young bride or groom and a much older widow or widower. The youth of the community showed their displeasure at having a young person removed from the pool of eligible spouses by making a clamour with pots, bells, rattles, horns, and other noisy things outside the house of the offending couple, possibly for several days or until the couple paid a fine. Their performance functioned as a mockery of the marriage, but it also had a restorative quality, clearing the air so that life could continue as before.[84] The Canadian charivari appears to have functioned in much the same way, although the grievance in this case was not with age difference (the spouses were only a few years apart), but instead with the unseemly haste of the second union. A young widow of twenty-five years old had remarried following only three weeks of widowhood.[85] The bishop reported that six days after the marriage, a large number of men and women assembled each night under the name of charivari. In their "scandalous disorders and freedoms," they committed "very impious actions" that were a derision of the mysteries and truths of the Christian religion and the most holy ceremonies of the church. He asked the secular arm to stop the assemblies. Not only did the gatherings continue, however, but they became even larger. So the bishop prohibited all the faithful from going to any charivari, prohibited fathers and mothers from sending their children or permitting them to go, and prohibited masters and mistresses from sending their servants or permitting them to go, under pain of excommunication.[86] Both the bishop and the people had codes of behaviour to enforce, and it is not at all clear whose methods were more effective.

Religious leaders might not have approved of the worldly entertainments available in Québec during the later seventeenth century, but the colonists were enjoying them anyway, while also expanding their worldly wealth. Industry within the French settlements increased, as did long-distance trade with other parts of the French empire. Marie de l'Incarnation described the building of a market, a brewery, and a tannery in 1670. She said that the cod fisheries about a hundred leagues away had the potential to generate immense revenues, and she noted also a "triple commerce" between France, the Caribbean, and Québec: vessels filled with pine board, peas, and grain left Québec for the Caribbean, where they discharged their merchandise and took on sugar for France, then brought back the things necessary for life in Canada.[87] In 1672, the newly appointed

Governor Frontenac wrote to Colbert that he found the country much less "sauvage" than he had thought, that it contained hidden treasures, and that in time commerce would increase. Not all the developments met with the governor's approval, however. Frontenac found the placement of the town of Québec beautiful and magnificent, but thought that it had been a mistake to allow people to build their houses in so disordered a fashion; he recommended instead increasing the beauty of the city by building on plans with carefully marked streets and spaces and with attention to symmetry. The beer being brewed in the new brewery, he conceded, was very good.[88] The following year, Frontenac boasted of the advantages brought by the establishment of markets, butchers, and bakers, saving people much money when they could buy food in these establishments and eat it at home. They could even purchase bread at such a reasonable price that everyone could eat white bread with their meal. There was less drunkenness than before, and the streets were cleaner; some residents had even begun to pave the area in front of their houses. The alignment of houses still displeased Frontenac, though, and he wrote that more care must be taken in planning so that people do not build their houses according to caprice.[89]

Capricious or not, many structures were being newly built or renovated in Québec. The cathedral was enlarged several times. In 1664, Bishop Laval wrote that it was constructed very soundly of stone, and that for music it had ten or twelve boy choristers mixing their voices sweetly with an organ, while in the sacristy were beautiful ornaments including eight silver candlesticks.[90] In 1688, a new church was erected in the Lower Town on top of the ruins of Champlain's second habitation. It was first devoted to the Enfant Jésus, and renamed Notre-Dame-de-la-Victoire in 1690 after a successful battle. The Jesuits were expanding the buildings around their college in the Upper Town, and they had a stone church constructed in 1666. New buildings were also built for the seminary and for the Hôtel-Dieu. In 1692, an Hôpital-Général was established with a focus on tending to the poor, indigent, and otherwise marginalized people.[91] The Ursuline monastery was largely rebuilt after a fire destroyed much of it in 1686. As Bishop Saint-Vallier said, the fire "spared nothing, it consumed all, provisions, furniture, buildings, except a very small central block."[92] The Château Saint-Louis was enlarged to make it both more effectively defensive and also more comfortable (and impressive) as a residence for the governor.[93]

5.2 Detail of an "habitation" on the Côte de Lauzon from "L'entrée de la Rivière du St Laurent, et la ville de Québec dans le Canada"

The physical changes to the town of Québec are clearly shown in plans and maps. One birds-eye view, produced at some point between 1670 and 1693, illustrates many of the sites from the life of Barbe Hallay. Beauport is bigger than she would have remembered from her early years there as a servant, now with more small houses near the manor. The Hôtel-Dieu remains perched on top of the cliff, a cross standing high on its roof. Both the Upper Town and the Lower Town are filled in with more buildings, and much of the land stretching from the edge of the town along the river is cleared and divided into plots. Several mills stand near sources of wind and water, and numerous ships have their sails unfurled in the river. On the Côte de Lauzon is drawn an example of a habitation with a house and an outbuilding by the river, surrounded by fields beyond whose bounds the thick forest still grows.[94]

A map of the surroundings of Québec created by Robert de Villeneuve in 1685–86 also illustrates recent changes. Beauport has a chapel, two mills, and quite a few dwellings. The town of Québec has the new institutional buildings as well as more houses. Many habitations cover the ground in Lauzon. Large ships travel along the St Lawrence, firing their cannons at nothing in particular, while canoes travel along the river more quietly.[95]

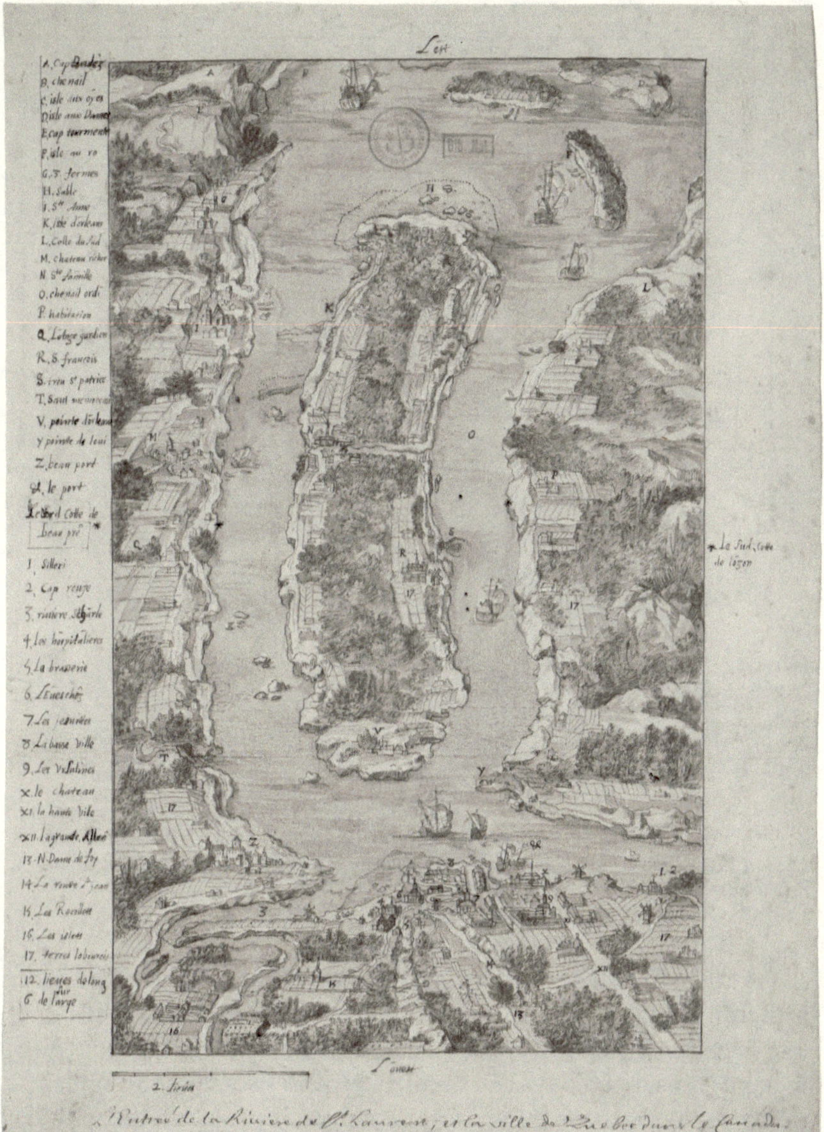

5.3 Jean-Baptiste Franquelin, "L'entrée de la Rivière du St Laurent, et la ville de Québec dans le Canada," circa later seventeenth century

5.4 Robert de Villeneuve, "Carte des Environs de Quebec en La Nouvelle France Mezuré sur le lieu très exactement en 1685 et 86 par le Sr Devilleneuve Ingénieur du Roy"

The town of Québec was bigger and more bustling than it had been at Barbe Hallay's first arrival. Its hinterland extended in reach and had become denser with settlements. It was a more permanent town in a more secure colony. This security provides some of the explanation for why there were not more instances of people claiming to be attacked by witches or possessed by demons. Studies of witch hunts in early modern Europe acknowledge a multicausal interpretation for why witchcraft accusations and claims of demonic possession arose in some places and at some times rather than others, but anxiety often features prominently in the analysis.[96] It makes sense, therefore, that the growing stability of the colony of New France would calm fears of interference by witches and demons.

Conversely, some of the changes in New France during the later seventeenth century might be expected to have led to a greater number of accusations of witchcraft, not fewer. In an analysis of why New France was "almost untouched" by the witchcraft accusations and trials endemic to Europe and New England during the seventeenth century, Jonathan L. Pearl highlights social and demographic differences. Among these are that settlements were smaller and farther apart in New France, so that the basic social unit was a family on a farm rather than an entire village; newcomers were welcomed gratefully rather than feared and distrusted; and there were fewer women than men and very few widows or unattached women of marriageable age.[97] All this is true for the first two-thirds of the seventeenth century, but changes from the 1660s onwards altered conditions significantly. Settlements grew in size and density; mistrust or scorn was increasingly being shown towards newcomers; and the demographic imbalance between the sexes began to even out. In early modern Europe, belief in witchcraft and outbreaks of witch-hunting were usually associated with the intimacy of neighbourly relationships gone wrong. Emotional conflicts and community tension found expression not just in village quarrels but also in witchcraft accusations.[98] If this same pattern were to hold in New France, then we should expect to see an increase in witchcraft accusations as settlements grew and aged. The lower number of marginalized people probably had a dampening effect, as perhaps did the diversity of regions in France from where migrants came. But another factor must also be explored, because it is clear that although many of the colonists in New France did believe in the power of witches and demons, this popular belief never led to any witch hunt or mass possession.

CHANGES IN DEMONOLOGY

The demonic troubles of Barbe Hallay were recorded by several powerful observers, and yet they did not trigger an outbreak of bewitchments or possessions. Part of the reason may be that the events, although well known, were not widely publicized. New France had no printing press, and so the written accounts were left in manuscript, not circulated as pamphlets. Hallay's torments were rarely on public display, and their conclusion through the ritual led by Marie Regnouard was held in private. This lack of public performance reduced the dramatic impact and reach of what happened.

Colonists, both lay and clerical, did continue to believe that witches and demons stalked their lives though, so the explanation for why New France never experienced a witch hunt or mass possession cannot simply be that people did not believe in these supernatural forces any longer. In 1670, the Procureur Fiscal of Ile d'Orléans and Beaupré accused the widow Catherine Gemier of witchcraft. The Superior Council heard from witnesses, interrogated Gemier, and ordered that the investigation continue for a year. No conclusion was reported. In 1671, Nicole Rolland accused her neighbour, Perrine Morel, of being a witch. Witnesses testified on behalf of Rolland that, among other things, Morel's relatives could set fires in clogs and make them smoke as if they had gunpowder inside, and her grandfather had put grease into a pot that a servant used to make a cart invisible. They also said that Morel herself, back in France, had killed calves and sheep belonging to her seigneur, and that in New France she bewitched the animals of one neighbour and killed the husband of another by a magical use of pins. In 1675, Marie Guillemette de Saint-Augustin, a nun at the Hôtel-Dieu, suffered from a very violent spitting of blood, which she interpreted as being a demon's strategy to turn her away from following the will of God. In 1676, the annaliste of the Ursulines recorded that Antoinette de Sainte-Marthe died after suffering from a strange illness that was very strong and against which none of their remedies would work. The nuns believed that "there was malefice in her malady." In 1682, a tribunal heard several witnesses say that they had seen Anne Lamarque, who was then running a successful tavern in Montréal, with a book of magic in her hands. One witness was particularly detailed in his description, reporting that this book was of about four or five inches square and of about the thickness of a finger, all written by hand, in French and Latin with a few words in Greek, and that among its contents were love spells to win the affection of girls, women, boys, and men. (Another witness reported that when he asked Lamarque whether she had a book of magic, she answered that it was a book of herbs and medicines). In 1684 Jean Campagna from Acadia was put on trial, accused of having killed two people in Beaubassin and bewitching a third, causing people to fall sick, and additionally killing cows, a bull, and oxen. Testimony was provided by multiple witnesses about events that stretched back over years, often in response to insults or slights, but Campagna was not convicted. One witness said that the accusations had come about because people owed the accused money.

In 1691, repairs were being made to the Hôtel-Dieu in Québec. One of the workmen at the stables wished to bewitch the nuns, but each time he came close to the person he chose, he felt himself repelled by an invisible force. He himself later declared that he had had commerce with the devil. In 1706, an outbreak of illness among livestock near Montréal was believed by several people to be due to witchcraft by Jean Charpentier, a coppersmith. They started to avoid Charpentier, refusing to speak with him or visit his shop. He went to court to clear his name. Those accused of having called him a witch or magician denied it, saying instead that they thought Charpentier a very honest man. The tribunal declared that any similar injuries in the future would be subject to a fine of fifty *livres*.[99]

This list of charges and rumours shows that belief in the power of witchcraft was widespread, and closely resembled ideas about witchcraft in Europe.[100] Each charge and rumour could have become a trigger for a rash of accusations, but none of them did. Some cases went to trial, but none ever led to a conviction or a rash of similar accusations. A few resulted in a penalty being imposed not on the accused witch, but rather on the accusers. The sources do not tell us why only some claims were taken seriously, but the general pattern can be explained by a populace largely willing to believe in magic, and an elite largely uninterested in prosecuting the crime.

A similar pattern can be found when considering people who displayed traditional signs of bewitchment or possession but were treated with remedies indicating a different diagnosis. In December 1674, the Jesuit François Boniface had been on a mission among the Iroquois for several years before returning to Québec. He was in a violent state. He spoke nonsense and screamed almost continually. He bit and hit those trying to help him with so much aggression that they needed to bind him. These symptoms resembled those of demonic possession, but the Jesuits instead diagnosed Boniface as suffering from "phrénésie," a type of madness. Their first attempt to treat him was with opium, a drug that would have been considered appropriate not only according to humoral theory, in which as a cold treatment it would counterbalance the hot illness, but also as a soporific. The Jesuits tried this treatment several times, but even at double and triple the usual dose the opium did not work. It was not until a series of prayers was spoken to Jean de Brébeuf and Boniface's head was touched with one of Brébeuf's bones that he was cured by regaining his senses and dying peacefully the following day. Through both the opium and the prayer treatments, the possibility of possession was never mentioned.[101] A collection of miracles from the shrine of Sainte-Anne-du-Petit-Cap, just down the river from Québec at what is now called Beaupré, tells of three women during the 1660s who suffered from fainting and convulsions, as well as the loss of speech, hearing, and understanding – all symptoms that were associated with possession. After finding that physicians could do nothing to help, the women made vows to St Anne and were healed. It might come as no surprise that these women tried medical treatment and then sought healing at a shrine. More surprising is that the record says nothing about these symptoms having a supernatural origin, like possession. Moreover, the record states that the women's suffering was common. They were "very inconvenienced by a sickness that occurs ordinarily in Canada," and the list of symptoms was described as being "like from a falling sickness" (epilepsy).[102] In 1686, the governor Denonville wrote a letter to France in which he listed some of the more frequent maladies in New France. The most ordinary, he said, was that of worms. Some have convulsive illnesses that were thought to be epilepsy ("maladies du hautmal"), but which could also be caused by worms.[103] Both at the shrine of Sainte-Anne and in the governor's letter, signs that could have been interpreted as indicating possession were described as widespread, yet they were not deemed a cause for concern about large-scale demonic attack. In these examples, as in the case of the frenetic priest, treatment could be through natural remedies, spiritual assistance, or both, but natural causes were considered before all else when interpreting symptoms that in many respects fit the earlier expectations for bewitchment or possession.

By the late seventeenth century, the number of witchcraft prosecutions was declining in Europe. The reasons for the decline are many, but among the most significant was a change in attitudes about the supernatural. Specifically, some people were becoming less worried about the threat posed by witches in conspiracies with demons. Louis XIV published an edict in 1682 against "those who called themselves diviners, magicians, and enchanters," also called "imposters," who used "pretended magic and other similar illusions" to deceive "ignorant or gullible individuals." While this document did not deny the existence of witchcraft outright, it did implicitly reclassify it as superstition and as something pretended rather than real. Such a reclassification had the effect of disassociating witchcraft from the devil, and also of denying people's claims of magical power.[104] Many continued to believe in the power of witches to perform the harmful magic of maleficium, but elites in much of Europe were becoming more and more skeptical about such beliefs. As Edward Bever has summed it up, in the early seventeenth century, "ordinary people and the governing elite shared a conviction that harmful magic intimated traffic with the devil and participation in an organized cult that threated the Christian order," but by about 1660, "a critical mass of leaders [...] had lost their certainty about the prevalence, if not the potency, of maleficium; the danger, if not the existence, of a diabolical conspiracy; and the practicality, if not the possibility, of identifying and punishing those involved in either pursuit."[105]

This change combined a growing skepticism about the physical reality of powers attributed to witches with a growing suspicion that, even if real witches did exist, many of the accusations of witchcraft were being made against innocent people. Lawyers and judges, noticing unfair or even fraudulent legal proceedings, became concerned about miscarriages of justice and insisted upon more judicial caution. Politicians became less preoccupied with maintaining a "godly" state and persecuting those deemed "ungodly," more convinced that the state's priority should be in the promotion of commerce and industry. Intellectuals were making belief in the powers of witches and the devil unfashionable. Those upon whom they looked down might still worry about witches interfering with their sexual relations or harming their livestock, but the elite were using disbelief in magic as a social marker of membership in a forward-looking, modern, well educated, urban class.[106]

A clear illustration of the changing attitudes can be found in the *Dictionnaire Universel* of 1690, which treats belief in witches and pacts with the devil as foolishly unreasonable. "Sorcellerie" is defined as "magical art that borrows the help and ministry of the Devil," but the example of usage undermines any reasonable argument for its reality and presumes instead that sorcery is something believed by those with insufficient education to discern the true reasons for things: "Ignorant people attribute to witchcraft all the effects whose causes they cannot perceive." In this and other entries for words associated with witchcraft, the dictionary includes phrases to make it clear that educated readers were expected to be more discerning than the general populace when it came to the supernatural. It defines the "sabbat," for example, as "the nocturnal assembly that it is believed that witches hold on Saturdays, where they say that the Devil appears in the form of a goat [...] the old women believe that they go to the sabbat on a broomstick."[107] The entries for "Demon" and "Demoniaque," interestingly, do not insinuate so strongly that the concept is unreasonable or silly. The dictionary defines "Demon" as spirits in the beliefs of ancients, and an enemy devil in the beliefs of Christians. Some of the examples of usage are metaphorical, but none suggests ignorance or too much credulity.[108] As these entries were being written, the numbers of possessions were declining in Europe, but not so precipitously as charges of witchcraft. Cases of possession without ties to witchcraft continued to be reported through the eighteenth and nineteenth centuries. Skepticism grew about the authenticity of all or most reported possessions, but a consensus never emerged among leaders in politics or religion about whether claims of possession should ever be believed.[109]

Overall, though, both witchcraft and demonism were losing credibility among the elite classes in Europe, and this trend reached across the ocean to New France. Ecclesiastical and civic leaders continued to admit the possibility of demonic powers in theory, but they were becoming much less inclined to suspect their operation in practice.[110] The *Catéchisme* by Bishop Saint-Vallier, published in 1702, says that rendering to a demon a service that should be rendered to God is a form of superstition, as is recourse to witches.[111] Saint-Vallier's *Rituel*, published in 1703, discusses witchcraft and exorcisms, but within a buffer of caution. It says that sometimes married persons are prevented from consummating their marriage by spells, and that in such cases curates must console them and counsel them to try prayer, confession, and communion until it pleases God to break the malefice; if the problem persists, curates are to consult the priests who can judge whether they should employ exorcism and prayers of the church. The *Rituel* does acknowledge the appropriateness of exorcism under some very specific circumstances. It says that sometimes people are tormented by demons in their persons or in their goods, and that priests must help people so afflicted, but these priests must carefully examine whether it is truly a malefice or infestation, as opposed to a malady or natural causes. Moreover, when people are suffering from malefice, priests and ministers are to warn them not to suspect their neighbours or other people, and not to listen to empty promises of those who claim to know the author of the malefice. The priests and ministers must also warn these people not to turn to superstitions to be cured, and not to permit someone to remove this malefice by use of another malefice or spells. In the section on exorcising people who are obsessed or possessed by demons, the manual insists on many conditions, including personal characteristics of the exorcist, a cautious examination of the possessed person, and performance of the ritual at the door of the church if possible and in the presence of witnesses. The stated reason for these conditions is that priests who are too credulous are often fooled, and too often it happens that people say they are obsessed or tormented by a demon when really they require the help of physicians rather than exorcists.[112] This manual from the start of the eighteenth century does not deny the possibility of witchcraft and possession, but it does imply that many seeming cases would actually turn out to be something else entirely under closer inspection. It also suggests that credulity, false accusations, and the undertaking of superstitious counter-measures were actually the greater dangers.

As a general pattern in early modern Europe, trials and executions for witchcraft were most frequent in areas where individuals in charge of criminal justice were most closely connected to the fears and hatreds that led to the accusations in the first place.[113] If people running the judicial machinery did not believe in the reality of witchcraft, no mass persecutions would take place. By the later seventeenth century, some people in New France still feared and hated witches and demons, but political and ecclesiastical leaders were less and less likely to go along with claims of witchcraft and demonic interference. In fact, they actively discouraged people from seeking magical explanations. In 1676 rumours began to spread of an outbreak of witchcraft and sorcery at the Sulpician mission of La Montagne near Montréal. The Sulpician superior in Paris, Louis Tronson, who had in a previous role helped train priests for their work in New France, sent a cautionary note of advice in March 1680. This note instructed the missionaries not to question people who were accusing others, not to interrogate too scrupulously on certain useless details, and not to believe too readily what people said without proof that the allegation was something other than imagined.[114] The missionary Guillaume Bailly was particularly credulous of the rumours, and Tronson warned that if Bailly could not disabuse himself of the notion that there were many witches, it would be necessary to pull him away from the mission, for it was "almost impossible to undeceive a person who had become preoccupied with this matter." To Bailly himself, Tronson wrote, "I know that it is very difficult to get rid of these sorts of preoccupations, in which, as a rule, the devil gets involved, in order to increase evil and prevent us from undeceiving ourselves; but I hope that Our Lord will have regard for the purity of your intentions, and that the sincere desire that he gives you to serve him will not be denied its effect at a time when, it seems to me, we have more need of your help."[115] Tronson's opinion of Bailly's stance did not improve. By March 1691, he wrote to Bailly that God "asks that you return to France this year. A longer stay in Canada will not be useful to you and could do harm to many."[116] In Tronson's interpretation, the devil was not in league with real witches; he was inspiring people to believe falsely in witches. More widely, calling someone a "witch" or a "magician" was insulting, but it did not carry the risk of sparking a witch-hunting craze. A Montréal parent in 1686 objected to the marriage of their son because his fiancée's mother had insulted them in the past with "the most atrocious injuries that can be said against the honour and reputation of a family," calling them "old devil old wolf witch magician" and other things.[117] Witchcraft and demonic power were still swirling around in early modern French colonial culture, but they were no longer the objects of fear that they had been a few generations earlier.[118]

As the years went by, diabolical forces drifted further from people's worries, and became tamed into entertaining tales to be told on long winter nights. The devil makes frequent appearances in Québécois and French-Canadian folklore, but usually as a force from the past rather than the present, and as a figure more to be outwitted than feared.[119] In one of the most famous legends, that of the *chasse-galerie*, a group of drunk lumbermen yearning for female company one New Year's Eve decide to offer their souls to the devil in return for passage aboard an enchanted canoe. One of them says that he is willing to "risk the salvation of my soul for the fun of going to give a New Year's kiss to my *blonde*." Among the terms of the pact is that if the travellers mention the name of God or touch the cross on any church's steeple while flying by on the canoe, the devil will win their soul. In most versions, they escape the devil's grasp.[120] It's a good yarn, to be sure, but this devil's ambitions had diminished a great deal since the early seventeenth century, when he was trying to overturn the entire project of New France.

Conclusion

The possession of Barbe Hallay as told in this book is a local story within the flow of global currents. The immediate setting is an area in and around the small town of Québec during a time span of a few years in the mid-seventeenth century. The full situation is not so circumscribed. Forces shaping New France in the 1660s extended across vast lands and wide oceans, and their development can be traced back through many years.

In order to understand the fundamentals of what was happening, how the people at the time thought about the events, and why they behaved as they did, I have alternated the distance of interpretive focus between near and far. The analytical work has come from investigating the sources from up close to scrutinize the historical records of seventeenth-century New France, then lifting my gaze to survey the more distant influences on this specific time and place. For those who prefer instrumental metaphors, I have sometimes employed an approach that is microscopic for examining the fine details of historical evidence, and sometimes one that is telescopic for viewing the context from afar.[1] This combination of small and large scales, of close and distant perspectives, illuminates the texture of everyday moments within grander historical narratives. Thickly descriptive, it responds to a curiosity to know more about the ordinary and mundane features of past lives while allowing us to analyze the deeper meanings and wider significance of people's actions.[2]

Through the daily experiences of people in seventeenth-century Canada, we can recognize the compromises of a colonial society trying to establish traditional forms in new surroundings. French settlers planted seeds and raised livestock to produce familiar French foods, then added North American plants and animals to their diets. They built French-style houses, then modified the materials to take advantage of local supplies and insulate their domestic spaces against the cold of a Canadian winter. They kept their laws on marriage, then altered customs for how people should choose their spouses. They founded a hospital to care for the sick poor as in France, and also evangelize to Indigenous peoples in North America, then moved its location and shifted its mandate to focus on the settler population. They retained the basic class structure of ancien régime society, then admitted a greater range of activities to permeate through the hierarchy.

All these features of New France appear in the investigation of Barbe Hallay's possession, as does yet another layer of how people understood their world and the trajectory of the colony. An earlier generation's ideal of New France was receding from view, and the colonists were struggling to adjust their expectations to match the realities of survival in North America. New France did not provide an easy route to Asia or the riches that the first French visitors had expected, nor did it turn into the new Jerusalem blessed by God with citizens destined for heaven as missionaries had hoped. Indigenous allies to France were not becoming French as the colonial architects of French assimilationist policy had arrogantly assumed, and enemies were showing no signs of weakening their opposition. During the years of Hallay's possession, the colonial project of New France was precarious, and the colonists knew it. They feared attacks by the Iroquois, a withdrawal of support from France, and the bad outcomes heralded by comets and earthquakes. When reports started circulating about a case of demonic infestation, colonial leaders were quick to believe that a Huguenot immigrant was involved, yet they disagreed about the prosecution. They felt confident that the Hôtel-Dieu hospital was the best place to treat a demoniac, then they assisted with a laywoman's unorthodox performance of a religious ritual. They were ready to believe that demonic instigators were loose among them, only to grow largely unconcerned about later possible cases. The actions of people around Barbe Hallay show that the quotidian realities of life in New France were less confidently unified in the service of an imperial goal than official dispatches would suggest.

By examining this story at both the small and large scales, we can also see how people's lives were shaped by forces beyond their control. Some of these forces were obvious to the colonists, if not necessarily well understood. The settlers were aware that winter was longer and colder in North America than in Europe, and they were able to infer some of the consequences for agriculture and transportation, but they remained confused about why places at similar latitudes should have such dissimilar climates. They knew that the Iroquois could capture and kill them, and they were worried about attacks, while largely ignorant of Haudenosaunee motivations and priorities. They sought more support from leaders in France, yet they were only sometimes successful in pressing their claims amid competing demands in France itself and from other more lucrative outposts of the French empire. Within the constraints imposed by such forces, and limited by an imperfect understanding of the forces' causes and extents, people made decisions about how to think and act. Marriageable women exercised more control over whom to marry. Religious and civic authorities disagreed about prosecuting misconduct. Missionaries found greater opportunities for an apostolic life with the possibility of martyrdom. Clerical and lay leaders defended those in their care against what they thought were demonic attacks.

This story of a case of suspected demonic possession unfolded as it did because of circumstances that were both very specific to New France in the mid-seventeenth century and much larger than the Laurentian colony. Among the local conditions were a demographic imbalance between the sexes, which exerted pressure on Hallay to wed; the ill-defined role of a vicar apostolic and the disagreements between the person in that role and the governor, which raised the stakes in the accusations against the suspected witch; the recent destruction of the Huronia mission, which encouraged a Jesuit superior to support the uses of a martyr's relics and the publication of those uses; and the familial connections of a seigneuresse, which gave her the confidence and authority to fight a demon possessing her servant. The development of the case also depended on influences with more distant origins, including a race among European states to colonize other parts of the world; the reshaping of Indigenous alliances across much of North America; and a growing separation in Europe and its overseas outposts between elite and popular beliefs about demons.

The confluence of local conditions and larger forces is perhaps most clearly seen in the settlers' basic presumption that they would find demons in New France in the first place. It is a presumption rooted in a belief that Christianity was a universally true system: the French in New France believed that the God they worshipped was the God of the whole world, regardless of whether people worshipped him or not, and they believed that the demons they battled were to be found in all lands, regardless of whether people recognized the forces as demonic or not. This outlook explains why André Thevet described evil spirits on the "Île des Démons" (an island to the north of Newfoundland) in the 1540s as a type familiar to Europeans,[3] why Samuel de Champlain in 1603 described the Mi'kmaq spirit of the Gougou as "some kind of Devil,"[4] why Pierre Biard in 1616 asserted that the world was divided between heavenly and infernal domains with New France in the latter category,[5] and why the people around Barbe Hallay interpreted her troubles as a demonic attack.[6] The French brought their beliefs about demons with them intact to New France, and they rarely paused to wonder whether they might encounter supernatural forces in North America that were wholly different from what they had understood to exist in Europe.[7] They were ready to believe, therefore, that a teenaged servant was a likely candidate for possession, that a man who felt spurned after asking to marry her was the witch responsible for causing the possession, that treatment in a hospital and an exorcism-like ritual were appropriate responses to the possession, and that once the possession was ended the previously possessed could lead her life entirely free from demonic torments. These expectations were all imported from France as ideas that travelled across the ocean with the colonists. As with other expectations brought by the settlers, those about demons could not endure completely unchanged in the colonial context. Here, the signs heralding the arrival of demonic interference included a fiery canoe, the presence of religious non-conformists such as Protestants and witches was especially concerning to leaders of church and state who were trying to create a perfectly Catholic society, and women had increased authority to lead in spiritual matters. New France was part of a bigger world, linked through North America to Indigenous polities and European colonies, across the Atlantic to France, and around the globe by physical geographies and metaphysical religious presumptions. It was also, like all parts of the world, a place with its own particularities.

It might be worth pointing out, if readers have not already noticed, that throughout this book we hardly ever hear Barbe Hallay's own words. In fact, we hear more from the demon believed to be possessing her body than we do from Hallay herself. This feature of the book was not a choice by the author, but a consequence of the sources: Barbe Hallay's speech only comes to us through a few lines in the account left by Marie Regnouard and, I suppose, indirectly through the consent she expressed in her marriage contract. Barbe Hallay is one of the mostly silent historical majority, people silent not in their own times but in ours because we are not left with lengthy accounts of their thoughts and actions. Understanding her world and her place within it is the task of the historian. Fortunately for us – those who conduct the research as well as those who read its findings – the world of Barbe Hallay offers much to captivate our attention.

Glossary

This glossary provides a brief explanation for how terms are used in this book, meaning within the context of seventeenth-century New France.

Ancien Régime	The political, social, and legal system in France before the Revolution of 1789.
Augustinians	A monastic order that provided nursing care at the Hôtel-Dieu in Québec. Also called "Hospitalières."
Bishop	A priest who was a member of the highest order of ministers in the Catholic Church. A bishop was responsible for spiritual oversight of his diocese.
Canada	The area of French settlement along the St Lawrence River, including the largest towns of Québec, Montréal, and Trois-Rivières.
Catholics	Christians who saw themselves as members of the Catholic Church.
Governor	The king's official representative and highest-ranking official in New France. Prior to New France becoming a royal colony in 1663, the governor held many military and civil powers; once France became a royal colony, he was mostly responsible for defending the colony and managing relations with other colonial powers and Indigenous nations.
Habitants	Agricultural settlers who, as tenants, paid a small fee (the "cens") and annual rent (the "rente") to a seigneur.

Habitation	An individual farm and the basic unit of organization in the rural landscape of the colonists.
Haudenosaunee	A confederacy of five nations to the south of the Great Lakes. Called the "Iroquois" by the French.
Hospitalières	A monastic order that provided nursing care at the Hôtel-Dieu in Québec. Also called "Augustinians."
Hôtel-Dieu	A hospital especially for the sick poor, but charged with providing medical care for all inhabitants. An Hôpital Général, by contrast, was largely an institution of poor relief.
Huguenots	French Calvinist Protestants.
Huron	The French name for the Wendat.
Intendant	The officer responsible for managing the colony's internal civil affairs such as finance, justice, and agriculture. The first intendant of New France arrived in 1665.
Iroquois	The French name for the Haudenosaunee.
Jesuits	Members of the Society of Jesus, a religious order well known for education and missionary work. Their most famous writings, the *Relations*, are reports of their activities sent back to France and published in Paris.
Martyr	A person who suffered death for their faith.
Mission	An enterprise to propagate Christianity. Those undertaking the propagation were missionaries.
New France	The lands in North America claimed by the king of France.
Protestants	Christians who saw themselves as members of one of the Churches that broke away from the Church of Rome to reform Christianity in the sixteenth century.
Québec	The largest town and most important French settlement in New France.
Récollets	Members of a Franciscan religious order.

Seigneur	A person granted land and certain privileges in return for pledging fealty and homage to the king's representative. The seigneur's tenants were habitants, and the seigneur's estate was a seigneurie.
St Lawrence River	A waterway that runs from the Great Lakes to the Atlantic Ocean.
Ursulines	A cloistered monastic order of nuns who took a vow of education in addition to the usual three monastic vows of poverty, chastity, and obedience.
Vicar Apostolic	A church official who was responsible for the pastoral care of the people in a region that had not yet been organized into a diocese.
Wendat	A confederacy of nations with a traditional territory between Georgian Bay and Lake Simcoe, then dispersed in the 1640s and 1650s. Called "Huron" by the French.

Notes

INTRODUCTION

1 "Nous avons eu des présages funestes" "l'on a découvert qu'il y a des Sorciers et Magiciens en ce païs." "il voulut parvenir à ses fins par les ruses de son art diabolique." Marie de l'Incarnation, *Correspondance*, 667–8.
2 Those familiar with the historiography of New France in particular may find that this book addresses the question first posed some decades ago by Louise Dechêne of "how a colonial society was formed and shaped by European settlers under the twin influences of tradition and North American experiences." Dechêne, *Habitants and Merchants in Seventeenth-Century Montreal*, xvii.
3 Robert-Lionel Séguin said that the possession was really the result of a miller susceptible to feminine charms and a young woman tormented by will-o-the-wisps. Séguin, *La Sorcellerie au Canada français*, 25–31.
4 André Cellard used the story to show the early modern association between madness and demonic possession. Cellard, *Histoire de la folie au Québec*, 24, 49–50. Cornelius Jaenen characterized New France as "a colony where popular religious belief sometimes bordered on the superstitious," and wrote that Hallay was "probably subject to epilepsy." Jaenen, *The Role of the Church in New France*, 146–7. Vincent Grégoire wrote an article focusing more on Daniel Vuil and Catherine de Saint-Augustin than on Hallay. He said that the "possession" of Hallay could be identified with epilepsy, and added that the "obsession" of a nun who tried to heal Hallay was really mental disequilibrium and neurosis. Grégoire, "Le meunier, la domestique et l'hospitalière," 86.
5 Pearl, "Witchcraft in New France in The Seventeenth Century," 41–55.
6 Trudel, *Histoire de la Nouvelle-France III*, 1:316–19.

7 Timothy G. Pearson mentioned the case in the context of female religious authority as one piece of evidence for how Catherine de Saint-Augustin voluntarily underwent suffering to improve her society. Pearson, "I Willingly Speak to You about her Virtues," 305–33. Julia Boss included a few lines about the role played by a relic of Jean de Brébeuf in Regnuouard's ending of Hallay's demonic possession as being a "typical example" of recourse to fragmentary relics of Jesuit martyrs. Boss, "Writing a Relic," 225. In a short article for the magazine *Canada's History*, André Pelchat presented the case (without a mention of Regnouard's role) as an example of New France being "a frightening place." Pelchat, "Sorcery in New France." Leslie Choquette discussed the colonists' concerns about the possession of Hallay in her evaluation of how European fears made their way across the Atlantic in attenuated form to New France. Choquette, "From Sea Monsters and Savages," 53–9. I have provided a chapter-length analysis of the role played by Marie Regnouard in Cowan, "A Deliverance from Demons."

8 Ginzburg, *The Cheese and the Worms*; Davis, *The Return of Martin Guerre*; Greer, *Mohawk Saint*.

9 Ginzburg, "Microhistory: Two or Three Things That I Know about It," 22, 33.

10 This discussion of common features in microhistories is adapted from Magnússon and Szíjártó, *What Is Microhistory?*, 4–5; Cohen, "The Macrohistory of Microhistory," 53–6; and Trivellato, "Microstoria/Microhistoire/Microhistory," 127. On the history of everyday life as sometimes nostalgic, and often a rejection and critique of grand narratives, see Brewer, "Microhistory and the Histories of Everyday Life," 91–2.

11 For a critique of some of the limitations of microhistory, or at least of how many historians practise it, see Guldi and Armitage, *The History Manifesto*, especially 112. For a critique of this critique, see Cohen and Mandler, "*The History Manifesto*: A Critique," especially 535.

12 Muir, "Observing Trifles," vii–xxviii, quotation on xxi.

13 Ginzburg, "Microhistory and World History"; Medick, "Turning Global?" 241–52; Levi, "Microhistoria e Historia Global," 21–5; Gamsa, "Biography and (Global) Microhistory," 231–41; Aslanian et al., "How Size Matters," 1431–72. See also the articles in the *Past & Present* issue supplement "Global History and Microhistory," including Ghobrial, "Introduction," 1–22.

14 Levack, *The Devil Within*, viii, 3–5.

15 Clark, *Thinking with Demons*, 402.

16 As Richard Raiswell and Peter Dendle have shown, "particular instances of apparent possession" are cultural products that "can serve as important microhistorical sites for the recovery of popular and learned *mentalité*." Raiswell and Dendle, "Demonic Possession in Anglo-Saxon and Early Modern England," 738–67, quotation on 740.

17 Geschiere, "Witchcraft and the Dangers of Intimacy," 213–29.

18 Ferber, "Possession and the Sexes," 214–38; Gasser, *Vexed with Devils*, 1.

19 Huizinga, *Dutch Civilisation in the Seventeenth Century*, 10.

20 This is not to deny that the colonists maintained an identity that was both colonial and French. Wien, "Quelle est la largeur de l'Atlantique?"

21 For discussions and deconstructions of the word "sauvage" in seventeenth-century French, see Melzer, *Colonizer or Colonized*, 87–90; Sayre, *Les Sauvages Américains*; Peace, "Deconstructing the *Sauvage/Savage* in the Writing of Samuel de Champlain and Captain John Smith"; Paul, *We Were Not the Savages*; and Dickason, *Myth of the Savage*.

22 The Jesuit Pierre Biard, in his *Relation* of 1616, explains to his readers that "Canada" is the part of New France extending along the banks of the St Lawrence River and into the Gulf of St Lawrence. JR 3:41. For more on the history of the word "Canadien," see Carpin, *Histoire d'un mot*, and Horguelin, "Le XVIIIe siècle des Canadiens."

23 Desbarats and Greer, "Où est la Nouvelle-France?" 31–62; Desbarats and Greer, "North America from the Top Down," 130; Greer, *Property and Dispossession*, 145–51; Havard and Vidal, *Histoire de l'Amérique française*, 22–9.

CHAPTER ONE

1 "Lettre de Talon au Ministre Colbert (4 octobre 1665)," RAPQ 1930–31, 38; Marie de l'Incarnation, *Écrits spirituels et historiques*, 2:357; Des Gagniers, *Le voyage au bout du vent*, 126–7; Proulx, *Between France and New France*, 54–7.

2 Des Gagniers, *Le voyage au bout du vent*, 126–7; Proulx, *Between France and New France*, 47; Palomino, "Mastering the North Atlantic," 70–3. For more on the determination of longitude, see Dunn and Higgitt, *Ships, Clocks, and Stars*.

3 "Observations que Talon a Faites sur la Navigation de La Rochelle en Canada (4 Octobre 1665)," RAPQ 1930–31, 30.

4 Sagard, *Le Grand voyage*, 118.

5 Moogk, "Reluctant Exiles," 468–9; Boleda, "Nouvelle estimation de l'immigration française au Canada," 35.

6 For good general overviews of the social and economic conditions of early modern France, see Beik, *A Social and Cultural History of Early Modern France*; Dewald and Vardi, "The Peasantries of France," 21–47; Follain, *Le village sous l'Ancien Régime*; Goubert, *The French Peasantry in the Seventeenth Century*; Hoffman, *Growth in a Traditional Society*; Kettering, *French Society*.

7 BAnQ-M, from Parchemin database, 27 07 1670 (1663–87) Duquet de Lechesnay, P.; microfilm M-167.1

8 His baptism was on 10 September 1659. BAnQ-M, from Parchemin database, 27 07 1670 (1663–1687) Duquet de Lechesnay, P.; microfilm M-167.1; PRDH.

9 Garnot, *Un Déclin*; Sauzet, "Le Problème Protestant," 683–96; Benedict, "French Cities from the Sixteenth Century to the Revolution," 25.

10 Charbonneau et al., *The First French Canadians*, 66; Choquette, *Frenchmen into Peasants*, 151–9.

11 Charbonneau et al., *The First French Canadians*, 67, 70; Choquette, *Frenchmen into Peasants*, 28–54, 99, 101–28; Carpin, *Le Réseau du Canada*, 26–7.

12 This peak lasted from 1635–65. Choquette, *Frenchmen into Peasants*, 2, 165; Charbonneau et al., *The First French Canadians*, 34–6.

13 Estimates of what fraction returned to France range from a little under half to more than two-thirds for the period 1632–62. Charbonneau et al., *The First French Canadians*, 40, 198–9; Campeau, *Les Cent Associés et le peuplement de la Nouvelle-France*, 152; Carpin, *Le Réseau du Canada*, 39–40; Wien, "Une Nouvelle-France," 31–3; Boleda, "Nouvelle estimation de l'immigration française au Canada," 36.

14 Livi Bacci, *A Concise History of World Population*, 58. In 1662, there were perhaps 3,000 French settlers in all of New France, which was much less than the 40,000 English settlers in New England. Carpin, *Le Réseau du Canada*, 345.

15 Earle, *A Geographical Inquiry*; Ballone, *The 1624 Tumult of Mexico in Perspective*, 42–3; Hoerder, "Global Migrations," 25.

16 Cartier, "Québec 1608–2008," 135.

17 Trudel, *Histoire de la Nouvelle-France III*, 2:70–5.

18 Landry, "Les Français passés au Canada avant 1760," 484–5.

19 Davis, "Ghosts, Kin, and Progeny," 87–114; Minvielle, *La famille en France*, 163–70.

20 Many of these migrants left, but those who stayed were often linked to people already there: about two out of every five male immigrants and almost two out of every three female immigrants before 1663 had at least

one kin member in Canada. Charbonneau et al., *The First French Canadians*, 37, 69, 70, 72–3, 75, 77–8.

21 Then, on 30 November 1657, three arpents of frontage on the St Lawrence was conceded to Jean-Baptiste Hallay in the seigneurie of Beaupré. He was back in France in 1658, and returned west over the ocean with his family the following year. Trudel, *Le terrier du Saint-Laurent en 1663*, 52, 97, 498; Trudel, *Histoire de la Nouvelle-France III*, 1:257.

22 The Compagnie de la Nouvelle-France was set up in 1627 as a private venture that possessed New France as a fief and seigneurie. As both a commercial and a colonizing enterprise, with responsibilities to make profits for its investors as well as extend French sovereignty in North America, this company made populating the colony its primary stated objective. In return for a perpetual monopoly on the fur trade and a fifteen-year monopoly on all other trade excluding fisheries, the company agreed to transport 4,000 indentured servants to New France. In 1645, the crown made a reconcession to the Communauté des Habitants, French men living permanently in the colony, which took upon itself the recruitment of twenty persons annually. Dewar, "Government by Trading Company"; Choquette, *Frenchmen into Peasants*, 249–53; Choquette, "Proprietorships in French North America," 117–31; Renaud, *Les origines économiques du Canada*, 236.

23 Kettering, *French Society*, 40; Goubert, *The Ancien Régime*, 42–3.

24 Kettering, *French Society*, 44.

25 Dewald and Vardi, "The Peasantries of France," 21–47.

26 JR 9:185–91.

27 Pioffet, "Nouvelle-France ou France nouvelle," 37–55.

28 Within the territory claimed by the French king, much remained unknown. In 1665, Jean Talon wrote a letter to Jean-Baptiste Colbert saying that Canada was of a "very vast extent" whose limits to the north he did not know, they being so distant from the French settlements. RAPQ 1930–31, 32; Landry, "Les Français passés au Canada avant 1760," 489–500.

29 Wien, "Quelle est la largeur de l'Atlantique," 63–4.

30 "Si quid in Gallia de Canadia audis, tibi fingis animo horrentem quamdam et incultam solitudinem." Campeau, "Un témoignage," 604–12, quotation on 609.

31 He did so by providing what a modern editor calls a description, an inventory, and a dream, writing a work of clarification and persuasion. Wien, "Pierre Boucher," 129–219.

32 Dechêne, *Le Peuple, l'État et la Guerre*, 90.

33 RAPQ 1930–31, 41.

34 Charbonneau et al., *The First French Canadians*, 24–5.

35 Anthony Grafton put the main development succinctly, saying that "between 1550 and 1650 Western thinkers ceased to believe that they could find all important truths in ancient books." Grafton, *New Worlds, Ancient Texts,* 1.

36 Peter Burke finds that some writers were more willing to accommodate new information about the Americas than others, depending partly on national styles of response, partly on whether they had been to the Americas themselves, and partly on whether their priorities were aligned with those of academics, missionaries, or merchants. Burke also finds that the Americas grew to hold a more prominent place in European thought overall as time went on, but only gradually: in spite of the flood of information about the "New World" reaching Europe in the sixteenth century, European works of history only moved beyond "brief and casual references" to the Americas during the later eighteenth century. Burke, "America and the Rewriting of World History," 33–51. Karen Ordahl Kupperman argues for an earlier intellectual shift in European conceptions of the significance of the Americas, and a confrontation in the late fifteenth and early sixteenth centuries with the very serious epistemological problem that ancient authors had simply not known of the Americas. Kupperman, "Introduction: The Changing Definition of America," 1–29. On the inclusion of the imagined Americas in sixteenth-century European images of witchcraft, see Zika, "Fashioning New Worlds from Old Fathers."

37 Cornelius Jaenen notes that the early French arrivals' initial impressions tended to be positive and optimistic, then changed with experience. At first, they saw in New France the possibility of a better world for the poor and oppressed of Europe; by the mid-seventeenth century, the experiences of people living in permanent French settlements were challenging earlier perceptions. Jaenen, "The Image of New France," 161–74. Brian Brazeau similarly finds that visitors to New France initially expected to find it much like France, but that these views were later challenged by observations of more and more people who had lived in both places. Brazeau, *Writing a New France*, 23–6.

38 Christopher Parsons points out that this ecotone made for an environment "familiar enough to beckon colonists" yet "different enough to demand their intervention." Parsons, *A Not-So-New World*, 24–5.

39 Samuel de Champlain said in 1613 that "it was difficult to know this country without having wintered there." Samuel de Champlain, "The Voyages, 1613," book 1, in Champlain, *Works*, 1:307. Marie Morin,

at the Hôtel-Dieu of Montréal, expressed a similar sentiment at the end of the century, when she said that the cold of this country cannot be understood except by those who suffer it. Morin, *Annales de l'Hôtel-Dieu de Montréal*, 123.

40 JR 3:39–61. On Jesuits and the reputation of Canada, see Pioffet, "La Nouvelle-France dans l'imaginaire jésuite," 326–43.

41 Frisinger, "Aristotle's Legacy in Meteorology," 198–204; Kupperman, "The Puzzle of the American Climate," 1262–89; Mauelshagen, "Climate as a Scientific Paradigm," 565–88; White, *A Cold Welcome*, 9–10.

42 JR 4:191–5; Sagard, *Le Grand voyage*, 147; JR 5:180–3.

43 Sam White finds that classical theories remained in place when they proved flexible enough to accommodate new observations, and that travellers in North America eventually changed their minds about the need to depart from ancient texts when trying to comprehend weather. White, "Unpuzzling American Climate," 544–66. It is also worth pointing out that Barbe Hallay's arrival in New France coincided with some particularly cold spells. The "Little Ice Age" is well documented for many regions, including the St Lawrence Valley. White, "North American Climate History," 301–3; White, "The Real Little Ice Age," 327–52.

44 Samuel de Champlain noted both when describing a harsh winter on St Croix Island, where the "the cold was severe and more extreme than in France, and lasted much longer." He explained the cold by saying that it was "caused by the north and north-west winds, which pass over high mountains continually covered with snow," and that the winter "lasts much longer than it would if the land were under cultivation." Champlain, *Works*, 1:302–3. The Jesuit Charles Lalemant thought that the winds from the north-east brought the snows, and the winds from the north-west brought the cold. JR 4:191–5.

45 Sagard blamed the problem on the merchants, who, he said, through negligence and a lack of affection for the country, did not spend enough on its culture, peopling, or advancement. Sagard, *Le Grand voyage*, 147; Pioffet, "Gabriel Sagard, l'insoumis," 39–50.

46 "Le 18 et le 20 d'avril, il tonna fort et ferme, avec de grands éclairs; et cependant la rivière estoit encor glacée et la terre couverte de neige. Ce qui fait voir qu'il y a de la chaleur en l'air et que ces neiges et froids sont accidentels et contre la nature du climat." "Voilà les vrayes causes & alimens du froid. Si le pays estoit découvert jusque à ces montagnes, nous aurions peut-estre l'une des plus foecondes vallées qui soient en l'univers." MNF II: 443–4.

47 Asseline de Ronval, *Journal en Abregé*, 23–4; Yon, "Notre premier touriste," 167–8.

48 "car puisque ces terres sont au mesme climat que la France, elles auront aussi la mesme benignité de l'air." JR 49:212–13.

49 Based on his belief that deforestation on the Canary, Madeira, and Azores islands had reduced mists and rains there, Christopher Columbus thought that afternoon rains in the Caribbean were caused by the luxuriant forests. Thompson, "Forests and Climate Change in America," 47–64.

50 Some historians have placed the English theorizing of a connection between clearing the land and warming the climate in the eighteenth century. Coates and Degroot, "Les bois engendrent les frimas et les gelées," 197–219; Golinski, "American Climate and the Civilization of Nature," 153–74. However, English people on both sides of the Atlantic were making connections between deforestation and warming at about the same time as the French in the seventeenth century. Richard Whitbourne suggested in 1620 that land clearing would help moderate the cold in Newfoundland, since exposing the soil to the rays of the sun would "make the Countrey much the hotter Winter and Summer." John Evelyn, a councillor of the Royal Society of London, argued in 1664 that cutting the forests would bring a better climate and better health for colonists. In 1676, the *Philosophical Transactions of the Royal Society of London* published the report of an anonymous correspondent who had heard that many North American colonists were claiming that weather had become more temperate because of the introduction of European agriculture, deforestation, and increased population. Fleming, *Historical Perspectives on Climate Change*, 27–8; Vogel, "The Letter from Dublin," 111–28. For more on colonial understandings of climate in early modern northeastern North America, see Zilberstein, *A Temperate Empire*.

51 Boucher, *Histoire véritable et naturelle*, 19, 141–3, 150–4.

52 RAPQ 1930–31, 33.

53 This optimism was shared by Acadian settler Nicolas Denys, who reminded his readers that Old France had not always produced its current range of foods and drinks, and asked them to understand that in time, and with a lot of work, New France could be as good a country as France, and fertile in all things. Denys, *Histoire Naturelle*, 4–18. For an exploration over the longer term of how Quebec culture went through different phases of acclimatizing to winter, moving from apprehension to adaptation to domestication, see Lamontagne, *L'Hiver dans la culture québécoise*.

54 Quoted in Moogk, "Reluctant Exiles," 463.

55 Dollier de Casson, *Histoire du Montréal*.

56 Harrison, *Until Next Year*, 55; Trudel, *Histoire de la Nouvelle-France III*, 2:482.

57 Dollier de Casson, *Histoire du Montréal*, 131–2; Dechêne, *Le Peuple, l'État et la Guerre*, 65; Oury, *L'Homme qui a conçu Montréal*, 197–8.
58 Charbonneau et al., *The First French Canadians*, 199.
59 Choquette, *Frenchmen into Peasants*, 159–246; Choquette, "The Ancien Régime Culture of Labor Mobility."
60 Marie de l'Incarnation, *Correspondance*, 832–3.
61 Hahn and Cowan, "Foods, Foodways, and Francisation."
62 AUQ *Mémoire de Marchandises* 1/E, 16, 2, 0, 1, 1; 1/E, 16, 2, 0, 1, 12; 1/E, 16, 2, 0, 1, 28. Pierre Boucher knew that sunflowers were originally grown in the Americas. Boucher, *Histoire véritable et naturelle*, 83.
63 Marie de l'Incarnation, *Correspondance*, 832–3.
64 Davidson, "Watermelon"; Maynard and Maynard, "Cucumbers, Melons, and Watermelons," 298–313; Lovegren, *Melon*, 30–2, 50–2, 61, 65, 78–82, 84–9.
65 Passage on the *Saint-André* to Montreal in 1659 cost seventy-five *livres* for adults, fifty for adolescents, and twenty-five for children. Godbout, *Les Passagers du Saint-André*, 2–5. To cover the cost, many entered into indentured labour, in which a sponsor paid for the passage and material upkeep in return for several years of work (usually three) with a salary in addition to food, shelter, and some clothing. Moogk, "Reluctant Exiles," 473–80.
66 The exact year of arrival is unknown for three-quarters of immigrants in seventeenth century; in the case of women, it is unknown more than eight times out of ten. Charbonneau et al., *The First French Canadians*, 54–6; Trudel, *Catalogue des immigrants*.
67 Choquette, *Frenchmen into Peasants*, 11–12; Charbonneau et al., *The First French Canadians*, 54.
68 MNF IX:383, 387; Marie de l'Incarnation, *Correspondance*, 616; Marcel Trudel, *Histoire de la Nouvelle-France III*, 1:258–60; Des Gagniers, *Le voyage au bout du vent*, 116–17.
69 AAQ, *Cathalogue ou Registre des Confirmés*, 4, 7.
70 Fortier, "François de Laval," 18–20; Gosselin, *Vie de Mgr de Laval*, 144. Also arriving at the same time as the Hallay family were Jérôme Lalemant, a Jesuit, and Charles de Lauson de Charny, son of the previous Governor of Canada and a priest. Gosselin, *Vie de Mgr de Laval*, 141–3.
71 Godbout, *Les Passagers du Saint-André*, 2–5.
72 Pauketat and Chapdelaine, "Overview of the St Lawrence Archaic through Woodland," 249–61; Lothrop et al., "Early Human Settlement of Northeastern North America," 192–251.
73 Cook, *The Voyages of Jacques Cartier*, 35–95.

74 Turgeon, *Une histoire de la Nouvelle-France.*

75 On the history of the people of Stadacona, the St Lawrence Iroquoians, see Tremblay, *St Lawrence Iroquoians*; Warrick and Lesage, "The Huron-Wendat and the St Lawrence Iroquoians," 134–44; Steckley, "St Lawrence Iroquoians among the Wendat," 17–25; Sioui, *Huron-Wendat*, 13, 87.

76 Rouleau, "An Archaeological View of the French Colonial Port of Québec," 229–30.

77 Samuel de Champlain, "The Voyages, 1613," in Champlain, *Works*, 1:24–45.

78 Havard and Vidal, *Histoire de l'Amérique française*, 80–6; Fischer, *Champlain's Dream*, 227–53; Greer, *Property and Dispossession*, 145–7. On cultural fluidity of Algonquins and Montagnais as "Saint Lawrence Algonquians," see Lozier, *Flesh Reborn*, 26–31.

79 "Après un an de séjour, les Français ont dû faire pousser du blé [...] et c'est à Uepishtikueiau qu'ils ont dû faire pousser le blé. Leur jardin ne devait pas être très grand alors, dit-on. Les premiers temps, ils ne semaient pas beaucoup [...] Ils ne devaient faire pousser que ce dont ils avaient besoin pour se nourrir eux-mêmes [...] Ils ont dû entourer leur jardin d'une clôture de bois. Puis, tandis que les Innus n'étaient pas là, tandis qu'ils étaient partis dans l'intérieur des terres, ils ont dû l'agrandir, ils ont dû agrandir la terre sur laquelle ils faisaient pousser leur blé [...] Ils ont dû l'agrandir de plus en plus et les Innus, eux, ont dû finir par quitter leur terre de Uepishtikueiau." Jean-Baptiste Bellefleur, Unamanshipit, 1993, in Vincent and Bacon, *Le Récit de Uepishtikueiau*, 23–4.

80 Christopher Parsons has argued that "gardens were an essential element of the expanding footprint of French colonialism in northeastern North America," and that horticulture was a political act. In both metaphor and on the ground, "cultivation became the self-legitimizing practice of French settler colonialism, transferring sovereignty and authority to colonists and missionaries who adopted the role of cultivator and benevolent patriarch." Parsons, *A Not-So-New World*, 2, 8, 9.

81 Asseline de Ronval stayed in the inn run by Jean Gloria in the Lower Town, probably at the corner of Sault-au-Matelot and Côte de la Montagne. Asseline de Ronval, *Journal en Abregé*, 19–20; Yon, "Notre premier touriste," 147–70.

82 LAC C-15801, "Vray plan du haut & bas de Quebec comme il est l'an 1660."

83 Bourdon, "Le Véritable plan de Québec fait en 1663"; Chénier, *Québec*, 20–5.

84 Cloutier and L'Anglais, "The Saint-Louis Forts and Chateaux Site," 106–24; Goyette, "The Origins of the Château Saint-Louis," 125–39.

85 Desrosiers et al., *Sites archéologiques religieux du Québec.*

86 Labelle, *Dispersed but not Destroyed*, 99–109; Trigger, *The Children of Aataentsic*, 801–16; Lozier, *Flesh Reborn*, 119–52.

87 Canadian houses of this style were basically the same as in France, although a shortage of tall trees in France meant that posts there tended to be curved and that short diagonal pieces were used to fill in gaps, while in Canada, thanks to the abundance of timber, the posts could be longer and straighter. Stone houses with slate roofs did not overtake wood or half-timber construction in Québec until the eighteenth century. The main practical advantage of stone construction was that it was less vulnerable to fires. Bédard, *Maisons et églises du Québec*, 7–9; Moogk, *Building a House in New France*, 22-9; Chénier, *Québec*, 152–7; Gauthier-Larouche, *Évolution de la maison rurale*, 15–17; Gaumond, *Place Royale*, 7–10.

88 Simoneau, "The Seminary of Québec Site," 216, 223.

89 Rath, *How Early America Sounded.*

90 Smith, *The Acoustic World of Early Modern England*, 49.

91 MNF VII:205–6, 218, 222; MNF VIII:165; MNF IX:135, 276; JR 47:285.

92 A bell had been installed at Notre-Dame church in the Upper Town by 1645. MNF VI:425. Plante, "Le paysage sonore de la Nouvelle-France," 130–1; Garrioch, "Sounds of the City," 5–25, especially 10–12.

93 Mark Peck and Sanja Hinic-Frlog, emails to author, 23 November 2021.

94 Garrioch, "Sounds of the City," 7.

95 Richer, Duval, and Grenier, *Le Cheval Canadien*, 26–56.

96 Gallat-Morin and Pinson, *La vie musicale en Nouvelle-France*, 25–31.

97 Marie de l'Incaranation, *Correspondance*, 96.

98 Instrumental music was occasionally compromised by cold temperatures once winter arrived. A scribe of the *Journal des jésuites*, with a sensitive ear for intonation, recorded that on Christmas Eve 1645, a wooden flute was found to be out of tune when it reached the church. MNF VI:430.

99 Gallat-Morin and Pinson, *La vie musicale en Nouvelle-France*, 143–4.

100 Gallat-Morin and Pinson, *La vie musicale en Nouvelle-France*, 40; JR 45:36.

101 On the teaching of French to Indigenous people as a means to facilitate communication, governance, and transmission of the Catholic faith, see Cohen, "Penser un empire de Babel," 35–54.

102 Barbaud, *Le choc des patois*; Asselin and McLaughlin, "Patois ou français," 3–58; Chaudenson, "Français d'Amérique du Nord et créoles français," 167–80; Poirier, "La langue parlée en Nouvelle-France," 237–73; Brousseau, "The Sociolect of 17th–18th Century French Settlers," 45–60; David A. Bell, "Lingua Populi, Lingua Dei," 1403–37.

103 Chiang, "The Nose Knows," 405–6.

104 Jenner, "Civilization and Deodorization," 127–44; Dobson, *Contours of Death and Disease in Early Modern England*, 10–18; Tullett, *Smell in Eighteenth-Century England*, 45.

105 Cloutier, "The Foreshore of the St Lawrence," 245–57.

106 "la mauvaise odeur qui exhale des corps qui y ont été inhumés jusques à présent"; "empêcher un air contagieux et pestiféré qui serait à craindre." Têtu and Gagnon, *Mandements*, 33–4; Jenner, "Civilization and Deodorization," 132.

107 Simoneau, "The Seminary of Québec Site," 221.

108 Hahn and Cowan, "Foods, Foodways, and Francisation," 1–8.

109 Desloges, *À table en Nouvelle-France*, 45–76, 113–40; Ferland, *Bacchus en Canada*, 25–131.

110 Tristan Sturm has distinguished between the concepts "the geopolitics of religion," which "refers to conflicts between actors who are clearly and rather unproblematically concerned with theologically inspired representations of how the world should be divided," and "religious geopolitics," which "refers to plainly secular geopolitical discourse and action … that nevertheless can be seen to employ political-theological vocabularies, symbols and action." Sturm, "The Future of Religious Geopolitics," 134–40, quotations on 135. Some have argued that even the idea of religion driving foreign policy had become anachronistic by the seventeenth century and the establishment of the Westphalian system. See, for example Dijkink, "When Geopolitics and Religion Fuse," 192–208, and Pickering, *Understanding Geography and War*, 115–37. The situation in New France would mostly satisfy the definition for the "géopolitique de religion" offered by Yves Lacoste, which is centred principally on territorial rivalries between political powers that refer explicitly or implicitly to religious representations. Lacoste, "Géopolitique des religions," 3. See also Henneton, "Spiritual Geopolitics." For a discussion of the complexities of spiritual geopolitics in early modern empires, see Lachenicht, Henneton, and Lignereux, "Spiritual Geopolitics in the Early Modern Imperial Age."

111 Goodman, *Mission and Conversion*.

112 Lachenicht, "À la découverte de l'Européen," 553–4; Po-chia Hsia, "Mission Frontiers," 191–2.

113 Cook and Biggar, *The Voyages of Jacques Cartier*, 37–8, 135–6.

114 "les descendans des François qui s'habitueront au dit pays, ensemble les Sauvages qui seront amenés à la connoissance de la foi, et en feront profession, seront censés et réputés naturels François." *Édits*, 1:1, 7.

On the implicit exclusion of Protestants from and explicit inclusion of Indigenous people into French subjecthood, see Dewar, *Disputing New France*, 133–53.

115 On the importance of missionaries' diplomatic skills in early modern colonial expansion, see Terpstra, *Global Reformations*, 3.

116 Codignola, "The Holy See and the Conversion of the Indians," 195–242; Eccles, *France in America*, 39.

117 "leur âme est un sol très bon de sa nature, mais chargé de toutes les malices qu'une terre delaissée depuis la naissance du monde peut porter." MNF II:545, 596.

118 On horticulture as a metaphor for missionary activities, see Parsons, *A Not-So-New World*, 69–96.

119 MNF III:51. By the mid-seventeenth century, representatives of church and crown were growing increasingly concerned about the Indigenous Christians in New France, and the destruction of the Huronia mission in 1649 reoriented missionary efforts away from outposts in the interior and towards the French settlers who were becoming more numerous in the St Lawrence Valley. As will be further discussed in chapters 3 and 5, missionaries in the later seventeenth century spent more time in French settlements to preach, counsel, and teach; care for the sick and the poor; worry about moral standards; and provide services associated with major lifecycle events such as baptisms, marriages, and funerals. Codignola, "The Holy See and the Conversion of the Indians," 208–11; Cowan, "Education, *Francisation*," 1–29; Belmessous, "Être français en Nouvelle-France," 510–15, 539; Havard, "Les forcer à devenir Cytoyens," 989–1000; Belmessous, *Assimilation and Empire*, 28–30.

120 MNF IX:383.

121 On processions demarcating the community's territory, see Follain, *Le village sous l'Ancien Régime*, 134–6.

122 Codignola, "The Holy See and the Conversion of the Indians," 205, 209, 211.

123 LAC, SOCG, Ser. 3, Vol. 256, fol. 5rv-12rv.

124 Vincent Grégoire has explained that the Huguenots "in no way represented a threat, except in the slightly paranoid minds of religious authorities." Grégoire, "Mais comment peut-on être protestant en Nouvelle-France," 53.

125 "gens fera et crudelissima, belloque assueta," "hollandis atque anglis haereticis feoderati" LAC, SOCG, Ser 3, Vol. 256 fol 5v "

126 Bédard, *Les protestants en Nouvelle-France*, 28–9, 81.

127 LAC, Ser 2 Acta Vol. 10 fol 169 rv.

128 The phrase "Religion Prétendue Réformée" had been used as early as the 1560s. Although it was objectionable to French Protestants, the Edict of Beaulieu nevertheless mandated it in 1576 as the term to be used in all edicts and legal documents to describe their religion. The term was repeated in the 1598 Edict of Nantes, and its use continued in the seventeenth century. Mentzer and Spicer, "Introduction: Être protestant," 7.

129 Bédard, *Les Protestants en Nouvelle-France*, 25–30.

130 Grégoire, "Mais comment peut-on être protestant en Nouvelle-France," 46–58.

131 "le navire où nous avions été en allant en France était tout huguenot" Bourgeoys, *Textes choisis*, 35–6.

132 "il a voulu reporter à l'Ancienne France le thrésor de la vérité que Dieu luy a fait trouver en la nouvelle" MNF III:82–3.

133 AAQ, "Registre des Abjurations d'Heresie depuis 1662 jusqu'à 1757," 5.

134 Bédard, *Les Protestants en Nouvelle-France*, 65–8.

135 Several members of Barbe Hallay's family were confirmed when they reached Québec. Her father, Jean-Baptiste, and her sister, Marie, were confirmed on 10 August 1659 in the church of Notre-Dame. Her sister Isabelle (Elisabeth) was confirmed on 1 May 1660 at the church of the Ursulines. Her mother, Mathurine Vallet, was confirmed in parish church at Québec in 1665. AAQ, *Cathalogue ou Registre des Confirmés*, 4, 7, 22, 36. The fact that they had not been confirmed in France should not be taken as evidence of opposition to Catholicism or a lack of religious devotion. Confirmation was only administered by a bishop, and so was not always available. Some people waited until well into adulthood before receiving the sacrament, and many were never confirmed. Bamji, "The Catholic Life Cycle," 192; Bergin, *Church, Society and Religious Change in France*, 176, 257–8. The sacrament likely also took on greater significance in New France when compared with France because of Laval's catholicising ambitions for the colony.

136 Godbout, "Les émigrants de 1664," 224.

137 It was decided that in future nobody would be buried in the parish church unless they had paid twenty-six *livres* beforehand to the churchwarden for the right of opening a burial pit, and additionally had the pit dug to a sufficient depth at their own expense. Têtu and Gagnon, *Mandements*, 33–4.

138 For more on the religious culture in New France, although mostly after the time of Barbe Hallay, see Cliche, *Les pratiques de dévotion en Nouvelle-France*.

139 Bossy, *Christianity in the West*; Bouwsma, *The Waning of the Renaissance*, 239–40.

140 For discussions of the distinction in seventeenth-century New England, and of a general lay tendency to see magic and religion as compatible in contrast to the more binary views of Puritan ministers, see Godbeer, *The Devil's Dominion*, 1–9, and Weisman, *Witchcraft, Magic, and Religion in Seventeenth-Century Massachusetts*, 66. For a similar distinction between lay and clerical views that has been influential for historical scholarship on medieval and early modern Europe, see Thomas, *Religion and the Decline of Magic*.

141 Edwards, "Introduction: What Makes Magic Everyday Magic," 1–10; Kieckhefer, "The Specific Rationality of Medieval Magic," 813–36.

142 MNF VI:724. For another procession in May 1662, this one against drought, see the *Journal des jésuites*, 308.

143 ASQ, Polygraphie 6, no. 7. For a procession to bring rain in May 1662, see *Le Journal des jésuites*, 308–9.

144 Baratay, "L'excommunication et l'exorcisme des animaux," 223–54.

145 As religious rituals, exorcisms against animals had several parallels to exorcisms against demons, most significantly adjuring the subject in the name of God, the Trinity, or the saints to depart and cause no further harm to humans. Cohen, "Law, Folklore and Animal Lore," 31–4.

CHAPTER TWO

1 *Ville de Québec*, "Toponymie: Rue du Manoir," 2020, https://www.ville.quebec.qc.ca/citoyens/patrimoine/toponymie/fiche.aspx?IdFiche=4723.

2 BAnQ-Q, P546, D3, P11, Fonds Fred C. Würtele, Montcalm's Headquarters with a distant view of Quebec; BAnQ-Q, P600, S6, D2, P52, Collection initiale, Beauport – Avenue Royale – Manoir Robert Giffard – Domaine Darnoc – Résidence, c1870; Harvey, "Le manoir seigneurial de Beauport," 11–12.

3 For a debate on the usefulness of "the seigneurial system" as a concept, see Greer, "There was no Seigneurial System," Grenier and Laberge, "Beyond the 'system,'" and Greer, "Reply to Benoît Grenier and Alain Laberge," on *Borealia: Early Canadian History*, in September and October 2018 (in French on *HistoireEngagée.ca*).

4 However strong and tidy seigneurialism may have looked in theory, French sovereignty over most of the territory claimed by France in North America remained incomplete and aspirational. Even in the settlements of the St Lawrence Valley, where the French exercised the most effective control, Indigenous communities maintained considerable economic, cultural, and political independence. Grenier, *Brève histoire du régime*

seigneurial, 33, 51–99; Desbarats and Greer, "North America from the Top Down," 109–36; Greer, *Property and Dispossession*, 154–77.

5 *Inventaire du site patrimonial de Beauport*; Trudel, *Le terrier du Saint-Laurent en 1663*, 87–98; Grenier, *Brève histoire du régime seigneurial*, 64.

6 Bessière, "Faire une bonne et fidèle servante," 233–57; Bessière, "La domesticité au Canada," 61–79; Fauve-Chamoux, "Domesticité et parcours de vie," 5–34; Bessière, "Le salaire des domestiques au Canada," 33–50; Gutton, *Domestiques et serviteurs*, 69.

7 "Après ce refus, il voulut parvenir à ses fins par les ruses de son art diabolique." Marie de l'Incarnation, *Correspondance*, 667–8; Ragueneau, *La vie*, 163–4.

8 AMHDQ, *Chroniques de l'Hôtel-Dieu de Québec 1639–1958, Registre no.* 2, 153.

9 Marie de l'Incarnation, *Correspondance*, 813–15, 886–7.

10 Ferber, *Demonic Possession*, 25; Levack, *The Devil Within*, 16–17.

11 Ragueneau, *La vie*, 171–2, discussed in Pearson, "I Willingly Speak to You about her Virtues," 317.

12 Ragueneau, *La vie*, 164.

13 Strocchia, "Women on the Edge," 53–77; Levack, *The Devil Within*, 23–6; Ferber, *Demonic Possession*, 10–11, 17.

14 Levack, *The Devil Within*, quotation on 29. See also viii–ix, 6–15, 29–30, 139–68.

15 "présages funestes." Marie de l'Incarnation, *Correspondance*, 667–8. This comet may have been the same as that now known as Comet C/2002 C1 (Ikeya-Zhang). Kronk, *Cometography*, 348–50; Asher et al., "Comet Ikeya-Zhang," 19–21. Thank you to John Percy for help in tracing this comet.

16 The growing divide between popular and elite thought can be seen in the learned *Journal des Sçavans*, which labelled a belief that a comet in 1680–81 presaged many misfortunes as "a popular error." Daston and Park, *Wonders*, 247, 334, 345; Johnson, "Periwigged Heralds," 399–419. For a dispute in New Spain over the significance of a comet observed in 1680, see More, "Cosmopolitanism and Scientific Reason in New Spain."

17 MNF IX:574–5.

18 Chamberland, *Lithobolia*; Davidson and Duffin, "Stones and Spirits," 99–109; Baker, *The Devil of Great Island*; Hunter, "New Light," 311–53. The sources from Québec do not describe the sounds of the drum heard in this infestation, but it is interesting to ponder whether they sounded more like European or Indigenous North American drumming.

19 Ferber, "Possession and the Sexes," 214–38; Lederer, *Madness, Religion and the State in Early Modern Europe*, 148–52; Monter, *Witchcraft in*

France and Switzerland, 139; Sluhovsky, "A Divine Apparition or Demonic Possession?," 1039–55. The same trend held true for New England, where women and children were thought especially likely to be possessed. Reis, *Damned Women*, 110–20; Godbeer, *The Devil's Dominion*, 113–18; Karlsen, *The Devil in the Shape of a Woman*, 135–6. Men could be possessed too, and the gendered dimension of possession may not always have been a particularly strong feature. See Brogan, "His Belly, Her Seed," 1–25.

20 Quoted in Ferber, "Possession and the Sexes," 222.

21 Levack, *The Devil Within*, 6–15, 191–214; Ferber, *Demonic Possession*, 26; Gasser, *Vexed with Devils*, 17–20.

22 Hutton, *The Witch*, 3–43. Witches were also, in a sense, normal. As Robin Briggs has said when discussing Lorraine, "witchcraft was so much a part of everyday life for the mass of the population that it became relatively domesticated, as just one of the dangers one faced; there were ways of dealing with it, and it was part of the magical universe that was largely taken for granted." Briggs, "Emotion and Affect in Lorraine Witchcraft Trials," 137–53, quotation on 150–1.

23 Levack, *The Devil Within*, 170–84, 191–3; Ferber, *Demonic Possession*, 26, 115–17; Monter, "Witchcraft Trials in France," 218–31. Demonologists wrote about male witches, and historians have found that men could be vulnerable to accusations either in conformity with notions of masculinity, or because they moved away from cultural expectations for masculine behaviour. Kounine, "Satanic Fury," 57–76; Schulte, *Man as Witch*, 92–159; Kent, "Tyrannical Beasts," 77–94; Kent, "Masculinity and Male Witches," 69–92; Walinski-Kiehl, "Males, 'Masculine Honor,' and Witch Hunting in Seventeenth-Century Germany," 254–71; Voltmer, "Witch-Finders, Witch Hunters or Kings of the Sabbath?" 74–99; Labouvie, "Men in Witchcraft Trials," 49–68. Robin Briggs has found no pattern of behaviour among male witches in Lorraine that violates masculine expectations. Briggs, "Male Witches in the Duchy of Lorraine," 31–51.

24 Vuil was probably not the first miller at the seigneurie of Beauport. There had been a mill there since at least 1655, by which time grains were being milled at the common mill ("moulin banal") of Seigneur Giffard. ASQ, Polygraphie 3, no. 107.

25 Freedman, "The Miller," 373–4; Goubert, *The French Peasantry in the Seventeenth Century*, 138–40; Grenier, *Brève histoire du régime seigneurial*, 82, 86–7, 218; Dechêne, "L'évolution du régime seigneurial au Canada," 164; Dechêne, *Habitants and Merchants*, 140–1.

26 The most famous miller from early modern Europe is Menocchio, memorably presented in Ginzburg's *The Cheese and the Worms*. This miller got into trouble with the Inquisition because of his beliefs, but he seems to have been a fairly well-respected member of his community.

27 "elle luy fut refusée" "Il en fut tellement irrité, que pour se vanger de ce refus, il voulut avoir par ses malignitez ce qu'il n'avoit pu obtenir par la bonne voie." Marie de l'Incarnation, *Correspondance*, 667–8, 813–15.

28 White, "Language of Emotions," 33–5.

29 "Irritated, adj." in *Oxford English Dictionary*.

30 The definition for "irriter" is "Provoquer, exciter la colére d'une personne," and the definition for "colére" is "Désir de vangeance de laquelle nous croions pouvoir venir à bout, mais un désire triste & mélé de déplaisir dans la pensée que nous avons qu'on nous a méprisé & traité indignement, ou quelqu'un de ceux qui nous apartiennent." Richelet, *Dictionnaire françois*, 442, 149. The *Dictionnaire universel* of 1690 similarly defines "irriter" as "to anger, offend, put into anger," "fascher, offenser, mettre en colere," Furetière, *Dictionnaire universel*, n.p. Cotgrave's 1611 French-English dictionary also makes it clear that the word in French means that a person is expressing a strong push to anger, rendering "irrité" as "stirred, incensed, urged, nettled, provoked, angered." Cotgrave, *A Dictionarie*, n.p. Examples for "irriter" in *Le Dictionnaire de l'Académie française* of 1694 show that the emotion being created was a heated and potentially violent anger: for example, do not irritate that man, our sins have irritated God, to irritate the wasps, to irritate a lion, a bull. *Dictionnaire de l'Académie françoise*, vol. 1, 1694, 209, 613.

31 The scribes of the annals of the Ursulines and of the Hôtel-Dieu wrote that God was irritated against the country preceding an earthquake. AUQ, *Annales des Ursulines de Québec 1639–1822*, 1/E, 1, 3, 2.0001 14r; Juchereau de Saint-Ignace and Duplessis, *Les annales de l'Hôtel-Dieu de Québec*, 123. Charles Lalemant wrote about the anger of God, justly irritated against the colonists for their faults. MNF II:217. François de Laval wrote that God, justly irritated, would withdraw his grace and save his harshest punishments for the church if the French continued to trade in hard liquor. "Mandement Pour Excommunier Ceux Qui Vendent Des Boissons Enivrantes Aux Sauvages" in Têtu and Gagnon, *Mandements*, 14–15. For a human, rather than God, to be "irrité" was considered sufficiently incendiary that the emotion could lead to a desire to kill someone with an ax. MNF IV:129.

32 Pollock, "Anger and the Negotiation of Relationships in Early Modern England," 567–90, quotation on 571.

33 Perfetti, "Introduction," 1–22; Harvey, "The Body," 165–7; Scheer, "Are Emotions a Kind of Practice," 193–220; Rosenwein, "Problems and Methods," 1–31; Lynch, "Emotional Community," 3–6. Lyndal Roper has said that the witch was an embodiment of the emotion of envy in *The Witch in the Western Imagination*, 91, 112. It is not clear that Vuil was envious, exactly, but Marie de l'Incarnation thought that the physical harm befalling Hallay through the demonic tormentors was ultimately caused by an emotion – the irritation of the witch Vuil.

34 Macfarlane, *Witchcraft in Tudor and Stuart England*, 173–4. Historians have sometimes tried to use findings from modern psychology and neurophysiology to argue that witchcraft was real in the sense that people suffered real harm from believing themselves to be bewitched. Bever, "Bullying, the Neurobiology of Emotional Aggression, and the Experience of Witchcraft," 193–212; Bever, *The Realities of Witchcraft*. Others caution against presuming that emotions are universal, biological, invariable, and therefore somehow ahistorical. Rosenwein, *Generations of Feeling*, 1–3. One need not wander too far into debates about the value of applying modern findings to people of the past, or the relative weights of biological and social dimensions in emotions, to see connections between anger and witchcraft in this case.

35 Ferber, "Demonic Possession, Exorcism, and Witchcraft," 586. It is not clear whether Hallay attributed to Vuil the motivation of being irritated, but, if she did, she would have gained both an explanation for what was happening and also a target against whom she and others in her community could direct anger and fear, possibly someone to punish for the problem. Ostling and Kounine, "Introduction," 10. In English witchcraft narratives, it was usually the devil or "demonic proxies" that allowed the accused witches to distance themselves from their malicious intentions. On how the devil was believed to help witches act on their anger and malice in England, see Millar, *Witchcraft, the Devil, and Emotions in Early Modern England*, 82–115.

36 Wiesner-Hanks, *Christianity and Sexuality in the Early Modern World*, 134–5, 151–4; Desan, "Making and Breaking Marriage," 1–3; Lebrun, "Amour et mariage," 294–317; Hanley, "Engendering the State," 4–27; Burguière, "L'État monarchique et la famille," 313–35; Minvielle, *La famille en France*, 38–43; Bardet, "Early Marriage in Pre-Modern France," 347–8; Sperling, "Marriage at the Time of the Council of Trent," 67–108. For an overview of changes to marriage legislation in France, see Lefebvre-Teillard, "Marriage in France from the Sixteenth to the Eighteenth Century."

37 ANOM, Section Outre-mer, Dépôt de papiers publics des colonies, G[I] 460, F°13. Recensement du Canada. 1666; ANOM, Section Outre-mer, Dépôt de papiers publics des colonies, G[I] 460, image 19 on *New France Archives*. Recensement du Canada. 1667.

38 Trudel, *La population du Canada en 1666*, 45–6.

39 Charbonneau et al., *The First French Canadians*, 51.

40 Paul Ragueneau said that Hallay was sixteen, but he wrote this more than a decade after Hallay's arrival in a biography of Catherine de Saint-Augustin that he published in 1671, and there is no evidence that he knew Hallay or anyone from her family well. Ragueneau, *La vie*, 105. The twentieth-century historian Marcel Trudel placed her age at twelve. Trudel, *Catalogue des immigrants*, 403.

41 In comparison with France, men in New France were marrying later, and women were marrying earlier. Charbonneau et al., *The First French Canadians*, 97–100. This change resulted in a wider gap between the age of spouses in New France so that women born before 1660 were on average twelve to thirteen years younger than first husbands. Roy and Charbonneau, "La nuptialité," 285–94.

42 "Cet homme vouloit épouser une fille qui étoit passée avec son père et sa mère dans le même vaisseau, disant qu'elle lui avoit été promise: mais parce que c'étoit un homme de mauvaises mœurs, on ne le voulut jamais écouter." Marie de l'Incarnation, *Correspondance*, 668.

43 Cartier, "Québec 1608–2008," 135.

44 By 1663, the French population of New France had risen to a little over 3,000, with almost 200 in the region of Québec. Choquette, *Frenchmen into Peasants*, 165; Trudel, *The Beginnings of New France*, 256–7; Charbonneau et al., *The First French Canadians*, 34–6; Roy and Charbonneau, "La nuptialité," 285. On the difficulties of attracting migrants and keeping them in Canada, see Moogk, "Reluctant Exiles," 463–505; Ouellet, "Un pouvoir de remplacement," 145–68.

45 As Simon Denys explained to his brother-in-law in a letter of 1651, girls were sought in marriage in New France regardless of their fortunes, provided that they were wise. ("modo sapientes sint") MNF VIII:87; Campeau, "Un témoignage," 611.

46 Charbonneau et al., *The First French Canadians*, 37, 65, 79–83, 90, 187.

47 Minvielle, *La famille en France*, 25. French writers of the time often used the word "*amitié*" to describe a desirable bond between spouses, a word that implied an expectation of mutual respect and intent to care for one another even while assuming that the husband would have authority over the wife. Desan, "Making and Breaking Marriage," 9, 11.

48 Marie de l'Incarnation, *Correspondance*, 813.

49 Deslandres, "… alors nos garçons se marieront à vos filles, & nous ne ferons plus qu'un peuple," 5–35; Aubert, "The Blood of France," 439–78; Cowan, "Education, *Francisation*," 1–29.

50 In 1663, for example, the crown started to give more ample portions of cleared land or "gratifications," and established pensions for parents of large families. ANOM, Colonies, C^{11A} 2, F°41-42v. Mémoire proposant divers moyens d'assurer la conservation et le développement du Canada. 1663.

51 This population growth happened almost entirely within the bounds of marriage, and pre-marital conceptions were rare. In the period between 1621 and 1699, under 5 per cent of babies were conceived before marriage. This low rate can be attributed largely to the low age at first marriage, both because younger adolescents have a somewhat lower fertility, and also because younger people would be more likely to be under the control of their parents. Bates, "Les conceptions prénuptiales," 253–72.

52 Trudel, *Histoire de la Nouvelle-France, III*, 1:317; Contrat de mariage entre Joachim Girard, fils de Michel Girard et de Françoise Anseaume, de la paroisse de Vaudrun en Normandie, évêché Deureux, et Marie Hallé (18 ans), fille de Baptiste Hallé et de Mathurine Valet, de la paroisse de St Julien de Coudray proche de la ville de Chartre en Beausse, BAnQ Montréal, 12 09 1660 (1634–63) Audouart dit Saint-Germain, G.; microfilm M-116.2 v.

53 Levack, *The Devil Within*, 171–85. There must have been a certain appeal in feigning possession. A French case from the end of the sixteenth century raised possibilities both of a performance that the demoniac knew to be false, and a performance that she herself believed. Some neighbours testified that a woman had faked possession in order to manipulate emotions and recover lost honour, and others testified that she had been persuaded of being truly bewitched. Walker and Dickerman, "A Woman under the Influence," 534–54.

54 Ferber, "Possession and the Sexes," 214–38; Sluhovsky, "A Divine Apparition or Demonic Possession?," 1043–5, 1050.

55 "Bella horrida et cruenta intersegerunt barbari." LAC, SOCG, Ser. 3, Vol. 256, fol. 5rv-12rv.

56 Havard and Vidal, *Histoire de l'Amérique française*, 97; Havard, *The Great Peace of Montreal of 1701*, 47–50; Trudel, *Histoire de la Nouvelle-France III*, 1:258-61; Dechêne, *Le Peuple, l'État et la Guerre*, 94–105. For a compelling study of how the traumatic memories of settlers who survived attacks could contribute to colonial insecurities and even fears of witchcraft, see Norton, *In the Devil's Snare*.

57 MNF IX:519.

58 AMHDQ, *Chroniques de l'Hôtel-Dieu de Québec 1639–1958, Registre no. 2, Première Partie : 1639–1698*, 3–4, 8.

59 AUQ, *Annales des Ursulines de Québec 1639–1822*, 1/E, 1, 3, 2.0001, 12V.

60 Marie de l'Incarnation, *Correspondance*, 619–21, 625. The *Journal des jésuites* for May 1660 mentions the Ursulines and Hospitalières coming to the Jesuit College to sleep. MNF IX:519.

61 Marie de l'Incarnation, *Correspondance*, 633–4.

62 Marie de l'Incarnation, *Correspondance*, 672.

63 Marie de l'Incarnation, *Correspondance*, 666–7.

64 MNF IX:519–20.

65 MNF IX:520.

66 Marie de l'Incarnation, *Correspondance*, 666.

67 MNF IX:573–4.

68 MNF IX:420–1.

69 Trudel, *Histoire de la Nouvelle-France, III*, 1:260; Richter, *The Ordeal of the Longhouse*, especially 64–5; Lignereux, "Une mission périlleuse," 5–26; Dechêne, *Le Peuple, l'État et la Guerre*, 93–109. For discussions and estimates, see Dickinson, "La guerre iroquoise et la mortalité," 31–54.

70 "La vie en ce pays la ést plus en danger que celle de l'oiseau sur la branche." LAC, CA ANC MG18-J2, 31, Asseline de Ronval, Journal en Abregé dés Voyages de Monsieur Asselinne de Ronval tant par Terre que par Mér, avec Plusieurs Remarques, Circonstances et Avantures très Curieuses; Yon, "Notre premier touriste en Nouvelle-France," 69.

71 Dechêne, *Le Peuple, l'État et la Guerre*, 94, 102.

72 "On ne leur dit rien aussi, car il n'est pas facile de convaincre des personnes en cette nature de crime." Marie de l'Incarnation, *Correspondance*, 668.

73 "une tourre quarrée pour deffense et pour servir de prison." "Inventaire et état des lieux du fort St Louis," 155; Lachance, "Les prisons au Canada sous le Régime français," 561–5.

74 According to Gustave Lanctôt, Vuil was arrested for relapsing into heresy, left prison, and was subsequently imprisoned again and executed for trade in alcohol. Lanctôt, "Une accusation contre Mgr de Laval," 11–25. Raymond Boyer wrote that Vuil was imprisoned under an accusation of magic, witchcraft, and profaning of the sacraments, but that he was shot for having violated the ordinance against trading alcohol with Indigenous people. Boyer, *Les crimes et les châtiments*, 297. The entry on Vuil in the *Dictionnaire Biographique du Canada* says that Vuil's execution was for trading alcohol, and that he had possibly been imprisoned earlier for the

same reason. Vachon, "Vuil, Daniel," in DCB, vol. 1. Denys Delâge and Étienne Gilbert listed Vuil among those who were prosecuted for illegal trade in alcohol, and said that for his sentence he was shot. Delâge and Gilbert, "Les Amérindiens face à la justice coloniale française dans le gouvernement de Québec, 1663–1759," 34.

75 Marcel Trudel wrote that Vuil was convicted for crimes of a religious nature, and Vincent Grégoire argued that accusations of magic and witchcraft were at the origin of Vuil's imprisonment, but that he was condemned to death for his relapse into heresy, blaspheming, and profaning the sacraments. Trudel, *Histoire de la Nouvelle-France III*, 1:316–19; Grégoire, "Le meunier, la domestique et l'hospitalière," 68–73; Grégoire, "Mais comment peut-on être protestant en Nouvelle-France," 56. Strangely, the English translation of Trudel's book says that "The Huguenot Vuil, caught red-handed selling spirits to the Indians, was 'arquebused' in October 1661 on the Governor's order." Trudel, *The Beginnings of New France*, 277. The editorial notes in the *Monumenta Novae Franciae* say that relapse into heresy was the likely reason for the execution. MNF IX:638. Peter Moogk found that the crimes were blasphemy, profaning of holy objects, and providing liquor to Indigenous people. Moogk, "The Crime of Lèse-Majesté in New France," 67. Marie-Aimée Cliche thought that Vuil was condemned for religious crimes. Cliche, *Les pratiques de dévotion en Nouvelle-France*, 70. Leslie Choquette determined that Vuil was the only person in New France to have been executed for sorcery. Choquette, *Frenchmen into Peasants*, 131; Choquette, "From Sea Monsters and Savages to Sorcerers and Satan," 55–6.

76 Trudel, *Histoire de la Nouvelle-France III*, 1:316–19; Grégoire, "Le meunier, la domestique et l'hospitalière," 68–73; Grégoire, "Mais comment peut-on être protestant en Nouvelle-France," 56; Choquette, *Frenchmen into Peasants*, 131; Choquette, "From Sea Monsters and Savages to Sorcerers and Satan," 55–6.

77 Moogk, "The Crime of Lèse-Majesté in New France," 67.

78 Ragueneau, *La vie*, 163–4.

79 The journal was perhaps used as a memory aide for the superior when he wrote his annual report for the principal in Paris, and it would therefore have been a source for the annual *Relations*. Pouliot, "Le Journal des Jésuites," 45; Pouliot, "Du Journal des Jésuites à la Relation," 345; MNF VI:413.

80 His surprise may have been due to the means, since hanging was the normal means of execution. Lachance, *Déliquants, juges et bourreaux*, 148. No explanation is provided for why the condemned was shot rather

than hanged in this case, but it is possible that no hangman was available. The editor of the entry in the *Monumenta Novae Franciae* suggests that the means of Vuil's execution was because he had been a soldier. MNF IX:638.

81 Laverdière and Casgrain, *Le journal des jésuites*, 303.

82 JR 46:186–7.

83 "Journal des Jésuites 1661" in MNF IX:638. The editorial footnote explains that the annotation was made by someone other than the scribe who wrote the main entry.

84 Lucien Campeau, in his editorial introduction to the *Journal des jésuites* in the *Monumenta Novae Franciae*, says that when Lalemant was first superior, the marginal notes were almost all in his hand, but that later these notes were added by a hand other than that of the superior. MNF VI:413.

85 ASQ, MS-48, *Journal des jésuites*, 154, 158; Laverdière and Casgrain, *Le journal des jésuites*, 303; MNF IX:630, 638.

86 "Grande brouillerie entre les puissances." MNF IX:630.

87 Trudel, *Histoire de la Nouvelle-France III*, 1:300–1.

88 Marie de l'Incarnation, *Correspondance*, 614.

89 For more on Gallican and Ultramontane views, see Hildesheimer, *Rendez à César*, 133–260; Fay, *A History of Canadian Catholics*, 5–28; Jaenen, "Church-State Relations in Canada."

90 Quoted in Trudel, *Histoire de la Nouvelle-France III*, 1:309.

91 RAPQ 1939–40, 191.

92 Quoted in Trudel, *Histoire de la Nouvelle-France III*, 1:308n13.

93 Marie de l'Incarnation, *Correspondance*, 633.

94 Marie de l'Incarnation, *Correspondance*, 632, 653.

95 Laverdière and Casgrain, *Le journal des jésuites*, 263–4, 269, 270, 273, 279, 288, 291; Têtu and Gagnon, *Mandements*, 29–30.

96 Laverdière and Casgrain, *Le journal des jésuites*, 268–9.

97 Jaenen, *The Role of the Church in New France*, 1985, 11.

98 "Gubernator fuit semper nobis iniquior et Societati nostrae et Domino Petraensi episcopo," quoted in Rochemonteix, *Les Jésuites et la Nouvelle-France*, 2:307n2.

99 "Mémoire du roi pour servir d'instruction à Talon," RAPQ 1930–31, 5.

100 The tithe shows how the conflict continued in New France. Laval tried to introduce a tithe when he arrived, but he only succeeded in a couple of places along the Beaupré coast. Four years later, in 1663, a royal proclamation established that the tithe would be set at the rate of one-thirteenth of the harvest. This was already lower than the rate in France,

which was one-eleventh, but colonists objected. Laval lowered the rate to one-twentieth, but this was still too much: in Trois-Rivières, parishioners refused to post, publish, or even read the royal edict on the tithe. After a petition, the civil authorities (rather than Laval) lowered the rate in 1667 to one twenty-sixth. Choquette, "From Sea Monsters and Savages to Sorcerers and Satan," 51–2; Trudel, *Histoire de la Nouvelle-France III*, 2:450–1; Trudel, *Histoire de la Nouvelle-France IV*, 749–52.

101 "cuius crimina utrumque forum sibi vindicabat. Longa historia de qua alibi fuse." ASQ, MS-48, Journal des jésuites, 154; Laverdière and Casgrain, *Le journal des jésuites*; MNF IX:630, 638.

102 There were probably written records, if this procedure followed the usual and slightly later course of taking down evidence in writing, verifying the statements of witnesses, and showing these to the accused. Girard, Phillips, and Brown, *A History of Law in Canada, 1*:121–2.

103 ASQ, Polygraphie 2, no. 33. "Inventaires de toutes les pieces mentionées qui ont esté envoyées touchant les affaires qu'on a eu avec Mr d'Argenson."

104 Trudel, *Histoire de la Nouvelle-France III*, 1:318–19; Jaenen, *The Role of the Church in New France*, 1985, 14.

105 Choquette, *Frenchmen into Peasants*, 131; Choquette, "From Sea Monsters and Savages to Sorcerers and Satan," 55–6; Trudel, *Histoire de la Nouvelle-France III*, 1:308–16, 323–30; Mathieu, "Voyer d'Argenson, Pierre de," in DCB, vol. 2.

106 Moogk, "The Liturgy of Humiliation," 89–90.

107 AAQ Registre A, 186–9; ASQ, Documents Faribault, no. 38, 41, 70, 73; Têtu and Gagnon, *Mandements*, 14–15, 30–2, 40, 41–2, 43–4; Trudel, *Histoire de la Nouvelle-France III*, 1:308–16, 323–30.

108 AAQ Registre A, 186–9.

109 Other crimes in this category included apostacy, heresy, atheism, magic, witchcraft, sacrilege, blasphemy, crimes against nature, and simony. Moogk, "The Crime of Lèse-Majesté in New France," 56.

110 Garnot, *Justice et Société en France aux XVIe, XVIIe et XVIIIe Siècles*, 34; Garnot, *Crime et Justice aux XVIIe et XVIIIe Siècles*, 60–2.

111 ASQ, Polygraphie 4, nos. 1–1C.

112 The parish registers of Notre-Dame de Montréal record for 31 August 1660 an annulment of the marriage because of the "perpetual impotence caused by malefice." Séguin, *La sorcellerie au Québec*, 65–81; Choquette, "From Sea Monsters and Savages to Sorcerers and Satan," 43.

113 The court was likely the seneschal's court. Dickinson, "New France: Law, Courts, and the *Coutume de Paris*," 32–54.

114 Choquette, "From Sea Monsters and Savages to Sorcerers and Satan," 57. A succinct summary of the relationship between witch-hunting and power in Scotland, where witch hunts were particularly intense, is provided by Julian Goodare: "Witch-hunting in Scotland was about power: state power over the common folk, religious power over deviant belief, and the whole community's power over the uncanny magical threats that lurked in an uncertain world." Goodare, "Men and the Witch-Hunt in Scotland," 149–70, quotation on 164.
115 Lacey and Pickard, "The Chimera of Proportionality," 216–40; Kettering, *French Society*, 129.
116 Moogk, "The Crime of Lèse-Majesté in New France," 56; Friedland, *Seeing Justice Done*, 13–14, 144–5.

CHAPTER THREE

1 "En ce moys fut amenée de Beauport Barbe Halé, infestée d'un démon folet depuis cinq ou six moys, mais à diverses reprises. Elle fut mise au commencement dans une chambre du vieux hospital, où elle passoit la nuit avec compagnie d'une garde de son sexe et quelque prestre et serviteurs." "Journal des Jésuites 1660," in MNF IX:526.
2 "follet" in Furetière, *Dictionnaire universel.*
3 "Sorte d'esprit qu'on croit qui reviennent & font du bruit dans les maisons, &c." Richelet, *Dictionnaire françois*, 302.
4 "Esprit folet," in the entry for "Folet," in Cotgrave, *A Dictionarie*, n.p.
5 If the scribe was Jérôme Lalement, superior of the Jesuits in Canada at the time, this characterization of the spirit as essentially harmless is especially noteworthy. While he was in the mission field among Indigenous people a few decades earlier, Lalemant was apt to presume that New France was a diabolical place where demonic power was real and pervasive. Cowan, "Jesuit Missionaries and the Accommodationist Demons," 214, 223, 224.
6 "Longa historia, de qua alibi fuse." MNF IX:526.
7 "de quelque mallefice," AMHDQ, *Chroniques de l'Hôtel-Dieu de Québec 1639–1958, Registre no.* 2, 153.
8 "dune estrange maladie," AUQ, *Annales des Ursulines de Québec 1639–1822*, 1/E, 1, 3, 2.0001, 21r.
9 Marie de l'Incarnation, *Correspondance*, 886.
10 Ragueneau, *La vie*, 334.
11 "malade" Ragueneau, *La vie*, 164.
12 Marie de l'Incarnation, *Correspondance*, 668.
13 Rousseau, *La croix et le scalpel*, 66.
14 Ragueneau, *La vie*, 163–5.

15 Rousseau, *La croix et le scalpel*, 88, 92, 99.

16 "Le jour le démon ne paroissoit pas, mais la nuit il faisoit du ravage, agittant cette fille d'une étrange manière, et lui donnant une vue importune de ce magicien qui lui apparoissoit accompagné de beaucoup d'autres." Marie de l'Incarnation, *Correspondance*, 813–15. The magician is not named in this passage, but people may have been linking the appearance to Daniel Vuil. See chapter 2.

17 Marie de l'Incarnation, *Correspondance*, 886–7.

18 Marie de l'Incarnation, *Correspondance*, 813–15.

19 "En effet elle en eut un soin digne d'un cœur vrayement Chrétien, & d'une charitable Hospitaliere," Ragueneau, *La vie*, 164–5, quotation on 164.

20 The relative importance of these different functions was shifting in the seventeenth century, with a growing emphasis on the medical dimension. McHugh, *Hospital Politics*, 8–11, 55–80; Brockliss and Jones, *The Medical World of Early Modern France*, 247–52; Jones, *The Charitable Imperative*, 38–43, 130–9. The "medicalization model" should not be pushed too far, appealing though it may be to think of the history of hospitals as one that leads progressively and triumphantly toward clinical good health. Medical care had been an important part of medieval hospitals too, and right through the early modern period European hospitals remained closely connected to wider social institutions, especially religious institutions. For more on the "medicalization model" and its critics, see Lindemann, *Medicine and Society in Early Modern Europe*, 157–65.

21 MNF II:557–8.

22 "Hélas! mon Dieu, si les excès, si les superfluitez de quelquez dames de France s'employoient à cet œuvre si sainct, quelle grande bénédiction feroient-elles fondre sur leur famille! Quelle gloire en la face des anges d'avoir recueilly le sang du Fils de Dieu pour l'appliquer à ces pauvres infidelles! Se peut-il faire que les biens de la terre nous touchent de plus près que la propre vie? Voilà des vierges tendres et délicates, toutes prestes à jeter leur vie au hazard sur les ondes de l'océan, de venir chercher de petites âmes dans les rigueurs d'un air bien plus froid que l'air de la France, de subir des travaux qui étonnent des hommes mesmes. Et on ne trouvera point quelque brave dame qui donne un passeport à ces amazones du grand Dieu, leur dotant une maison, pour louer et servir sa divine Majesté en cet autre monde? Je ne sçaurois me persuader que Nostre-Seigneur n'en dispose quelqu'une pour ce sujet." MNF III:46–7, quotation on 47.

23 Rousseau, *La croix et le scalpel*, 35–42.

24 This sum proving insufficient, she donated a further 18,100 *livres* in 1640. AMHDQ, "Copie contrat de fondation de l'Hôtel-Dieu de Québec par la

Duchesse d'Aiguillon," HDQ-F1-A2/1:1; "Copie du contrat de donation aux religieuses de Québec par Madame la Duchesse d'Aiguillon," HDQ-F1-A2/1:2; "Copie du contrat par lequel nos mères acceptent et ratifient le contrat du 30 janvier 1640," HDQ-F1-A2/1:3; Rousseau, *L'œuvre de chère en Nouvelle-France*, 84. On French laywomen's contributions to missionary work, see Deslandres, "Inspiration, fondation, relais."

25 McHugh, *Hospital Politics*, 36; Brockliss and Jones, *The Medical World of Early Modern France*, 255–62; Jones, "Perspectives on Poor Relief, Health Care and the Counter-Reformation in France," 217–18; Dinges, "Health Care and Poor Relief," 255–6.

26 Jean d'Aubry, *Le Triomphe de l'Archée et la merveille du monde, ou, La Médecine universelle et veritable* (Paris, 1659), quoted in Jones, "Perspectives on Poor Relief, Health Care and the Counter-Reformation in France," 223.

27 Deslandres, "In the Shadow of the Cloister," 130–3, 137.

28 "d'attrirer a la vraye religion les peuples sauuages & infidelles de la nouuelle France," "Abregé de la Copie des Lettres Royaux pour l'establissement de Nostre Monastere de Kebéc en 1639," in AMHDQ, *Chroniques de l'Hôtel-Dieu de Québec 1639–1958, Registre no. 1*, 11.

29 "Si un monastère semblable à celuy-là estoit en la Nouvelle-France, leur charité feroit plus pour la conversion des sauvages que toutes nos courses et nos paroles." MNF III:56.

30 "les descendans des François qui s'habitueront au dit pays, ensemble les Sauvages qui seront amenés à la connoissance de la foi, et en feront profession, seront censés et réputés naturels François." *Édits*, 1:1, 7. See chapter 1, as well as Deslandres, "Female Voices and Agencies," 50-2.

31 On the hospital as part of the larger function of religion in colonization, see Axtell, *The Invasion Within*, 58–62. Bronwen McShea shows how the Jesuit missions were firmly ensconced within imperial interests, and how imperial motivations were highly placed among Jesuit priorities, in *Apostles of Empire*.

32 "l'un des mieux réglez de l'Europe" MNF III:56.

33 Roy, *À Travers l'histoire de l'Hôtel-Dieu de Québec*, 8. They were known as the "Filles de la Miséricorde," the Daughters of Mercy, and later the "Religieuses de la Miséricorde de Jésus," the Nuns of the Mercy of Jesus.

34 MNF IV:510; Rousseau, *La croix et le scalpel*, 46–53; Robert, "Le site de l'ancienne mission des Jésuites à Sillery," 13.

35 MNF IV:194; see also MNF IV:535–7.

36 MNF II:306. Le Jeune also reminisced of this idea in his *Relation* of 1640, MNF IV:564.

37 MNF II:559–60.

38 MNF IV:78, 106. Not long after, the idea of converting Indigenous people who were not sedentary began to take hold among French missionaries. As the leader at Tadoussac told Le Jeune in late 1640 or early 1641, they could be invited to pray to God, but they would not leave their country to go to Sillery. Charles Meiachka8at, also from Tadoussac but living at Sillery, tried to convince others at Tadoussac to leave. He said that it was the devil who kept them there by giving them thoughts that they would be poor if they left their country, and by making them think that the riches of the earth were of great importance. His compatriots concluded not that they needed to move closer to the French, but rather that it was the Jesuits who would have to go to Tadoussac to teach them. And this is what the Jesuits did: they built a house at Tadoussac where two priests stayed from spring until fall. MNF V:150–1, 447.

39 Jesuits used this phrase several times when defending the rights of Indigenous residents of Sillery to fish for eels against incursions by settlers who were supported by the governor: "On sçaura que de temps immémorial les sauvages ont eu une entière liberté de faire leur pesche d'anguille en toute ceste coste," "ce lieu ayant esté de temps immémorial occuppé par les sauvages qui y faisoient le principal de leur pesche dont ils tirent leur nourriture une grand partie de l'année," "le droit qu'ils y ont de temps immémorial et dont ils ont joui jusques à présent toutes les années précédentes," MNF VII:673, 681–2, 684–5, 686, 688.

40 Lozier, *Flesh Reborn*, 53–4.

41 "La terre est meilleure à Québec, mais les sauvages se plaisent de résider à Sillery." MNF IV:513. A mémoire by Paul Ragueneau from 1650 also explains the Indigenous preference for settling at this place. MNF VII:685; Lozier, *Flesh Reborn*, 56–7.

42 Sillery had a church and facilities for brewing beer, like many European towns, but only some houses were built like French houses and others employed a hybrid construction. MNF IV:513, 578; MNF V:655–6, 647; MNF VII:204, 210; MNF VIII:98–9; Jetten, *Enclaves amérindiennes*, 41.

43 In 1644, the residents presented bundles of corn at the altar in the chapel at Sillery, and they must have had some wheat fields by 1646, because in that year a cow belonging to a neighbouring French farmer got into a wheat crop and caused damage. MNF VI:98; MNF VI:727. A good deal of evidence shows that agriculture was not the only or even the most important means of providing food. In 1651, a Jesuit wrote to his superior in Rome that some people at Sillery were cultivating fields, as well as engaging in fishing and trade, but that in the winter they transferred their huts to the woods. MNF VIII:94; Beaulieu, *Convertir les fils de Caïn*, 139–40. On going to the woods for several months during the winter to

hunt, see also MNF IV:595–6; MNF V:655–6; MNF VI:77–8, 80; MNF VII:207; MNF VIII:94; Jetten, *Enclaves amérindiennes*, 42–4. Storehouses were used to store the eel catch, and the importance of eel comes through again and again in the records. MNF V:657–8; MNF VII:685. For more on the importance of the eel fishery to the Indigenous inhabitants and French settlers, see Greer, *Property and Dispossession*, 76–80.

44 Lozier, *Flesh Reborn*, 59–61. Not only were the civic leaders themselves Indigenous people, but their selection was also made through traditionally Indigenous means. When the Jesuits thought that they were overseeing an election, their influence was actually quite limited. MNF IV:321, 536–7, 572–3, 596–7; Jetten, *Enclaves amérindiennes*, 49; Savard, "La « réduction » de Sillery 1638–1660," 128–9.

45 Lozier, *Flesh Reborn*, 60–1; Morrison, "Baptism and Alliance," 430–1. On differences between European and Indigenous means of control, see Delâge, *Bitter Feast*, 64–7; Sioui, *Huron-Wendat*, 171–3. Describing the Sillery leaders' attempts to force a woman to go to prison in Québec if she did not return to her husband, the Jesuit *Relation* reported that "this violence is a horror to the Indians and more distant from their ways of doing things than the sky is distant from the earth." MNF V:396–7; Beaulieu, *Convertir les fils de Caïn*, 136.

46 Jean-Baptiste Etinechkadat explained the decision: "I believe that the only way to resurrect your nation that will be lost, is for you to all assemble yourselves together and to believe in God, not as a pretense, but from the base of your hearts. And because he is good and can do all things, he will revive us and preserve us." "Je croy que l'unique moyen de ressuciter vostre nation qui va se perdre, c'est de vous rassembler tous et de croire en Dieu, non pas feintise, mais du fond du coeur. Et comme il est bon et qu'il peut tout, il nous fera revivre et nous conservera." MNF IV:570-1.

47 Jetten, *Enclaves amérindiennes*, 35–8.

48 Lozier, *Flesh Reborn*, 5, 54.

49 Lozier, *Flesh Reborn*, 67–9. For a wider discussion of how ideas of kinship networks were transformed, see Cook, "Vivre comme frères," 61–3. Some Christians felt regret at being sundered from their kin. According to the Jesuit Jean de Quen, when Christians from Sillery went into the woods in winter, they found it regrettable to see their kin enslaved to Satan. He said that their non-Christian kin mocked them but did not hate them, just as the Christians detested their kin's superstitions but did not wish any evil on them as people. MNF V:383–4. Others at Sillery felt their kinship groups ruptured and their obligations torn by religious distinctions. They told

people they were no longer kin because they had stopped being Christian, then refused them food and friendship. MNF V:70–2, MNF VI:108–13.

50 The others there declared that his friends were now their friends and his enemies their enemies. MNF V:96.

51 MNF VI:623. The new bonds of kinship could extend beyond the bounds of the settlement too. One of the captains said that after his baptism he acquired a "great kinship": when he entered a French church, it seemed to him that the French were his kin; when he saw a baptized Wendat, he regarded him as kin; and if the Iroquois were baptized, he would hold them as kin. MNF VIII:285.

52 MNF VIII:285.

53 "le soulagement des malades et la conversion des pauvres sauvages." "Acte de la réception et approbation pour l'établissement de l'hôpital de Québec par Monsieur le Commandant," AMHDQ, HDQ-F1-A2/2:5.

54 On ideas and debates about the differences between settler bodies and Indigenous bodies in New England and Spanish colonies, see Jones, *Rationalizing Epidemics*, 40–1 and Earle, *The Body of the Conquistador*, especially 19–53, 187–9; MNF IV:632; MNF V:103.

55 MNF V:102–4; MNF VI:89.

56 MNF V:103; Juchereau de Saint-Ignace and Duplessis, *Les annales de l'Hôtel-Dieu de Québec*, 26, 31–2; Lozier, *Flesh Reborn*, 64; Havard, *Great Peace of Montreal*, 16–18; Leavelle, *The Catholic Calumet*, 24–5.

57 MNF V:427–8.

58 AMHDQ, *Chroniques de l'Hôtel-Dieu de Québec 1639–1958, Registre no. 1*, 16–18; MNF V:106.

59 AMHDQ, *Chroniques de l'Hôtel-Dieu de Québec 1639–1958, Registre no. 1*, 17–18.

60 MNF V:103, 106, 428, 723; MNF VI:98.

61 *Le registre de Sillery*, 107, 110, 111, 117, 118, 119, 120, 121, 123, 124, 125, 126, 184, 298, 299.

62 MNF III:619; MNF IV:294.

63 MNF IV:596–7.

64 For a discussion of deathways in colonial New France and New England, see Seeman, *Death in the New World*, 106–84.

65 MNF V:717–19.

66 Gagné, "La réduction de Sillery," 108–10.

67 MNF VI:88–9; AMHDQ, *Chroniques de l'Hôtel-Dieu de Québec 1639-1958, Registre no. 2, Première partie: 1639–1698*, 88. After a brief period in the Lower Town, the hospital was relocated to the Upper Town at the place where it still stands today.

68 AMHDQ, *Chroniques de l'Hôtel-Dieu de Québec 1639–1958, Registre no. 1*, 3–5, 11, 14; Rousseau, *La croix et le scalpel*, 55–67; Rousseau, "Hôpital et société en Nouvelle-France," 29–30.

69 Jones, "The Construction of the Hospital Patient," 55–74.

70 Dinet-Lecomte, "Les sœurs hospitalières," 277–92.

71 Dinet-Lecomte, "Les sœurs hospitalières," 278; Ibbett, *Compassion's Edge*, 206–7.

72 MNF VII:333. For an examination of the "compassionate action" of the nursing sisters in seventeenth-century Montréal, see Ibbett, *Compassion's Edge*, 196–222.

73 Bowden, "Collecting the Lives of Early Modern Women Religious," 7–20; Wang, "Telling the Truth about Vocation," 129–45; Rapley, *A Social History of the Cloister*, 148–63.

74 Juchereau de Saint-Ignace and Duplessis, *Les annales de l'Hôtel-Dieu de Québec*, 232. Marie Hiroüin's name as recorded by the Francophone scribe was probably a French approximation of the Scottish name "Mary Irvine" or "Mary Irwin." She was described as "Scottish" in the marginal note of the Hôtel-Dieu Annales, and she came from a family that had become refugees in France following Scotland's Protestant Reformation. For more on Marie Hiroüin, her family's connections to Scotland, and her two voyages to Canada, see Cowan, "The Thistle and the Cross"; Juchereau de Saint-Ignace and Duplessis, *Les annales de l'Hôtel-Dieu de Québec*, 42, 76, 95, 231–2; AMHDQ, *Chroniques de l'Hôtel-Dieu de Québec 1639–1958, Registre no. 2, Première partie: 1639–1698*, 139–40. On Scottish confessional emigrants, see Talbott, "Diasporic of Distinct?" 100–35; Murdoch and Mijers, "Migrant Destinations, 1500–1750," 320–7.

75 Brockliss and Jones, *The Medical World of Early Modern France*, 272, 686–7; Jones, "Perspectives on Poor Relief, Health Care and the Counter-Reformation in France," 231; Dinges, "Health Care and Poor Relief," 256; Strocchia, *Forgotten Healers*, 132-49; Broomhall, *Women's Medical Work in Early Modern France*, 71–2; Fissell, "Women, Health, and Healing," 16.

76 ASQ. Documents Faribault no. 115 A, Les Hospitalières de Québec reçoivent de Couillard 24 pieds de terre pour le "Cimetière des Pauvers," 25 juillet 1661.

77 Rousseau, *La croix et le scalpel*, 58–60, 82. Hôtels-Dieu in France sometimes continued to offer a bed and meals to travellers in need. Brockliss and Jones, *The Medical World of Early Modern France*, 686.

78 *Constitutions de la Congregation des Religieuses Hospitalieres de la Misericorde de Jesus de la Misericorde de Jesus. De l'Ordre de Sainct Augustin*, 141–2.

79 Benedictus Pererius Valentinus, *Adversus Fallaces & Superstitiosas artes, id est, de observatione somniorum, & de divinatione astrologica*, and Petrus Thyraeus, *Daemoniaci, hoc est: de obsessis a spiritibus daemoniorum hominibus, liber unus*. AMHDQ, "Inventaire des livres anciens antérieur de 1800."

80 *Constitutions de la Congregation des religieuses Hospitalieres de la Misericorde de Jesus. De l'Ordre de Sainct Augustin*, 155–6, 178, quoted in Rousseau, *La croix et le scalpel*, 85–6.

81 Marie de l'Incarnation, *Correspondance*, 886–7. Learned physicians and theologians believed that supernatural causes could lie at the root of physical ailments, and that the discernment of spirits was a complex and complicated task drawing upon many different domains of knowledge – including the medical and the theological. Caciola and Sluhovsky, "Spiritual Physiologies," 26–7, 34; Petry, "Many Things Surpass Our Knowledge," 47–64.

82 Anderson, "My Spirit Found a Unity with This Holy Man," 187–8; Marie-Emmanuel Chabot, "Simon de Longpré, Marie-Catherine de, dite de Saint-Augustin," in DCB, vol. 1.

83 "à l'assistance spirituelle et corporelle des pauvres et des malades qui est le comble de la charité chrétienne." "ces sanctes ames qui ont le bonheur d'y travailler comme des ames vrayement apostoliques qui méritent l'aprobation et le secours de toute l'eglise." AMHDQ, "Lettre de Vincent de Paul adressée à la supérieure Catherine Vironceau de Saint-Joseph," HDQ-F1-G4,1/39:5. On how the nuns' letters between the Hôtel-Dieu in Québec and its sister institutions in France show an awareness of the changes that needed to happen to culture, language, and daily life for the community in Canada, see Piché, "Ma Très Chère Mère du Canada," 11–32.

84 Diefendorf, *From Penitence to Charity*, 20–1. Biographies of nuns may also have given some readers a voyeuristic pleasure by revealing cloistered women's interior experiences. Paige, "Enlightened (Il)literates," 120–3.

85 Bilinkoff, *Related Lives*, 70–5; Anderson, "My Spirit Found a Unity with This Holy Man," 192–3; Codignola, "Few, Uncooperative, and Ill Informed," 179–81; Goddard, "Canada in Early Modern Jesuit Thought," 186–99.

86 Diefendorf, *From Penitence to Charity*, 21; Greer, "Colonial Saints"; Pearson, *Becoming Holy in Early Canada*.

87 Heffernan, *Sacred Biography*, 21–2; Yarrow, *Saints and Their Communities*, 13–17; Cowan, "A Contested Conception," 586–7.

88 Catherine said that she saw in a dream the Holy Virgin, as if she had just given birth, whose breasts were so full of milk that they were causing her pain. It seemed to Catherine that the Virgin was looking around to see if

someone could relieve her, and Catherine boldly offered to the Virgin to suckle her milk so softly that she would feel no pain. The Virgin asked Catherine to approach and gave her permission to suckle, which she did with great joy. Ragueneau, *La vie*, 125–31.

89 Ragueneau, *La vie*, 300–23.

90 Ragueneau, *La vie*, 289–94.

91 Ragueneau, *La vie*, 362. The Jesuit *Relation* reports the conversion as taking place after Catherine mixed a powdered relic of Brébeuf into a drink that she fed to the soldier. JR:50, 87–9.

92 Ragueneau, *La vie*, 229–30.

93 Ragueneau, *La vie*, 65.

94 Ragueneau, *La vie*, 170–1.

95 Ragueneau, *La vie*, 80, 82–3, 88, 200–1, 214, 223–9, 279.

96 "se croyant la plus criminelle du monde & digne de mille enfers" Ragueneau, *La vie*, 266.

97 Ragueneau, *La vie*, 3–4, 77–8, 173–4.

98 Ragueneau, *La vie*, 9.

99 Ragueneau, *La vie*, 89.

100 Berry, "Le Ciel et la Terre nous ont parlé," 11–35; Grégoire, "L'interprétation du tremblement de terre de 1663," 64–76; Ebel, "A New Analysis of the Magnitude of the February 1663 Earthquake at Charlevoix, Quebec," 1024–38. For observations made three years later on alterations to the landscape, see ANOM, "Relation par Jacques de Cailhault de La Tesserie du voyage qu'il a fait, par ordre de Talon," Colonies, C11A 111, F°206-215. Le 18 août 1666. Thank you to Joseph Gagné for suggesting the source and providing a transcription.

101 "Je ne pûs m'empecher de souhaiter ce châtiment quel qu'il fût; car je n'eus pour lors aucune idée de ce que ce pourroit être." Ragueneau, *La vie*, 238–40.

102 Juchereau de Saint-Ignace and Duplessis, *Les annales de l'Hôtel-Dieu de Québec*, 123–4.

103 JR 48:182–221.

104 Marie de l'Incarnation, *Correspondance*, 688–9.

105 "transitoria conversione ita ut a multis optaretur accretio magis quam decretio hujus flagella" ARSI, Gal. 110 vol. 1, 26 r.

106 Juchereau de Saint-Ignace and Duplessis, *Les annales de l'Hôtel-Dieu de Québec*, 122–7.

107 "comme en effet il a changé des âmes toutes diaboliques, et mis en un meilleur état celles qui étoient désjà dans le bon chemin," Marie de l'Incarnation, *Correspondance*, 686. A few months later, she still held the same view, writing that the earthquakes brought people together: since

they held everyone in fear and humility, everyone lived in peace. Marie de l'Incarnation, *Correspondance*, 711.

108 Camba, "Religion, Disaster, and Colonial Power in the Spanish Philippines," 215–31; Lehmann, "Miracles within Catastrophes," 321–34. In France, the Bishop of Grasse said in a sermon that God had brought a recent earthquake to pull people away from the drowsiness of sin and love of worldly things, and move them towards God. Quenet, *Les tremblements de terre en France aux XVIIe et XVIIIe siècles*, 158. José Zaragoza, a mathematician at the Jesuit Imperial College of Madrid, wrote that many earthquakes were a natural effect but that sometimes God caused them, or allowed a demon to cause them, in order to punish people. Alonso de Tomás, bishop of Malaga, wrote that people's sins forced God to cause an earthquake. Protestant writers also interpreted earthquakes as divine punishment or correction. A Puritan minister, Thomas Doolittle, in sermons after an earthquake in London, said that God sometimes caused earthquakes that produced a "holy fear" leading to moral improvement. Udías, "Earthquakes as God's Punishment," 42, 43–4. The Reverend Emmanuel Heath described the earthquake that had destroyed much of Port Royal, Jamaica, and killed about a third of its inhabitants, as a "terrible Judgment of God" sent to punish the sinners of the town. Mulcahy, "The Port Royal Earthquake," 392–4, 405–8; Parrish, *American Curiosity*, 99–100.

109 Udías, "Earthquakes as God's Punishment," 41–8. For the emerging view in universities and learned circles that earthquakes, like the rest of nature, were ruled by immutable universal laws, see Rienk, *Thinking on Earthquakes in Early Modern Europe*, 157–84.

110 Thoum, *Le tremble-terre*, 56; Quenet, *Les tremblements de terre aux XVIIe et XVIIIe siècles*, 149.

111 AUQ, *Annales des Ursulines de Québec 1639–1822*, tome 1 1/E, 1, 3, 2.0001 14r.

112 "je vous diray entre vous et moy que je ne suis pas trop sçavante en ses affaires." "je vous supplie de m'en dispenser, voiant que des personnes de science et de vertu y suspendent leur jugement, et demeurent dans le doute, n'osant pas se fier à des visions extraordinaires de cette qualité." Marie de l'Incarnation, *Correspondance*, 886–7.

113 On marks on the skin in early modern France and its Atlantic colonies, see Dauge-Roth, *Signing the Body*. On concerns with distinguishing "true" from "false" witches, see Houdard, "Des fausses saintes aux spirituelles à la mode." For the case of an English nun in the Spanish Netherlands who bore marks of demonic beating on her body, see Hallett, *Witchcraft, Exorcism and the Politics of Possession*, 1, 62, 88–9, 112.

114 Sluhovsky, *Believe Not Every Spirit*, 169.
115 Lierheimer, "False Sanctity and Spiritual Imposture," 71–91.
116 Diefendorf, "Discerning Spirits," 241–65.
117 Hillman, "Testing the Spirit of the Prophets."
118 Ferber, *Demonic Possession and Exorcism in Early Modern France*, 10–11; Godineau, *Les Femmes dans la Société Française*, 113–16; Timmermans, *L'accès des femmes à la culture*, 394–6, 501–659. Timmermans also makes the interesting argument that the power of mystical women was similar to the power of demoniacs in being able to say and do things not normally permitted to women.
119 Caciola and Sluhovsky, "Spiritual Physiologies," 6, 32–3; Hsia, *The World of Catholic Renewal*, 139–48.
120 Some contemporary observers interpreted the mass possession at Loudun as a sign of holiness, with the devil choosing this community because of its success and God allowing it in order for his servants to show their strength. Others interpreted the behaviour of the Loudun nuns as the result of sexual frustration among young women and the seductions of an infamous local *curé*. Briggs, "From Devilry to Sainthood," 33–48; Certeau, *The Possession at Loudun*; Mandrou, *Magistrats et sorciers*, 237–8.
121 "C'est une demande tres-raisonnable que de vouloir sçavoir quelle asseurance on peut avoir de la vérité de tant de visions, apparitions, & revelations si extraordinaires & si frequentes, dont toute cette Vie est remplie" "d'ailleurs il n'est que trop veritable que l'imagination, principalement des filles qui sont portées à la pieté, se trompe aisément, & qu'elles croyent fort legerement avoir veu & entendu ce qu'elles se sont imaginé" "comme si leurs yeux & leur jugement étoient l'unique regle infaillible de toutes choses" Ragueneau, *La vie*, 10–12, quotations on 10.
122 Lierheimer, "Preaching or Teaching?," 220.
123 Martin, *La vie de la venerable mere Marie de l'Incarnation*, 303–4.
124 Leslie Choquette characterizes female missionary activity in seventeenth-century New France as "a story of female eagerness and official reticence," and has written of Catherine de Saint-Augustin's ability "virtually to usurp the function of exorcist" as "consistent with the enhanced role of women religious in the early years of the colony." Choquette, "Ces Amazones du Grand Dieu," 632. For Jan Noel, this time in New France was "a rare moment of seventeenth-century female religious activism." Noel, *Along a River*, quotation on 56. See also 17–18. Allan Greer has argued that a basic European patriarchy prevailed in New France, but that it also displayed "the latest tendencies in Counter-Reformation idealism without the counterweight of older, entrenched customs and institutions,"

with the consequence that "restrictions such as *clausura* were less rigidly enforced." Greer, "Women of New France," 98. For more on the historiography of women's power and authority in New France, see Grenier, "Femmes et propriété seigneuriale au Canada," 8–11. On women missionaries playing a more important role in New France than in other colonies in the Americas, see Dinet-Lecomte, "Les hospitalières françaises en Amérique," 262–3; Deslandres, "New France," 126.

125 "qu'elles avoient des corps capables des souffrances, & qu'elles avoient des volontez & des désirs aussi genereux que les hommes pour entreprendre de faire le sacrifice de leurs corps." *Histoire de la fondation du monastere des religieuses feuillentines*, 26.

126 Evangelisti, *Nuns*, 6–7, 45–65; Diefendorf, "Rethinking the Catholic Reformation," 31–59; Rapley, *A Social History of the Cloister*, 111–18; Lierheimer, "Preaching or Teaching?," 212–26.

127 Diefendorf, *From Penitence to Charity*, 8. Dominique Deslandres writes of this age as one of "religious feminism" ("féminisme religieux"), which had as its first principle the affirmation of equality between the sexes. Deslandres, "De Marie Guyart de l'Incarnation aux Femmes 'ordinaires' de la Nouvelle-France," 268.

128 Anderson, "My Spirit Found a Unity with This Holy Man," 186–9.

129 This enthusiasm for martyrdom was not just insincere posturing. Thousands were willing, and some even eager, to die for their beliefs. Gregory, *Salvation at Stake*, 4–5, 97–111.

130 "elle étoit attachée à la croix du Canada, par trois cloux dont elle ne se détacheroit jamais. Le premier, la volonté de Dieu; le second, le salut des ames; & le troisiéme, sa vocation en ce païs, & le vœu qu'elle avoit fait d'y mourir : & elle ajoûtroit que quand méme toute les Religieuses voudroient revenir en France, pourveu qu'il luy fût permis, elle demeureroit seule en Canada pour y consommer sa vie au service des pauvres Sauvages, & des malades du païs." Ragueneau, *La vie*, 62; Pearson, *Becoming Holy in Early Canada*, 97.

131 Pearson, "I Willingly Speak to You about her Virtues," 305–6.

132 Ragueneau, *La vie*, 179–99.

133 "Enfin des Démons et les Magiciens se retirèrent par l'intercession de ce saint homme qui a répandu son sang pour le soutien de la foy en ce païs." Marie de l'Incarnation, *Correspondance*, 813–15, quotation on 814.

134 Catherine's connection with martyrdom is an example of one historian's memorable phrase describing early modern martyrdom as both highly conventional and highly painful: "*imitatio Christi* with a vengeance." Kelley, "Martyrs, Myths, and the Massacre," 1328. Recent assessments

do not always conclude that Brébeuf was a martyr, since he and his companions were treated much like other imprisoned enemies would have been, and he was not necessarily killed for being a Christian. See, for example, Carson, "Brébeuf Was Never Martyred."

135 See chapter 1 for more on Canada's reputation in France.

136 Pizzorusso, "Le choix indifférent," 891–2.

137 Pearson, "I Willingly Speak to You about Her Virtues," 313–14. Marc Lescarbot acknowledged that some of his French readers might be put off by what they would see as the primitiveness of New France, but he thought that the brave would not be dissuaded. "There are certainly no violins, no masquerades, no dances, no palaces, no towns, and no goodly buildings as in France," Lescarbot admitted, but he was convinced that such shortages would only bother the faint-hearted; the glory of establishing a New France did not belong to these timid people who "find all things great impossible." Lescarbot, *The History of New France*, 1:15–16.

138 On the wider European Christian assumption that Indigenous peoples in North America would convert quickly, see Codignola, "The Holy See and the Conversion of the Indians," 195–242

139 Champlain, *Works*, 1:111–17.

140 Lescarbot, *The History of New France*, 1:3.

141 Lescarbot, *The History of New France*, 1:13.

142 Hippocrates, *Ancient Medicine*, 133.

143 Imbruglia, "A Peculiar Idea of Empire." 29–30; MNF II:596; Melzer, "The Role of Culture and Art," 170–2; Havard and Vidal, *Histoire de l'Amérique française*, 173–4.

144 MNF II:636–8; McShea, *Apostles of Empire*, 35–8.

145 MNF II:289, 306; MNF III:51–2.

146 Smith, *Nature, Human Nature, & Human Difference*, 105; Brazeau, *Writing a New France*, 70–95.

147 "Comme ces pauvres sauvages, pour estre hommes, n'ont pu mécognoistre Dieu tout à fait." MNF III:355.

148 MNF II:434, 564. Missionaries in New France were not alone in this. Jean de Léry identified what he thought were fragments of the story of Noah's flood in Brazil, while Spanish friars identified what they thought were fragments from the story of creation and Noah's flood in Mexico and Peru. MacCormack, "Limits of Understanding," 79–129.

149 Deslandres, "Entre persuasion et adhésion," 95–117.

150 This idea could be useful to early modern states as a justification for claiming spiritual powers beyond the borders of their civil authority. See Clossey, "Faith in Empire," 571–87.

151 On this creation story, see Sioui, *Huron-Wendat*, 16–19.

152 "Et quand nous leur preschons un Dieu créateur du ciel et de la terre et de toutes choses, de mesme quand nous leur parlons d'un enfer et d'un paradis et du reste de nos mystères, les opiniastres respondent que cela est bon pour nostre pays, non pour le leur; que chaque pays a ses façons de faire. Mais leur ayant monstré par le moyen d'un petit globe que nous avons apporté qu'il n'y a qu'un seul monde, ils demeurent sans réplique." MNF III:103. Brébeuf was not the only Jesuit to use cartographic instruction. When Mestigoit asked Paul Le Jeune how the earth was made, and brought the priest some bark and coal, Le Jeune drew for him Europe, Asia, Africa, and America, showing it like a big island. Pioffet, "La Nouvelle-France dans l'imaginaire jésuite," 327–8.

153 Podruchny and Labelle, "Jean de Brébeuf and the Wendat Voices," 119.

154 E.g., MNF II:546, 571–2, 583; MNF III:99, 328–9; MNF V:210–12; MNF VII:400. Sometimes Jesuits showed a more nuanced understanding of these spirits, e.g., MNF III:600; MNF IV:595. Cowan, "Jesuit Missionaries and the Accommodationist Demons," 213–14.

155 MNF IV:405–6; MNF VII:173.

156 MNF III:128, 269; Marie de l'Incarnation, *Correspondance*, 26–7; Caulier, "Bâtir la Jérusalem des Terres froides," 235–49.

157 Belmessous, *Assimilation and Empire*, 14–15, 28–36; Belmessous, "Être français en Nouvelle-France," 510–15, 539; Havard, "Les forcer à devenir Cytoyens," 989–1000; Melzer, *Colonizer or Colonized*, 102–9. On the development of racial prejudice after the failure of earlier assimilationist approaches, see Belmessous "Assimilation and Racialism," and Aubert, "The Blood of France."

158 Codignola, "Few, Uncooperative, and Ill Informed," 173–85.

159 Galland, *Pour la gloire de Dieu et du Roi*, 284–92; Trigger, *The Children of Aataentsic*, vol. I, 378; Deslandres, *Croire et faire croire*, 241–61; Fast, "Helping 'our Canadian brothers,'" 75–108.

160 "À mesure que la Colonie se peuplera, nous humaniserons les Barbares; ce qui est premierement necessaire, leur esprit s'ouvrira et le bon sens dont ils ont le fond: on les policera par les loix & les manieres de vivre à la Françoise, afin de les rendre capables d'entendre raison sur des Mysteres si élevez." Quoted in Le Clercq, *Premier établissement de la foy dans la Nouvelle France*, I:264–5; Magnuson, *Education in New France*, 19–20, 191–2.

161 Individual members of the order did disagree somewhat on this question, as they did on other matters of conversion. Cowan, "Jesuit Missionaries and the Accommodationist Demons," 221–32.

162 MNF I:509–16.

163 AUQ "Contrat de Madame Chauvigny de la Peltrie pour la fondation des Ursulines en Nouvelle-France," 1/A,2,1,3,1, 1–2, 4.

164 AUQ "Constitutions rédigées par le R.P. Jérôme Lalemant, Supr des Jésuites, à Québec, et adaptées aux besoins du pays, pour les Ursulines du Canada [1647] et approuvées par Mgr de Laval [1667] avec les Règlements," fol. 159, 1r, 61v-64v.

165 Deslandres, "… alors nos garçons se marieront à vos filles, & nous ne ferons plus qu'un seul peuple," 5–35.

166 Cowan, "Education, *Francisation*," 1–29. For differing views on how successful the Urusline nuns were in their efforts at "francisation," see Oury, *Les Ursulines de Québec*, 58–66; Trudel, *Les écolières*; Goudeau, *Les délices de nos cœurs*; Magnuson, *Education in New France*; Grégoire, "Malentendus culturels."

167 Cowan, "Jesuit Missionaries and the Accommodationist Demons," 232–8; Dunn, "Bedside Manners," 567–85; Trigger, *The Children of Aataentsic*, 535; Sayre, *Les Sauvages Américains*, 204; Blackburn, *Harvest of Souls*, 108–9; Axtell, "The Power of Print in the Eastern Woodlands," 300–9.

168 E.g., JR 45:63; JR 48:63; JR 50:17; JR 51:125, 129, 267; JR 52:139. The Jesuits still wrote about demons actually present in the communities the missionaries were trying to evangelize, but less frequently and with less immediate concern than a few decades earlier. E.g., JR 45:64–5, 69-71; JR 50:271; JR 51:77. Goddard, "The Devil in New France," 43.

169 "comme nous auons en Canada des personnes infesteés de la mesme façon." Ragueneau, "Lettre sur des possédées habitant le Canada."

170 Cowan, "Jesuit Missionaries and the Accommodationist Demons," 221–32.

171 MNF II:289–90, 415, 435, 456, 566–70, 673–4, 716–17; MNF III:601–3, 603-5; MNF IV:326; McShea, *Apostles of Empire*, 52–64.

172 MNF III:104–6, 110, 358, 361–2, 392–404.

173 MNF IV:409, 412–13, 425, 435, 438–40, 652–5; MNF V:167, 525–8, 538; MNF VI:397; MNF VII:155. MNF V:538.

174 MNF VII:417–19.

175 "Or de sçavoir s'il y a vrayement des sorciers en ce pays, je veux dire des hommes qui fassent mourir par sortilèges, c'est ce que je ne puis pas décider. Seulement, je puis dire qu'ayant examiné tout ce qui s'en dit, je n'ay point encore veu aucun fondement assez raisonnable de croire qu'en effet il y en ait icy qui se meslent de ce mestier d'enfer." MNF VII:419–20.

176 "Il est aisé qu'on accuse d'irréligion ce qui n'est que sottise et qu'on prenne pour opération diabolique ce qui n'a rien au-dessus de l'humain." Ragueneau decided that the Jesuits had been too severe in the past, and

that henceforth they should be less rigorous about apparently innocent recreations. MNF VII:395.

177 MNF VIII:341.

178 Anderson, *The Death and Afterlife of the North American Martyrs*, 55–6, 64–6; Anderson, "My Spirit Found a Unity with This Holy Man," 185–6.

CHAPTER FOUR

1 Much of this chapter appears also in Cowan, "A Deliverance from Demons."

2 AMHDQ, "Recit du Soulagement d'une possedée par l'Entremise des Reliques du R.P. Jean de Breboeuf dheureuse et saincte memoire."

3 ASJCF, Q-0001, 251.Il "Recit de la Deliurance D'une possedée par l'entremise des reliques du deffunct R.P. Jean de Breboeu[f] d'heureuse et sainte memoire."

4 For 1636, see ASQ, P29-Fonds Georges-Barthélémi Faribault, Documents Faribault, no 2. For 1661, see LAC, Fonds des greffes de notaires du Québec [document textuel (quelques microformes)] (R11118-0-7-F), Transport de Marie Regnouard, épouse de Robert Giffard, sieur de Moncel et de Beauport, à ... (No 1043). Guillaume Audouart, notaire.

5 The examples of handwriting on these documents do not appear to match the hand of Paul Ragueneau. See, e.g., autograph correspondence of 1665 in the Georgetown University Archival Resources, file box 15, folder 8.

6 AMHDQ, "État des dettes contractées par les religieuses hospitalières de la Miséricorde de Jésus de l'Hôtel-Dieu de Québec," HDQ-F1-A3,2/1:3.

7 Unless otherwise indicated, quotations in the notes come from the version held at the Hôtel-Dieu, since it is dated the earliest of the three. "y ayant par plusieurs autres fois, qu'elle estoit en pareil estat mis sur elle des reliques de beaucoup de sts." "Incontinent le Demon luy fist faire plusieurs contorsions, et des bras et des jambes, et generalement de tout le corps, et me parlant me dit par plusieurs fois; oste moy femme, oste moy cela, Je brusle ie brusle" [underlined in original]

8 This quotation is from the second of the documents in the Jesuit archives, since a tear in the paper makes part of the Hôtel-Dieu copy impossible to read and a fold in the first of the Jesuit archives version obscures some of the words. "ie luy dis tu en as menty maudict esprit que tu est tu ny as rien elles amoy nostre bon dieu et son père et sa mere melont donnee."

9 This quotation is from the first of the Jesuit archive versions, since a tear in the Hôtel-Dieu version has cut through some of this section. "par plusie[urs] fois oste moy cela femme car ie n'en puis plus, oste, oste viste ie n'en puis pl[us] ie suis brulé"

10 "aussitost je vis un souffle sortir de la bouche de cette fille, qui commen[script faded] de parler, et dire Jesus, Maria, Joseph, et faire le signe de la croix sur son front, sur sa bousche, et sur son cœur."
11 See chapter 2.
12 See chapter 3.
13 Ferber, *Demonic Possession*, 26.
14 Levack, *The Devil Within*, 11–12.
15 Levack, *The Devil Within*, 6–15.
16 Roper, *Oedipus and the Devil*, 175–6; Levack, *The Devil Within*, 81.
17 Levack, *The Devil Within*, 184.
18 Roper, *Oedipus and the Devil*, 190–1.
19 Gowing, *Common Bodies*, 69–71.
20 Ferber, *Demonic Possession*, 3, 25; Levack, *The Devil Within*, 19–22.
21 Ragueneau, *La vie*, 172, discussed in Pearson, "I Willingly Speak to You about Her Virtues," 317.
22 Ferber, *Demonic Possession*, 115.
23 In the *Dictionnaire françois* of 1680, "délivrance" is defined as "C'est mettre en liberté. Tirer de servitude. Exemption de peine, de mal, ou de travail." "Soulagement" is defined as "Alégement, diminution de peine, diminution de mal." "Guerison" is defined as "Rétablissement d'une personne en santé. Retour de la maladie à la santé. Cure de quelque mal, ou de quelque blessure." Richelet, *Dictionnaire françois*, 225, 388, 392.
24 *Rituale Romanum*, 206–27; Sluhovsky, *Believe Not Every Spirit*, 91; Young, *A History of Exorcism*, 116–20. In the 1658 edition of the *Rituale Romanum* held at the Archives du Séminaire de Québec, the section on exorcism does not show any obvious marks of use, unlike the section on baptism, which has drops of candle wax and damp-looking markings at the bottom crease where the book would have been held. This book also has on the inside of its front cover a list of some baptisms performed in the 1680s. ASQ, *Rituale Romanum*, Venice, 1658.
25 Vincent Grégoire points out that Catherine de Saint-Augustin's actions are never described as an exorcism either. He makes no mention of the unpublished accounts in the Jesuit and Hôtel-Dieu archives, but his observation about terminology extends to these sources as well. "Le meunier, la domestique et l'hospitalière," 82–4.
26 Ferber, *Demonic Possession*, 3; Levack, *The Devil Within*, 100–5.
27 Sluhovsky, *Believe Not Every Spirit*, 91; Ferber, "Demonic Possession, Exorcism, and Witchcraft," 578–9.
28 Levack, *The Devil Within*, 81. On the speech of a demoniac being heard as spoken by another, see De Certeau, *The Writing of History*, 244–68.

29 Sluhovsky, *Believe Not Every Spirit*, 37–8; Levack, *The Devil Within*, 94–7; Broomhall, *Women's Medical Work in Early Modern France*, 113; Ferber, "Demonic Possession, Exorcism, and Witchcraft," 575–92; Cameron, *Enchanted Europe*, 59–60.

30 Ferber, "Possession and the Sexes," 218.

31 *Rituale Romanum*, 206–27; Levack, *The Devil Within*, 63, 88–91.

32 When Charles de Lauson de Charny signed the document about the deliverance of Hallay, he was living at the Jesuit College. In July 1664, he became ecclesiastical superior of the Hôtel-Dieu hospital. He returned to France in 1671 and remained there for the rest of his life. He tried to have his daughter join the community of Hospitalière nuns at the Hôtel-Dieu in Québec. In spite of the substantial dowry he offered, however, the community refused his request that his daughter be given a special diet because of her delicate condition: the sisters were worried that her special treatment could cause jealousy in the community. She returned with her father to France and joined the community of the Hôtel-Dieu at La Rochelle instead. MNF VIII:385, 901, 966, 976; MNF IX:383, 393; Juchereau de Saint-Ignace and Duplessis, *Les annales de l'Hôtel-Dieu de Québec*, 92, 93, 168–9; Honorius Provost, "Lauson de Charny, Charles de," in DCB, vol. 1.

33 Levack, *The Devil Within*, 97.

34 Among the noblemen present were Mathurin Mauduict sieur de la Resniere, Charles Michel sieur du Parc, Noël Ruffre sieur du Buisson, and Jean Barban sieur de Boisboullay. Besnard, "Les diverses professions de Robert Giffard," 323; *Bulletin des recherches historiques* 9, no. 9 (1903): 267–70; Montagne, "Du nouveau sur Robert Giffard," 29–30.

35 Montagne, "Du nouveau sur Robert Giffard," 27–8; Besnard, "Les préliminaires de l'émigration percheronne," 66–75; Langlois, *Dictionnaire biographique des ancêtres québécois (1608–1700)*, 2:347–9.

36 Montagne, "Du nouveau sur Robert Giffard," 29–31; Besnard, "Les préliminaires de l'émigration percheronne," 74.

37 Besnard, "Les diverses professions de Robert Giffard," 327; Besnard, "Les préliminaires de l'émigration percheronne," 68–70; Langlois, *Dictionnaire biographique des ancêtres québécois (1608–1700)*, 2:347–9.

38 *Inventaire et Analyse du Site Patrimonial déclaré de Beauport*; Trudel, *Le terrier du Saint-Laurent en 1663*, 87–98; Grenier, *Brève histoire du régime seigneurial*, 64; Langlois, *Dictionnaire biographique des ancêtres québécois (1608–1700)*, 2:347–9.

39 Choquette, *Frenchmen into Peasants*, 67–9, 261; Charbonneau, *Tourouvre-au-Perche aux XVIIe et XVIIIe siècles*, 3–9, 11.

40 Trudel, *Catalogue des immigrants*, 36.

41 Montagne, "Du nouveau sur Robert Giffard," 32, 34.
42 MNF III:31; Grenier, *Seigneurs campagnards*, 280.
43 Sluhovsky, *Believe Not Every Spirit*, 89
44 For more on the so-called "seigneurial system," see chapter 2.
45 Goubert, *The French Peasantry*, 110, 166–77, 193–6.
46 "on donna à madame Giffar de l'estoffe noire de vieille sotanne pour doubler des manches" MNF VI:424.
47 Although it has been thought that the term "seigneuresse" was a Canadian neologism appearing at the end of the seventeenth century, recent findings in French archives show that the term was being used on that side of the Atlantic to designate the wife of a seigneur. Even before the term came into widespread use, women could and did hold seigneurial authority in New France, but among lay women this generally happened only when the woman was the daughter or wife of a seigneur who had died. Sometimes the word "seigneuresse" is used today to designate a woman holding the powers or usufruct rights of a seigneur, and sometimes it is used more generally for the wife of a seigneur. Since Marie Regnouard's husband was still alive at this point, it is not clear whether she would have been considered a "seigneuresse" legally in her own time, although the term fits well socially and culturally. Benoît Grenier, personal communication to author, 15 October 2021; Grenier, "Femmes et propriété seigneuriale au Canada," 6, 11, 15; Grenier, "Réflexion sur le pouvoir féminin au Canada," 306; Grenier, *Brève histoire du régime seigneurial*, 107–14.
48 Dinges, "Health Care and Poor Relief," 241.
49 Rankin, *Panaceia's Daughters*, 7, 25–6; Strocchia, *Forgotten Healers*, especially chapters 1 and 2.
50 Pelling, "Thoroughly Resented," 63–88.
51 De Serres, *Le théâtre d'agriculture et mesnage des champs*, 887–8.
52 Cabré, "Women or Healers," 18–51; Strocchia, "Women and Healthcare in Early Modern Europe," 498. Rebecca J. Tannenbaum argues that "domestic medicine did not differ much from learned medicine" in England and its colonies during the seventeenth century, and that medical practice, including healing magic, was a household skill. Tannenbaum, *The Healer's Calling*, 3, 19, 22–4. For a discussion of how to view medical practice in medieval Europe as a household craft, see Green, "Documenting Medieval Women's Medical Practice," 322–52. The phrase "locus of care" is borrowed from Horden and Smith, *The Locus of Care*. The "everyday body" is a term developed by Riddy, "Looking Closely," 212–28.
53 Noel, *Along a River*, 34.

54 "Medical practitioner" is being used here as it was by Margaret Pelling and Charles Webster in their study of London and Norwich in the sixteenth century, where they defined "medical practitioner" as "any individual whose occupation is basically concerned with the care of the sick." Pelling and Webster, *Health, Medicine and Mortality in the Sixteenth Century*, 166. See also Green, "Women's Medical Practice and Health Care in Medieval Europe," 444–6.

55 Montagne, "Du nouveau sur Robert Giffard," 29.

56 Besnard, "Les préliminaires de l'émigration percheronne," 74; Besnard, "Les diverses professions de Robert Giffard," 322–9; Montagne, "Du nouveau sur Robert Giffard," 29–31.

57 MNF V:388; MNF VII:225; Trudel, *Catalogue des immigrants*, 35–6; Cambray, *Robert Giffard*, 187–8; Roy, *À Travers l'histoire de l'Hôtel-Dieu de Québec*, 29; Giroux, *Robert Giffard*; Montagne, "Du nouveau sur Robert Giffard," 33. François Rousseau says that Giffard was a surgeon in *La croix et le scalpel*, 100. The *Dictionary of Canadian Biography* says that in 1640 Giffard became the first doctor in the Hôtel-Dieu, an apothecary, and held the honorary title of "doctor in ordinary" to the king. Honorius Provost, "Giffard de Moncel, Robert" in DCB, vol. 1. Lessard says that Giffard was both surgeon and physician, but not one with a degree from a faculty of medicine, rather a surgeon by training. *Au temps de la petite vérole*, 203–4, 224–5.

58 MNF V:81, 108.

59 AMHDQ, *Chroniques de l'Hôtel-Dieu de Québec 1639–1958, Registre no. 2, Première Partie: 1639–1698*, 1, 17, 32, 90–1, 151. Terrence Crowley has argued that a religious life in New France offered protection, service to others, and an ordered existence with self-direction in daily life. "Women, Religion and Freedom in New France," 101–18. On distinctions between nuns of the choir and *converses*, or lay sisters, see Rapley, *A Social History of the Cloister*, 182–97.

60 "à cause de la particuliere affection qu'elles s'étroient portées l'une à l'autre" Ragueneau, *La vie*, 96–101, quotation on 96.

61 Montserrat Cabré defines "authorized healers" as "women legally allowed to practice under certain conditions, whose licenses, granted by royal or municipal authorities, are extant." "Women or Healers," 24. See also Pomata, "Practicing between Earth and Heaven," 119–43.

62 Brockliss and Jones, *The Medical World of Early Modern France*, 17–19.

63 Fissell, "Women, Health, and Healing," 1–17.

64 Greer, "Women of New France," 88–90; Noel, *Along a River*; Choquette, "Ces Amazones du Grand Dieu," 632, 654. See also Pearson, "I Willingly

Speak to You about her Virtues," 305–33; Deslandres, "In the Shadow of the Cloister," 135–7; Choquette, "From Sea Monsters and Savages to Sorcerers and Satan," 57–8; Davis, *Women on the Margins*, 63–139.

65 Ragueneau, *La vie.*

66 Marie de l'Incarnation, *Correspondance*, 813–15.

67 We do not know whose relics they were, but the options were quite numerous since many relics had moved to and from the colony. By one count, the relics of twenty-one saints were found in New France during the seventeenth century. Deslandres, "Signes de Dieu," 145–60.

68 ASJCF, Q-0001, 251.Il "Recit de la Deliurance D'une possedée par l'entremise des reliques du deffunct R.P. Jean de Breboeu[f] d'heureuse et sainte mémoire."

69 "Recit de la Deliurance D'une possedée par l'entremise des reliques du deffunct R.P. Jean de Breboeu[f] d'heureuse et sainte mémoire"; "Recit du soulagement d'une possedée par l'Entremise des Reliques du R.P. Jean de Breboeuf dheureuse et Saincte Mémoire." For more on the triumphalist purposes of such accounts, which sometimes emphasize the role of the healer or the saintly ally more than the story of the possessed, see Ferber, "Possession and the Sexes," 214–38.

70 MNF VII:468, 598–609; René Latourelle, "Brébeuf, Jean de (Échon)," DCB, vol. 1; Steckley, "Hechon," 85; Steckley, "Huron Carol," 55–74.

71 Cowan, "Jesuit Missionaries and the Accommodationist Demons," 230; Donnelly, *Jean de Brébeuf*, 11, 57; Trigger, *The Children of Aataentsic*, 501; Monet, "The Jesuits in New France," 186–98; Bonvillain, "Jesuit Perceptions of Iroquoian Culture," 84; Labelle, *Dispersed but Not Destroyed*, 30, 36–8.

72 Labelle, *Dispersed but Not Destroyed*, 29–67; Trigger, *The Children of Aataentsic*, 665–788.

73 MNF VII:468–70, 488–92, 500–17, 591–5.

74 MNF VII:634.

75 Greer, "Colonial Saints," 333–5; Anderson, *The Death and Afterlife of the North American Martyrs*, 21–53. On Brébeuf's death as a model both for European Catholics and for the Wendat, see Carson, "Brébeuf Was Never Martyred," 222–43.

76 MNF VII:494, 496. See also MNF VII:592 for the *Relation*'s explanation of why their deaths are martyrdoms.

77 Gregory, *Salvation at Stake*, 301–3.

78 Boss, "Writing a Relic," 225.

79 "ce saint homme qui a répandu son sang pour le soutien de la foy en ce païs." Marie de l'Incarnation, *Correspondance*, 814.

80 Ragueneau, *La vie*, 362; JR 50:87–9.

81 AJC-GLC, "Prodige operé par une relique du P. de brébeuf, sur le père francois Boniface," Q0001, D320, discussed in Overgaard and Cowan, "A 'Very Particular Assistance.'"
82 On the struggles of Jesuits and other missionaries to secure support for their work in New France, see Goddard, "Canada in Early Modern Jesuit Thought" and Codignola, "Few, Uncooperative, and Ill Informed," 173–85 and 186–99. On the many entanglements between Jesuits in New France and the wider imperial objectives of France, see McShea, *Apostles of Empire.*
83 Anderson, *The Death and Afterlife of the North American Martyrs*, 55–7, 63–6, 70–2; Anderson, "My Spirit Found a Unity with This Holy Man," 185–6.
84 MNF IX:393, 512.
85 MNF VI:695; MNF VIII:157, 158.
86 "le R.P. Ragueneau m'a fait la Charité de me donner, a son retour des hurons," AMHDQ, "Recit du Soulagement d'une possedée par l'Entremise des Reliques du R.P. Jean de Breboeuf dheureuse et saincte memoire."
87 Vatican Apostolic Archive, Congregazione dei Riti, vol. 4755, 372, 451–2, 457, 556, 651–2, 1037–9.

CHAPTER FIVE

1 "elle est resteé derechef Entierement delivree" ASJCF, Q-0001, 251.Il "Recit de la Deliurance D'une possedée par l'entremise des reliques du deffunct R.P. Jean de Breboeu[f] d'heureuse et sainte mémoire."
2 On 8 October 1668, she also became godmother to her niece Barbe Charlotte Albert, whose mother was Barbe's sister Elisabeth. *Québec, Notre-Dame, baptêmes 1667–1679*, Drouin Collection, 16; PRDH.
3 The Jesuit author of the *Relation* provided several reasons why he thought this opinion probable: the mother found the door of the house closed in the same fashion as she had left it going out; she did not see the woman dressed in white when she entered; all things were done as she was accustomed to doing them; this could not be attributed to anyone known in the neighbourhood, or in the country; the child was of an age little capable of lying; and, after all, God does sometimes favour the poor with such wonders. JR 50:50–3.
4 ANOM, Section Outre-mer, Dépôt de papiers publics des colonies, G[1] 460, F°13. Recensement du Canada. 1666; RAPQ 1935–36, 15.
5 Trudel, *La population du Canada en 1666*, 40–1. The careful noting of people's occupation was probably due to Intendant Jean Talon's keen interest in opportunities for economic improvement. Choquette, *Frenchmen into Peasants*, 9.

6 René Maheust, "ancien habitant de ce pays," was buried in Québec on 31 August 1661, and Marguerite Corriveau married Jean Maheu in Québec on 16 July 1663. *Québec, Notre-Dame, sépultures 1621–1671*, Drouin Collection, 197v; *Québec, Notre-Dame, mariages 1621–1671*, Drouin collection, 143r. The recently deceased husband and the new spouse probably did share a name. Spelling could change from document to document, even from census to census, so "Maheut" and "Maheu" and "Maheust" could certainly be thought of as variations of the same name. Charbonneau, Lavoie, and Légaré, "Recensements et registres paroissiaux du Canada," 99, 102.

7 René was born in Paris, whereas Jean was born in Québec with a father from the Perche region. "Marguerite Corriveau" in PRDH.

8 The register does say that the ceremony happened after an engagement and the publication of only one of the banns, having done away with the two others that were normal, but publishing the banns only once instead of three times was probably not very significant: of the other marriages registered on the same page, one had the banns published twice dispensing with the third, and the other dispensed of the publication of all three. *Québec, Notre-Dame, mariages 1621–1671*, Drouin Collection, 143r.

9 The age gap at first marriage reflects in part an age difference at immigration, where women were on average about three years younger than men upon their arrival in Canada. A more important contributor to the gap was the unbalanced sex ratio among marriageable settlers, which favoured women marrying shortly after arrival while men needed some years to become established. See chapter 2, and also Charbonneau et al., *The First French Canadians*, 97–100, 187; Roy and Charbonneau, "La nuptialité," 285–94.

10 Charbonneau et al., *The First French Canadians*, 201; Gauvreau, *Québec, une ville et sa population au temps de la Nouvelle-France*, 124–6.

11 One of Corriveau's landholdings was of eighteen feet fronting on rue Sous-le-Fort, with a depth extending about sixty-two feet. By 1667 her sons Louis and Paul owned a substantial house on this land. She also held lands on Ile d'Orléans with frontage on the St Lawrence River, and an additional holding that fronted the river in the seigneurie of Cap-Rouge, a bit to the west of the town. These lands had been conceded to René Maheut in 1655, 1651, and 1637. Trudel, *Le terrier du Saint-Laurent en 1663*, 68, 85, 134, 304.

12 *Jugements et délibérations du Conseil souverain de la Nouvelle-France*, I:97, 116, 147–9, 153–4, 159, 332–3.

13 The 1666 census suggests that domestic workers made up about 14 per cent of the population, and the 1667 census suggests they made

up about 11.5 per cent. Arnaud Bessière, noting that the censuses missed some of the population and that some people's occupations were not stated, has calculated that the actual number of servants was probably much higher, possibly upwards of 30 per cent of the workforce. Bessière, "La domesticité au Canada," 66–8. On the census missing perhaps a quarter of the population, see Trudel, *La population du Canada en 1666*, 54–6.

14 ANOM, Section Outre-mer, Dépôt de papiers publics des colonies, G[I] 460, image 19 on *New France Archives*. Recensement du Canada. 1667; Sulte, *Histoire des Canadiens-français*, 4:65.

15 "Debtes actiues de lhospital le 25me de Januier 1671," "a barbe halay pour Reste de ses gages 100 H" AMHDQ, *Recettes et Depenses de l'Hôtel-Dieu de Québec 1665 à 1725*, 72.

16 Religious communities were among the largest employers for domestic servants in seventeenth-century Québec. About 20 per cent of identified servants in 1666–67 worked in religious communities. Most were men, and most of their labour probably went towards managing the lands that the communities possessed in town and countryside, doing agricultural labour, taking care of buildings, and provisioning the communities. Barbe Hallay likely worked at the Hôtel-Dieu itself, where the servants also helped to look after the sick. Bessière, "Les domestiques des communautés religieuses," 45–69.

17 AMHDQ, *Recettes et Depenses de l'Hôtel-Dieu de Québec 1665 à 1725*, 11, 12, 14, 16–18, 23–6, 31, 35, 39, 55, 76; Rousseau, *L'œuvre de chère en Nouvelle-France*, 147–98.

18 Marie de l'Incarnation, *Correspondance*, 829. Hallay may have been in attendance during the final illness and death of Catherine de Saint-Augustin. Catherine began to fall ill at the end of April 1668 with spitting of blood. She appeared at first to respond well to remedies administered by the sisters, but on 3 May, which was also her thirty-sixth birthday as well as the feast of the Holy Cross, Catherine felt violent pains, was brought into the infirmary, and died five days later. Juchereau de Saint-Ignace and Duplessis, *Les annales de l'Hôtel-Dieu de Québec*, 155–8.

19 Marriage contracts were not required by law or custom, but they were quite common in New France. The reasons why they were more popular there than in France are unknown. Perhaps they helped speed the process of securing a match in a society where many people were removed from networks of kin, and perhaps the occasion of signing a contract created a welcome excuse for a social event. Choquette, *Frenchmen into Peasants*, 9; Trudel, *Histoire de la Nouvelle-France III*, 2:517–25; Dechêne, *Habitants and Merchants*, 240–1.

20 Jean Carrier was the son of Jean Carrier, deceased, and Jeanne Dodier. They were from the parish of Saint Georges in Xaintes, which was in the Saintonge province on the Atlantic coast of France. BANQ-Q, CN301, S95, Greffe de Pierre Duquet de la Chesnaye (1663–87), Contrat de mariage entre Jean Carrier, de la seigneurie de Lauson, fils de feu Jean Carrier et de Jeanne Dodier, de la paroisse de St Georges, évêché de Xaints; et Barbe Halay, fille de Jean-Baptiste Hallay et de Mathurine Vallet, de la seigneurie de Lauson, de la paroisse de St Jullien du Coudray, évêché de Chartres. 27 July 1670.

21 ANOM, Section Outre-mer, Dépôt de papiers publics des colonies, G^{I} 460, F°7. Recensement du Canada. 1666.

22 Her father and mother were there, as was her sister Elisabeth with her husband Guillaume Albert and their children. Sulte, *Histoire des Canadiens-français*, 4:71; Roy, *La Seigneurie de Lauzon*, I:168.

23 "Amour fait rage, mais l'argent fait mariage." Howell, "Some Choice Proverbs ... in the French Toung," n.p.

24 Trudel, *Histoire de la Nouvelle-France III*, 2:520–1. Jean Carrier had with him François Byssot, "S[ieu]r de la Riviere," previously member of the Communauté des habitants, seigneurial attorney, and provost judge, an inhabitant of Pointe-Lévy on the Lauzon shore where he had recently built the colony's first tannery; André Albert, "dit la Roche" or called the Rock, inhabitant of Lauzon; and Louis Gerezon, also inhabitant of Lauzon. The witnesses on Hallay's side were almost all family members: her father and mother, who gave their consent; Joachim Girard, husband of her sister Marie Hallay; and Guillaume Albert called "La Fontayne," husband of her sister Elisabeth. She also had as a witness Esther de Lambourg, widow of Guillaume Gaultier. Esther was not related to Barbe, but her place of origin in France was only about thirty kilometres away from Hallay's birthplace.

25 Régis de Roquefeuil, "Byssot (Bissot) de la Rivière, François," in DCB, vol. 1; Marie Esther Lambour Lafeuill in PRDH.

26 *Québec, Notre-Dame, mariages, 1667–1679*, Drouin Collection, 82. The autumnal timing was quite typical, with about three-fifths of men and two-thirds of women marrying for first time in autumn. It was generally linked to summer crossings of the ships, since the women married shortly after their arrival. Charbonneau et al., *The First French Canadians*, 90. The pairing was quite typical in another respect too. When female servants in New France married, most married an habitant, and sometimes he had also been a domestic. Bessière, "Faire une bonne et fidèle servante," 245.

27 See chapter 2.

28 Langlois, *Dictionnaire biographique des ancêtres québécois (1608–1700)*, I:353-4; Roy, *La Seigneurie de Lauzon*, I:143, 180, 183–4; *Jugements et délibérations du Conseil souverain de la Nouvelle-France*, I:417, 437–8.

29 The records provide no evidence for the quality of emotional attachment between the two spouses, nor anything direct about the presence of "amitié," that connection of mutual respect and intent to care for one another as described in chapter 2. On the role of affection in premodern families, see Ozment, *Ancestors*.

30 Oren-Magidor, "Conception, Pregnancy, and Childbirth," 57–8; Pollock, "Childbearing and Female Bonding," 287–8. As in early modern Europe, infanticide in New France was rare but harshly punished. On 7 September 1671, Françoise Duverger was convicted in Montréal of having hidden her pregnancy, medicating herself with the intention of causing an abortion, and then killing and burying her infant immediately after its birth. She was also convicted of having contributed to the murder of her first husband. Duverger was sentenced to be hanged and strangled, then, to serve as an example, her body was to be exposed on a gibbet on Cap Diamant. In November, Duverger was examined by a surgeon and a midwife, determined not to be pregnant, and then was executed. BAnQ Québec, Fonds Conseil souverain, TP1, S28, P738, and TP1, S28, P746; *Jugements et délibérations du Conseil souverain de la Nouvelle-France*, I:659–61; Cliche, "L'infanticide dans la région de Québec," 45.

31 Quoted in Dechêne, *Habitants and Merchants*, 56.

32 Charbonneau et al., *The First French Canadians*, 191–2.

33 PRDH; *Québec, Notre-Dame, baptêmes 1667–1679*, Drouin Collection, 155, 283. If there were other births, they do not seem to have been recorded in the baptismal register of either Québec or Lauzon. Child mortality was high. In spite of the healthy air as described in chapter 1, almost half of French settlers died before reaching young adulthood. Charbonneau et al., *The First French Canadians*, 195.

34 Firstborns were an exception, where conceptions often happened from November to February, probably reflecting the pattern of marriages following the ships' arrivals in the St Lawrence ports. Charbonneau et al., *The First French Canadians*, 112–15.

35 It has been calculated that 43 per cent of firstborns conceived in New France by female immigrants from France were born before the parents had been married a year. For subsequent births, the interval rose gradually until the second-to-last birth, and then a sudden increase occurred between penultimate and final birth. The mean age of the mother for the last birth was around forty. Charbonneau et al., *The First French Canadians*, 130, 132–7.

36 Dechêne, *Habitants and Merchants*, 144.

37 Greer, *The People of New France*, 27–9.

38 Marie de l'Incarnation, *Correspondance*, 759.

39 ANOM, Section Outre-mer, Dépôt de papiers publics des colonies, G^{I} 460, F°111. Recensement du Canada fait par l'intendant Du Chesneau. 14 November 1681; Sulte, *Histoire des Canadiens-français*, 5:76. For more on the census, see Charbonneau, Lavoie, and Légaré, "Le recensement nominatif du Canada en 1681," 77–98.

40 Dechêne, *Habitants and Merchants*, 170–83; Dechêne, *Power and Subsistence*, 7–9.

41 Roy, *La Seigneurie de Lauzon*, I:418–19; Jaenen, *The Role of the Church in New France*, 17. Other members of Hallay's family were doing well too. Her brother Jean-Baptiste occupied a bench with his wife Marie Marguerite Maranda on the other side of the nave in the same parish church. He had studied at the Québec seminary for a year or so when still a child, then helped cultivate his mother's land after the death of his father, married Marie Marguerite Maranda from the Ile d'Orléans, and became the first beadle of the parish of St Joseph in Lauzon. Responsibilities of this position included distributing bread to parishioners during mass, chasing away beggars and dogs, drawing water for baptisms and Sunday services, cutting branches for Palm Sunday, and looking after the regular cleaning of the church. Roy, *La Seigneurie de Lauzon*, I: 358–9, 418–19; Back, "Le bedeau de Notre-Dame," 60–1. The parish registry's entry for Jean-Baptiste's burial in 1726 says that the good services he provided as beadle for many years should move the parishioners to remember him and pray for the repose of his soul. *Québec, Lauzon, St-Joseph-de-la-Pointe-Lévy, 1679–1736*, Drouin Collection, 98v-99r.

42 *Québec, Lauzon, St-Joseph-de-la-Pointe-Lévy, 1679–1736*, Volume I, Cahier VI, Drouin Collection, 4r.

43 Oliver-Lloyd, *Le patrimoine archéologique des cimetières euroquébécois*, 12–13, 50–5.

44 On the whole, French settlers in Canada tended to have lower mortality rates than French people who remained in France. This difference was due to a combination of a lower population density, a less polluted environment, and, for the first generation of migrants, sufficiently good health to have made the trans-Atlantic crossing in the first place. Charbonneau et al., *The First French Canadians*, 162–80.

45 Campeau, "Un témoignage," 604.

46 Larocque, *La naissance et la mort à Québec autrefois*. Epidemic diseases were another cause of death. Smallpox, typhus, and measles all struck the

colonists during the span of Hallay's life. Lessard, *Au temps de la petite vérole*, 38–43.

47 *Québec, Notre-Dame, sépultures 1671–1679*, Drouin Collection, 224v–225r.

48 *Québec, Lauzon, St-Joseph-de-la-Pointe-Lévy, 1686*, Drouin Collection, 5v. Upon the death of both her parents, Barbe Hallay would have inherited the same share of their land as her brothers. Dechêne, *Habitants and Merchants*, 165–7, 244–9.

49 Three Jesuit priests along with Bishop Laval, the parish priest, the superior of the seminary, and seminarians attended his obsequies. *Journal des jésuites*, 360; JR 51:149.

50 Roy and Roy, *Inventaire de greffes des notaires du Régime français*, 2:44.

51 Roy, *La Seigneurie de Lauzon*, 1:lv–lvi; Langlois, *Dictionnaire biographique des ancêtres québécois (1608–1700)*, 1:353–4.

52 Dechêne, *Habitants and Merchants*, 59–61; Dechêne, *Le Peuple, l'État et la Guerre*, 121–217; Landry and Lessard, "Les causes de décès aux XVIIe et XVIIIe siècles," 509–26.

53 "Voicy vostre Nouvelle-France aux pieds de Vostre Majesté. Une troupe de barbares, comme vous fera voir ce petit livret, l'a réduite aux abois. Écoutez, SIRE, si vous l'avez pour agréable, sa voix languissante et ses dernières paroles: Sauvez-moi, s'écrie-t-elle. Je vais perdre la religion catholique. On me va ravir les Fleurs de Lys. Je se serai plus françoise. On me dérobe ce beau Nom, dont j'ay esté honorée depuis si longtemps. Je tomberay entre les mains des estrangers, quand les Iroquois auront tiré le reste de mon sang, qui ne coule quasi plus. Je seray bientost consommée dans leurs feux et le démon va enlever un grand nombre de nations qui attendront le salut de votre piété, de votre puissance et de votre générosité." MNF IX:572–3, quotation on 572. On Louis IX, and on his canonization as Saint Louis, see Le Goff, *Saint Louis*, and Gaposchkin, *The Making of Saint Louis*.

54 Dauchy, "Le conseil souverain de Québec," 513–26.

55 Havard and Vidal, *Histoire de l'Amérique française*, 100–1.

56 RAPQ 1930–31, 5–10. At the start of 1666, Colbert continued to express confidence that Canada would grow stronger in spite of its challenges. He even wrote that all the things necessary for life came with the same facility in Canada as they did in France. RAPQ 1930–31, 41–6.

57 "Mémoire de Talon sur l'État Présent du Canada (1667)," RAPQ 1930–31, 63–6.

58 Marie de l'Incarnation, *Correspondance*, 832.

59 *Québec, Notre-Dame, mariages 1667–1679*, Drouin Collection, 325; "Espérance Durosaire," in PRDH; Trudel, *Histoire de la Nouvelle-France IV*, 242.

60 Havard and Vidal, *Histoire de l'Amérique française*, 98; Noel, *Along a River*, 75–83; Landry, "Gender Imbalance," 14–32; Lanctôt, *Filles de joie ou Filles du Roi*, 101–26; RAPQ 1926–27, 24; Marie de l'Incarnation, *Correspondance*, 862; Charbonneau, Lavoie, and Légaré, "Le recensement nominatif du Canada en 1681," 81–2.

61 "Les Iroquois, qui sont distinguez en diverses nations et qui sont tous ennemis perpétuels et irréconciliables de la Colonie, ayant, par le massacre de quantité de François et par les inhumanitez qu'ils exercent contre ceux qui tombent en leur pouvoir, empesché que le pays ne se soit pas peuplé plus qu'il l'est à présent, et par leurs surprises et leurs courses inopinées tenant toujours en échec, le Roy, pour y apporter un remède convenable, a résolû de leur porter la guerre jusques dans leurs foyers pour les exterminer entièrement" RAPQ 1930–31, 7.

62 Verney, *The Good Regiment*; Dechêne, *Le Peuple, l'État et la Guerre*, 105–9. On diplomatic relations between the French and Indigenous nations at the end of the seventeenth century, see Havard, *The Great Peace of Montreal of 1701*.

63 Greer, *Property and Dispossession*, 145–54. The quotation by Talon is from RAPQ 1926–27, 9; Margry, *Découvertes et établissements des Français*, 1:256. The phrases "compact colony" and "extensive colony" come from Jaenen, "Colonisation compacte et colonisation extensive," 15–22. See also Havard and Vidal, *Histoire de l'Amérique française*, 99–112. For differing interpretations of the French presence in the Great Lakes region, see White, *The Middle Ground*, and Havard, *Empire et métissages*. On the figure of the coureur de bois, see Havard, *Histoire des coureurs de bois*.

64 Jean-Baptiste Colbert to Intendant Jean Talon, January 5, 1666, RAPQ 1930–31, 41 and 45, cited in Belmessous, "Assimilation and Racialism," 327–8.

65 Van Kirk, "Changing Patterns of Aboriginal/Non-Aboriginal Marriage," 1–11; Deslandres, "… alors nos garçons se marieront à vos filles, & nous ne ferons plus qu'un seul peuple," 5–35. By contrast, some women in the pays des Illinois by the late seventeenth century found Christian marriage to a French partner attractive. Morrissey, *Empire by Collaboration*, 64–5, 99–101.

66 The letter from Frontenac to Colbert is in RAPQ 1926–27, 34–5. Belmessous, "Assimilation and Racialism"; Belmessous, "Être français en Nouvelle-France," 510–15, 539; Havard, "Les forcer à devenir Cytoyens,"

989–1000; Belmessous, *Assimilation and Empire*, 28–30; Melzer, *Colonizer or Colonized*, 102–9. The league here was probably the *grande lieue ordinaire*, a length of just under five kilometres. Chardon, "The Linear League in North America," 128–53.

67 "Inventaire des documents concernant l'Église du Canada," RAPQ 1939–40, 219, 239.

68 Belmessous, *Assimilation and Empire*, 15–16, 27; Aubert, "The Blood of France," 439–78; Pagden, *The Burdens of Empire*, 97–119.

69 Cowan, "Education, *Francisation*," 1–29.

70 Dechêne, *Habitants and Merchants*, 260–1; Morin, *Annales de l'Hôtel-Dieu de Montréal*, 114–15. See also François Dollier de Casson, *Histoire du Montréal.*

71 The labels "missionary church" and "colonial church" are borrowed from Jaenen, *The Role of the Church in New France*, 1976. See also Codignola, "The Holy See and Conversion of the Indians," 208–13; Deslandres, "New France," 134–41.

72 Trudel, *Initiation à la Nouvelle-France*, 249–77.

73 *Édits*, 1:41.

74 Quoted in Jaenen, *The Role of the Church in New France*, 48.

75 Verney, *The Good Regiment*, 24–5.

76 Jaenen, *The Role of the Church in New France*, 66–8; Grégoire, "Mais comment peut-on être protestant en Nouvelle-France," 50–1; *Jugements et délibérations du Conseil souverain de la Nouvelle-France*, II:72; *Arrêts et règlements du Conseil supérieur*, 72.

77 Marie de l'Incarnation, *Correspondance*, 863.

78 Têtu and Gagnon, *Mandements*, 100–1, 161–2. In 1681, two parents from Lauzon refused to have their one-month-old child baptized even though they had been admonished on three occasions. The father was Jean Dumets. His wife was not named in the ordinance. Têtu and Gagnon, *Mandements*, 104–5.

79 Jaenen, *The Role of the Church in New France*, 123.

80 "Mandement Contre le Luxe et Vanité des Femmes et des Filles dans l'Église," "celles qui portent cet appareil fastueux jusques dans nos églises, paraissant dans ces lieux consacrés à la prière et à la pénitence avec des habits indécents, faisant voir des nudités scandaleuses des bras, d'épaules et de gorges, se contentant de les couvrir de toile transparente, qui ne sert bien souvent qu'à donner plus de lustre à ces nudités honteuses, la tête découverte, ou qui n'est couverte que de coiffes transparentes, et les cheveux frisés d'une manière indigne d'une personne chrétienne," "en cet état indécent." Têtu and Gagnon, *Mandements*, 106–8, quotations on 107. The bishop prohibited all girls and women from approaching the

sacraments, presenting blessed bread, and making the offering in such indecent manner, and he also prohibited all clergy from receiving the girls and women in this state. In 1694, an ordinance was issued listing occasions when confessors were to refuse or delay absolution. Among them was when women and girls had their breasts uncovered after being warned of the evil in this manner of dress. Holy Communion was not to be given to them when they presented themselves in this state. Têtu and Gagnon, *Mandements*, 323.

81 "Dieu veille que cela ne tire point en consequence." JR 50:206.

82 Têtu and Gagnon, *Mandements*, 302–4; Jaenen, *The Role of the Church in New France*, 131–2.

83 Cliche, "La confrérie de la Sainte-Famille"; Caulier, "Bâtir l'Amérique des dévots."

84 Davis, "The Reasons of Misrule," 41–75, quotation on 42. For more on the charivari in New France, see Hardy, *Charivari et justice populaire au Québec*; Massicotte, "Le charivari au Canada," 713–14.

85 Hardy, *Charivari et justice populaire au Québec*, 151, 157.

86 "grand nombre de personnes de l'un et l'autre sexe se seraient assemblées toutes les nuits sous le nom de charivari et auraient dans leurs désordres et libertés scandaleuses, comme il arrive ordinairement, commis des actions très impies et qui vont à une entière dérision de nos mystères, et des vérités de la Religion chrétienne et des plus saintes cérémonies de l'Eglise," Têtu and Gagnon, *Mandements*, 114–15, quotation on 114.

87 Marie de l'Incarnation, *Correspondance*, 873.

88 RAPQ 1926–27, 11–14.

89 RAPQ 1926–27, 28.

90 LAC, Ser 3, SOCG, Vol 256, "Informatio de statu Ecclesia Nouae Franciae," f 21r–24v.

91 Desrosiers and et al., *Sites archéologiques religieux du Québec*, 23–7, 113–15, 125; Tésio, "Indigence et maladie."

92 "il n'épargna rien, il consuma tout, provisions, meubles, bâtimens, excepté un petit corps de logis." Saint-Vallier, *Estat present de l'Eglise et de la colonie*, 8. Even some of the Ursulines' records were destroyed. The scribe of their *Annales* wrote at the start of the volume in 1689 that the earlier record had been consumed in the fire, and that their attempts to recreate what had been lost were neither so ample nor so correct in some circumstances as what had been in the original, being written for the most part based on the memory of those who had seen the start of the community joined to some remarks that they could find in old books. AUQ, *Annales des Ursulines de Québec 1639–1822*, 1/E, 1, 3, 2.0001, 2.

93 Roy, "Le château Saint-Louis;" Goyette, "The Origins of the Château Saint-Louis," 125–39.

94 "L'entrée de la Rivière du St Laurent, et la ville de Québec dans le Canada," probably by Jean-Baptiste Franquelin. BNF, département des Cartes et plans, GE SH 18 PF 127 DIV 6 P 1 D.

95 Although Carrier and Hallay are not among the list of habitants provided in the legend, some buildings on the map have no associated names, and the couple could perhaps have lived in one of those. Robert de Villeneuve, "Carte des Environs de Quebec en La Nouvelle France Mezuré sur le lieu très exactement en 1685 et 86 par le Sr Devilleneuve Ingénieur du Roy," BNF, département des Cartes et plans, GE SH 18 PF 127 DIV 7 P 4.

96 Among the necessary preconditions was a popular belief in the powers of witches and demons combined with an elite legal machinery willing to prosecute. Also necessary was a general atmosphere of heightened anxiety brought by public discussion of witchcraft or more indirectly by difficult developments in the economy, politics, or religion. Briggs, "Many Reasons Why," 49–63; Levack, *The Witch-Hunt in Early Modern Europe*, 160–7.

97 Pearl, "Witchcraft in New France in the Seventeenth Century," 41–55.

98 Briggs, *Witches and Neighbours*.

99 *Jugements et délibérations du Conseil souverain de la Nouvelle-France*, I:628–9; AMHDQ, *Chroniques de l'Hôtel-Dieu de Québec 1639–1958, Registre no.* 2, Première Partie: 1639–1698, 104; Juchereau de Saint-Ignace, *Histoire de l'Hôtel-Dieu de Quebec*, 230–1,345-7; AUQ, *Annales des Ursulines de Québec 1639–1822*, 1/E, 1, 3, 2.0001, 21r.; "Procès de Jean Campagna, prisonnier, 45 ans, laboureur, natif d'Angoulins en Aunis, demeurant à Beaubassin en Acadie, accusé de sorcellerie," BAnQ-Q, TP1, S777, D117, Fonds Conseil souverain; Jaenen, *The Role of the Church in New France*, 148–50; Séguin, *La sorcellerie au Québec*, 83–9, 93–9, 113, 125–8; Cliche, *Les pratiques de dévotion en Nouvelle-France*, 70–4. Choquette, "From Sea Monsters and Savages to Sorcerers and Satan," 42–3.

100 In early modern Europe, triggers for witchcraft accusations were usually some kind of personal misfortune that was interpreted as maleficent magic. These triggers included sudden death or the contraction of disease, loss of livestock, and romantic failure. Sometimes people brought charges deliberately against rivals and competitors. Levack, *The Witch-Hunt in Early Modern Europe*, 167–72. Marie-Aimée Cliche has found that many of the accusations of witchcraft in New France happened at times of epidemics or epizootics. Cliche, *Les pratiques de dévotion en Nouvelle-France*, 71.

101 AJC-GLC, Q0001, D320; JR 52:123; Overgaard and Cowan, "A 'Very Particular Assistance.'"

102 ASQ, Paroisses Diverses, no. 84, XIV. "plusieurs femmes fort incommodées d'un mal qui court ordinairement en Canada" The three women named in the record were "Marie Guyon femme du Sieur François Bellanger, Loüise Morin femme de Charles Cloustier, et Loüise Racine femme de Simeon Guyon tous habitans de beaupré." Dunn, "The Miracles at Sainte-Anne-du-Petit-Cap," 611–35.

103 He also claimed that a girl with a convulsive sickness had been cured after taking an emetic. Lessard, *Au temps de la petite vérole*, 24.

104 *Edit du Roy Pour la punition de différents crimes. Registré en Parlement le 31. Aoust. 1682*, translated into English in Levack, *The Witchcraft Sourcebook*, 181–3. On the debate around demons in England and a growing sense that belief in demonic power should be categorized as superstition, see Cameron, *Enchanted Europe*, 248–69.

105 Bever, "Witchcraft Prosecutions and the Decline of Magic," 263. For an earlier observation of this periodization in the history of witchcraft, see Mandrou, *Magistrats et sorciers*.

106 Bever, "Witchcraft Prosecutions and the Decline of Magic," 263–93; Goodare, *The European Witch-Hunt*, 317–59; Bostridge, *Witchcraft and Its Transformations c.1650–c.1750*.

107 "Sorcellerie" is defined as "Art magique, qui emprunte le secours et le ministère du Diable." The example of usage is "Les ignorants attribuent à sorcellerie tous les effets dont ils ne peuvent pénétrer les causes." Houdard, "Quand les matous vont au sabbat," 149–66, cited in Goodare, *The European Witch-Hunt*, 344.

108 For "Demoniaque," "Qui est possedé du Demon. Le Seigneur a gueri plusieurs Demoniaques. L'Eglise exorcise les Demoniaques." and "se dit figurément de ceux qui crient, qui tempestent, qui menacent. Ce mary, quand il a bû, fait le demoniaque dans le logis." Furetière, *Dictionnaire universel*, n.p.

109 Levack, *The Devil Within*, 215–49. On belief in demons and the efficacy of exorcism persisting into the eighteenth century, sometimes without a concurrent concern about witches, see Midelfort, *Exorcism and Enlightenment*, and Bárth, *The Exorcist of Sombor*.

110 Magic was theoretically still possible and possibly very harmful, even if rarely prosecuted. In 1694, the bishop published a mandate on which sins were so enormous that he reserved them to the bishops to decide whether to absolve or not. The first was speaking publicly or writing something injurious against God, the Holy Virgin, and the saints. The

second was magic, and in this category were included both those who made use of illicit means and also those who consulted the users. The other sins on the list were hitting a father and mother or refusing them help; incest; sodomy and bestiality; adultery or public concubinage; attempted rape against children; eating meat during fast days without permission; making libels or defamatory songs; dueling; failing to pay the tithe; "impurity" (sexual relations) between French men and Indigenous women; and sacrilege. Têtu and Gagnon, *Mandements*, 328–31.

111 *Catéchisme du diocese de Quebec*, 166.

112 *Rituel du diocese de Quebec*, 309–10, 485–527.

113 Hutton, *The Witch*, 181–2.

114 Pearson, "Il sera important de me mander le détail de toutes choses," 45–65.

115 "Cet exemple, suivi de quelques autres, m'a persuadé qu'il étoit presque impossible de détromper une personne qui s'étoit laissé préoccuper sur cette matière." "Je sais qu'il est très difficile de se défaire de ces sortes de préoccupations, où, pour l'ordinaire, le démon se mêle, pour en augmenter le mal et empêcher qu'on ne se détrompe; mais j'espère que Notre Seigneur aura égard à la pureté de vos intentions, et que le désir sincère qu'il vous donne de le servir ne sera pas frustré de son effet, dans un temps où il me semble que l'on a plus besoin de votre secours." Bernard, *Correspondance de M. Louis Tronson*, 2:187–8, 204–5, quotations on 187 and 205.

116 "Je crois qu'il demande que vous repassiez en France cette année. Un plus long séjour en Canada ne vous seroit pas utile et pourroit faire tort à plusieurs." Bernard, *Correspondance de M. Louis Tronson*, 2:303. Tronson also asked Sulpicians in France to cease their exorcisms, 22–6.

117 "des plus atroces Injures quon puisse dire Contre Lhonneur et reputato.' dunne famille en Les Chargant de Confusion et de reproches, traitant Lun et L'autre de vieux diable vieux Loup Sorcier Magicien et autres parolles Injurieuses" quoted in Séguin, *La sorcellerie au Québec*, 197.

118 In France, older demonological books continued to be reprinted, but for fun rather than as serious treatises. As Lyndal Roper put it, "demonology had become entertainment." Roper, *The Witch*, 44.

119 Fournier, "Le diable, le saint, le revenant et la fée," 117–35; Du Berger, *Le Diable à la danse*.

120 Gitlin and Brasseaux, "Chasing *La Chasse-Galerie*," 221–43, quotations on 222.

CONCLUSION

1 For uses of the microscope and telescope metaphors in microhistorical and macrohistorical investigations, see Menegon, "Telescope and Microscope"; Magnússon and Szíjártó, *What Is Microhistory?*, 4–5.

2 Historians have often claimed to use "thick description," as advised by Clifford Geertz in *The Interpretation of Cultures*, where behaviour is "symbolic action" that "signifies," and is intelligible within an "imaginative universe" where "acts are signs." (10, 13) For a critical evaluation of these claims, see Clark, "Thick Description, Thin History." For an argument in favour of the "Singularization of History," which limits contextualization to the immediate environment of the historical subject, see Magnússon, "Far-Reaching Microhistory."

3 Thevet, "Cosmographie universelle" and "Description de Plusieurs Isles," 195–7, 202–9; Lestringant, "L'île des Démons," 99–125.

4 Samuel de Champlain, *The Works of Champlain*, vol. 1, 186–9; Thierry, "Le discours démonologique," 210–11.

5 MNF I: 460–2.

6 Europeans elsewhere in the world, and especially missionaries, also believed that they were fighting against demonic forces that were essentially similar to what the missionaries thought they knew in Europe. See, for example, Zhang, "About God, Demons, and Miracles"; Gareis, "Merging Magical Traditions"; Clossey, *Salvation and Globalization*, 131–3; Javellana, "The Jesuits and the Indigenous Peoples of the Philippines," 422, 427; Cervantes, *The Devil in the New World*; Bauer, "Baroque New Worlds," 46; Li, *Stratégies missionaires*. For a connected history of demonology across Eurasia, see White, *Daemons are Forever*.

7 Some of the Jesuit missionaries may have taken this possibility of difference seriously. See Cowan, "Jesuit Missionaries and the Accommodationist Demons."

Bibliography

ARCHIVES CONSULTED

Archive of the Jesuits in Canada
Archives de l'archidiocèse de Québec
Archives des Ursulines de Québec
Archives du Monastère de l'Hôtel-Dieu de Québec
Archives du Séminaire de Québec
Archives nationales, Outre-Mer, Colonies (Aix-en-Provence) via microfilms
LAC, *New France Archives*, https://nouvelle-france.org
Archivum Romanum Societas Iesu
Bibliothèque et Archives nationales du Québec
Bibliothèque nationale de France
Bibliothèque Sainte-Geneviève
Georgetown University Manuscripts
Library and Archives Canada
Propaganda Fide Historical Archives
Vatican Apostolic Archive

PUBLISHED PRIMARY AND SECONDARY SOURCES

Advitam, Bibliothèque et Archives nationales de Québec. https://advitam.banq.qc.ca.

Anderson, Emma. *The Death and Afterlife of the North American Martyrs*. Cambridge, MA: Harvard University Press, 2013.

– "'My Spirit Found a Unity with This Holy Man': A Nun's Visions and the Negotiation of Pain and Power in Seventeenth-Century New

France." In *Dreams, Dreamers, and Visions: The Early Modern Atlantic World*, edited by Ann Marie Plane and Leslie Tuttle, 185–204. Philadelphia: University of Pennsylvania Press, 2013.

Archives de la province de Québec. *Rapport de l'Archiviste de la province de Québec, 1930–1931*. Quebec: Rédempti Paradis, 1931.

Arrêts et règlements du Conseil supérieur de Québec, et ordonnances et jugements des intendants du Canada. Quebec: E.R. Fréchette, 1855.

Asher, David, Mark Bailey, Apostolos Christou, John McFarland, Mark Muir, and Paul Rafferty. "Comet Ikeya-Zhang Rises for the NAM." *Astronomy & Geophysics* 43, no. 2 (April 2002): 2.19–2.21.

Aslanian, Sebouh David, Joyce E. Chaplin, Ann Mcgrath, and Kristin Mann. "AHR *Conversation*. How Size Matters: The Question of Scale in History." *American Historical Review* 118, no. 5 (December 2013): 1431–72.

Asselin, Claire, and Anne McLaughlin. "Patois ou français: la langue de la Nouvelle-France au 17e siècle." *Langage et société*, no. 17 (1981): 3–57.

Aubert, Guillaume. "'The Blood of France': Race and Purity of Blood in the French Atlantic World." *William and Mary Quarterly* 61, no. 3 (July 2004): 439–78.

Axtell, James. *The Invasion Within: The Contest of Cultures in Colonial North America*. New York: Oxford University Press, 1985.

– "The Power of Print in the Eastern Woodlands." *William and Mary Quarterly* 44, no. 2 (1987): 300–9.

Back, Francis. "Le bedeau de Notre-Dame." *Cap-aux-Diamants*, no. 62 (Summer 2000): 60–1.

Baker, Emerson W. *The Devil of Great Island: Witchcraft and Conflict in Early New England*. New York: Palgrave Macmillan, 2007.

Ballone, Angela. *The 1624 Tumult of Mexico in Perspective (c. 1620–1650): Authority and Conflict Resolution in the Iberian Atlantic*. Leiden: Brill, 2018.

Bamji, Alexandra. "The Catholic Life Cycle." In *The Ashgate Research Companion to the Counter-Reformation*, edited by Alexandra Bamji, Geert H. Janssen, and Mary Laven, 183–201. Farnham: Ashgate, 2013.

Baratay, Eric. "L'excommunication et l'exorcisme des animaux aux XVIIe-XVIIIe siècles, une négociation entre bêtes, fidèles et clergé." *Revue d'Histoire ecclésiastique* 107, no. 1 (2012): 223–54.

Barbaud, Philippe. *Le choc des patois en Nouvelle-France: essai sur l'histoire de la francisation au Canada*. Quebec: Presses de l'Université du Québec, 1984.

Bardet, Jean-Pierre. "Early Marriage in Pre-Modern France." *History of the Family* 6, no. 3 (2001): 345–63.

Bárth, Dániel. *The Exorcist of Sombor: The Mentality of an Eighteenth-Century Franciscan Friar*. New York: Routledge, 2020.

Bates, Réal. "Les conceptions prénuptiales dans la vallée du Saint-Laurent avant 1725." *Revue d'histoire de l'Amérique française* 40, no. 2 (1986): 253–72.

Bauer, Ralph. "Baroque New Worlds: Ethnography and Demonology in the Reformation and Counter-Reformation." In *Religious Transformations in the Early Modern Americas*, edited by Stephanie Kirk and Sarah Rivett, 46–78. Philadelphia: University of Pennsylvania Press, 2014.

Beaulieu, Alain. *Convertir les fils de Caïn. Jésuites et Amérindiens nomades en Nouvelle-France, 1632–1642*. Quebec: Nuit Blanche, 1990.

Bédard, Hélène. *Maisons et églises du Québec XVIIe, XVIIIe, XIXe Siècles*. Quebec: Editeur officiel du Québec, 1972.

Bédard, Marc-André. *Les protestants en Nouvelle-France*. Quebec: La Société historique de Québec, 1978.

Beik, William A. *A Social and Cultural History of Early Modern France*. Cambridge: Cambridge University Press, 2009.

Bell, David A. "Lingua Populi, Lingua Dei: Language, Religion, and the Origins of French Revolutionary Nationalism." *American Historical Review* 100, no. 5 (1995): 1403–37.

Belmessous, Saliha. *Assimilation and Empire: Uniformity in French and British Colonies, 1541–1954*. Oxford: Oxford University Press, 2013.

– "Assimilation and Racialism in Seventeenth and Eighteenth-Century French Colonial Policy." *American Historical Review* 110, no. 2 (2005): 322–49.

– "Être français en Nouvelle-France: Identité française et identité coloniale aux dix-septième et dix-huitième siècles." *French Historical Studies* 27, no. 3 (Summer 2004): 507–40.

Benedict, Philip. "French Cities from the Sixteenth Century to the Revolution: An Overview." In *Cities and Social Change in Early Modern France*, edited by Philip Benedict, 7–68. London: Routledge, 1992.

Bergin, Joseph. *Church, Society and Religious Change in France, 1580–1730*. New Haven: Yale University Press, 2009.

Bernard, Louis, ed. *Correspondance de M. Louis Tronson, Troisième Supérieur de la Compagnie de Saint-Sulpice*. Volume 2. Paris: Librairie Victor Lecoffre, 1904.

Berry, Lynn. "« Le Ciel et la Terre nous ont parlé. » : Comment les missionnaires du Canada français de l'époque coloniale interprétèrent le tremblement de terre de 1663." *Revue d'histoire de l'Amérique française* 60, nos. 1–2 (February 2007): 11–35.

Besnard, Joseph. "Les diverses professions de Robert Giffard." *Nova Francia* 4, no. 6 (November-December 1929): 322–9.

– "Les préliminaires de l'émigration percheronne au Canada." *Nova Francia* 5, no. 2 (March-April 1930): 66–75.

Bessière, Arnaud. "La domesticité au Canada aux XVIIe et XVIIIe siècles : mesures d'un phénomène." In *La domesticité au siècle des Lumières. Une approche comparative*, edited by Bruno Bernard and Xavier Stevens, 61–79. No spécial 86. Brussels: Archives et bibliothèques de Belgique, 2009.

– "Les domestiques des communautés religieuses au Canada au XVIIe siècle." *Études d'histoire religieuse* 74 (2008): 45–69.

– "« Faire une bonne et fidèle servante » au Canada sous le régime français." *Histoire sociale/Social History* 50, no. 102 (2017): 233–57.

– "Le salaire des domestiques au Canada au XVIIe siècle." *Histoire, économie & société* 27e année, no. 4 (2008): 33–50.

Bever, Edward. "Bullying, the Neurobiology of Emotional Aggression, and the Experience of Witchcraft." In *Emotions in the History of Witchcraft*, edited by Laura Kounine and Michael Ostling, 193–212. London: Palgrave Macmillan, 2016.

– *The Realities of Witchcraft and Popular Magic in Early Modern Europe: Culture, Cognition and Everyday Life*. New York: Palgrave Macmillan, 2008.

– "Witchcraft Prosecutions and the Decline of Magic." *Journal of Interdisciplinary History* 40, no. 2 (Autumn 2009): 263–93.

Bilinkoff, Jodi. *Related Lives: Confessors and Their Female Penitents, 1450–1750*. Ithaca: Cornell University Press, 2005.

Blackburn, Carole. *Harvest of Souls: The Jesuit Missions and Colonialism in North America, 1632–1650*. Montreal and Kingston: McGill-Queen's University Press, 2004.

Boleda, Mario. "Nouvelle estimation de l'immigration française au Canada, 1608–1760." In *Le peuplement du Canada aux XVIIe et XVIIIe siècles*, edited by Yves Landry, 29–37. Caen: Centre de recherche d'histoire quantitative, 2004.

Bonvillain, Nancy. "Jesuit Perceptions of Iroquoian Culture: Ethnocentrism and Enlightenment." In *Jesuit Encounters in the New World: Jesuit Chroniclers, Geographers, Educators and Missionaries in the Americas, 1549–1767*, edited by Joseph A. Gagliano and Charles E. Ronan, 81–97. Rome: Institutum Historicum Societatis Iesu, 1997.

Boss, Julia. "Writing a Relic: The Uses of Hagiography in New France." In *Colonial Saints: Discovering the Holy in the Americas, 1500–1800*, edited by Allan Greer and Jodi Bilinkoff, 211–34. New York: Routledge, 2003.

Bossy, John. *Christianity in the West, 1400–1700*. Oxford: Oxford University Press, 1988.

Bostridge, Ian. *Witchcraft and Its Transformations c.1650–c.1750*. Oxford: Clarendon Press, 1997.

Boucher, Pierre. *Histoire véritable et naturelle des mœurs et productions du pays de la Nouvelle-France, vulgairement dite le Canada*. Paris: Florentin Lambert, 1664.

– *Histoire véritable et naturelle des mœurs et productions du pays de la Nouvelle-France vulgairement dite le Canada. 1664*. Edited by Pierre Benoit. Quebec: Septentrion, 2014.

Bourgeoys, Marguerite. *Marguerite Bourgeoys: Textes choisis et présentés par Hélène Bernier*. Montreal: Fides, 1958.

Bouwsma, William J. *The Waning of the Renaissance, 1550–1640*. New Haven: Yale University Press, 2000.

Bowden, Caroline. "Collecting the Lives of Early Modern Women Religious: Obituary Writing and the Development of Collective Memory and Corporate Identity." *Women's History Review* 19, no. 1 (February 2010): 7–20.

Boyer, Raymond. *Les crimes et les châtiments au Canada français du XVIIe au XXe siècle*. Ottawa: Le Cercle du Livre de France, 1966.

Brazeau, Brian. *Writing a New France, 1604–1632: Empire and Early Modern French Identity*. Farnham: Ashgate, 2009.

Brewer, John. "Microhistory and the Histories of Everyday Life." *Cultural and Social History* 7 (2010): 86–109.

Briggs, Robin. "Emotion and Affect in Lorraine Witchcraft Trials." In *Emotions in the History of Witchcraft*, edited by Laura Kounine and Michael Ostling, 137–53. London: Palgrave Macmillan, 2016.

– "From Devilry to Sainthood: Mère Jeanne Des Anges and the Catholic Reform." In *Women and Religion in the Atlantic Age, 1550–1900*, edited by Emily Clark and Mary Laven, 33–48. Farnham: Ashgate, 2013.

– "Male Witches in the Duchy of Lorraine." In *Witchcraft and Masculinities in Early Modern Europe*, edited by Alison Rowlands, 31–51. New York: Palgrave Macmillan, 2009.

– "'Many Reasons Why': Witchcraft and the Problem of Multiple Explanation." In *Witchcraft in Early Modern Europe: Studies in Culture and Belief*, edited by Jonathan Barry, Marianne Hester, and Gareth Roberts, 49–63. Cambridge: Cambridge University Press, 1998.

– *Witches and Neighbours: The Social and Cultural Context of European Witchcraft*. 2nd ed. Oxford: Blackwell Publishing, 2002.

Brockliss, Laurence, and Colin Jones. *The Medical World of Early Modern France*. Oxford: Clarendon Press, 1997.

Brogan, Boyd. "His Belly, Her Seed: Gender and Medicine in Early Modern Demonic Possession." *Representations* 147, no. 1 (2019): 1–25.

Broomhall, Susan. *Women's Medical Work in Early Modern France*. Manchester: Manchester University Press, 2004.

Brousseau, Anne-Marie. "The Sociolect of 17th–18th Century French Settlers: Phonological Clues from French Creoles." *University of Pennsylvania Working Papers in Linguistics* 10, no. 2 (2014): 45–60.

Burguière, André. "L'État monarchique et la famille (*XVI*e *XVIII*e siècle)." *Annales. Histoire, Sciences Sociales* 56, no. 2 (2001): 313–35.

Burke, Peter. "America and the Rewriting of World History." In *America in European Consciousness, 1493–1750*, edited by Karen Ordahl Kupperman, 33–51. Chapel Hill: University of North Carolina Press, 1995.

Cabré, Montserrat. "Women or Healers? Household Practices and the Categories of Health Care in Late Medieval Iberia." *Bulletin of the History of Medicine* 82, no. 1 (Spring 2008): 18–51.

Caciola, Nancy, and Moshe Sluhovsky. "Spiritual Physiologies: The Discernment of Spirits in Medieval and Early Modern Europe." *Preternature: Critical and Historical Studies on the Preternatural* 1, no. 1 (2012): 1–48.

Camba, Alvin Almendrala. "Religion, Disaster, and Colonial Power in the Spanish Philippines in the Sixteenth to Seventeenth Centuries." *Journal for the Study of Religion, Nature and Culture* 6, no. 2 (July 2012): 215–47.

Cambray, Alfred A. *Robert Giffard: premier seigneur de Beauport et les origines de la Nouvelle-France*. Cap-de-la-Madeleine, 1932.

Cameron, Euan. *Enchanted Europe: Superstition, Reason, and Religion, 1250–1750*. Oxford: Oxford University Press, 2010.

Campeau, Lucien. *Cent Associés et le peuplement de la Nouvelle-France (1633–1663)*. Montreal: Bellarmin, 1974.

– "Un témoignage de 1651 sur la Nouvelle-France." *Revue d'histoire de l'Amérique française* 23, no. 4 (March 1970): 601–12.

Carpin, Gervais. *Histoire d'un mot: L'ethnonyme Canadien de 1535 à 1691*. Quebec: Septentrion, 1995.

Carson, James Taylor. "Brébeuf Was Never Martyred: Reimagining the Life and Death of Canada's First Saint." *Canadian Historical Review* 97, no. 2 (Summer 2016): 222–43.

Cartier, Gwenaël. "Québec 1608–2008: 400 ans de statistiques démographiques tirées Des recensements." *Cahiers Québécois de Démographie* 37, no. 1 (Spring 2008): 131–61.

Catéchisme du diocese de Quebec par Monseigneur l'Illustrissime & Reverendissime Jean de la Croix de saint Vallier, Evêque de Quebec. Paris: Urbain Coustelier, 1702.

Caulier, Brigitte. "« Bâtir la Jérusalem des Terres froides » : Réflexion sur le catholicisme français en Nouvelle-France." In *Mémoires de Nouvelle-France: De France en Nouvelle-France*, edited by Philippe Joutard, Thomas Wien, and Didier Poton, 235–49. Rennes: Presses universitaires de Rennes, 2005.

– "Bâtir l'Amérique des dévots: Les confréries de dévotion montréalaises depuis le Régime français." *Revue d'histoire de l'Amérique française* 46 no. 1 (1992): 45–66.

Cellard, André. *Histoire de la folie au Québec de 1600 à 1850*. Montreal: Boréal, 1991.

Certeau, Michel de. *The Possession at Loudun*. Translated by Michael B. Smith. Chicago: University of Chicago Press, 2000.

Certeau, Michel de. *The Writing of History*, translated by Tom Conley. New York: Columbia University Press, 1998.

Cervantes, Fernando. *The Devil in the New World: The Impact of Diabolism in New Spain*. New Haven: Yale University Press, 1994.

Chamberland, Richard. *Lithobolia, or, the Stone-throwing Devil*. London: E. Whitlook, 1698.

Champlain, Samuel de. *The Works of Samuel de Champlain*. Volume 1, *1599–1607*. Edited by H.P. Biggar. Toronto: The Champlain Society, 1922.

– *The Works of Samuel de Champlain*. Volume 2, *1608–1613*. Edited by H.P. Biggar. Toronto: The Champlain Society, 1925.

Chapdelaine, Claude. "Overview of the St Lawrence Archaic through Woodland." In *The Oxford Handbook of North American Archaeology*, edited by Timothy R. Pauketat, 249–61. Oxford: Oxford University Press, 2012.

Charbonneau, Hubert. *Tourouvre-au-Perche aux XVIIe et XVIIIe siècles: étude de démographie historique*. Institut national d'études démographiques, Travaux et documents 55. Paris: PUF, 1970.

Charbonneau, Hubert, Bertrand Desjardins, André Guillemette, Yves Landry, Jacques Légaré, and François Nault. *The First French Canadians: Pioneers in the St Lawrence Valley*. Translated by Paola Colozzo. Newark, DE: University of Delaware Press, 1993.

Charbonneau, Hubert, Yolande Lavoie, and Jacques Légaré. "Recensements et registres paroissiaux du Canada durant la période 1665–1668. Étude critique." *Population* 25, no. 1 (1970): 97–124.

Charbonneau, Hubert, Yolande Lavoie, and Jacques Légaré. "Le recensement nominatif du Canada en 1681." *Histoire sociale/ Social History* 4, no. 7 (1971): 77–98.

Chardon, Roland. "The Linear League in North America." *Annals of the Association of American Geographers* 70, no. 2 (June 1980): 129–53.

Chaudenson, Robert. "Français d'Amérique du Nord et créoles français: le français parlé par les immigrants du XVIIe siècle." In *Les Origines du français québécois*, edited by Raymond Mougeon and Edouard Beniak, 167–80. Quebec: Presses de l'Université Laval, 1994.

Chénier, Rémi. *Québec: A French Colonial Town in America, 1660 to 1690*. Ottawa: Minister of the Environment, 1991.

Chiang, Connie Y. "The Nose Knows: The Sense of Smell in American History." *Journal of American History* 95, no. 2 (2008): 405–16.

Choquette, Leslie. "The Ancien Régime Culture of Labor Mobility and Migration to New France." In *French Connections: Cultural Mobility in North America and the Atlantic World, 1600–1875*, edited by Robert Englebert and Andrew N. Wegmann, 73–96. Baton Rouge: Louisiana State University Press, 2020.

– "'Ces Amazones Du Grand Dieu': Women and Mission in Seventeenth-Century Canada." *French Historical Studies* 17, no. 3 (1992): 627–55.

– *Frenchmen into Peasants: Modernity and Tradition in the Peopling of French Canada*. Cambridge, MA: Harvard University Press, 1997.

– "From Sea Monsters and Savages to Sorcerers and Satan: A History of Fear in New France." In *Fear and the Shaping of Early American Societies*, edited by Lauric Henneton and L.H. Roper, 38–59. Boston: Brill, 2016.

– "Proprietorships in French North America." In *Constructing Early Modern Empires: Proprietary Ventures in the Atlantic World, 1500–1750*, edited by L.H. Roper and Bertrand Van Ruymbeke, 117–31. Leiden: Brill, 2007.

Clark, Stuart. "Thick Description, Thin History: Did Historians Always Understand Clifford Geertz?" In *Interpreting Clifford Geertz: Cultural*

Investigation in the Social Sciences, edited by Matthew Norton, 105–19. New York: Palgrave Macmillan, 2011.
– *Thinking with Demons: The Idea of Witchcraft in Early Modern Europe*. New York: Oxford University Press, 1999.
Cliche, Marie-Aimée. "La confrérie de la Sainte-Famille à Québec sous le régime français, 1663–1760." *Session d'étude, Société canadienne d'histoire de l'Église catholique* 43 (1976): 79–93.
– "L'infanticide dans la région de Québec (1660–1969)." *Revue d'histoire de l'Amérique française* 44, no. 1 (Summer 1990): 31–59.
– *Les pratiques de dévotion en Nouvelle-France: comportements populaires et encadrement ecclésial dans le gouvernement de Québec*. Quebec: Presses de l'Université Laval, 1988.
Clossey, Luke. "Faith in Empire: Religious Sources of Legitimacy for Expansionist Early-Modern States." In *Politics and Reformations: Communities, Polities, Nations, and Empires. Essays in Honor of Thomas A. Brady, Jr*, edited by Christopher Ocker, Michael Printy, Peter Starenko, and Peter Wallace, 571–87. Leiden: Brill, 2007.
– *Salvation and Globalization in the Early Jesuit Missions*. Cambridge: Cambridge University Press, 2011.
Cloutier, Céline. "The Foreshore of the St Lawrence at the Îlot Hunt Site in the 17th and 18th Centuries: An Open Dump?" *Post-Medieval Archaeology* 43, no. 1 (June 2009): 245–57.
Cloutier, Pierre, and Paul-Gaston L'Anglais. "The Saint-Louis Forts and Chateaux Site: Archaeology in the Heart of New France." *Post-Medieval Archaeology* 43, no. 1 (June 2009): 106–24.
Coates, Colin, and Dagomar Degroot. "« Les bois engendrent les frimas et les gelées » : comprendre le climat en Nouvelle-France." *Revue d'histoire de l'Amérique française* 68, nos. 3–4 (2015): 197–219.
Codignola, Luca. "Few, Uncooperative, and Ill Informed? The Roman Catholic Clergy in French and British North America, 1610–1658." In *Decentring the Renaissance: Canada and Europe in Multidisciplinary Perspective, 1500–1700*, edited by Germaine Warkentin and Carolyn Podruchny, 173–85. Toronto: University of Toronto Press, 2001.
– "The Holy See and the Conversion of the Indians in French and British North America, 1486–1760." In *America in European Consciousness, 1493–1750*, edited by Karen Ordahl Kupperman, 195–242. Chapel Hill: University of North Carolina Press, 1995.
Cohen, Deborah, and Peter Mandler. "*The History Manifesto*: A Critique." *American Historical Review* 120, no. 2 (April 2015): 530–42.

Cohen, Esther. "Law, Folklore and Animal Lore." *Past & Present* 110, no. 1 (1986): 6–37.

Cohen, Paul. "Penser un empire de Babel. Langues et célébration du pouvoir royal dans le monde atlantique français XVIe-XVIIe siècles." In *Français Français? La nation en débat entre colonies et métropole (XVIe-XIXe siècle)*, edited by Cécile Vidal, 35–54. Paris: Éditions de l'École des Hautes Études en Sciences Sociales, 2014.

Cohen, Thomas V. "The Macrohistory of Microhistory." *Journal of Medieval and Early Modern Studies* 47, no. 1 (2017): 53–73.

Constitutions de la Congregation des religieuses Hospitalieres de la Misericorde de Jesus. De l'Ordre de Sainct Augustin. 1666.

Cook, Peter. "Vivre comme frères: le rôle du registre fraternel dans les premières alliances franco-amérindiennes au Canada (vers 1580–1650)." *Recherches amérindiennes au Québec* 31, no. 2 (2001): 55–65.

Cook, Ramsay, and H.P. Biggar, eds. *The Voyages of Jacques Cartier.* Toronto: University of Toronto Press, 2013.

Cotgrave, Randle. *A Dictionarie of the French and English Tongues.* London: Adam Islip, 1611.

Cowan, Mairi. "A Contested Conception: Jocelin of Furness and St Kentigern in Twelfth-Century Glasgow." In *From Learning to Love: Schools, Law, and Pastoral Care in the Middle Ages*, edited by Tristan Sharp with Isabelle Cochelin, Greti Dinkova-Bruun, Abigail Firey, and Giulio Silano, 571–89. Toronto: Pontifical Institute for Mediaeval Studies Press, 2017.

– "A Deliverance from Demons: Possession and Healing at the Seigneurie of Beauport." In *French Connections: Cultural Mobility in North America and the Atlantic World, 1600–1875*, edited by Robert Englebert and Andrew N. Wegmann, 11–34. Baton Rouge: Louisiana State University Press, 2020.

– "Education, *Francisation*, and Shifting Colonial Priorities at the Ursuline Convent in Seventeenth-Century Québec." *Canadian Historical Review* 99, no. 1 (March 2018): 1–29.

– "Jesuit Missionaries and the Accommodationist Demons of New France." In *Knowing Demons, Knowing Spirits in the Early Modern Period*, edited by Michelle D. Brock, Richard Raiswell, and David R. Winter, 211–38. Basingstoke: Palgrave Macmillan, 2018.

– "The Thistle and the Cross." *Canada's History*, February-March 2022, 39–45.

Crowley, Terrence. "Women, Religion and Freedom in New France." In *Race and Gender in the Northern Colonies*, edited by Jan Noel, 101–18. Toronto: Canadian Scholars' Press, 2000.

Daston, Lorraine, and Katharine Park. *Wonders and the Order of Nature, 1150–1750*. New York: Zone Books, 1998.

Dauge-Roth, Katherine. *Signing the Body: Marks on Skin in Early Modern France*. London: Routledge, 2019.

Davidson, Alan. "Watermelon." In *The Oxford Companion to Food*, edited by Alan Davidson and Tom Jaine, 3rd edition. Oxford: Oxford University Press, 2014.

Davidson, Jane P., and Christopher John Duffin. "Stones and Spirits." *Folklore* 123, no. 1 (2012): 99–109.

Davis, Natalie Zemon. "Ghosts, Kin, and Progeny: Some Features of Family Life in Early Modern France." *Daedalus* 106, no. 2 (Spring 1977): 87–114.

– "The Reasons of Misrule: Youth Groups and Charivaris in Sixteenth-Century France." *Past & Present* 50, no. 1 (1971): 41–75.

– *The Return of Martin Guerre*. Cambridge, MA: Harvard University Press, 1983.

– *Women on the Margins: Three Seventeenth-Century Lives*. Cambridge, MA: Harvard University Press, 1997.

Dauchy, Serge. "Le conseil souverain de Québec. Une institution de l'ancienne France pour le Nouveau Monde." *Revue du Nord* 3, no. 411 (2015): 513–26.

Dechêne, Louise. "L'évolution du régime seigneurial au Canada. Le cas de Montréal aux XVIIe et XVIIIe siècles." *Recherches sociographiques* 12, no. 2 (1971): 143–83.

– *Habitants and Merchants in Seventeenth-Century Montreal*. Translated by Liana Vardi. Montreal and Kingston: McGill-Queen's University Press, 1992.

– *Le Peuple, l'État et la Guerre au Canada Sous le Régime français*. Edited by Hélène Paré, Sylvie Dépatie, Catherine Desbarats, and Thomas Wien. Montreal: Boréal, 2008.

– *Power and Subsistence: The Political Economy of Grain in New France*. Translated by Peter Feldstein. Montreal and Kingston: McGill-Queen's University Press, 2018.

Delâge, Denys. *Bitter Feast. Amerindians and Europeans in Northeastern North America, 1600–64*. Translated by Jane Brierley. Vancouver: UBC Press, 1993.

Delâge, Denys, and Étienne Gilbert. "Les Amérindiens face à la justice coloniale française dans le gouvernement de Québec, 1663–1759: II - Eau-de-vie, traite de fourrures, endettement, affaires civiles." *Recherches amérindiennes au Québec* 34, no. 1 (2004): 31–41.

Denys, Nicolas. *Histoire Naturelle Des Peuples, des Animaux, des Arbres & Plantes de l'Amerique Septentrionale, & de ses divers Climats*. Paris: Chez Claude Barbin, 1672.

Des Gagniers, Jean. *Le voyage au bout du vent. La Nouvelle-France et la mer aux XVIe et XVIIe siècles*. Quebec: Presses de l'Université Laval, 2017.

Desan, Suzanne. "Making and Breaking Marriage: An Overview of Old Regime Marriage as a Social Practice." In *Family, Gender, and Law in Early Modern France*, edited by Suzanne Desan and Jeffrey Merrick, 1–25. University Park: Pennsylvania State University Press, 2009.

Desbarats, Catherine, and Allan Greer. "North America from the Top Down." *Journal of Early American History* 5, no. 2 (2015): 109–36.

– "Où est la Nouvelle-France?" *Revue d'histoire de l'Amérique française* 64, nos. 3–4 (2011): 31–62.

Deslandres, Dominique. "« … alors nos garçons se marieront à vos filles, & nous ne ferons plus qu'un seul peuple »: religion, genre et déploiement de la souveraineté française en Amérique aux XVIe-XVIIIe siècles – une problématique." *Revue d'histoire de l'Amérique française* 66 no. 1 (2012): 5–35.

– *Croire et faire croire: Les missions françaises au XVIIe siècle (1600–1650)*. Paris: Fayard, 2003.

– "De Marie Guyart de l'Incarnation aux femmes « ordinaires » de la Nouvelle-France." In *Marie Guyart de l'Incarnation. Singularité et universalité d'une femme de cœur et de raison*, edited by Philippe Roy-Lysencourt, Thérèse Nadeau-Lacour, and Raymond Brodeur, 265–76. Quebec: Presses de l'Université Laval, 2019.

– "Entre persuasion et adhésion: La mission française au XVIIe siècle." *Théologiques* 13, no. 1 (2005): 95–117.

– "Female Voices and Agencies on the Canadian Missionary Frontier, according to Marie Guyart de L'Incarnation (1599–1672)." In *The Frontiers of Mission: Discovering the Holy in the Americas, 1500–1800*, edited by Alison Forrestal and Seán Alexander Smith, 42–67. Leiden: Brill, 2016.

– "Inspiration, fondation, relais: Le rôle des femmes laïques dans les missions françaises au XVIIe siècle." In *Les Laïcs dans la mission: Europe et Amériques, XVIe-XVIIIe siècles*, edited by Aliocha Maldavsky, 69–93. Tours: Presses universitaires François-Rabelais, 2017.

– "In the Shadow of the Cloister: Representations of Female Holiness in New France." In *Colonial Saints: Discovering the Holy in the Americas, 1500–1800*, edited by Allan Greer and Jodi Bilinkoff, 129–52. New York: Routledge, 2003.

– "New France." In *A Companion to the Early Modern Catholic Global Missions*, edited by Ronnie Po-Chia Hsia, 124–47. Leiden: Brill, 2018.

– "Signes de Dieu et légitimation de la présence française au Canada: Le 'trafic' des reliques ou la construction d'une histoire." In *Les Signes de Dieu aux XVIe et XVIIe siècles*, edited by Geneviève Demerson and Bernard Dompnier, 145–60. Clermont Ferrand: La Faculté de Lettres de Clermont-II, 1993.

Desloges, Yvon. *À table en Nouvelle-France: alimentation populaire, gastronomie et traditions alimentaires dans la vallée laurentienne avant l'avènement des restaurants*. Quebec: Septentrion, 2009.

Desrosiers, Pierre, et al. *Sites archéologiques religieux du Québec*. Quebec: Ministère de la Culture et des Communications du Québec et Ethnoscop, 2016.

Dewald, Jonathan, and Liana Vardi. "The Peasantries of France, 1400–1789." In *The Peasantries of Europe from the Fourteenth to the Eighteenth Centuries*, edited by Tom Scott, 21–47. London: Addison Wesley Longman, 1998.

Dewar, Helen. *Disputing New France: Companies, Law, and Sovereignty in the French Atlantic, 1598–1663*. Montreal and Kingston: McGill-Queen's University Press, 2022.

– "Government by Trading Company?: The Corporate Legal Status of the Company of New France and Colonial Governance." *Nuevo Mundo, Mundos Nuevos* (2018): 1–16.

Dickason, Olive Patricia. *The Myth of the Savage: And the Beginnings of French Colonialism in the Americas*. Edmonton: University of Alberta Press, 1984.

Dickinson, John. "La guerre iroquoise et la mortalité en Nouvelle-France, 1608–1666." *Revue d'histoire de l'Amérique française* 36, no. 1 (1982): 31–54.

Dickinson, John A. "New France: Law, Courts, and the *Coutume de Paris*, 1608–1760." *Manitoba Law Journal* 23 (1995): 32–54.

Dictionary of Canadian Biography. Toronto and Quebec: University of Toronto/Université Laval, 2003–. http://www.biographi.ca.

Dictionnaire de l'Académie Françoise, Volume 1. Paris: Chez la Veuve de Jean Baptiste Coignard and Chez Jean Baptiste Coignard, 1694.

Diefendorf, Barbara B. "Discerning Spirits: Women and Spiritual Authority in Counter Reformation France." In *Culture and Change: Attending to Early Modern Women*, edited by Margaret Mikesell and Adele Seeff, 241–65. Cranbury, NJ: University of Delaware Press, 2003.

– *From Penitence to Charity: Pious Women and the Catholic Reformation in Paris*. Oxford: Oxford University Press, 2004.

– "Rethinking the Catholic Reformation: The Role of Women." In *Women, Religion, and the Atlantic World (1600–1800)*, edited by Daniella J. Kostroun and Lisa Vollendorf, 31–59. Toronto: University of Toronto Press in association with the UCLA Center for Seventeenth- and Eighteenth-Century Studies and the William Andrews Clark Memorial Library, 2009.

Dijkink, Gertjan. "When Geopolitics and Religion Fuse: A Historical Perspective." *Geopolitics* 11 (July 2006): 192–208.

Dinet-Lecomte, Marie-Claude. "Les hospitalières françaises en Amérique aux XVIIe et XVIIIe siècles." *Revue d'histoire de l'Église de France* 84, no. 213 (1998): 261–82.

– "Les sœurs hospitalières au service des pauvres malades aux XVIIe et XVIIIe siècles." *Annales de démographie historique* (1994): 277–92.

Dinges, Martin. "Health Care and Poor Relief in Regional Southern France in the Counter-Reformation." In *Health Care and Poor Relief in Counter-Reformation Europe*, edited by Jon Arrizabalaga, Andrew Cunningham, and Ole Peter Grell, 239–78. London: Routledge, 2005.

Dobson, Mary J. *Contours of Death and Disease in Early Modern England*. Cambridge: Cambridge University Press, 1997.

Dollier de Casson, François. *Histoire du Montréal.* Edited by Marcel Trudel and Marie Baboyant. Montreal: Hurtubise HMH, 1992.

Donnelly, Joseph. *Jean de Brébeuf.* Chicago: Loyola University Press, 1975.

Du Berger, Jean. *Le Diable à la danse*. Quebec: Presses de l'Université Laval, 2006.

Dunn, Mary. "Bedside Manners: Sickness and the Jesuit Mission in Early Modern New France." *Journal of Jesuit Studies* 5, no. 4 (2018): 567–85.

Dunn, Mary Corley. "The Miracles at Sainte-Anne-du-Petit-Cap and the Making of a Seventeenth-Century Colonial Community." *Canadian Historical Review* 91, no. 4 (2010): 611–35.

Dunn, Richard, and Rebekah Higgitt. *Ships, Clocks, and Stars: The Quest for Longitude.* London: Harper Design, 2014.

Earle, Carville. *A Geographical Inquiry and American Historical Problems*. Stanford: Stanford University Press, 1992.

Earle, Rebecca. *The Body of the Conquistador: Food, Race and the Colonial Experience in Spanish America, 1492–1700*. Cambridge: Cambridge University Press, 2012.

Ebel, John E. "A New Analysis of the Magnitude of the February 1663 Earthquake at Charlevoix, Quebec." *Bulletin of the Seismological Society of America* 101, no. 3 (June 2011): 1024–38.

Eccles, W.J. *France in America*. 2nd ed. Toronto: Fitzhenry & Whiteside, 1990.

Edit du Roy Pour la punition de différents crimes. Registré en Parlement le 31. Aoust. 1682. Paris: François Muguet, 1682.

Édits, ordonnances royaux, déclarations et arrêts du Conseil d'État du roi, concernant le Canada. Volume 1. Quebec: P.E. Desbarats, 1803.

Edwards, Kathryn A. "Introduction: What Makes Magic Everyday Magic?" In *Everyday Magic in Early Modern Europe*, edited by Kathryn A. Edwards, 1–10. Farnham: Ashgate, 2015.

Evangelisti, Silvia. *Nuns: A History of Convent Life, 1450–1700*. Oxford: Oxford University Press, 2007.

Fast, Anicka. "Helping 'Our Canadian brothers': Early Recollect Missiology as an Experiment in Christian Community, 1615–1629." *Journal of Early Modern Christianity* 5, no. 1 (2018): 75–108.

Fauve-Chamoux, Antoinette. "Domesticité et parcours de vie. Servitude, service prémarital ou métier?" *Annales de démographie historique* 117, no. 1 (2009): 5–34.

Fay, Terence J. *A History of Canadian Catholics: Gallicanism, Romanism, and Canadianism*. Montreal and Kingston: McGill-Queen's University Press, 2002.

Ferber, Sarah. *Demonic Possession and Exorcism in Early Modern France*. London: Routledge, 2004.

– "Demonic Possession, Exorcism, and Witchcraft." In *The Oxford Handbook of Witchcraft in Early Modern Europe and Colonial America*, edited by Brian P. Levack, 575–92. Oxford: Oxford University Press, 2013.

– "Possession and the Sexes." In *Witchcraft and Masculinities in Early Modern Europe*, edited by Alison Rowlands, 214–38. New York: Palgrave Macmillan, 2009.

Ferland, Catherine. *Bacchus en Canada: boissons, buveurs et ivresses en Nouvelle-France*. Quebec: Septentrion, 2010.

Fischer, David Hackett. *Champlain's Dream*. New York: Alfred A. Knopf, 2008.

Fissell, Mary E. "Introduction: Women, Health, and Healing in Early Modern Europe." *Bulletin of the History of Medicine* 82, no. 1 (2008): 1–17.

Fleming, James Roger. *Historical Perspectives on Climate Change*. Oxford: Oxford University Press, 1998.

Follain, Antoine. *Le village sous l'Ancien Régime*. Paris: Fayard, 2008.

Fortier, Jean-Marie. "François de Laval." *Revue d'histoire de l'Amérique française* 13, no. 1 (June 1959): 18–29.

Fournier, Michel. "Le diable, le saint, le revenant et la fée: le conte de fées classique et la sécularisation de l'imaginaire merveilleux canadien-français." *Féeries* 10 (September 2013): 117–35.

Freedman, Paul. "The Miller." In *Historians on Chaucer: The "General Prologue" to the Canterbury Tales*, edited by Stephen Rigby and Alastair Minnis, 368–85. Oxford: Oxford University Press, 2014.

Friedland, Paul. *Seeing Justice Done: The Age of Spectacular Capital Punishment in France*. Oxford: Oxford University Press, 2012.

Frisinger, H. Howard. "Aristotle's Legacy in Meteorology." *American Meteorological Society* 54, no. 3 (March 1973): 198–204.

Furetière, Antoine. *Dictionnaire universel, contenant généralement tous les mots françois tant vieux que modernes, et les termes de toutes les sciences et des arts*. The Hague and Rotterdam: Chez Arnout et Reinier Leers, 1690.

Gagné, Gérard. "La réduction de Sillery: examen ostéoarchéologique d'un cimetière autochtone du *XVIII*e siècle." In *Archéologies québécoises*, edited by Anne-Marie Balac, Claude Chapdelaine, Norman Clermont, and Françoise Duguay, 103–21. Paléo-Québec 23. Montreal: Recherches amérindiennes au Québec and Ministère de la Culture et des Communications, 1995.

Galland, Caroline. *Pour la gloire de Dieu et du Roi. Les récollets en Nouvelle-France aux XVIIe et XVIIIe siècles*. Paris: Cerf, 2012.

Gallat-Morin, Elisabeth, and Jean-Pierre Pinson. *La vie musicale en Nouvelle-France*. Quebec: Septentrion, 2003.

Gamsa, Mark. "Biography and (Global) Microhistory." *New Global Studies* 11, no. 3 (2017): 231–41.

Gaposchkin, M. Cecilia. *The Making of Saint Louis: Kingship, Sanctity, and Crusade in the Later Middle Ages*. Ithaca: Cornell University Press, 2008.

Gareis, Iris. "Merging Magical Traditions: Sorcery and Witchcraft in Spanish and Portuguese America." In *The Oxford Handbook of Witchcraft in Early Modern Europe and Colonial America*, edited by Brian P. Levack. Oxford: Oxford University Press, 2013.

Garnot, Benoît. *Crime et Justice aux XVIIe et XVIIIe siècles*. Paris: Imago, 2000.

– *Un déclin: Chartres au XVIIIe siècle*. Paris: Éditions du C.T.H.S., 1991.

– *Justice et Société en France aux XVIe, XVIIe, XVIIIe siècles*. Paris: Orphys, 2000.

Garrioch, David. "Sounds of the City: The Soundscape of Early Modern European Towns." *Urban History* 30, no. 1 (2003): 5–25.

Gasser, Erika. *Vexed with Devils: Manhood and Witchcraft in Old and New England*. New York: New York University Press, 2017.

Gaumond, Michel. *Place Royale: Its Houses and Their Occupants*. Quebec: Ministère des affaires culturelles du Québec, 1972.

Gauthier-Larouche, Georges. *Évolution de la maison rurale traditionnelle dans la région de Québec: étude ethnographique*. Quebec: Presses de l'Université Laval, 1974.

Gauvreau, Danielle. *Québec. Une ville et sa population au temps de la Nouvelle-France*. Quebec: Presses de l'Université Laval, 1991.

Geertz, Clifford. *The Interpretation of Cultures*. New York: Basic Books, 1973.

Geschiere, Peter. "Witchcraft and the Dangers of Intimacy: Africa and Europe." In *Emotions in the History of Witchcraft*, edited by Laura Kounine and Michael Ostling, 213–29. London: Palgrave Macmillan, 2016.

Ghobrial, John-Paul A. "Introduction: Seeing the World like a Microhistorian." *Past & Present* 242, Issue Supplement 14 (November 2019): 1–22.

Ginzburg, Carlo. *The Cheese and the Worms: The Cosmos of a Sixteenth-Century Miller*. Translated by John and Anne Tedeschi. Baltimore: Johns Hopkins University Press, 1980.

– "Microhistory and World History." In *The Cambridge World History*, volume 6, edited by Jerry H. Bentley, Sanjay Subrahmanyam, Merry E Wiesner-Hanks, 446–73. Cambridge: Cambridge University Press, 2015.

– "Microhistory: Two or Three Things That I Know about It." Translated by John Tedeschi and Anne C. Tedeschi. *Critical Inquiry* 20, no. 1 (1993): 10–35.

Girard, Philip, Jim Phillips, and R. Blake Brown. *A History of Law in Canada*. Volume 1, *Beginnings to 1866*. Toronto: University of Toronto Press, 2018.

Giroux, T. Edmond. *Robert Giffard, seigneur colonisateur au tribunal de l'histoire, ou, La raison de fêter le troisième centenaire de Beauport, 1634–1934*. Quebec: L'Action sociale, 1934.

Gitlin, Jay, and André Brasseaux. "Chasing *La Chasse-Galerie*: Honoré Beaugrand and the Life of a Journalistic Voyageur." In *French Connections: Cultural Mobility in North America and the Atlantic World, 1600–1875*, edited by Robert Englebert and Andrew N. Wegmann, 221–43. Baton Rouge: Louisiana State University Press, 2020.

Godbeer, Richard. *The Devil's Dominion: Magic and Religion in Early New England*. Cambridge: Cambridge University Press, 1992.

Godbout, Archange. "Les émigrants de 1664." *Mémoires de la Société généalogique canadienne-française* 4, no. 4 (June 1951): 217–25.

– *Les passagers du Saint-André: la Recrue de 1659*. Montreal: Société Généalogique Canadienne-Française, 1964.

Goddard, Peter. "Canada in Early Modern Jesuit Thought: Backwater or Opportunity?" In *Decentring the Renaissance: Canada and Europe in Multidisciplinary Perspective, 1500–1700*, edited by Germaine Warkentin and Carolyn Podruchny, 186–99. Toronto: University of Toronto Press, 2001.

– "The Devil in New France: Jesuit Demonology, 1611–50." *Canadian Historical Review* 78, no. 1 (March 1997): 40–62.

Godineau, Dominique. *Les Femmes dans la Société Française 16e–18e siècle*. Paris: A. Colin, 2003.

Golinski, Jan. "American Climate and the Civilization of Nature." In *Science and Empire in the Atlantic World*, edited by James Delbourgo and Nicholas Dew, 153–74. New York: Routledge, 2008.

Goodare, Julian. *The European Witch-Hunt*. New York: Routledge, Taylor & Francis Group, 2016.

– "Men and the Witch-Hunt in Scotland." In *Witchcraft and Masculinities in Early Modern Europe*, edited by Alison Rowlands, 149–70. New York: Palgrave Macmillan, 2009.

Goodman, Martin. *Mission and Conversion: Proselytizing in the Religious History of the Roman Empire*. Oxford: Clarendon, 1994.

Gosselin, Auguste. *Vie de Mgr de Laval: premier évêque de Québec et apôtre du Canada, 1622–1708*. Quebec: L.-J. Demers & Frères, 1890.

Goubert, Pierre. *The French Peasantry in the Seventeenth Century*. Translated by Ian Patterson. Cambridge: Cambridge University Press, 1986.

Gowing, Laura. *Common Bodies: Women, Touch and Power in Seventeenth-Century England*. New Haven: Yale University Press, 2003.

Goyette, Manon. "The Origins of the Château Saint-Louis, the Residence of the Governor of New France." *Post-Medieval Archaeology* 43, no. 1 (June 2009): 125–39.

Grafton, Anthony, with April Shelford and Nancy Siraisi. *New Worlds, Ancient Texts: The Power of Tradition and the Shock of Discovery*. Cambridge, MA: Harvard University Press, 1992.

Green, Monica. "Documenting Medieval Women's Medical Practice." In *Practical Medicine from Salerno to the Black Death*, edited by Luis García Ballester, 322–52. Cambridge: Cambridge University Press, 1994.

– "Women's Medical Practice and Health Care in Medieval Europe." *Signs* 14, no. 2 (1989): 434–73.

Greer, Allan. "Colonial Saints: Gender, Race, and Hagiography in New France." *William and Mary Quarterly* 57, no. 2 (April 2000): 323–48.

– *Mohawk Saint: Catherine Tekakwitha and the Jesuits*. Oxford: Oxford University Press, 2005.

– *The People of New France*. Toronto: University of Toronto Press, 1997.

– *Property and Dispossession: Natives, Empires and Land in Early Modern North America*. Cambridge: Cambridge University Press, 2017.

– "Reply to Benoît Grenier and Alain Laberge." *Borealia: Early Canadian History* (blog), 16 October 2018.

– "There Was No Seigneurial System." *Borealia: Early Canadian History*, 24 September 2018.

– "Women of New France." In *Race and Gender in the Northern Colonies*, edited by Jan Noel, 87–100. Toronto: Canadian Scholars' Press, 2000.

Grégoire, Vincent. "L'interprétation du tremblement de terre de 1663 en Nouvelle-France d'après les écrits des missionnaires." *Seventeenth-Century French Studies* 30, no. 1 (July 2008): 64–76.

– "Mais comment peut-on être protestant en Nouvelle-France au dix-septième siècle?" *Seventeenth-Century French Studies* 31, no. 1 (July 2009): 46–58.

– "Malentendus culturels rencontrés par les missionnaires ursulines en Nouvelle-France au XVIIème siècle." *Seventeenth-Century French Studies* 36, no. 2 (2014): 109–24.

– "Le meunier, la domestique et l'hospitalière: entre magie, « possession » et « obsession » en Nouvelle-France au 17ème siècle." *Cahiers Du Dix-Septième* XIII, no. 1 (2010): 68–91.

Gregory, Brad S. *Salvation at Stake: Christian Martyrdom in Early Modern Europe*. Cambridge, MA: Harvard University Press, 1999.

Grenier, Benoît. *Brève histoire du régime seigneurial*. Montreal: Boréal, 2012.

– "Femmes et propriété seigneuriale au Canada (XVIIe-XIXe siècles): Les formes de l'autorité des « seigneuresses »." *Histoire, Économie & Société* 4 (2019): 5–27.

– "Réflexion sur le pouvoir féminin au Canada sous le Régime français. Le cas de la 'seigneuresse' Marie-Catherine Peuvret (1667–1739)." *Histoire social/Social History* 42, no. 84 (November 2009): 299–326.

– *Seigneurs campagnards de la Nouvelle-France. Présence seigneuriale et sociabilité rurale dans la vallée du Saint-Laurent à l'époque préindustrielle*. Rennes: Presses universitaires de Rennes, 2007.

Grenier, Benoit, and Alain Laberge. "Beyond the 'System': The Enduring Legacy of Seigneurial Property." *Borealia: Early Canadian History*, 9 October 2018.

Guldi, Jo, and David Armitage. *The History Manifesto*. Cambridge: Cambridge University Press, 2014.

Gutton, Jean-Pierre. *Domestiques et serviteurs dans la France de l'Ancien Régime*. Paris: Aubier Montaigne, 1981.

Hahn, Whitney, and Mairi Cowan. "Foods, Foodways, and Francisation in Seventeenth-Century Québec." *Dublin Gastronomy Symposium: Food and Power* (2018): 1–8.

Hallett, Nicky. *Witchcraft, Exorcism and the Politics of Possession in a Seventeenth-Century Convent: 'How Sister Ursula Was Once Bewiched and Sister Margaret Twice.'* New York: Routledge, 2017.

Hanley, Sarah. "Engendering the State: Family Formation and State Building in Early Modern France." *French Historical Studies* 16, no. 1 (Spring 1989): 4–27.

Hardy, René. *Charivari et justice populaire au Québec*. Quebec: Septentrion, 2015.

Harrison, Jane E. *Until Next Year: Letter Writing and the Mails in the Canadas, 1640–1830*. Hull, Quebec: Canadian Postal Museum and Canadian Museum of Civilization, 1997.

Harvey, Jacques. "Le manoir seigneurial de Beauport." *Histo'Art, revue de la Société d'art et d'histoire de Beauport* 3 (December 1991): 11–12.

Harvey, Karen. "The Body." In *Early Modern Emotions: An Introduction*, edited by Susan Broomhall, 165–7. London: Routledge, 2017.

Havard, Gilles. *Empire et métissages: Indiens et Français dans le Pays d'en Haut, 1660–1715*. 2nd ed. Quebec: Septentrion, 2017.

– "'Les forcer à devenir Cytoyens': État, Sauvages et citoyenneté en Nouvelle-France (XVIIe-XVIIIe siècle)." *Annales. Histoire, Sciences Sociales* 64, no. 5 (2009): 985–1018.

– *The Great Peace of Montreal of 1701: French-Native Diplomacy in the Seventeenth Century*. Translated by Phyllis Aronoff and Howard Scott. Montreal and Kingston: McGill-Queen's University Press, 2001.

– *Histoire des coureurs de bois: Amérique du Nord, 1600–1840*. Paris: Les Indes savantes, 2016.

Havard, Gilles, and Cécile Vidal. *Histoire de l'Amérique française*. Revised edition. Paris: Flammarion, 2014.

Hébert, Léo-Paul, ed. *Le registre de Sillery (1638–1690)*. Quebec: Presses de l'Université du Québec, 1994.

Heffernan, Thomas J. *Sacred Biography: Saints and Their Biographers in the Middle Ages*. Oxford: Oxford University Press, 1988.

Henneton, Lauric. "Spiritual Geopolitics: Reconsidering Religious and Political Boundaries in Seventeenth-Century Northeastern America." *Journal of Early American History* 4, no. 3 (2014): 212–38.

Hildesheimer, Françoise. *Rendez à César: l'Église et le pouvoir : IVe-XVIIIe siècle*. Paris: Flammarion, 2017.

Hillman, Jennifer. "Testing the Spirit of the Prophets: Jean Chéron, Melancholy and the 'Illusions' of Dévotes." *Études Épistémè* 28 (2015).

Hippocrates. *Ancient Medicine. Airs, Waters, Places. Epidemics 1 and 3. The Oath. Precepts. Nutriment*. Translated by W.H.S. Jones. Cambridge, MA: Harvard University Press, 1923.

Histoire de la fondation du monastere des religieuses feuillentines de Toulouse Avec les Eloges de plusieurs Religieuses de cette Maison, remarquables par leurs vertus. Par un Religieux Feüillent. Bordeaux, 1696.

Hoerder, Dirk. "Global Migrations." In *The Cambridge World History*, volume 6, edited by Jerry H. Bentley, Sanjay Subrahmanyam, and Merry E. Wiesner-Hanks, 3–28. Cambridge: Cambridge University Press, 2015.

Hoffman, Philip T. *Growth in a Traditional Society: The French Countryside, 1450–1815*. Princeton: Princeton University Press, 1996.

Horden, Peregrine, and Richard Smith, eds. *The Locus of Care: Families, Communities, Institutions, and the Provision of Welfare Since Antiquity*. London: Routledge, 1998.

Horguelin, Christophe. "Le XVIIIe siècle des Canadiens: discours public et identité." In *Mémoires de Nouvelle-France: de France en Nouvelle-France*, edited by Philippe Joutard and Thomas Wien, 209–19. Rennes: Presses universitaires de Rennes, 2005.

Houdard, Sophie. "Des fausses saintes aux spirituelles à la mode: les signes suspects de la mystique." *XVIIe Siècle* 200 (1998): 417–32.

– "Quand les matous vont au sabbat … Démons et sorciers dans le *Dictionnaire universel*." *Littératures classiques* 47 (2003): 149–66.

Howell, James. "Some Choice Proverbs … in the French Toung." In *Lexicon Tetraglotton*. London: Printed by J.G. for Samuel Thomson at the Bishop Head in St Pauls Church-Yard, 1660.

Hsia, Ronnie Po-chia. "Mission Frontiers: A Reflection on Catholic Missions in the Early Modern World." In *The Frontiers of Mission: Perspectives on Early Modern Missionary Catholicism*, edited by Alison Forrestal and Seán Alexander Smith, 180–93. Leiden: Brill, 2016.

– *The World of Catholic Renewal, 1540–1770*. Cambridge: Cambridge University Press, 1998.

Huizinga, Johan. *Dutch Civilisation in the Seventeenth Century and Other Essays*. Selected by Pieter Geyl and F.W.N. Hugenholtz. Translated by Arnold J. Pomerans. London: Collins, 1968.

Hunter, Michael. "New Light on the 'Drummer of Tedworth': Conflicting Narratives of Witchcraft in Restoration England." *Historical Research* 78, no. 201 (August 2005): 311–53.

Hutton, Ronald. *The Witch: A History of Fear, from Ancient Times to the Present*. New Haven: Yale University Press, 2017.

Ibbett, Katherine. *Compassion's Edge: Fellow-Feeling and Its Limits in Early Modern France*. Philadelphia: University of Pennsylvania Press, 2018.

Imbruglia, Girolamo. "A Peculiar Idea of Empire: Missions and Missionaries of the Society of Jesus in Early Modern History." In *Jesuit Accounts of the Colonial Americas: Intercultural Transfers Intellectual Disputes, and Textualities*, edited by Marc-André Bernier, Clorinda Donato, and Hans-Jürgen Lüsebrink, 21–49. Toronto: University of Toronto Press, 2014.

Inventaire et analyse du site patrimonial déclaré de Beauport. Rapports sectoriels: Synthèse de l'historique et du développement des lieux. Québec: Bergeron Gagnon, 2018.

"Inventaire et état des lieux du fort St Louis." *Canadian Antiquarian and Numismatic Journal* 1, second series (April 1889–90): 153–6.

Jaenen, Cornelius J. "Church-State Relations in Canada, 1604–1685." *Historical Papers/Communications historiques* 2, no. 1 (1967): 20–40.

– "Colonisation compacte et colonisation extensive aux XVIIe et XVIIIe siècles en Nouvelle-France." In *Colonies, territoires, sociétés: l'enjeu français*, edited by Alain Saussol and Joseph Zitomersky, 15–22. Paris: L'Harmattan, 1996.

– "The Image of New France: Real and Imaginary." *Australian Journal of French Studies* 31, no. 2 (1994): 161–74.
– *The Role of the Church in New France*. Ottawa: Canadian Historical Association, 1985.
Javellana, René B. "The Jesuits and the Indigenous Peoples of the Philippines." In *The Jesuits: Cultures, Sciences, and the Arts, 1540–1773*, edited by John W. O'Malley, Gauvin Alexander Bailey, Steven J. Harris, and T. Frank Kennedy, 418–38. Toronto: University of Toronto Press, 1999.
Jenner, Mark S.R. "Civilization and Deodorization? Smell in Early Modern English Culture." In *Civil Histories: Essays Presented to Sir Keith Thomas*, edited by Peter Burke, Brian Harrison, and Paul Slack, 127–44. Oxford: Oxford University Press, 2000.
Jetten, Marc. *Enclaves amérindiennes, les « réductions » du Canada, 1637–1701*. Quebec: Septentrion, 1994.
Johnson, Christopher. "'Periwigged Heralds': Epistemology and Intertextuality in Early American Cometography." *Journal of the History of Ideas* 65, no. 3 (2004): 399–419.
Jones, Colin. *The Charitable Imperative: Hospitals and Nursing in Ancien Régime and Revolutionary France*. London: Routledge, 1989.
– "The Construction of the Hospital Patient in Early Modern France." In *Institutions of Confinement. Hospitals, Asylums, and Prisons in Western Europe and North America, 1500–1950*, edited by Norbert Finzsch and Robert Jütte, 55–74. Cambridge: Cambridge University Press, 1996.
– "Perspectives on Poor Relief, Health Care and the Counter-Reformation in France." In *Health Care and Poor Relief in Counter-Reformation Europe*, edited by Jon Arrizabalaga, Andrew Cunningham, and Ole Peter Grell, 215–38. London: Routledge, 2005.
Jones, David S. *Rationalizing Epidemics: Meanings and Uses of American Indian Mortality Since 1600*. Cambridge, MA: Harvard University Press, 2004.
Juchereau de Saint-Ignace, Jeanne-Françoise. *Histoire de l'Hôtel-Dieu de Québec*. Montauban: Chez Jerosme Legier, 1751.
Juchereau de Saint-Ignace, Jeanne-Françoise, and Marie-Andrée Duplessis. *Les annales de l'Hôtel-Dieu de Québec, 1636–1716, composées par les révérendes mères Jeanne-Françoise Juchereau de St-Ignace et Marie Andrée Duplessis de Ste-Hélène*. Edited by Dom Albert Jamet. Quebec: Hôtel-Dieu de Québec, 1939.
Jugements et délibérations du Conseil souverain de la Nouvelle-France. Volume 1. Quebec: Imprimerie A. Coté et Cie, 1885.

Jugements et délibérations du Conseil souverain de la Nouvelle-France. Volume 2. Quebec: Imprimerie A. Coté et Cie, 1886.

Karlsen, Carol F. *The Devil in the Shape of a Woman: Witchcraft in Colonial New England.* New York: Vintage Books, 1989.

Kelley, Donald R. "Martyrs, Myths, and the Massacre: The Background of St Bartholomew." *American Historical Review* 77, no. 5 (1972): 1323–42.

Kent, E.J. "Masculinity and Male Witches in Old and New England, 1593–1680." *History Workshop Journal* 60, no. 1 (October 2005): 69–92.

– "Tyrannical Beasts: Male Witchcraft in Early Modern English Culture." In *Emotions in the History of Witchcraft*, edited by Laura Kounine and Michael Ostling, 77–94. London: Palgrave Macmillan, 2016.

Kettering, Sharon. *French Society, 1589–1715.* London: Routledge, 2001.

Kieckhefer, Richard. "The Specific Rationality of Medieval Magic." *American Historical Review* 99, no. 3 (1994): 813–36.

Kounine, Laura. "Satanic Fury: Depictions of the Devil's Rage in Nicolas Remy's Daemonolatria." In *Emotions in the History of Witchcraft*, edited by Laura Kounine and Michael Ostling, 57–76. London: Palgrave Macmillan, 2016.

Kronk, Gary W. *Cometography: A Catalog of Comets.* Volume 1, *Ancient–1799.* Cambridge: Cambridge University Press, 1999.

Kupperman, Karen Ordahl. "Introduction: The Changing Definition of America." In *America in European Consciousness, 1493–1750*, edited by Karen Ordahl Kupperman, 1–30. Chapel Hill: University of North Carolina Press, 1995.

– "The Puzzle of the American Climate in the Early Colonial Period." *American Historical Review* 87, no. 5 (December 1982): 1262–89.

Labelle, Kathryn Magee. *Dispersed but Not Destroyed: A History of the Seventeenth-Century Wendat People.* Vancouver: UBC Press, 2013.

Labouvie, Eva. "Men in Witchcraft Trials: Towards a Social Anthropology of 'Male' Understandings of Magic and Witchcraft." In *Gender in Early Modern German History*, edited by Ulinka Rublack, 49–68. Cambridge: Cambridge University Press, 2002.

Lacey, Nicola, and Hanna Pickard. "The Chimera of Proportionality: Institutionalising Limits on Punishment in Contemporary Social and Political Systems." *Modern Law Review* 78, no. 2 (March 2015): 216–40.

Lachance, André. *Délinquants, juges et bourreaux en Nouvelle-France.* Montreal: Les Éditions Libre Expression, 2011.

– "Les prisons au Canada sous le Régime français." *Revue d'histoire de l'Amérique française* 19, no. 4 (1966): 561–5.

Lachenicht, Susanne. "À la découverte de l'Européen? Perceptions de l'Autre et identités au Canada et en Acadie (XVIIe-XVIIIe siècles)." *Francia* 35, no. 2 (2008): 551–63.

Lachenicht, Susanne, Lauric Henneton, and Yann Lignereux, "Spiritual Geopolitics in the Early Modern Imperial Age. An Introduction." *Itinerario* 40, no. 2 (2016): 181–7.

Lacoste, Yves. "Géopolitique des religions." *Hérodote* 106, no. 3 (2002): 3–15.

Lamontagne, Sophie-Laurence. *L'hiver dans la culture québécoise (XVIIe-XIXe siècles)*. Quebec: Institut québécois de recherche sur la culture, 1983.

Lanctôt, Gustave. "Une accusation contre Monseigneur de Laval." *Rapport – Société canadienne d'histoire de l'Église catholique* (1944–45): 11–25.

– *Filles de joie ou Filles du Roi. Étude sur l'émigration féminine en Nouvelle-France*. Montreal: Éditions du Jour, 1952.

Landry, Yves. "Les Français passés au Canada avant 1760: le regard de l'émigrant." *Revue d'histoire de l'Amérique française* 59, no. 4 (Spring 2006): 481–500.

– "Gender Imbalance, Les Filles du roi, and Choice of Spouse in New France." In *Canadian Family History: Selected Readings*, edited by Bettina Bradbury, 14–32. Toronto: Copp Clark Pitman, 1992.

– *Orphelines en France, pionnières au Canada: les Filles du roi au XVIIe siècle*. Ottawa: Lemaéc, 1992.

Landry, Yves, and Rénald Lessard. "Les causes de décès aux XVIIe et XVIIIe siècles d'après les registres paroissiaux québécois." *Revue d'histoire de l'Amérique française* 48, no. 4 (1995): 509–26.

Langlois, Michel. *Dictionnaire biographique des ancêtres québécois (1608–1700)*. Volume 1. Sillery: La Maison des ancêtres, 1998.

– *Dictionnaire biographique des ancêtres québécois (1608–1700)*. Volume 2. Sillery: La Maison des ancêtres, 1999.

Larocque, Robert. *La naissance et la mort à Québec autrefois: les restes humains des cimetières de la basilique Notre-Dame-de-Québec*. Quebec: CELAT, 2000.

Laverdière, C.-H., and H.R. Casgrain, eds. *Le journal des jésuites*. Quebec: Chez Léger Brousseau, 1871.

Lavoie, Michel. *C'est ma seigneurie que je réclame. La lutte des Hurons de Lorette pour la seigneurie de Sillery, 1650–1900*. Montreal: Boréal, 2010.

– "Des Indiens seigneurs au temps de Louis XIV." In *Un continent en partage: Cinq siècles de rencontres entre Amérindiens et Français*, edited by Gilles Havard et Mickaël Augeron, 97–105. Paris: Les Indes savantes, 2013.

Le Clercq, Chrestien. *Premier établissement de la foy dans la Nouvelle France, contenant la publication de l'Évangile, l'Histoire des Colonies Françoises, & les fameuses découvertes depuis le Fleuve de Saint Laurent, la Loüisiane & le Fleuve Colbert jusqu'au golphe Mexique, achevées sous la conduite de feu Monsieur de la Salle*. 2 volumes. Paris: Chez Amable Auroy, 1691.

Le Goff, Jacques. *Saint Louis*. Translated by Gareth Evan Gollrad. Notre Dame: University of Notre Dame Press, 2009.

Leavelle, Tracy Neal. *The Catholic Calumet: Colonial Conversions in French and Indian North America*. Philadelphia: University of Pennsylvania Press, 2011.

Lebrun, François. "Amour et mariage." In *Histoire de la population française*, volume 2, *De la Renaissance à 1789*, edited by Jacques Dupâquier, 294–317. Paris: Presses universitaires de France, 1988.

Lederer, David. *Madness, Religion, and the State in Early Modern Europe: A Bavarian Beacon*. Cambridge: Cambridge University Press, 2006.

Lefebvre-Teillard, Anne. "Marriage in France from the Sixteenth to the Eighteenth Century: Political and Juridical Aspects." In *Marriage in Europe, 1400–1800*, edited by Silvana Seidel Menchi and Emlyn Eisenach, 261–93. Toronto: University of Toronto Press, 2016.

Lehmann, Hartmut. "Miracles within Catastrophes: Some Examples from Early Modern Germany." *Studies in Church History* 41 (2005): 321–34.

Lescarbot, Marc. *The History of New France*. Volume 1. Edited by W.L. Grant. Toronto: Champlain Society, 1907.

Lessard, Rénald. *Au temps de la petite vérole: la médecine au Canada aux XVIIe et XVIIIe siècles*. Quebec: Septentrion, 2012.

Lestringant, Frank. "L'île des Démons dans la Cosmographie de la Renaissance." In *Voyager avec le diable: voyages réels, voyages imaginaires et discours démonologiques, XVe-XVIIe siècles*, edited by Grégoire Holtz and Thibault Maus de Rolley, 99–125. Paris: Presses de l'Université Paris-Sorbonne, 2008.

Levack, Brian P. *The Devil Within: Possession & Exorcism in the Christian West*. New Haven: Yale University Press, 2013.

– *The Witchcraft Sourcebook*. 2nd ed. London: Routledge, 2015.

– *The Witch-Hunt in Early Modern Europe*. New York: Routledge, 1995.

Levi, Giovanni. "Microhistoria e Historia Global." *Historia Crítica*, no. 69 (2018): 21–35.

Li, Shenwen. *Stratégies missionnaires des Jésuites français en Nouvelle-France et en Chine au XVIIe siècle*. Quebec: Les presses de l'Université de Laval, 2001.

Lierheimer, Linda. "False Sanctity and Spiritual Imposture in Seventeenth-Century French Convents." In *Everyday Magic in Early Modern Europe*, edited by Kathryn A. Edwards, 71–91. Farnham: Ashgate, 2015.

– "Preaching or Teaching?: Defining the Ursuline Mission in Seventeenth-Century France." In *Women Preachers and Prophets through Two Millennia of Christianity*, edited by Beverly Mayne Kienzle and Pamela J. Walker, 212–26. Berkeley: University of California Press, 1998.

Lignereux, Yann. "Une mission périlleuse ou le péril colonial jésuite dans la France de Louis XIV: Sainte-Marie des Iroquois (1649–1665)." *Revue d'histoire de l'Amérique française* 69, no. 4 (2016): 5–26.

Lindemann, Mary. *Medicine and Society in Early Modern Europe*. 2nd ed. Cambridge: Cambridge University Press, 2010.

Livi-Bacci, Massimo. *A Concise History of World Population*. 6th Edition. Malden, MA: Wiley-Blackwell, 2017.

Lothrop, Jonathan C., Darrin L. Lowery, Arthur E. Spiess, and Christopher J. Ellis. "Early Human Settlement of Northeastern North America." *PaleoAmerica* 2, no. 3 (July 2016): 192–251.

Lovegren, Sylvia. *Melon: A Global History*. London: Reaktion Books, 2016.

Lozier, Jean-François. *Flesh Reborn: The Saint Lawrence Valley Mission Settlements through the Seventeenth Century*. Montreal and Kingston: McGill-Queen's University Press, 2018.

Lynch, Andrew. "Emotional Community." In *Early Modern Emotions: An Introduction*, edited by Susan Broomhall, 3–6. London: Routledge, 2017.

MacCormack, Sabine. "Limits of Understanding: Perceptions of Greco-Roman and Amerindian Paganism in Early Modern Europe." In *America in European Consciousness, 1493–1750*, edited by Karen Ordahl Kupperman, 79–129. Chapel Hill: University of North Carolina Press, 1995.

Macfarlane, Alan. *Witchcraft in Tudor and Stuart England: A Regional and Comparative Study*. 2nd ed. New York: Routledge, 1999.

Magnuson, Roger. *Education in New France*. Montreal and Kingston: McGill-Queen's University Press, 1992.

Magnússon, Sigurður Gylfi. "Far-Reaching Microhistory: The Use of Microhistorical Perspective in a Globalized World," *Rethinking History: The Journal of Theory and Practice* 27, no. 3 (2017): 312–41.

Magnússon, Sigurður Gylfi, and István M. Szíjártó. *What Is Microhistory? Theory and Practice*. New York: Routledge, 2013.

Mandrou, Robert. *Magistrats et sorciers en France au XVIIe siècle. Une analyse de psychologie historique*. Paris: Plon, 1968.

Margry, Pierre, ed. *Découvertes et établissements des Français dans l'ouest et dans le sud de l'Amérique Septentrionale (1614–1754). Mémoires et documents originaux*. Volume 1. Paris: D. Jouaust, 1875.

Marie de l'Incarnation. *Correspondance*. Edited by Dom Guy Oury. Solesmes: Abbaye Saint-Pierre, 1971.

– *Écrits spirituels et historiques, publiés par dom Claude Martin, réédités par dom Albert Jamet, avec des annotations critiques, des pièces documentaires & une biographie nouvelle*. Paris: Desclée-de Brouwer, 1929.

Martin, Claude. *La vie de la venerable mere Marie de l'Incarnation premiere superieure des Ursulines de la Nouvelle France: Tirée de ses Lettres & de ses Ecrits*. Paris: Loüis Billaine, 1677.

Massicotte, Édouard-Zotique. "Le charivari au Canada." *Bulletin des recherches historiques* 32, no. 12 (December 1926): 713–25.

Mauelshagen, Franz. "Climate as a Scientific Paradigm – Early History of Climatology to 1800." In *The Palgrave Handbook of Climate History*, edited by Sam White, Christian Pfister, and Franz Mauelshagen, 565–88. London: Palgrave Macmillan, 2018.

Maynard, David, and Donald Maynard. "Cucumbers, Melons, and Watermelons." In *The Cambridge World History of Food*, edited by Kenneth F. Kiple and Kriemhild Coneè Ornelas, 298–313. Cambridge: Cambridge University Press, 2000.

McHugh, Tim. *Hospital Politics in Seventeenth-Century France: The Crown, Urban Elites and the Poor*. Aldershot: Ashgate, 2007.

McShea, Bronwen. *Apostles of Empire: The Jesuits and New France*. Lincoln: University of Nebraska Press, 2019.

Medick, Hans. "Turning Global? Microhistory in Extension." *Historische Anthropologie* 24, no. 2 (August 2016): 241–52.

Melzer, Sara E. *Colonizer or Colonized: The Hidden Stories of Early Modern French Culture*. Philadelphia: University of Pennsylvania Press, 2012.

– "The Role of Culture and Art in France's Colonial Strategy of the Seventeenth Century." In *Jesuit Accounts of the Colonial Americas:*

Intercultural Transfers Intellectual Disputes, and Textualities, edited by Marc-André Bernier, Clorinda Donato, and Hans-Jürgen Lüsebrink, 169–85. Toronto: University of Toronto Press, 2014.

Menegon, Eugenio. "Telescope and Microscope. A Micro-Historical Approach to Global China in the Eighteenth Century." *Modern Asian Studies* 54, no. 4 (2020): 1315–44.

Mentzer, Raymond A., and Andrew Spicer. "Introduction: Être protestant." In *Society and Culture in the Huguenot World, 1559–1685*, edited by Raymond A. Mentzer and Andrew Spicer, 1–9. Cambridge: Cambridge University Press, 2002.

Midelfort, H.C. Erik. *Exorcism and Enlightenment: Johann Joseph Gassner and the Demons of Eighteenth-Century Germany*. New Haven: Yale University Press, 2005.

Millar, Charlotte-Rose. *Witchcraft, the Devil, and Emotions in Early Modern England*. London: Routledge, 2017.

Minvielle, Stéphane. *La famille en France à l'époque moderne XVIe-XVIIIe siècle*. Paris: Armand Colin, 2010.

Monet, Jacques. "The Jesuits in New France." In *The Cambridge Companion to the Jesuits*, edited by Thomas Worcester, 186–98. Cambridge: Cambridge University Press, 2008.

Montagne, Françoise. "Du nouveau sur Robert Giffard, promoteur de l'émigration percheronne." *Cahiers percherons* 25 (1967): 29–43.

Monter, William. "The Catholic Salem: How the Devil Destroyed a Saint's Parish (Mattaincourt, 1627–31)." *Catholic Historical Review* 98, no. 4 (2012): 679–702.

– *Witchcraft in France and Switzerland: The Borderlands During the Reformation*. Ithaca: Cornell University Press, 1976.

– "Witchcraft Trials in France." In *The Oxford Handbook of Witchcraft in Early Modern Europe and Colonial America*, edited by Brian P. Levack, 218–31. Oxford: Oxford University Press, 2013.

Monumenta Novae Franciae. Edited by Lucien Campeau. Rome and Quebec: Monumenta Hist. Soc. Jesu, 1967–2003.

Moogk, Peter N. *Building a House in New France: An Account of the Perplexities of Client and Craftsmen in Early Canada*. Toronto: McClelland and Stewart, 1977.

– "The Crime of Lèse-Majesté in New France:" In *Canadian State Trials*, volume 1, *Law, Politics, and Security Measures, 1608–1837*, edited by F. Murray Greenwood and Barry Wright, 55–71. Toronto: University of Toronto Press, 1996.

– "The Liturgy of Humiliation, Pain, and Death: The Execution of Criminals in New France." *Canadian Historical Review* 88, no. 1 (March 2007): 89–112.

– "Reluctant Exiles: Emigrants from France in Canada before 1760." *William and Mary Quarterly* 46, no. 3 (July 1989): 463–505.

More, Anna. "Cosmopolitanism and Scientific Reason in New Spain: Carlos de Sigüenza y Góngora and the Dispute over the 1680 Comet." In *Science in the Spanish and Portuguese Empires, 1500–1800*, edited by Daniela Bleichmar, Paula De Vos, Kristin Huffine, and Kevin Sheehan, 115–31. Stanford: Stanford University Press, 2009.

Morin, Marie. *Annales de l'Hôtel-Dieu de Montréal*. Montreal: Imprimerie des éditeurs limitée, 1921.

Morin, Michel. "Fraternité, souveraineté et autonomie des Autochtones en Nouvelle-France." *Revue générale de droit* 43, no. 2 (2013): 531–98.

– *L'Usurpation de la souveraineté autochtone. Le cas des peuples de la Nouvelle-France et des colonies anglaises de l'Amérique du Nord*. Montreal: Boréal, 1997.

Morrison, Kenneth M. "Baptism and Alliance: The Symbolic Mediations of Religious Syncretism." *Ethnohistory* 37, no. 4 (1990): 416–37.

Morrissey, Robert Michael. *Empire by Collaboration: Indians, Colonists, and Governments in Colonial Illinois Country*. Philadelphia: University of Pennsylvania Press, 2015.

Muir, Edward. "Observing Trifles." In *Microhistory and the Lost Peoples of Europe*, edited by Edward Muir and Guido Ruggiero, translated by Eren Branch, vii–xxviii. Baltimore: Johns Hopkins University Press, 1991.

Mulcahy, Matthew. "The Port Royal Earthquake and the World of Wonders in Seventeenth-Century Jamaica." *Early American Studies* 6, no. 2 (2008): 391–421.

Murdoch, Steve, and Esther Mijers. "Migrant Destinations, 1500–1750." In *The Oxford Handbook of Modern Scottish History*, edited by T.M. Devine and Jenny Wormald, 320–7. Oxford: Oxford University Press, 2012.

Noel, Jan. *Along a River: The First French-Canadian Women*. Toronto: University of Toronto Press, 2013.

Norton, Mary Beth. *In the Devil's Snare: The Salem Witchcraft Crisis of 1692*. New York: Vintage Books, 2003.

Oliver-Lloyd, Vanessa. *Le patrimoine archéologique des cimetières euroquébécois*. Quebec: ministère de la Culture, des Communications et de la Condition féminine, 2008.

Oren-Magidor, Daphna. "Conception, Pregnancy, and Childbirth." In *Early Modern Childhood: An Introduction*, edited by Anna French, 57–73. London: Routledge, 2020.

Ostling, Michael, and Laura Kounine. "Introduction: 'Unbridled Passion' and the History of Witchcraft." In *Emotions in the History of Witchcraft*, edited by Laura Kounine and Michael Ostling, 1–15. London: Palgrave Macmillan, 2016.

Ouellet, Marie-Ève. "Un pouvoir de remplacement: les enjeux féminins de la migration de retour au Canada sous le Régime français." In *Femmes, culture et pouvoir: relectures de l'histoire au féminin, XVe-XXe siècles*, edited by Catherine Ferland and Benoît Grenier, 145–68. Quebec: Presses de l'Université Laval, 2010.

Oury, Guy-Marie. *Jérôme Le Royer de la Dauversière, l'homme qui a conçu Montréal*. Montreal: Éditions du Méridien, 1991.

– *Les Ursulines de Québec 1639–1953*. Quebec: Septentrion, 1999.

Overgaard, Nicholas, and Mairi Cowan. "A 'Very Particular Assistance' from Jean de Brébeuf: Opium, Relics, and a Cure for Phrénésie in Seventeenth-Century New France." *The Champlain Society: Findings/Trouvailles* (June 2017).

Ozment, Steven. *Ancestors: The Loving Family in Old Europe*. Cambridge, MA: Harvard University Press, 2001.

Pagden, Anthony. *The Burdens of Empire: 1539 to the Present*. Cambridge: Cambridge University Press, 2015.

Paige, Nicholas. "Enlightened (Il)Literates: Problems of Gender and Authority in Early Modern Devotional Writing." In *EMF: Studies in Early Modern France*, volume 7, edited by David Lee Rubin and Julia V. Douthwaite, 115–40 (Charlottesville: Rookwood Press, 2002).

Palomino, Jean-François. "Mastering the North Atlantic: Seamen and Nautical Knowledge." In *Mapping a Continent: Historical Atlas of North America, 1492–1814*, edited by Raymonde Litalien, Jean-François Palomino, and Denis Vaugeois, translated by Kathe Röth, 70–4. Quebec: Septentrion, and Montreal and Kingston: McGill-Queen's University Press, 2007.

Parrish, Susan Scott. *American Curiosity: Cultures of Natural History in the Colonial British Atlantic World*. Chapel Hill: University of North Carolina Press, 2006.

Parsons, Christopher M. *A Not-So-New World: Empire and Environment in French Colonial North America*. Philadelphia: University of Pennsylvania Press, 2018.

Paul, Daniel N. *We Were Not the Savages: Collision between European and Native American Civilizations*. Halifax: Fernwood Publishing, 2006.

Peace, Thomas. "Deconstructing the *Sauvage/Savage* in the Writing of Samuel de Champlain and Captain John Smith." *French Colonial History* 7 (2006): 1–20.

Pearl, Jonathan L. "Witchcraft in New France in The Seventeenth Century: The Social Aspect." *Historical Reflections/Réflexions Historiques* 4, no. 2 (Winter 1977): 191–205.

Pearson, Timothy G. *Becoming Holy in Early Canada*. Montreal and Kingston: McGill-Queen's University Press, 2014.

– "'I Willingly Speak to You about Her Virtues': Catherine de Saint-Augustin and the Public Role of Female Holiness in Early New France." *Church History* 79, no. 2 (June 2010): 305–33.

– "'Il sera important de me mander le détail de toutes choses': Knowledge and Transatlantic Communication from the Sulpician Mission in Canada, 1668–1680." *French Colonial History* 12, no. 1 (2011): 45–65.

Pelchat, André. "Sorcery in New France." *Canada's History*, December 2015–January 2016, 50–4.

Pelling, Margaret. "Thoroughly Resented? Older Women and the Medical Role in Early Modern London." In *Women, Science and Medicine 1500–1700: Mothers and Sisters of the Royal Society*, edited by Lynette Hunter and Sarah Hutton, 63–88. Stroud: Sutton Publishing, 1997.

Pelling, Margaret, and Charles Webster. "Medical Practitioners." In *Health, Medicine and Mortality in the Sixteenth Century*, edited by Charles Webster, 165–235. Cambridge: Cambridge University Press, 1979.

Perfetti, Lisa. "Introduction." In *The Representation of Women's Emotions in Medieval and Early Modern Culture*, edited by Lisa Perfetti. Gainesville: University Press of Florida, 2005.

Petry, Yvonne. "'Many Things Surpass Our Knowledge': An Early Modern Surgeon on Magic, Witchcraft and Demonic Possession." *Social History of Medicine* 25, no. 1 (February 2012): 47–64.

Piché, Geneviève. "« Ma très chère mère du Canada » : perceptions et représentations des Augustines de l'Hôtel-Dieu de Québec dans la correspondance des Mères de France, XVIIe-XIXe siècles." *Cahiers franco-canadiens de l'Ouest* 29, no. 1 (4 October 2017): 11–41.

Pickering, Steve. *Understanding Geography and War*. New York: Palgrave Macmillan, 2017.

Pioffet, Marie-Christine. "Gabriel Sagard, l'insoumis: archéologie d'une historiographie polémique." *Études littéraires* 47, no. 1 (2016): 39–50.

– "La Nouvelle-France dans l'imaginaire jésuite: *terra doloris* ou Jérusalem céleste?" In *Jesuit Accounts of the Colonial Americas: Intercultural Transfers Intellectual Disputes, and Textualities*, edited by Marc-André Bernier, Clorinda Donato, and Hans-Jürgen Lüsebrink, 326–43. Toronto: University of Toronto Press, 2014.

– "Nouvelle-France ou France nouvelle: les anamorphoses du désir." *Tangence*, no. 90 (Summer 2009): 37–55.

Pizzorusso, Giovanni. "Le choix indifférent: mentalités et attentes des jésuites aspirants missionnaires dans l'Amérique française au XVIIe siècle." *Mélanges de l'École française de Rome* 109, no. 2 (1997): 881–94.

Plante, Jean-François. "Le paysage sonore de la Nouvelle-France." *Ethnologies* 35, no. 1 (2013): 125–44.

Podruchny, Carolyn, and Kathryn Magee Labelle. "Jean de Brébeuf and the Wendat Voices of Seventeenth-Century New France." *Renaissance and Reformation/Renaissance et Réforme* 34, nos. 1–2 (Winter-Spring 2011): 97–126.

Poirier, Claude. "La langue parlée en Nouvelle-France: vers une convergence des explications." In *Les Origines du français québécois*, edited by Raymond Mougeon and Edouard Beniak, 237–73. Quebec: Presses de l'Université Laval, 1994.

Pollock, Linda A. "Anger and the Negotiation of Relationships in Early Modern England." *Historical Journal* 47, no. 3 (2004): 567–90.

– "Childbearing and Female Bonding in Early Modern England." *Social History* 22, no. 3 (October 1997): 286–306.

Pomata, Gianna. "Practicing between Earth and Heaven: Women Healers in Seventeenth-Century Bologna." *Dynamis* 19 (1999): 119–43.

Pouliot, Léon. "Du Journal des Jésuites à la Relation: la harangue de M. d'Ailleboust (1658)." *Revue d'histoire de l'Amérique française* 20, no. 3 (1966): 345–8.

– "Le Journal des Jésuites de Québec de 1632 à 1645." *Rapport – Société canadienne d'histoire de l'Église catholique* 28 (1961): 45–52.

Programme de recherche en démographie historique. Université de Montréal. http://www.genealogie.umontreal.ca.

Proulx, Gilles. *Between France and New France: Life aboard the Tall Sailing Ships*. Toronto: Dundurn Press, 1984.

Ragueneau, Paul. *La vie de la mere Catherine de Saint Augustin: religieuse hospitaliere de la misericorde de Quebec en la Nouvelle-France*. Paris: Chez Florentin Lambert, 1671.

Raiswell, Richard, and Peter Dendle. "Demon Possession in Anglo-Saxon and Early Modern England: Continuity and Evolution in Social Context." *Journal of British Studies* 47, no. 4 (October 2008): 738–67.

Rankin, Alisha. *Panaceia's Daughters: Noblewomen as Healers in Early Modern Germany*. Chicago: University of Chicago Press, 2013.

Rapley, Elizabeth. *A Social History of the Cloister: Daily Life in the Teaching Monasteries of the Old Regime*. Montreal and Kingston: McGill-Queen's University Press, 2001.

Rath, Richard C. *How Early America Sounded*. Ithaca: Cornell University Press, 2003.

Reis, Elizabeth. *Damned Women: Sinners and Witches in Puritan New England*. Ithaca: Cornell University Press, 1997.

Renaud, Paul-Émile. *Les origines économiques du Canada: l'oeuvre de la France*. Mamers: G. Enault, 1928.

Richelet, Pierre. *Dictionnaire françois*. Geneva: Jean Herman Widerhold, 1680.

Richer, Claude, Pearl Duval, and Carole-Anne Grenier. *Le Cheval Canadien: histoire et espoir*. Quebec: Septentrion, 2015.

Richter, Daniel K. *The Ordeal of the Longhouse: The Peoples of the Iroquois League in the Era of European Colonization*. Chapel Hill: Published for the Institute of Early American History and Culture, Williamsburg, Virginia, by the University of North Carolina Press, 1992.

Riddy, Felicity. "Looking Closely: Authority and Intimacy in the Late Medieval Urban Home." In *Gendering the Master Narrative: Women and Power in the Middle Ages*, edited by Mary C. Erler and Maryanne Kowaleski, 212–28. Ithaca: Cornell University Press, 2003.

Rituale Romanum, Editio Princeps (1614). Vatican: Libreria Editrice Vaticana, 2004.

Rituel du diocese de Quebec, publié par l'ordre de Monseigneur de Saint-Valier, evêque de Québec. Paris: Chez Simon Langlois, 1703.

Robert, Isabelle. "Le site de l'ancienne mission des Jésuites à Sillery." MA Thesis, Université Laval, 1990.

Rochemonteix, Camille de. *Les Jésuites et la Nouvelle-France au XVIIe siècle d'après beaucoup de documents inédits*. Paris: Letouzey et Ané, 1895–96.

Roper, Lyndal. *Oedipus and the Devil: Witchcraft, Religion and Sexuality in Early Modern Europe*. London: Routledge, 1994.

– *The Witch in the Western Imagination*. Charlottesville: University of Virginia Press, 2012.

Rosenwein, Barbara H. *Generations of Feeling: A History of Emotions, 600–1700*. Cambridge: Cambridge University Press, 2016.

– "Problems and Methods in the History of Emotions." *Passions in Context: International Journal for the History and Theory of Emotions* 1, no. 1 (2010): 1–32.

Rouleau, Serge. "An Archaeological View of the French Colonial Port of Québec." *Post-Medieval Archaeology* 43, no. 1 (June 2009): 229–44.

Rousseau, François. *La croix et le scalpel. Histoire des Augustines et de l'Hôtel-Dieu de Québec.* Volume 1, *1639–1892*. Quebec: Septentrion, 1989.

– "Hôpital et société en Nouvelle-France: l'Hôtel-Dieu de Québec à la fin du XVIIe siècle." *Revue d'histoire de l'Amérique française* 31, no. 1 (1977): 29–47

– *L'œuvre de chère en Nouvelle-France: le régime des malades à l'Hôtel-Dieu de Québec*. Quebec: Presses de l'Université Laval, 1983.

Roy, Alain. "Le château Saint-Louis: vestiges d'un haut lieu de pouvoir." In *Les traces de la Nouvelle-France: Au Québec et en Poitou-Charentes*, edited by Marc St-Hilaire, Alain Roy, Mickaël Augeron, and Dominique Guillemet, 218–19. Quebec: Les Presses de l'Université Laval, 2008.

Roy, Joseph-Edmond. *La Seigneurie de Lauzon*. Volume 1. Lévis: Mercier et Cie, 1897.

Roy, Pierre-Georges. *À Travers l'histoire de l'Hôtel-Dieu de Québec.* Lévis, 1939.

Roy, Pierre-Georges, and Antoine Roy. *Inventaire de greffes des notaires du Régime français*. Volume 2. Quebec: R. Lefebvre, 1942.

Roy, Raymond, and Hubert Charbonneau. "La nuptialité en situation de déséquilibre des sexes: le Canada du XVIIe siècle." *Annales de Démographie Historique* (1978): 285–94.

Sagard, Gabriel. *Le Grand voyage du pays des Hurons suivi du Dictionnaire de la langue huronne*. Edited by Jack Warwick. Montreal: Presses de l'Université de Montréal, 1998.

Saint-Vallier, Jean-Baptiste de la Croix de Chevrières de. *Estat present de l'Eglise et de la colonie française dans la Nouvelle-France*. Paris: Chez Robert Pepie, 1688.

Sauzet, Robert. "Le problème protestant dans les visites pastorales chartraines du XVIIe siècle." *Bulletin de la Société de l'Histoire du Protestantisme Français* 118 (1972): 683–96.

Savard, Rémi. "La « réduction » de Sillery 1638–1660: maquette de l'idée de « réserves indiennes »." *Recherches amérindiennes au Québec* 38, nos. 2–3 (2008): 127–31.

Sayre, Gordon M. *Les Sauvages Américains: Representations of Native Americans in French and English Colonial Literature*. Chapel Hill: University of North Carolina Press, 1997.

Scheer, Monique. "Are Emotions a Kind of Practice (and Is That What Makes Them Have a History)? A Bourdieuian Approach to Understanding Emotion." *History and Theory* 51, no. 2 (2012): 193–220.

Schulte, Rolf. *Man as Witch*. London: Palgrave Macmillan, 2009.

Seeman, Erik R. *Death in the New World: Cross-Cultural Encounters, 1492–1800*. Philadelphia: University of Pennsylvania Press, 2010.

Séguin, Robert Lionel. *La sorcellerie au Québec du XVIIe au XIXe siècle*. Montreal: Leméac/Payot, 1978.

Serres, Olivier de. *Le théâtre d'agriculture et mesnage des champs*. Paris: Jamet Métayer Imprimeur ordinaire du Roy, 1600.

Simoneau, Daniel. "The Seminary of Québec Site: From New France's Earliest Farm to its First Religious Institution." *Post-Medieval Archaeology* 43, no. 1 (June 2009): 213–28.

Sioui, Georges E. *Huron-Wendat. The Heritage of the Circle*. Translated by Jane Brierley. Vancouver: UBC Press, 2000.

Sluhovsky, Moshe. *Believe Not Every Spirit: Possession, Mysticism, & Discernment in Early Modern Catholicism*. Chicago: University of Chicago Press, 2007.

– "A Divine Apparition or Demonic Possession? Female Agency and Church Authority in Demonic Possession in Sixteenth-Century France." *Sixteenth Century Journal* 27, no. 4 (1996): 1039–55.

Smith, Bruce R. *The Acoustic World of Early Modern England: Attending to the O-Factor*. Chicago: University of Chicago Press, 1999.

Smith, Justin E.H. *Nature, Human Nature, & Human Difference: Race in Early Modern Philosophy*. Princeton: Princeton University Press, 2015.

Sperling, Jutta. "Marriage at the Time of the Council of Trent (1560–70): Clandestine Marriages, Kinship Prohibitions, and Dowry Exchange in European Comparison." *Journal of Early Modern History* 8, no. 1 (February 2004): 67–108.

Steckley, John. "Hechon: The Story of a Wendat Name." *Onomastica Canadiana* 95, nos. 1–2 (2016).

– "Huron Carol: A Canadian Cultural Chameleon." *British Journal of Canadian Studies* 27, no. 1 (2014): 55–74.

– "St Lawrence Iroquoians among the Wendat: Linguistic Evidence." *Ontario Archaeology*, no. 96 (2016): 17–25.

Strocchia, Sharon T. *Forgotten Healers: Women and the Pursuit of Health in Late Renaissance Italy*. Cambridge, MA: Harvard University Press, 2019.

– "Women and Healthcare in Early Modern Europe: Introduction." *Renaissance Studies* 28, no. 4 (September 2014): 496–514.

– "Women on the Edge: Madness, Possession, and Suicide in Early Modern Convents." *Journal of Medieval and Early Modern Studies* 45, no. 1 (January 2015): 53–77.

Sturm, Tristan. "The Future of Religious Geopolitics: Towards a Research and Theory Agenda." *Area* 45, no. 2 (2013): 134–40.

Sulte, Benjamin. *Histoire des Canadiens-français,1608–1880*. Volume 4. Montreal: Wilson & Cie, 1882.

– *Histoire des Canadiens-français, 1608–1880*. Volume 5. Montreal: Wilson & Cie, 1882.

Talbott, Siobhan. "Diasporic or Distinct? Scots in Early Modern Europe." In *British and Irish Diasporas: Societies, Cultures and Ideologies*, edited by Donald MacRaild, Tanja Bueltmann, and Jonathan Clark, 100–35. Manchester: Manchester University Press, 2019.

Tannenbaum, Rebecca J. *The Healer's Calling: Women and Medicine in Early New England*. Ithaca: Cornell University Press, 2002.

Terpstra, Nicholas. *Global Reformations: Transforming Early Modern Religions, Societies, and Cultures*. Abingdon: Routledge, 2019.

Tésio, Stéphanie. "Indigence et maladie: les hôpitaux." In *Les traces de la Nouvelle-France: Au Québec et en Poitou-Charentes*, edited by Marc St-Hilaire, Alain Roy, Mickaël Augeron, and Dominique Guillemet, 264–6. Quebec: Les Presses de l'Université Laval, 2008.

Têtu, H., and C.-O. Gagnon, eds. *Mandements, lettres pastorales et circulaires des évêques de Québec. Volume Premier*. Quebec: Imprimerie Côté, 1887.

Thevet, André. "Cosmographie universelle" and "Description de Plusieurs Isles." In *Roberval, la Damoiselle et le Gentilhomme : Les Robinsons de Terre-Neuve*, edited by Michel Bideaux, 191–210. Paris: Éditions Classiques Garnier, 2009.

Thierry, Éric. "Le discours démonologique ans les récits de voyage au Canada et en Acadie." In *Voyager avec le diable: voyages réels, voyages imaginaires et discours démonologiques, XVe-XVIIe siècles*, edited by Grégoire Holtz and Thibault Maus de Rolley, 209–20. Paris: Presses de l'Université Paris-Sorbonne, 2008.

Thomas, Keith. *Religion and the Decline of Magic*. New York: Scribner, 1971.

Thompson, Kenneth. "Forests and Climate Change in America: Some Early Views." *Climate Change* 3, no. 1 (December 1980): 47–64.

Thoum, Louys du. *Le tremble-terre ov sont contenvs ses causes, signes, effets & remedes.* Bordeaux: Gilbert Vernot, 1616.

Thwaites, Reuben Gold, ed. *The Jesuit Relations and Allied Documents: Travels and Explorations of the Jesuit Missionaries in New France, 1610–1791.* 73 volumes. Cleveland: The Burrows Brothers Company, 1896–1901.

Timmermans, Linda. *L'Accès des femmes à la culture (1598–1715): un débat d'idées de Saint François de Sales à la Marquise de Lambert.* Paris: Champion, 1993.

Tremblay, Roland. *The St Lawrence Iroquoians: Corn People.* Montreal: Pointe-à-Callière Montréal Museum of Archaeology and History, 2006.

Trigger, Bruce G. *The Children of Aataentsic: A History of the Huron People to 1660.* Montreal and Kingston: McGill-Queen's University Press, 1987.

Trivellato, Francesca. "Microstoria/Microhistoire/Microhistory." *French Politics, Culture & Society* 33, no. 1 (Spring 2015): 122–34.

Trudel, Marcel. *The Beginnings of New France, 1524–1663.* Toronto: McClelland and Stewart, 1973.

– *Catalogue des immigrants, 1632–1662.* Montreal: Hurtubise HMH, 1983.

– *Les écolières des Ursulines de Québec, 1639–1686: Amérindiennes et Canadiennes.* Montreal: Hurtubise, 1999.

– *Histoire de La Nouvelle-France III. La seigneurie des Cent-Associés 1627–1663.* Volume 1, *Les Événements.* Montreal: Fides, 1979.

– *Histoire de la Nouvelle-France III. La seigneurie des Cent-Associés 1627–1663.* Volume 2, *La société.* Montreal: Fides, 1983.

– *Histoire de la Nouvelle-France IV. La seigneurie de la Compagnie des Indes occidentales, 1663–1674.* Montreal: Fides, 1997.

– *Initiation à la Nouvelle-France.* Montreal: Holt, Rinehart and Winston, 1968.

– *La population du Canada en 1666: Recensement reconstitué.* Quebec: Septentrion, 1995.

- *Le terrier du Saint-Laurent en 1663.* Ottawa: Éditions de l'Université d'Ottawa, 1973.

Tullett, William. *Smell in Eighteenth-Century England: A Social Sense.* Oxford: Oxford University Press, 2019.

Turgeon, Laurier. *Une histoire de la Nouvelle-France: Français et Amérindiens au XVIe siècle.* Paris: Belin, 2019.

Udías, Agustín. "Earthquakes as God's Punishment in 17th- and 18th-Century Spain." In *Geology and Religion: A History of Harmony and Hostility*, edited by Martina Kölbl-Ebert, 41–8. London: Geological Society, 2009.

Van Kirk, Sylvia. "From 'Marrying-In' to 'Marrying-Out': Changing Patterns of Aboriginal/Non-Aboriginal Marriage in Colonial Canada." *Frontiers: A Journal of Women Studies* 23, no. 3 (2002): 1–11.

Vermij, Rienk. *Thinking on Earthquakes in Early Modern Europe: Firm Beliefs on Shaky Ground*. London: Routledge, 2020.

Verney, Jack. *The Good Regiment: The Carignan-Salières Regiment in Canada, 1665–1668*. Montreal and Kingston: McGill-Queen's University Press, 1991.

Vincent, Sylvie, and Joséphine Bacon. *Le Récit de Uepishtikueiau: l'arrivée des Français à Québec selon la tradition orale innue*. Montreal: Institut Culturel et éducatif montagnais and Recherches amérindiennes au Québec, 2013.

Vogel, Brant. "The Letter from Dublin: Climate Change, Colonialism, and the Royal Society in the Seventeenth Century." *Osiris* 26, no. 1 (January 2011): 111–28.

Voltmer, Rita. "Witch-Finders, Witch-Hunters or Kings of the Sabbath? The Prominent Role of Men in the Mass Persecutions of the Rhine-Meuse Area (Sixteenth-Seventeenth Centuries)." In *Witchcraft and Masculinities in Early Modern Europe*, edited by Alison Rowlands, 74–99. New York: Palgrave Macmillan, 2009.

Walinski-Kiehl, Robert. "Males, 'Masculine Honor,' and Witch Hunting in Seventeenth-Century Germany." *Men and Masculinities* 6, no. 3 (2004): 254–71.

Walker, Anita M., and Edmund H. Dickerman. "'A Woman under the Influence': A Case of Alleged Possession in Sixteenth-Century France." *Sixteenth Century Journal* 22, no. 3 (1991): 535–54.

Walter, François. *Les tremblements de terre aux XVIIe et XVIIIe siècles. La naissance d'un risque*. Seyssel: Champ Vallon, 2005.

Wang, Ping-Yuan. "Telling the Truth about Vocation: The Death Notices of the Visitandines in Brussels, 1683–1714." In *A Linking of Heaven and Earth: Studies in Religious and Cultural History in Honor of Carlos M.N. Eire*, edited by Emily Michelson, Scott K. Taylor, and Mary Noll Venables, 129–45. Farnham: Ashgate, 2012.

Warrick, Gary, and Louis Lesage. "The Huron-Wendat and the St Lawrence Iroquoians: New Findings of a Close Relationship." *Ontario Archaeology*, no. 96 (2016): 136–44.

Weisman, Richard. *Witchcraft, Magic, and Religion in Seventeenth-Century Massachusetts*. Amherst: University of Massachusetts Press, 1985.

White, David Gordon. *Daemons Are Forever: Contacts and Exchanges in the Eurasian Pandemonium*. Chicago: The University of Chicago Press, 2021.

White, R.S. "Language of Emotions." In *Early Modern Emotions: An Introduction*, edited by Susan Broomhall, 33–5. London: Routledge, 2017.

White, Richard. *The Middle Ground: Indians, Empires, and Republics in the Great Lakes Region, 1650–1815*. Cambridge: Cambridge University Press, 2011.

White, Sam. *A Cold Welcome: The Little Ice Age and Europe's Encounter with North America*. Cambridge, MA: Harvard University Press, 2017.

– "North American Climate History (1500–1800)." In *The Palgrave Handbook of Climate History*, edited by Sam White, Christian Pfister, and Franz Mauelshagen, 297–308. London: Palgrave Macmillan, 2018.

– "The Real Little Ice Age." *Journal of Interdisciplinary History* 44, no. 3 (2013): 327–52.

– "Unpuzzling American Climate: New World Experience and the Foundations of a New Science." *Isis* 106, no. 3 (2015): 544–66.

Wien, Thomas. "Une Nouvelle-France: conjectures sur le Canada d'avant 1763." In *Le Québec: société et cultures. Les enjeux d'une francophonie lointaine*, edited by Ingo Kolboom, Maria Lieber, and Edward Reichel, 29–37. Dresden: Dresden University Press, 1998.

– "Pierre Boucher: Mœurs et Productions." In *Histoire Véritable et Naturelle de La Nouvelle-France*, edited by Christophe Horguelin. Montreal: Almanach, 2014.

"Quelle est la largeur de l'Atlantique? Le 'François Canadien' entre proximité et distance, 1660–1760." In *Français? La nation en débat entre colonies et métropole (XVIe-XIXe siècle)*, edited by Cécile Vidal, 55–75. Paris: Éditions de l'École des Hautes Études en Sciences Sociales, 2014.

Wiesner-Hanks, Merry. *Christianity and Sexuality in the Early Modern World: Regulating Desire, Reforming Practice*. London: Routledge, 2010.

Yarrow, Simon. *Saints and Their Communities: Miracle Stories in Twelfth-Century England*. Oxford: Oxford University Press, 2005.

Yon, Armand. "Notre premier touriste en Nouvelle-France: Asseline de Ronval [1662]." *Les Cahiers des dix*, no. 39 (1974): 146–70.

Young, Francis. *A History of Exorcism in Catholic Christianity*. London: Palgrave Macmillan, 2016.

Zhang, Qiong. "About God, Demons, and Miracles: The Jesuit Discourse on the Supernatural in Late Ming China." *Early Science and Medicine* 4, no. 1 (1999): 1–36.

Zika, Charles. "Fashioning New Worlds from Old Fathers: Reflections on Saturn, Amerindians and Witches in a Sixteenth-Century Print." In *Exorcising our Demons: Magic, Witchcraft, and Visual Culture in Early Modern Europe*, by Charles Zika, 411–44. Leiden: Brill, 2002.

Zilberstein, Anya. *A Temperate Empire: Making Climate Change in Early America*. Oxford: Oxford University Press, 2016.

Index

Page numbers in italics refer to figures. Page numbers in bold refer to glossary entries.

Abenaki, 42. *See also* Indigenous peoples

Aigron, Pierre (excommunicated for trading liquor), 69

Albert, André (inhabitant of Lauzon), 212n24

Albert, Guillaume (Barbe Hallay's brother-in-law), 212n24

Algonquin, 34. *See also* Indigenous peoples

ancien régime, **159**

Antoinette de Sainte-Marthe (nun who died of "malefice"), 146

architecture in Québec, 29, 33, 78, 154, 173n87, 191n42. *See also* Québec French settlement

assimilation policies, francisation, and beliefs, 97–9, 134–6, 154

Augustinians. *See* Hospitalières and Hospitalière nuns

Bailly, Guillaume (Sulpician missionary), 151–2

Beauport (seigneurie), 44–5, *46*, 111–12; changes to, 142; demonic appearances at, 44, 47–8; Barbe Hallay as domestic servant, 44, 47, 102; miller of, 51–2, 179n23 (*see also* Vuil, Daniel). *See also* Giffard de Moncel, Robert; Regnouard, Marie

Beschefer, Thierry (Jesuit), 119

Besnard dit Bourjoly, René (accused of witchcraft), 69–70

Biard, Pierre (Jesuit), 21, 98, 156, 165n22

birds, 34

bishop, **159**

blasphemy, 69, 139, 187n109; Daniel Vuil accusation and execution, 61, 68, 70, 185n75

Boniface, François (Jesuit): phrénésie diagnosis, 119, 147–8

Boucher, Pierre (Governor of Trois-Rivières), 19, 23, 167n31

Bourdon, Jean: "Le Véritable plan de Québec fait en 1663," *32*, *81*

Bourgeoys, Marguerite (Congrégation de Notre-Dame de Montréal): on Protestants, 40

Brébeuf, Jean de (Jesuit), 7, 117–18, 199n134; Catherine de Saint-Augustin's connection to, 85, 93, 101, 116–17; on demons and Indigenous people, 99–100; Barbe Hallay's possession and, 116–17; martyrdom of, 118–20; a patron saint of Canada, 120; relics of, 85, 103–5, 106, 109, 110, 116–17, 119–21, 147, 164n7, 196n91, 208n67; spirituality of Indigenous people, 96–7; *See also* Jesuits in New France

Byssot, François (seigneurial attorney and provost judge), 212n24

Cabré, Montserrat, 207n61

Campagna, Jean (accused of witchcraft), 146

Canada, 12, **159**, 165n22. *See also* New France; Québec French settlement

Carignan-Salières regiment, 133–4, 137

Carrier, Jean (Barbe Hallay's husband), 126–7, 212n20, 212n24, 213n29. *See also* Hallay, Barbe

Cartier, Jacques, 37

Catherine de Saint-Augustin: apostolic aspirations of, 84, 92–4; Jean de Brébeuf and, 93, 101, 116–17, 119, 120–1, 196n91; care of Barbe Hallay by, 74, 164n7; death of, 211n18; demonic obsession of, 72–3, 85–8, *87*, 195n88, 204n25; earthquake as divine punishment, 86, 88–90; Françoise Marie de Saint-Ignace and, 115; martyrdom and, 93–4, 199n134. *See also* Hospitalières and Hospitalière nuns; Hôtel-Dieu in Québec; Ragueneau, Paul

Catholicism in New France, 5, 15, **159**, 176n135; authority of, 65, 67, 137–40, 186n100, 217–18n80, 217n78, 220n110; behaviour in church, 138, 217–18n80; bells and music of Québec, 33, 34; conversion attempts, 96–7 (*see also* Indigenous peoples; missions and missionaries); entertainment, response to, 139; Hôtel-Dieu role, 75–6 (*see also* Hôtel-Dieu in Québec); magic or religion distinction, 41–3; Montréal founding ideals, 136; official skepticism of demons and witchcraft, 148–52, 220n110; presumption of universality, 155–6, 222nn6–7; Protestants and, 5, 39–40, 137, 175n124; religious identity, 36–41, 174n110. *See also* Hôtel-Dieu in Québec; Jesuits in New France; missions and missionaries; Ursulines and Ursuline convent

census data, New France: 1666 and 1667, 54, 123, 125, 126, 210n13; 1681, 128–9, 133

Champlain, Samuel de, 26–7, 94, 112, 156, 168n39, 169n44

charivari or shaming, 139–40

Charpentier, Jean (accused of witchcraft), 147
Chartres, France, 15–16
chasse-galerie folktale, 152
Château Saint-Louis (governor's residence), 29, 112, 141; prison tower, 61
Chéron, Jean: *Examen de la théologie mystique* (1657), 91
Chiouabougoukoue, Ursule: death and burial of, 80
class: descriptions in New France of, 19; evolution in New France of, 154; healthcare, 113; migration role of, 17–18; seigneurialism, 45, 113, 177n4
climate and colonialism: early modern theories of, 21–3, 27, 95, 155, 169n43–5, 170n53, 170nn49–50; New France house construction and, 33
cloisters for women religious, 92–3, 199n127
Colbert, Jean-Baptiste (chief minister for the king), 20, 23, 131, 133–4, 167n28, 215n56
colonialism and colonization: assimilation policies, 97–9, 134–6, 154; insecurities of New France, 57–61; kinship ties, 17; missions, 94–6, 136, 154, 200n150; New France becomes a royal colony, 131–2; recruitment for, 17–18, 167n22; religious identity of New France and, 36–41, 155–6, 222nn6–7; settlement gardens, 27, 172n80; weather theories and, 21–3, 95, 169n43–5, 170nn49–50, 170n53
comets as portents, 49–50, 178nn15–16
Compagnie de la Nouvelle-France/des Cent-Associés, 37, 45, 76, 167n22; dissolved, 131
Confraternity of the Holy Family, 139
Corriveau, Marguerite, and Jean Maheu (Barbe Hallay's employer), 124–5, 210nn6–11
Côte de Lauzon, 142, *142–3*
Couillard, Guillaume, and Marie Guillemette Hébert, 33, 83

"daughters of the king" *(filles du roi)*, 132–3
demonology: agency in social hierarchy of a demoniac, 56–7, 91, 183n53; Catherine de Saint-Augustin's obsession, 72–3, 85–8, *87*; demoniacs' cultural profile, 49, 50; dictionary definitions (1690), 149–50; esprit follet definition, 72; in folklore, 152; French and colonial compared, 5–6, 8, 150–1, 156, 222n6; Louis XIV 1682 edict, 148–9; New France experience and, 99–100, 202n168; obsession versus possession, 48–9, 91; possession diagnosis in New France, 147–8; possession's characteristics, 106; skepticism of, 8, 49–50, 90–2, 148–52, 221n118. *See also* Hallay, Barbe
Denonville, New France, 148, 220n103
Denys, Nicolas (Acadian settler), 170n53

Denys, Simon (gentleman in Québec): comparing New France and France, 19, 129; on marriages in New France, 182n45
Désy, Edouard (Jesuit), 121
Dictionnaire Universel (1690), 149
Dollier de Casson, François, 23–4
domestic servant's work and pay, 44, 47, 125, 210n13, 211n16; employment and occupations, 102, 124, 209n5
Duchesse d'Aiguillon (Marie Madeleine de Vignerot du Pont Courlay), 75, 78, 189n24
Dumets, Jean (from Lauzon), 217n78
Duverger, Françoise (convicted of infanticide), 213n30

earthquake, 86, 88–90, 197n108
economics of New France: cost of migration, 17–18, 25, 171n65; marriage law and customs, 54; miller's role, 51–2; seigneurialism, 45
education: of Indigenous girls at the Ursuline convent, 98–9
emotions, significance of, 52–3, 181nn33–4. *See also* language and languages
employment and occupations in New France, 44, 47, 102, 124, 125, 209n5, 210n13, 211n16
esprit follet, definition, 72
Etinechkadat, Jean-Baptiste (Sillery mission), 192n46
Evelyn, John (Royal Society of London), 170n50
exorcisms (religious rituals): against animals, 177n145; as bodywork, 116; characteristics of, 106–8; eroticism of, 106–7; procession against caterpillars, 42–3; Marie Regnouard's ritual deliverance of Barbe Hallay, 102–5; *Rituale Romanum* (Roman Rite), 108–9, 112, 204n24; Saint-Vallier's *Rituel* (1703), 150–1; skepticism of, 150–1, 221n116

foods: establishments selling, 141; at Hôtel-Dieu, 125–6; Indigenous and French exchanges of, 79; missionary schools, 98–9; origins of, 24–5; settlement gardens/agriculture, 27, 29, 129, 153–4, 172n80, 191n43; settlers' diets, 35–6, 153–4; squash seeds from the Wendat, 24; watermelon and its origins, 25
Fournet, Pierre-Auguste (priest), 121
francisation as an assimilation policy, 97–9, 134–6, 154
Françoise Marie de Saint-Ignace (daughter to Marie Regnouard), 114–15
Franquelin, Jean-Baptiste: "L'entrée de la Rivière du St Laurent ...," *143*
Frontenac, Louis de Buade, Comte de (governor), 135, 139, 140–1

Gadois, Pierre (victim of witchcraft), 69–70, 187n112
Gallicanism and Ultramontanism, 65
Garnier, Charles (Jesuit), 119
Gemier, Catherine (accused of witchcraft), 146

gender: agency in social hierarchy of a demoniac, 56–7, 91, 183n53, 198n118; apostolic aspirations and, 84, 92–4; Confraternity of the Holy Family, 139; demographic imbalance, 53, 55, 133, 210n9; of demoniac/demon, 107–8; demoniacs' cultural profile, 50, 179n19; exorcisms, 109, 116; healthcare, 113–14, 116, 207n61; marriage age and choice, 54–6; missionary service and, 92–4, 198n124; mysticism and, 90–1, 198n118; teaching versus preaching distinction, 92; of witches, 51, 109, 179n23; women's behaviour in church, 138, 217–18n80
Gerezon, Louis (inhabitant of Lauzon), 212n24
Giffard de Moncel, Robert (seigneur), 110, 111, 114, 207n57; death of, 130, 215n49; Jesuits and, 120; seigneurial land of, 45, 111–12. *See also* Beauport; Regnouard, Marie
Girard, Barbe (Barbe Hallay's niece), 123, 128–9
Girard, Joachim (Barbe Hallay's brother-in-law), 212n24
Goumin, Annet (surgeon), 124–5
governor, 159
Guyart, Marie. *See* Marie de l'Incarnation
Guyon, Marie (possession-like illness), 220n102
Guyon sieur du Bisson, Jean (children's guardian), 125

habitants and habitations, *142*, 159–60; of Hallay-Carrier family, 127–8
Hallay, Barbe: age of, 54, 182n40; domestic servant employment, 44, 47; family and background, 15–16, 130, 166n8, 214n41, 215n48; migrant profile of, 14; migration to New France, 5, 16, 17, 167n21, 169n43, 171n65, 171n70; migration vessel (1659), 25–6; name spellings, 11; religion, 5, 41, 176n135; sister's marriage contract, 56
– possession of, 3, 5–7, 154, 155, 156; Jean de Brébeuf miracles and, 120–1; "deliverance" accounts, 103–4, 117, 121, 203n5; "deliverance" by Marie Regnouard, 102–7 (*see also* Regnouard, Marie); evidence and sources, 9–10, 156–7; obsession/infestation, 106; possession/obsession distinction, 48; previous studies of, 8, 163nn3–4, 164n7; sinister portents of, 49–50; status as a demoniac, 56–7, 181n35; treatment in hospital, 71–4, 83, 93, 101; Daniel Vuil's spurned proposal, 52–3, 55 (*see also* Vuil, Daniel); witnesses description of, 47–8, 73, 189n16. *See also* demonology; witches and witchcraft
– post-possession, 7–8, 122–3; bench in church, 129; Catherine de Saint-Augustin and, 211n18; children, 127–8, 213n33;

death of, 129; death of parents, 130, 215n48; employment, 123–6, 211n16; family habitation, 128–30; godmother to nieces, 123, 128–9, 209n2; marriage, 126–7, *128*, 212nn20–6, 213n29; sister Marie's supernatural encounter, 123, 209n3
Hallay, Elisabeth (Barbe Hallay's sister), 15, 176n135
Hallay, Jean-Baptiste (Barbe Hallay's brother), 15, 214n41
Hallay, Jean-Baptiste (Barbe Hallay's father), 15, 47, 130, 167n21, 176n135
Hallay, Marie (Barbe Hallay's sister), 15, 123, 176n135, 212n24
Haudenosaunee (Iroquois), 160; Jean de Brébeuf and, 118–19; colonists' fear of, 58–9; as enemies of the colony, 39, 133; Laval's description of, 58. *See also* Indigenous peoples
healthcare in New France, 73, 102, 113–15, 206n52, 207n54; bodywork, 116; illnesses, 73, 148, 214n46, 220n103. *See also* Hospitalières and Hospitalière nuns; Hôtel-Dieu in Québec
Hébert, Marie Guillemette, and Guillaume Couillard, 33, 83, 112
Hippocrates, 95
Hiroüin, Marie (Hospitalière nun): obituary of, 82, 194n74
historiography. *See* microhistory
Hospitalières and Hospitalière nuns, 160; fear of the Haudenosaunee, 58–9; Barbe Hallay and, 6, 34; ideals described in obituaries of, 82; migration to New France, 24, 76. *See also* Hôtel-Dieu in Québec
Hôtel-Dieu in Québec: about and background, 75–6, 154, 160, 189n20, 193n67, 194n77; earthquake, 88, 89; expansion of, 141; food and medicine at, 125–6; Françoise Marie de Saint-Ignace, 114–15; Giffard as medical practitioner, 114, 207n57; Barbe Hallay admission record, 71–2; Barbe Hallay as employee, 125, 211n16; Barbe Hallay treatment in, 71–4, 101; at mission of Sillery, 76–7; missionary mandate of, 71, 75–80, 85, 154; patient care description, 82–3, 195n81; worker wished to bewitch nuns, 147. *See also* Hospitalières and Hospitalière nuns; Regnouard, Marie
housing construction in Québec, 29, 33, 78, 154, 173n87, 191n42. *See also* Québec French settlement
Huguenots in New France, 160. *See also* Protestants and Protestantism
Huron, 160. *See also* Wendat
Huronia mission, 99, 117–18, 120

illnesses. *See* healthcare in New France
imperialism. *See* colonialism and colonization

indentured labour, 38, 124, 167n22, 171n65
Indigenous peoples: Catholicism, colonialism, and, 37–9, 76, 175n119; Christian diversity of, 79–80; pluralism among, 97; resistance and engagement with French culture, 27, 77–80, 94–9, 118–19, 135–6, 154, 177n4, 191n38, 192–3nn49–51, 192nn44–6, 216n65; settlers' diet and, 36; terminology and translation, 12
infanticide in New France, 213n30
Innu oral history: on French gardening, 27
intendant, 160
Iroquois, 160. *See also* Haudenosaunee
"Irrité" definition, 52–3, 180nn30–1, 181n35. *See also* language and languages

Jesuits in New France, 160, 222n7; colonial role of, 38; conversion approaches, 96–7, 98, 191n38–9, 192nn44–5, 201n152, 201n161; exorcism role of, 110; procession (exorcism) against caterpillars, 42; quarrel between bishop and governor, 66–7. *See also* Brébeuf, Jean de; Lalemant, Jérôme; Le Jeune, Paul; missions and missionaries; Ragueneau, Paul
Journal des jésuites (1661), 61–2, 63, 64, 67–8, 185n75. *See also* Lalemant, Jérôme

Kamiskouaouangachit: site of Sillery, 77–8
kinship ties, 17, 78

La Montagne Sulpician mission, 151–2
La Rochelle, France, 41
Lalemant, Charles (Jesuit), 169n44, 180n31
Lalemant, Gabriel (Jesuit), 118–19
Lalemant, Jérôme (Jesuit): arrival in New France, 171n70; on colonial insecurities, 60; on demons and Indigenous people, 99–100, 188n5; earthquake and conversions, 89; on European demons, 97; *Journal des jésuites* (1661), 61–4; on Daniel Vuil's crimes, 63–4; on Daniel Vuil's execution, 62
Lamarque, Anne: seen with a book of magic, 146
Lambourg, Esther de (a witness to Barbe Hallay's marriage contract), 212n24
language and languages: "amitié," use of, 182n47; esprit follet definition, 72; exorcism versus deliverance, 108–9, 116, 204n23, 204n25; Indigenous languages in church, 34; "Irrité" definition, 52–3, 180nn30–1; linguistic diversity among settlers, 34–5; about names and translations, 11–12; nuns learning Indigenous, 79–80; obsession versus possession, 48–9, 91; "seigneuresse" usage, 206n47; settler terminology, 12, 165n20; spoken by demons, 106;

teaching versus preaching distinction, 92
Lauson de Charny, Charles de (acting governor and a priest), 110, 205n32; account of Barbe Hallay's deliverance (exorcism), 103–5, 110, 117, 203n5; arrivals in New France, 110, 171n70
Lauzon, New France, 126, 127, 142, 214n41, 217n78; church of Saint-Joseph, 129
Laval, François de (bishop/vicar apostolic), 5; arrival in Québec, 26, 38–9; authority and title of, 64–5, 67, 136, 186n100; case of witchcraft against Daniel Vuil, 68; on the cathedral, 141; Catherine's biography and, 84; description of Barbe Hallay's possession, 48; exorcism of Beauport, 48; on Iroquois, 39; liquor trade and dispute about, 68–9, 180n31; from missionary to colonial church, 136; orders Barbe Hallay into hospital, 72; passage to New France, 26; on Protestants in New France, 137; quarrel with Governor Voyer d'Argenson, 64–8; report on New France (1660), 57–8; on women's behaviour in church, 138
Le Caron, Joseph (Récollet friar), 97–8
Le Jeune, Paul (Jesuit): advice to New France migrants, 18; climate theories, 22; on conversion of Protestants, 40; on converting Indigenous people, 38, 76, 77, 190n36; on demons and Indigenous people, 99; expectation of Indigenous people, 95–6; on a Hôtel-Dieu for New France, 75–6; plea for New France, 130–1
Le Mercier, François Joseph (Jesuit), 22, 119
Lescarbot, Marc, 200n137; *1609 History of New France*, 94
liquor trade: civil and religious dispute over, 68–9; punishment for, 62–3, 69, 70, 180n31, 185–6n74
Longueville, Simon (marriage of), 132
Loudun, France, 91, 198n120

Maheu, Jean, and Marguerite Corriveau (employer of Barbe Hallay), 124–5, 210nn6–11
Mance, Jeanne, 40
Maranda, Marie Marguerite (Barbe Hallay's sister-in-law), 214n41
Marie de l'Incarnation (Ursuline nun): "apostolic woman," 92; Jean de Brébeuf and, 119; Jean de Brébeuf's help for Barbe Hallay, 93, 116–17; on Catherine de Saint-Augustin, 72–4, 83, 89–90, 93; on commercial expansion, 140; contagious and deadly illness in Québec, 73; description of the possession, 47–8; on diverse migration, 132; earthquake description, 89, 196n107; foods in New France, 24–5, 128; on habitation life, 128–9; Marie Guyart (a.k.a.), 11; on physical and spiritual patient care, 83, 126; portents

of possession, 49; preparations for war with Haudenosaunee, 59; quality of migrants, 137–8; on quarrel between governor and bishop/vicar apostolic, 65; Daniel Vuil as "Irrité," 52, 53; on Daniel Vuil's criminal accusation, 60–1; witness to Barbe Hallay's possession, 3. *See also* Ursulines and Ursuline convent
Marie Guillemette de Saint-Augustin (nun), 146
Marie Sara de Saint-André (nun), 120–1
marriage law and customs, 53–6, 154, 212n26; age and choice in New France, 54–6, 124, 182n41, 182n45, 210n9; children, 127–8, 213n30, 213nn34–5; contracts, 126–7, *128*, 211n19; expectations of, 182n47, 183n50; shaming or charivari, 139–40; women's power in New France, 182n45; women's right to withhold consent, 55–6
Martin, Claude (son and biographer of Marie de l'Incarnation), 92
martyrdom and martyrological literature, 93, 199n129, 200n137; terminology, 160. *See also* Brébeuf, Jean de
medicine. *See* healthcare in New France
Meiachka8at, Charles (from Tadoussac), 191n38
Melançon, Arthur (Jesuit), 121
Meulles, Jacques de (intendant), 23
microhistory, 8–11, 165n16, 222nn1–2; historiography, 4–5, 163n2; research sources, 4, 8–11, 16, 61–2, 83, 153, 156, 163n2
migration, France to New France: Atlantic crossing experiences, 13–14, *14*; cost of travel, 25, 171n65; "daughters of the king" *(filles du roi)*, 132–3; demographics of, 16–17, 166n20, 166nn12–14, 171nn65–6; diversity and quality of, 132, 137–8; expectations and reality of, 18–23, 168nn37–9, 169nn43–4, 170n53; recruitment, 17–18, 64, 112, 132, 167n22, 200n137; resistance to, 24; ships sailing in 1659, 25–6. *See also* New France
miller: at Beauport, 51, 179n23; role and occupation in New France, 51–2, 180n26. *See also* Vuil, Daniel
missions and missionaries (Catholic), 6, 160; assimilation policies of France, 97–9, 135–6, 154; disappointments in New France of, 99–101, 119–20; expectations of Indigenous peoples, 94–9, 200n148; gender and, 92–4, 198n124; Hôtel-Dieu's role, 71, 75–80; Montréal founding ideals, 136; role in New France of, 37–9, 120, 136–7, 175n119. *See also* Catholicism in New France; Hôtel-Dieu in Québec; Jesuits in New France; Ursulines and Ursuline convent
Mohawks, 133. *See also* Haudenosaunee
Molière: *Tartuffe,* 139

monogenesis, theory of, 96
Montréal or Ville-Marie: founding of, 136; Haudenosaunee attacks on, 58–60; witchcraft accusations, 69–70, 146, 147, 151, 152
Morel, Perrine (accused of witchcraft), 146
Morin, Loüise: possession-like illness of, 220n102
mysticism: of Catherine de Saint-Augustin, 74, 85, 88, 90 (*see also* Catherine de Saint-Augustin); gender and, 90–1

names and their spellings, 11–12. *See also* microhistory
New France, 4, 7–8, 11–12, 14, 154–5, 160; assimilation policies and beliefs, 97–9, 134–6, 154; authority of Catholic Church in, 65, 67, 137–40, 186n100, 217–18n80, 217n78, 220n110 (*see also* Catholicism in New France); authority of governor, 64–5, 67, 186n100; becomes a royal colony, 131; climate of, 21–4, 169nn43–5, 170n53 (*see also* climate and colonialism); colonial insecurities of, 57–61, 64, 130–8; earthquake, 86, 88; education, 24; entertainment, 138–9; executions in, 68–9, 185n75, 185n80, 213n30 (*see also* Vuil, Daniel); France knowledge of, 18–21, 168nn35–6; global networks of, 24, 155–6; isolation of, 23–4, 59, 64; life expectancy, 129, 213n33, 214n44 (*see also* statistics); migrant demographics, 16–17; military reinforcements, 133–4; population, birthrate increasing, 131, 133; population incentives of French government, 20, 132–3; possession and witchcraft in, 145–7, 147–8 (*see also* demonology; Hallay, Barbe; witches and witchcraft); Protestants officially excluded from, 39–40, 43; terminology, 12. *See also* migration, France to New France; Québec French settlement
Notre-Dame (church), Québec: enlargement of, 141; Barbe Hallay's marriage, 127; interments in, 35, 41, 176n137; music of, 34, 141, 173n92, 173n98

occupations and employment in New France, 44, 47, 102, 124, 125, 209n5, 210n13, 211n16
odours and air of Québec, 35
Oneidas, 133. *See also* Haudenosaunee

papal authority in New France, 65
papal bulls and colonialism, 36–7
Pardoux, Barthélemy (*De Morbis animi*), 50
Parlement of Rouen, 64–5, 67
pluralism of Indigenous peoples, 97
Pontonnier, Marie (victim of witchcraft), 69–70, 187n112
possession of Barbe Hallay. *See* Hallay, Barbe
Prince Guillaume (ship), 26
Protestants and Protestantism, 40, 160, 176n128; known as Huguenots, 40; presence in New

France, 5, 39–40, 137, 175n124; Religion Prétendue Réformée (RPR), 40, 176n128. *See also* Catholicism in New France

Québec French settlement, 4, 28, 33–6, 160; growth of and changes to, 140–2, *143–4*, 144; historical background of, 26–7; housing construction in, 29, 33, 78, 154, 173n87, 191n42; population statistics, 17; procession (exorcism) against caterpillars, 42–3; shaming or charivari, 139–40; soundscape of Québec, 33–4, 173n92, 173n98; terminology, 12; Upper Town and Lower Town layout, 28–9, *30–2*, *81*, 141. *See also* New France

Racine, Loüise: possession-like illness example, 220n102
Ragueneau, Paul (Jesuit): belief in demons by, 99–101, 202n176; Jean de Brébeuf relics and, 110, 120
– *La vie de la mere Catherine de Saint-Augustin* (1671): Catherine's care of Barbe Hallay, 74; Catherine's veracity, 90–1; description of Halley's possession, 48–9, 182n40; frontispiece, *87*; infestation by demons, 73; possession/obsession distinction, 48–9, 91, 108; purpose of biography, 84–5; as source of Vuil's execution, 61. *See also* Catherine de Saint-Augustin; Jesuits in New France
Récollets, 97–8, 160
Regnouard, Marie (seigneuresse), 7, 110–11, 111–13, 130, 205n34; daughter as medical practitioner, 114–15; "deliverance" of Barbe Hallay, explanation of role, 110–16; "deliverance" of Barbe Hallay by, 102–7, 117, 120, 121; exorcism unnamed, 108–10, 204n23; as healthcare provider, 113–15, 116; "seigneuresse" usage, 206n47; unpublished accounts of Barbe Hallay's "deliverance," 103–4, 117, 121, 203n5. *See also* Giffard de Moncel, Robert
Relations (Jesuit writings), 160. *See also* Jesuits in New France
relics of Jean de Brébeuf, 85, 103–5, 106, 109, 110, 116–17, 119–21, 147, 196n91, 208n67. *See also* Brébeuf, Jean de
religion in New France. *See* Catholicism in New France
Religion Prétendue Réformée (RPR), 40, 176n128. *See also* Protestants and Protestantism
Rituale Romanum (Roman Rite), 108–9, 112, 204n24. *See also* exorcisms
Rolland, Nicole: (accused neighbour of witchcraft), 146
Ronval, Asseline de (traveller from Dieppe), 22, 28, 60
Rosaire, Espérance du (migrant), 132
Rouen, Parlement of, 64–5, 67

Sacrifice d'Abraham (ship), 26

Sagard, Gabriel (Récollet missionary), 14, 22, 169n45
Saint André (ship), 26, 171n65
Saint-Joseph mission. *See* Sillery Jesuit mission
Saint-Vallier, Bishop: *Catéchisme* (1702), 150; on New France entertainment, 139; *Rituel* (1703), 150
Sainte-Anne-du-Petit-Cap shrine, 148
Scott, Henri Arthur (Jesuit), 121
seigneurialism, 45, 113, 161, 177n4. *See also* Giffard de Moncel, Robert; Regnouard, Marie
Serres, Olivier de (agronomist), 113
settler terminology, 12, 165n20
Sillery Jesuit mission (a.k.a. Saint-Joseph), 76–80, 98, 99, 191–2nn42–6, 191n39, 192–3nn49–51, 192n44; Christian diversity of, 79–80
Simon, Charles (Jesuit): earthquake description, 88–9
soundscape of Québec, 33–4, 173n92, 173n98. *See also* Québec French settlement
Sovereign Council, Québec, 131, 137
statistics: age of marriage in New France, 54–5; children in New France, 127–8, 213nn34–5; "daughters of the king" (*filles du roi*), 132–3; demographics of New France, 16–17, 53, 55, 56, 166n20, 166nn12–14, 182n44, 183n51; executions in New France, 68–9; fertility rate in New France, 183n51; Iroquois wars fatalities, 60; life expectancy in New France, 129, 213n33, 214n44; migration crossing, 14, 25, 171nn65–6; population, 16–17, 55, 133, 182n44; workforce employed as servants, 125, 210n13, 211n16
St Lawrence River, 161
Sulpician mission, La Montagne, 151–2
sunflowers, 24–5

Tadoussac, 80, 88, 94, 111, 191n38
Talon, Jean (Intendant of New France), 14, 131, 133–4, 209n5
Tametsi (1563 decree from the Council of Trent), 53
Thevet, André: evil spirits on the "Île des Démons," 156
Thoum, Louis du: on earthquakes, 89
translations, 11–12
Trigatin, Pierre (Captain of Prayers, Sillery): death and burial of, 80
Trois-Rivières, 19, 50, 70, 187n100
Tronson, Louis (Sulpician superior), 151–2, 221n116

Ursulines and Ursuline convent, 161; earthquake responses, 89–90; engagement with Indigenous peoples, 135–6; monastery rebuilt, 141, 218n92; music of, 34; nuns' diet, 36; school, 98–9

Vallet, Mathurine (mother of Barbe Hallay), 15, 130, 176n135

vicar apostolic, **161**
Villeneuve, Robert de: map of Québec, 142, *144*
Vimont, Barthélemi (Jesuit), 78
Voyer d'Argenson, Pierre de (governor): authority of, 64–5, 67, 186n100; liquor trade dispute, 68–9; population of New France, 17; quarrel with Laval, 64–8
Vuil, Daniel: character of, 56; migration to New France, 5, 56; name spellings, 11; occupation as a miller, 51, 179n23; Protestant, 5, 39
– possession accusation, 3, 5–6, 48; execution of, 61–4, 68, 185–6n80, 185n75; imprisonment of, 61; Lauson de Charny and, 110; Laval's witchcraft case against, 68; power struggle of bishop and governor and, 67–8; reasons for imprisonment(s), 63–4, 184–5nn74–5; severity of sentence, 70; witch-like characteristics and accusation, 6, 51, 52–3

watermelon and its origins, 25
weather theories and colonization, 21–3, 95, 155, 169n43–5, 170n53, 170nn49–50
Wendat (Huron), **161**; aaskouandy items, 100; Jean de Brébeuf and, 117–18; Haudenosaunee and, 59; hymns in language of the, 34; response to Christian stories, 96–7; squash seeds from, 24. *See also* Indigenous peoples
witches and witchcraft: beliefs in New France, 7–8, 60–1, 144–7, 150–2, 219n100; characteristics of, 50–1, 178n18, 179n23, 181nn34–5, 188n114, 219n100; crime and punishment of, 70, 187n109, 219n96, 220n110; cultural acceptance of, 179n22; dictionary definitions of (1690), 149–50; in folklore, 152; gender of, 51, 109, 179n23; at Barbe Hallay's deliverance (exorcism), 108; Louis XIV 1682 edict, 148–9; New France trial for, 69–70; skepticism of, 8, 148–52; Vuil's accusation of, 68

www.ingramcontent.com/pod-product-compliance
Lightning Source LLC
LaVergne TN
LVHW090748030926
847095LV00029B/292
9780228014041